Legends of Disco

ALSO BY JAMES ARENA

First Ladies of Disco: 32 Stars Discuss the Era and Their Singing Careers (McFarland, 2013)

Fright Night *on Channel 9: Saturday Night Horror Films on New York's WOR-TV, 1973–1987* (McFarland, 2012)

Legends of Disco
Forty Stars Discuss Their Careers

JAMES ARENA

Foreword by France Joli; *Afterword by* Henry Stone

McFarland & Company, Inc., Publishers
Jefferson, North Carolina

LIBRARY OF CONGRESS CATALOGUING-IN-PUBLICATION DATA

Names: Arena, James, 1960–
Title: Legends of disco : forty stars discuss their careers / James Arena ; foreword by France Joli ; afterword by Henry Stone.
Description: Jefferson, North Carolina : McFarland & Company, 2016. | Includes bibliographical references and index.
Identifiers: LCCN 2016011062 | ISBN 9781476664965 (softcover : acid free paper) ∞
Subjects: LCSH: Disco musicians—Biography. | Disco music—History and criticism.
Classification: LCC ML394.A76 2016 | DDC 782.42164092/2—dc23
LC record available at http://lccn.loc.gov/2016011062

BRITISH LIBRARY CATALOGUING DATA ARE AVAILABLE

© 2016 James Arena. All rights reserved

No part of this book may be reproduced or transmitted in any form or by any means, electronic or mechanical, including photocopying or recording, or by any information storage and retrieval system, without permission in writing from the publisher.

Cover artwork by Ryan White

Printed in the United States of America

*McFarland & Company, Inc., Publishers
Box 611, Jefferson, North Carolina 28640
www.mcfarlandpub.com*

For my loving parents
and all of the talented artists,
musicians and professionals worldwide
who made disco an art form

Acknowledgments

This book is the result of the kindness, contributions and assistance of many people.

I want express my gratitude to all of the stars who graciously agreed to be featured in this book and whose chapters only hint at the depth of their lives, careers and accomplishments.

Not long after the preparation of this book, James "Ajax" Baynard of Crown Heights Affair and T.K. Records founder Henry Stone passed away. They were innovators of disco who were very enthusiastic about participating in this project, and I am very grateful they did. May they rest in peace.

I also extend my thanks to Teri DeSario, Cory Robbins, Joe Causi, Luci Martin, Myra Scheer, Precious Wilson, Ray Harris, Lynná Davis, Trudy Miller, Sofiane Hadjazi, Tom Hayden of TSR Records, and Patrick Adams for providing some great supplementary commentary and insights into the disco world.

I extend my deepest thanks to Nick Bunning of Australia.

Special thanks to James Washington.

I am grateful to Joe La Greca, Fritz Pointer and Anita Pointer, Samuel A. Harvey, Thad Whyte, Troy Bronstein, Lynn Marocola, Vinnie Medugno, Roxie McKain, Venice Harris, Michael Bullock, Daniel Vaillancourt and Amanda Tilk.

Thanks to Elvis Bramble and Robert and Maureen Arena for their support.

My gratitude goes to Charles R. Muniz for contributing some beautiful photographs from his personal collection so that we all might see and feel the youthful spirit and energy of many of these great performers.

Thank you to all the publication, TV and radio station personnel that have seen some merit in my books and have offered me opportunities to publicize my projects.

I'd like to acknowledge Discogs (http://www.discogs.com) and Joel Whitburn's *Billboard's Hot Dance/Disco 1974–2003* (2004, Record Research Inc.), which were most helpful as data verification resources.

There were many other individuals who supported this project in a variety of ways, and my apologies to you if I have neglected to include your name here. Please know that I am deeply grateful to everyone who helped me on this journey.

Table of Contents

Acknowledgments — vi
Foreword by France Joli — 1
Preface — 3

Professionals Behind the Scenes — 7
Alfa Anderson, formerly of Chic—"Le Freak" — 19
William "Bubba" Anderson, James "Ajax" Baynard, LA Blacksmith, Tyrone Cox, Mark Lipetz and Phil "Flip" Thomas of Crown Heights Affair—"Dreaming a Dream" — 28
Clare Bathé, formerly of Machine—"There But for the Grace of God Go I" — 36
Anthony Brooks of Harold Melvin's Blue Notes—"Bad Luck" — 42
Ed Cermanski and Robert Upchurch of the Trammps—"Disco Inferno" — 46
Sarah Dash—"Sinner Man" — 53
John Davis—"Ain't That Enough for You" — 59
Leonard "Butch" Davis and Joe Harris of Double Exposure—"Ten Percent" — 66
Venus Dodson—"Night Rider" — 75
Joy Dorris of Lime—"Your Love" — 81
Bob Esty—"Last Dance" — 84
Jimmie Bo Horne—"Spank" — 92
Geraldine Hunt—"Can't Fake the Feeling" — 97
Carol Jiani—"Hit'n Run Lover" — 102
Janice Marie Johnson, formerly of A Taste of Honey—"Boogie Oogie Oogie" — 108
France Joli—"Come to Me" — 115
Randy Jones, formerly of Village People—"Y.M.C.A." — 123

Table of Contents

Shirley Jones, formerly of the Jones Girls—"You Gonna Make Me Love Somebody Else"	130
Denis LePage/Nini Nobless, formerly of Lime—"Babe, We're Gonna Love Tonite"	135
Robbie Leslie—Studio 54 DJ	144
W. Michael Lewis—"Cocomotion"	150
George McCrae—"Rock Your Baby"	157
Denise Montana—"#1 Dee Jay"	163
Eddie O'Loughlin—"Doctor's Orders"	168
Rob Parissi, formerly of Wild Cherry—"Play That Funky Music"	175
Bonnie Pointer—"Heaven Must Have Sent You"	182
Warren Schatz—"Turn the Beat Around"	190
Debbie Sledge, Joni Sledge and Kim Sledge of Sister Sledge—"We Are Family"	199
Arthur "Pooch" Tavares of Tavares—"Heaven Must Be Missing an Angel"	210
Richie Weeks, formerly of Weeks & Co.—"Rock Your World"	215
James "D-Train" Williams—"You're the One for Me"	220
Afterword by Henry Stone	227
The Turntable: Recommended Listening	231
Index	235

Foreword
by France Joli

Disco changed my life. We met in 1976, this revolutionary musical genre and I, and for me it was love at first sight—and sound. I was 13 years old, living in my hometown of Montreal, and going to Friday night dances at my local community center, where friends and I would get down to such hits as "Doctor's Orders" by Carol Douglas, "Turn the Beat Around" by Vicki Sue Robinson, "Don't Leave Me This Way" by Thelma Houston, and the Andrea True Connection's "More, More, More."

As much as I loved these women and their music, it was Donna Summer who gave me one of the most important realizations of my life. Having dreamed of being a successful singer since I was a child, I was already a veteran of voice lessons. For years, my idol had been the great Barbra Streisand, whose perfect performances I would listen to and mimic right over her LPs. But the torch songs Streisand favored were at odds with my youthful high spirits. I wanted to be a star, to be sure, and to showcase my singing prowess, but my teenage self didn't just want to sing ballads like "My Man" and "He Touched Me." I wanted this groove to make me move! Donna, with her plush voice and lush melodies, proved to me that a female artist could strut her vocal stuff and remain current. Perhaps I, too, could belt—all the while crafting indelible disco classics. I suddenly saw an avenue I could pursue.

Imagine my surprise and gratitude when I got the chance to do just that just a few years later. It was in 1978 that I met Montreal songwriter-producer Tony Green, who, after hearing me croon over my beloved Barbra, created the custom-made "Come to Me." Clichéd as the old adage is, the rest is history. A mere few months after meeting Tony, I was belting my own number one disco hit before crowds throughout the world, reveling in chart success alongside all the artists I'd so admired for so long. And I was still but 16 years old. The only bitter to the sweet of my debut is that it came a little late, just as disco's star was fading.

France Joli (courtesy France Joli).

While in many ways it still feels as if it were just yesterday, my breakthrough happened 35 years ago. At 16, one doesn't give much thought to middle-age—much less to a long-lasting career. If anyone had told me then that I would still be singing "Come to Me" to sold-out, ecstatic crowds now, more than three decades later, at the age of 51, I never would have believed them. But here I am, still going strong, still buoyed by the profound and seemingly everlasting power of love that disco provides.

I'm often asked how I feel about being labeled as a disco artist. My answer is always, "I feel nothing but pride." I'm honored to have been able to contribute in my own relatively small way to the massive, unbridled joy disco artists and their repertoires have brought (and continue to bring) to aficionados the world over. Disco wasn't just a beat; it was a state of mind. I'm also gratified and humbled to see that so many artists that came after us—from Madonna and Britney Spears to Rihanna and Lady Gaga—can trace their musical roots back to disco. Yes, today we call it "dance music," but that art form has disco deeply imbedded in every strand of its DNA. It's proof of how much we and our music have mattered. Disco is far from dead. Rather, with each new dance pop hit, it's reborn.

These days, when I meet fans after a performance, I'm tickled by two particular types of admirers. The first is the person who used to be a hardcore rocker in his youth, one who thought disco sucked but who has come to understand the beauty inherent in the genre's words and melodies. The second is the person who wasn't even alive during disco's heyday but who, because their parents played our records throughout their childhood, has not only learned to appreciate the songs but knows every word to the vast majority of them.

I am so thankful to author James Arena for inviting me to be a part of this staggering, significant volume. Alongside its predecessor, *First Ladies of Disco*, it serves as an invaluable historical record of a particular musical moment in time. But more than that, both tomes, taken together, serve as a long overdue tribute to the women and men who made disco what it was and is, but whose considerable harmonious talents and contributions have for too long been either forgotten or ignored, and thereby remain unsung.

I intend to wear my own "Disco Artist" badge with great pride and gratitude for the rest of my life. Only time will tell at what age I will sing my last note. But one thing I already know is that long after I'm gone, "Come to Me" and all those other golden oldies will live on and on and on, kept vibrantly alive in the hearts and souls of fans who don't yet dance this earth.

Preface

Disco has hit middle age. It's fairly safe to say the genre unofficially turned 40 in 2014 when much of this book of interviews was developed, making the year a ruby anniversary worth celebrating—loudly and proudly. While most of us run screaming from that red-letter day in our personal lives (assuming we ever admit we've hit the 40-year milestone), disco has reason to rejoice. Generally speaking, the first major commercial hits classified as "disco" (e.g., "Never Can Say Goodbye" by Gloria Gaynor, Carol Douglas' "Doctor's Orders," "Rock Your Baby" by George McCrae and the Hues Corporation's "Rock the Boat," among a handful of others) made their debuts in 1974 and changed the music and pop culture landscape forever. Furthermore, disco music is alive and well today with a resume that reveals the bumps, bruises, triumphs and achievements of a survivor!

Throughout the past four decades, disco music (which is obviously based on energy and movement) has ironically been something of a concrete foundation in my life. It has elevated my spirit and given me unstoppable, immeasurable bliss, regardless of what else or who else threatened to pull me down. It has always been there—stable and solid, like a faithful friend. From the moment I heard and saw the late Andrea True singing "N.Y., You Got Me Dancing" on the *Disco '77* television show one summer night when just a teen, I was hooked. Never had I heard such an invigorating and intoxicating sound and, as it turned out, music like this would never stop fueling my soul's engine. I know that sounds a bit sensational, but I assure you the statement is quite true. Obtaining a steady supply of these remarkably inspiring musical creations became nothing short of an addiction for me (as it did for millions of people like me). It still is.

By the time I turned 50, I was no longer able to quell the curiosity that had been burning in me for years to learn more about the great male and female singers of disco and those in the background who supported them. I could no longer wait around for someone else to give me the details I craved, so I decided to write a book about the subject myself in 2011, *First Ladies of Disco*. I knew what these entertainers could do in the recording studio, but I had precious little understanding of who they were as people. I needed to find out what quality—what power—these individuals possessed that enabled them to move me in such a remarkable way for so many years. I didn't know how or if I would succeed. Perhaps something about my plunge into middle age drove me to take on this formidable quest, but I was determined to see it through.

I elected to first concentrate on the female vocalists of the disco era and managed to gather the stories of 32 remarkable women for the project. *First Ladies of Disco* was released in the summer of 2013. Never could I have imagined what would happen next—in the course of promoting this book on radio, TV and in live shows, I would get to know, even befriend, many of these accomplished stars and share so many incredible new experiences with them. I can only describe this time in my life as surreal. Yet my personal discoveries about them weren't dreamy at all. In the process of interviewing and working with these stars, I discovered that the power these singers possessed was something that's really in all of us—a desire to make people happy. It was nothing mysterious or supernatural, nothing complicated. They were mostly just good people—genuine people, with many of the same hopes and fears we all have. They are each the sum total of the ups and downs that we all must go through in one way or another as part of our experience on this planet. But one thing the women of *First Ladies of Disco* have that most of us lack is a knack for using a powerhouse song to express their positivity and creativity. They use their voices like a paintbrush, splashing the brightest possible colors across a dance floor canvas. They moved us back in those days—and they still do.

While pressing onward with the promotion of *First Ladies of Disco*, I continued working on the follow-up book you now hold. I knew another volume would be mandatory and, frankly, I was exhilarated and eager to develop *Legends of Disco*. There were several major female artists I wanted to include in the first book, but for various reasons had been unable to feature. Now I had my chance to reach them. I also needed to have some of their male counterparts represented. Frankly, I had worried that the men might not be as enthusiastic as the women, but such fears were completely unfounded. The gentlemen were extraordinarily agreeable and just as exuberant about the project as the women.

I received countless requests and suggestions to include many wonderful notables from around the world in this edition, but, as you might expect (and as was the case with *First Ladies of Disco*), many were unreachable, sometimes uninterested or, regrettably, impossible to communicate with in a timely fashion. There are also, of course, limits to how many individuals can be brought into a single book. In no way does a person's absence in either of these volumes indicate he or she is not a first lady or legend of disco. However, the 40 luminaries assembled here *are* truly among the finest ambassadors of disco.

One of the discoveries I've made in the course of writing these books is that the word "disco" is still a bit of a problem for some people, even stars of the genre. I've always liked the word and was quite comfortable with it. It was a short and sweet label, and I knew I would generally savor the music classified by this term. But you'll find a few artists in this volume who don't hesitate to say they *weren't* thrilled to be categorized as a disco act. However, most will agree the genre put them on the map, and it continues to pay the bills today. Still, labeling has always been a mixed bag in modern society. While it's generally considered fine to call a person an Italian, a Frenchman or a Latin American, or to identify an athlete as a baseball player, soccer star, etc., somehow being referred to as a "disco artist" is far trickier, especially in the U.S. That may be a stretch as far as comparisons go, but you get the idea. Never has there been a style of music that stirs up such a mixed bag of emotions. If a musician or singer is categorized as R&B, hip-hop, rock, jazz, country or classical, for the most part, nobody fights it. Call someone a first lady or legend of *disco*, and the brakes are applied, even though such a title should never imply that the genre was the *only* music form at which the artist excelled (or was capable of performing).

It's unfortunate that being strongly associated with a disco hit or the era isn't always cause for celebration. It really should be. Basically, public fatigue with a marketplace flooded by dance records, a few notoriously cheesy songs, media excesses and a dash of industry insider sabotage resulted in an anti-disco backlash in the United States that has lingered in the air for decades. (Not the case in Europe, where audiences generally displayed far more loyalty to the genre and its stars.) It takes a bit of courage for an artist associated with disco to embrace all of his or her history, especially with such embers of negativity still smoldering here and there. But it's definitely changing. Disco has made huge strides forward in the last few years. As the populations of the world that experienced this era become nostalgic for these sounds (and as a younger generation discovers that the majority of this music was, indeed, kick-ass), disco's respectability is undeniably increasing. And the singers, composers, arrangers, producers and DJs who made this beautiful music famous are finally getting their due.

This book is a celebration of the living, but I would be remiss if I did not respectfully note those who have departed. In *First Ladies of Disco*, I acknowledged the contributions of many great women who championed the genre and have left this life, such as the incomparable Donna Summer, whose passing still leaves many of us feeling stunned and empty. Since then, we have lost songstress Zulema (1947–2013), vocalist of the 1978 club smash "Change." There have been many extraordinary gentlemen who are now dancing in heaven as well, leaving behind an indelible mark on the genre. Among those who have passed in the 21st century are:

Nick Ashford (1941–2011)—singer, songwriter, member of Ashford & Simpson: "One More Try," "Don't Cost You Nothing," "Found a Cure," "Solid."
Harvey Fuqua (1929–2010)—singer, songwriter, producer and record company executive, instrumental in launching the careers of Sylvester ("Dance (Disco Heat)," "You Make Me Feel (Mighty Real)"), Jeanie Tracy and Martha Wash.
Maurice Gibb (1949–2003)—member of the Bee Gees: "Stayin' Alive," "You Should Be Dancing."
Robin Gibb (1949–2012)—member of the Bee Gees: "Night Fever," "Boys Do Fall in Love."
Glenn Hughes (1950–2001)—member of the group Village People (the original "biker" character): "Fire Island," "Macho Man," "Y.M.C.A.," "In the Navy."
Michael Jackson (1958–2009)—lead singer of Jackson 5, the Jacksons: "Blame It on the Boogie," "Enjoy Yourself," "Shake Your Body (Down to the Ground)," "Can You Feel It," "Don't Stop 'Til You Get Enough," "Rock with You."
Rick James (1948–2004)—"You and I," "Give It to Me Baby," "Super Freak," "Love Gun."
Gene McFadden (1948–2006)—singer, songwriter, producer, member of McFadden & Whitehead: "Don't Feel Bad," "Mr. Music."
Edwin Starr (1942–2003)— "Contact," "H.A.P.P.Y. Radio."
Edmund Sylvers (1957–2004)—lead singer of the Sylvers: "Boogie Fever," "High School Dance," "Hot Line," "That Burning Love."
Johnnie Taylor (1938–2000)— "Disco Lady."
Luther Vandross (1951–2005)—vocalist with Chic, Change, Hi-Gloss, and others, background vocalist for Diana Ross, Barbra Streisand, Donna Summer, Chaka Khan. "Never Too Much," "A Lover's Holiday" (Change).

Barry White (1944–2003)—"You're the First, the Last, My Everything," "Can't Get Enough of Your Love, Babe."

Maurice White (1941–2016)—singer, songwriter, musician, producer and arranger, founder of Earth, Wind & Fire: "Sing a Song" (EWF), "Getaway" (EWF), "Boogie Wonderland" (EWF with the Emotions), "September" (EWF), "Let's Groove" (EWF), "Magnetic" (EWF).

John Whitehead (1948–2004)—singer, songwriter, producer, member of McFadden & Whitehead: "Ain't No Stoppin' Us Now," "I Heard It in a Love Song."

Remembering these wonderful artists serves to remind us that disco was a source of life. It tapped into the very core of our beings, inciting us to smile, laugh, look our best, clink a glass, get a little high, kiss, hold each other, sing, feel good and *move*. There was no room for sexism, racism or discrimination on the dance floor. Everyone was welcome. Gay, straight, black, white, geeky, cool, dumb, smart, short, tall, thin, fat, common, weird, foreign or domestic, successful or struggling—everyone was equal under the disco ball, and the music brought them there. For every blemish on disco's reputation, there is an even brighter reason to celebrate the excitement, energy and communal feeling this music generated. The pioneering vocalists and creators of disco did something extraordinary. They took a world that had become crippled by depression and negativity and got it back on its feet again—literally. The disco era was a remarkable time in pop culture history, and while we may have simply casually enjoyed it at the time, only now are we beginning to fully appreciate the beauty and power this art form held.

It's important to acknowledge the artists assembled in *First Ladies of Disco* and *Legends of Disco* and to listen to their stories. There is much to be gleaned from their struggles and triumphs. The lessons in positivity their steadfastness teaches us are sure to inspire. Revered business guru and life coach Earl Nightingale once said that success is best measured not by fame or money, but rather by the quest of a worthy goal. The goal of these entertainers was to bring all of us joy. I can think of no group of people who were more successful. To this distinguished assemblage of professionals, I posed questions about their lives and careers. These are their answers. These are the thoughts they want to share with you.

One last note about *Legends of Disco*. This book was originally released as a self-published project called *First Legends of Disco*. At the time, I chose this method of creation (in part) to satisfy my curiosity about this burgeoning book creation platform. While self-publishing provides solid opportunities for many writers covering unique subjects, I found the medium to be limited in its reach and not terribly popular among organizations and institutions that are vital to book exposure, including libraries. Though proud of the effort I put into releasing *First Legends of Disco*, I believed the artists featured in these pages deserved a stronger opportunity to be heard. My publisher agreed, so I eagerly worked with their team to re-edit, redesign and update some of the information contained herein.

I hope *Legends of Disco* and *First Ladies of Disco* will be viewed as a tribute to *all* the great stars of this music genre who hail from every corner of the globe. And, after reading both of these volumes, it is my fervent wish that you will be left wanting more, more, more!

Professionals Behind the Scenes

"The enjoyment I felt being part of disco as it gained popularity was partly due to the fact that the genre created a mutually respectful community among artists, and there was a real sense of unity and fun."—Precious Wilson, Singer, Eruption

There are many professionals in the entertainment industry who have had the opportunity to work in the world of disco music and who possess compelling insights into its mechanics, challenges and relevance to pop culture. I consulted with a few of these individuals and posed to each some questions that may help us better understand the artists celebrated in this book and to appreciate the environment in which they must work today. The panelists sharing their viewpoints are:

Patrick Adams

Patrick is a phenomenon in disco, esteemed for his accomplishments as a brilliant producer, songwriter, arranger, musician and engineer. Harlem-born Adams contributed his artistry to such legendary classics as "Keep on Jumpin'" and "In the Bush" by Musique, the 1975 debut LP of Sister Sledge (*Circle of Love*), the *Super Mann* album by Herbie Mann, Bumblebee Unlimited's *Sting Like a Bee* LP, the smash single by Inner Life, "I'm Caught Up (In a One Night Love Affair)," and Fonda Rae's "Touch Me (All Night Long)." He's worked with Loleatta Holloway, Narada Michael Walden, Jeanie Tracy, Boris Midney, Rick James, Venus Dodson, Melba Moore and countless others. Patrick continues to produce exciting dance music in the 21st century.

Joe Causi

"Brooklyn's Own" Joe Causi, as he is often touted, is a legendary radio and TV host with a long history in dance music, including a long-running DJ gig at one of the most popular New York disco radio stations of all time, WKTU. He has appeared on SiriusXM Satellite Radio, Court TV, Clear Channel Radio and currently hosts a number one-rated nightly music show on New York's WCBS-FM, as well as his "Saturday Night Block Party" program. Joe's playlist is always packed with timeless dance classics.

Teri DeSario

Teri entered the disco arena after Barry Gibb heard her youthful, enchanting voice and wrote a song for her called "Ain't Nothing Gonna Keep Me from You," now widely considered a 1978 Casablanca Records dance classic. She teamed up with Harry Wayne Casey (KC), a former schoolmate, and together the duo reached the number two position on the pop charts in 1980 with the hit "Yes, I'm Ready." DeSario pursued a career in

Christian music for a time and spent many years residing in Germany. She recently returned to the disco performance circuit, singing her hits once again for enthusiastic audiences.

Luci Martin

Luci is a former vocalist with Chic, and her voice can be heard on the group's landmark *C'est Chic* and *Risqué* albums, among other legendary recordings helmed by producers Nile Rodgers and Bernard Edwards. She continues to perform and release music today with fellow former first ladies of Chic, Norma Jean Wright and Alfa Anderson.

Sofiane Hadjazi

Sofiane is a successful disco, dance, soul and funk show promoter based in Paris, France. This youthful entrepreneur has worked with many of classic disco's finest talents, producing popular shows that have attracted massive crowds throughout the continent.

Cory Robbins

Cory produced many classic disco records, including "Doin' the Best That I Can" by Bettye LaVette (for West End Records) and "Love Insurance" by Front Page (for Panorama Records, where he served as general manager). Finding the production side of the industry tedious, he favored the executive side of the business and started Profile Records in 1981. The label was initially designed to specialize in 12-inch singles ("I'm Starting Again" by Grace Kennedy—the company's first release, "I Specialize in Love" by Sharon Brown, "To Sir with Love" by Vicki Sue Robinson, etc.) during the post-disco crash years. The label later became extremely successful in the hip-hop genre. Cory formed the Robbins Entertainment label in 1996, which has been a major force in contemporary dance music ever since.

Myra Scheer

Myra served as assistant to Studio 54's original owners and visionaries, Steve Rubell and Ian Schrager. She was entrusted with the "Master Call List," which represented the influencers and stars of the era, including Warhol, Halston and Jagger. Myra also handled the club's in-house public relations and eventually worked the so-called "inner door" several nights a week. She currently is co-host of *The Marc and Myra Show* with Marc Benecke on SiriusXM. The program firmly places the spotlight on disco music and the culture of the legendary New York night club she once called home.

James Washington

James is founder and owner of J. Washington Management, Inc., and is responsible for launching and molding the careers of the Emmy Award–winning violin duo Nuttin' But Stringz. He became widely respected for having a natural eye for talent and the ability to guide his artists down a prosperous career path. Washington has expanded his reach into the world of dance music and currently guides legendary diva Martha Wash ("It's Raining Men"). He formed the trio First Ladies of Disco (inspired by the book of the same name), featuring Martha, Linda Clifford and Evelyn "Champagne" King, whose first release in 2015, "Show Some Love," was a Top 10 *Billboard* dance chart hit.

Precious Wilson

Born in Jamaica, Precious joined the newly formed group Eruption in 1974 with lead guitarist Greg Perrineau, his brother Morgan Perrineau on bass, Gerry Williams on keyboards and Eric Kingsley on drums. Wilson soon became the group's lead singer and the troupe began performing throughout Germany. Eventually, they were introduced to Frank Farian, the producer of Boney M., who signed them in 1977. A riveting disco cover of the Ann Peebles classic "I Can't Stand the Rain" was released in 1978, sending Eruption soaring up the American and European pop and club charts. The single "One Way Ticket," a top U.K. smash, cemented Eruption's position as a progressive dance music ensemble. Wilson went solo in 1979 and has scored numerous hits on her own, including the high-energy anthem "Only the Strong Survive," produced by the Stock Aitken Waterman team. She continues to record and tour today.

* * *

What is it about the artists you have known or worked with in disco that makes them so special and well suited to this genre of music?

Adams: "In my eyes, there are artists, and there are *artists*. Popularity is earned by exhibiting the ability to engage and entertain an audience. I don't want to point in any one direction, but you cannot just grab a bunch of cute kids, throw them on the stage and call them 'stars.' I recently watched a program featuring a performance by Frank Sinatra. It is easy to see why he was so revered as a performer. He engaged his audience. He shared his emotional journey with them. On a personal level I can tell you, if you have ever experienced Christine Wiltshire (Musique, Class Action) or Jocelyn Brown or Fonda Rae live, you know you have been entertained. They each can command an audience, whether in a small intimate club setting or a huge outdoor festival."

Causi: "Everything that comes out today is really fabricated in the studio. I remember seeing the Trammps at a club on Long Island back in the day. They had something like 20 guys on stage. There was no CD playing—it was all the work of these gentlemen. The Trammps had real brass, drums, keyboards and five main singers. That was what was so special about the disco era. These artists were professionals and so great at what they did. These people were great performers on stage, and many of them were great musicians. The music industry today has come down to the bad boys and bad girls, having fights and that kind of nonsense. It's all about getting the media attention. In the days of disco, it was the song and the performance that got the attention. The first time I put Theo Vaness or Patrick Juvet on my turntable at KTU, you could hear what went into these extended play tracks. You could hear the craftsmanship that went into making this music. I must have about 11,000 albums in my home. I love this music!"

Martin: "They have the attitude of enjoying life to its fullest, even if at times recklessly."

Hadjazi: "Undoubtedly, the symphony created from the use of so many instruments made disco unlike any other style of music in the world. From my experience in France, disco is music that appeals to almost everyone, and they always enjoy it! This style of music, 'le disco' as it is called in my country, reflects more of the '80s for us—while in the U.S. it was thought of as a '70s phenomenon. At the time, there weren't the means of communication we have today and, unfortunately, not all American disco records made it to our continent. Luckily, we are close to Belgium, Holland and England—countries that generally were served with U.S. hits. This permitted many of us to go stock up on American vinyl.

"My words can never quite do these classic disco singers justice. Artistically, they are performers who earned and deserved success because, 35 or 40 years later, I find them all still at the top of their game on stage. I have listened to my records endlessly, and I found that when these artists sing live in front of me, the sound is pretty much the same. I realized that this remarkable talent is what made them superstars in their heyday! They are the real thing.

"There is another side to these performers as well. It is the magic of their personalities. After working with them, I found them all to be very different. Yet they have something in common—they all are so full of kindness and love. I have forged great friendships with many of these artists beyond the business side."

Scheer: "It's interesting that the people we've interviewed on the *Marc & Myra Show*, like Nile Rodgers, France Joli and some of the first ladies of disco, have this sense of gratitude common to all of them. I don't think the creation of their music or their motivation was about money or fame. Back then, disco music seemed to come out of a more creative drive and a desire to express one's self.

"The stars of disco have a lot of wisdom to pass on. It was a different time—something Nile Rodgers refers to as 'a liberated territory.' Certainly today, the Internet age has created a scenario where nobody really is in the moment like we were in the days of Studio 54. It's funny because these singers and stars would be at Studio 54, and I have no memory of anyone asking for an autograph or to take a photo with them. People at the club were validated—simply by being there. Thoughts of picture taking weren't even on our radar. Today, the essence of celebrity isn't necessarily about those who are celebrated. It seems to be more about a need for attention. Bob Colacello, Andy Warhol's editor, joked on our show that today Andy would probably say, 'In the future, everyone will be anonymous for 15 minutes.' The dance floor was the star, and all inside were equals. As I believe Andy said, 'It was a dictatorship at the door, but a democracy inside.'"

Washington: "I think it's the characteristics and personalities of the artists themselves. It was a fun time for music. It took flamboyant, charismatic talent to be successful and come forward, and the women I work with definitely have it. America was changing when disco came to the forefront of pop culture, and the music was a fun way to emerge into the new era. They were great vocalists who could really make a dance track work, and their voices and energy were the perfect fit."

Wilson: "I believe that the reason the producers, musicians and artists, like me and the guys in Eruption, have become synonymous with classic disco music was because of our individual backgrounds and the caliber and quality of talent we grew up listening to.

"As far back as I can remember, I've always loved to sing and entertain. There was always music in our house, and I can still recall the day my mother took me to my very first live concert in our hometown of Kingston Jamaica. Growing up, I was exposed to many musical influences, including gospel and R&B. I consider myself very lucky because I grew up in an era of really great singers, such as Sam Cooke, Sam & Dave and Mahalia

Jackson. Country music and ska music were also favorites of mine. This, combined with the homegrown music of lovers rock, reggae and calypso, rock 'n' roll, and classical music, were all a way of life for me.

"The enjoyment I felt being part of disco as it gained popularity was partly due to the fact that the genre created a mutually respectful community among artists, and there was a real sense of unity and fun. Eruption strived to generate positivity in our music, and as the popularity of disco music increased globally, the community of disco music fans grew because of the pleasure that the music gave."

What are the biggest challenges artists from the days of classic disco face in their careers today?

Adams: "There are two serious challenges today. The first is that, like so many other structures in society, the music business model is seriously broken. Corporations are quick to use music (whether it's a car company flaunting their on-board mp3 player or online services giving unlimited streaming for a monthly fee), but have no respect for the creators and the intellectual property—which allow them to make millions. The second challenge is being heard in an ocean of wanna-be artists. Now that anyone with a computer, app and Internet service can place his or her creations out for the world to hear, competition has gone from impossible to total insanity, and musical talent has nothing to do with it. 'In a world where everybody is a star, nobody is a star.'"

Causi: "If you ask your average person, your average radio listener, what their favorite disco songs are, you'll be lucky if you get more than 'I Will Survive,' "Ring My Bell,' 'Come to Me,' 'Macho Man,' 'Y.M.C.A.,' 'Play That Funky Music' and maybe a handful of others. That's all they know. It's not even a seed on the bread. The real disco fans know Melba Moore's 'Pick Me Up, I'll Dance,' Barbara Roy and Ecstasy, Passion & Pain, Rochelle Fleming and First Choice, the Trammps' 'That's Where the Happy People Go' and things like that. But the general public? Not so much. That's the biggest hurdle for these artists to get over today."

DeSario: "The biggest challenge these artists face is to not feel the need to have to recapture the past. I look back at my career in disco, and I accept that the time is over. I made my contribution, and now I make a different type of contribution today. I think the challenge for these singers is to go out as an elder with gratitude and say yes to the people who danced to their music and made it a part of their lives. But they must do this without feeling the pressure to recapture everything about those days.

"That said, I know this music means a great deal to a lot of people. I receive messages from the children of people I sang for. I got a letter from someone the other day who said his father died three days ago and 'Ain't Nothing Gonna Keep Me from You' was his favorite song. His son has played the song every day since his father's passing. Isn't that beautiful?"

Martin: "It's increasingly difficult to establish oneself as an artist with abilities outside of disco. If you have gained popularity through it, no matter what you do you are always typecast with disco being your specialty. Music has changed, and so has the industry. It's challenging trying to bridge the gap—retaining your history and not losing its value and yet being taken seriously as a qualified artist who is capable of performing in other genres."

Hadjazi: "When we contact a disco artist and show this person what we have to offer in France, most of the time the artist is very pleased to come to our country! There is no doubt in our minds that these performers are still powerful, professional and will deliver an unforgettable show. The biggest challenge we face is keeping tickets to the shows affordable, as it's very expensive to bring all these artists to Europe. This is especially true for groups or to bring an artist that works with his or her own band. It has become common for artists to sing a showcase [perform to instrumental tracks]. Just as in America, there are budget restrictions here in France. So, unfortunately, we cannot always invite artists who are important to us because their rates often exceed our ability to pay. However, I feel inclined to say that, fortunately, it is not always the most expensive artist who sings the best or puts on the most enjoyable show.

"In France, I'd say the average age of the audience for a disco artist is between 40 and 60 years. After all, this is the music of that generation. However, there are people of all types within these audiences. I never heard or felt that disco belonged to a sexual orientation, age group or any other community. It has always been simply the people who like to party!

"Speaking for myself, I am probably one of the youngest promoters in France to organize parties and concert events that allow fans to approach the artists and take pictures. In some cases, we've even allowed some fans to get their vinyl signed on stage. I would describe our disco shows as very warm. My goal was and is to get the most fun out of the event for the artist and for the fan. I started doing this at the age of 25 years, now I'm 30 with over 15 artists on my roster. I'm not a major producer or rich (quite the contrary), and I have a very simple way of life. I take the money from my wages, and with it, I have managed to achieve my dreams. It is my passion and love for this music and these artists that places me where I am today, and I have no regrets. I get immense pleasure from their performances on stage and for me, their age is irrelevant!"

Washington: "They have to fight the 'stigma' that disco was left with in the end. Artists from this genre need a plan to move forward from that music to be relevant today. Disco will always be popular, but the men and women who are known for this music must work with their representation to prepare for the future. Having read some of these artists' stories in *First Ladies of Disco*, I discovered some of these people didn't want to be in disco. Then, when the music died, they were stuck. I think back then, just as today, you needed to plan properly. Even when you get dropped by a label, it doesn't have to be the end. An artist needs to look at reinvention—a rebirthing. A lot of that came down to having a strong team behind them, and they weren't all that lucky in those days. Record labels and some artist managers and the like—they were taking advantage of these singers back then and, unfortunately, some of these performers were not equipped to fight back.

"The words 'independent artist' weren't popular back then, and that's unfortunate. I think many of these artists would have excelled had that concept been more accepted. But even today, being open to the possibilities of reinvention can absolutely keep disco artists relevant. But they must have the spirit and will to do so."

Wilson: "When I came into the music business, the industry was totally different from how it is now. In those days, artists would receive large financial advance payments from the record companies. There were many more opportunities to sell your records.

Record companies were more willing to invest in a new artist for the long term. Your fan base grew as a direct result of having the talent and the ability to do tours and perform live. Generally, singers had to really be able to sing and there was, of course, no Internet, no MTV and no Twitter or Facebook. The artist was more able to make a living from being in the entertainment industry, and your intellectual copyright was safer. Nowadays, many people feel entitled to download music for free with little thought about whether or not the artist makes a living or gets paid for their work and their creativity."

What contribution can classic disco artists continue to make in the 21st century? What keeps these artists and their music relevant?

Adams: "A good artist will always have a place in the world. Once again, the genre of an artist should never be the main consideration. Any artist who put in the time to perfect their craft and has years of experience under their belt as an entertainer will always have a place in the world.

"In every culture on earth, there will always be a place for music to soothe people and lift their spirits. As we move forward, the challenge is the same as always. New technology arrives and makes it possible for almost anyone to create sounds which, when organized in a coherent fashion, could be mistaken for music. Currently, there is a plethora of electronic 'music' being 'created' by well-meaning artists who are on the fringe. Many are motivated by the promise of an easy path to fame and riches. Drum machines, samplers and computer software and apps make it possible for almost anyone to make noises that simulate music. The Internet and social media make it possible for any novice to share their creations with the whole world.

"For the sake of argument, let us call it 'reality music.' Most of it lacks substance and will never rise to the level of acceptance afforded to well-composed art. Inspired music moves people and sticks to the soul. Great music lives beyond the dance floor. Longevity is the test. The sounds and instrumentation may change, but the artistic foundation remains the same.

"Complicating matters are the corporate masters who believe that by controlling all the radio stations and record companies, they can profit by dictating what people hear. As young people hear the great music of past generations and feel what music is, they will grow to understand and begin to create new exciting music of their own."

Causi: "I host live disco shows once every three months or so. I did one just a few weeks ago and 2,000 to 2,500 people were there. It was a sell-out show for music that is 35 to 40 years old. Personally, I think disco has a few more years to go as far as live shows are concerned, because [the average fan of this music is generally in his or her late 40s, 50s or 60s, and] I'm not sure those people, as they get into their 70s, are going to go out as much. That's just what I've seen with other types of music artists like the Doo-wop groups. When it reaches that point, I think you have to say, 'We had our day in the sun; let's move on.' But I do want to say that many of these disco artists are still incredible. For example, I just saw Tavares, and they are phenomenal on stage. They always get the crowd on their feet, and they are great at what they do. People are still hungry for this music, and they want to feel like a kid again. Disco can do that!"

Martin: "I see disco music making its appearance in different ways throughout this century. I can't see any form of dance music disappearing forever. We may see snippets or hints of it in other styles. We may see all of it return when there is a lull in the creative activity that music seems to take every few decades. But it will always be a part of us because people love to dance. They love to celebrate and move, whether in a gym or on a dance floor, and there will always be times in our lives that call for us to show expression or feel the joy of letting loose, if only for a moment. That tells us we're alive!

"Those fortunate enough to find a place in the arts need to have some form of talent. They need a distinct personality and the nature to give even when it seems like no one wants what you are serving. And we all need a bit of luck. This is especially true in disco, since it was an era of fun, lightness and good times—no pun intended—and you had to be able to walk on stage ready to inject your audience with a sense of well-being and playfulness. There is no room for depression with disco. Even songs about lost loves or heartaches have something in them to that motivates the listener to dance it all away.

"I suppose the relevance I see disco artists having in today's industry is in their ability to remind audiences of better days. Couple that with the ability to be able to transition into the current marketplace with a contemporary sound, while avoiding the temptation to just imitate it. In my opinion only, it is like knowing how to pair a piece of your favorite vintage clothing with a current trend or style that someone younger might wear. You don't want to put on the entire outfit of either. You do not want to dress like a 20-year-old if you're not that age, but you also don't wish to look dated. Finding that compromise—that happy medium—is the key."

Scheer: "Interviewing the people of my generation who were involved in disco is an inspiring adventure for me that I could never have predicted. This era was predominantly branded as 'sex, drugs and disco.' Those who survived it and who came out the other side (and let's also note the classic disco era began before AIDS had a name) have done so with grace, gratitude and it seems like unlimited boundaries. I look at someone like Nile Rodgers. He's made 60 the new 21. These artists and survivors show that aging isn't necessarily the end of your life—it can be the best time of your life. Happiness isn't getting inside a club; it's what's inside you. It's not having what you want but wanting what you have.

"I think the disco genre is more highly regarded now. On our show, there are rock 'n' roll musicians like John Oates who are so happy to talk about how incredible the music was back then and how remarkable Studio 54 was. Studio 54 would not have been the place it was without the music. I think there's a second coming for disco. I hear it in commercials on TV and just about everywhere. Our SiriusXM station, which plays the original music of the era, has quite a following today, even with the younger generation. It is coming at a time when the economy is shaky. It's on people's minds. It's constantly in the news, so this music is like a rush of happiness that's coming on again, just as it did before. The disco joy back then seemed like it was short-lived, but it feels to me like this revival is now here to stay longer, and it will be recognized in a 21st Century way."

Robbins: "There are a few artists that I have a warm spot for and would love to hear something new from. Would anyone else? Probably not that many will care, unless the artist has a unique angle or a producer that is really prominent. It's not impossible for [the stars from the disco era] to have a hit today, but the odds are stacked against it.

"Some artists will always be able to continue to work. Someone like Gloria Gaynor will probably be able to work forever because of 'I Will Survive.' Donna Summer had many hits beyond disco. The absolute greatest artists can last through decades—Madonna, Cher, Elton John, Barbra Streisand. These cross-generation artists come along very rarely.

"I'm not sure where disco will go in the future. I think there are a lot of great dance records today that don't necessarily relate to the old sound, but some do. Daft Punk certainly are heavily influenced by disco, and we may see more of that. I don't necessarily agree with people who say that modern dance music owes everything to disco, as if nothing original could come after it. Everything is influenced by what came before it, every form of music, but, to me, the belief that any current artist 'owes' their success to another who came before just sounds bitter. As much as I love disco, I enjoy staying current, and disco artists had their time. That happens in almost every career. I have seen artists who are unhappy that they aren't remembered anymore, but that's just sort of the way it goes. I truly appreciate the great music of the disco era, but I also appreciate what's happening now."

Wilson: "There's room for classic disco artists because theirs is a heartfelt music that is universal and timeless. Disco had singers who could really sing, real musicians playing real instruments. The fact that it originated in both the gay and black community minority groups is not surprising, as it possessed a sensual, rhythmic quality that had power and energy. As long as people got a chance to hear it, their spirits and hearts couldn't help but connect to the rhythm and heartbeat of the music.

"The main thing about staying relevant today is to stay true to yourself and update your sound with today's technology to enhance and complement your 'authentic creative substance.' Technology and society are changing around us all the time, and it's not always easy to keep up. Many artists from the disco era don't want to change the way they do things. I had to consciously re-educate myself. Many of my generation of singers don't want to do that because they feel overwhelmed or they feel relaxed in the 'old school' ways of doing things. They are afraid to embrace the challenge of stepping out of their comfort zone and trying something new.

"The fact is, that if you are engaged in an occupation as a paid job rather than as a hobby, the only way to survive is to accept and surrender to the idea that things are done differently these days. For disco artists, producers and musicians to continue to have some bearing on or importance in today's world, I believe that we need to move with the times. We need to reframe our beliefs and attitudes, partner up and collaborate with others, reinvent ourselves and diversify. We must generally be willing to take the necessary steps to continue to not just survive, but thrive and make progress.

"Staying relevant for me includes having a website (www.preciouswilson.com) and also giving back—sharing my knowledge and expertise. That is why I am creating my own voice and artist development company. The aim of my company will be to help aspiring artists to perform like a 'business celebrity,' so that they can profit from their passion."

What is disco music's value and place in pop culture history, now that it has turned 40 years old?

Adams: "Disco was the real world soundtrack of a period of liberation in the '70s. As the promises of the '60s began to be realized by people of color and as sexual culture expanded, disco represented a spirit of change. I believe it was the reflection of the 'American Dream.' It was music of the people, by the people and for the people. Some people say it was the 'classical music' of the United States."

Causi: "Disco makes people feel good. Today, it makes people think about their past, before they met their husbands or wives. When they hear this music, they might start thinking of the first time they saw the Trammps, Crown Heights Affair, Double Exposure or France Joli. People take those memories with them, and nostalgia is a big part of the music. Every decade has its music, and there's a place in history for all of it. Having worked at clubs and parties, I've played songs by the Beach Boys, the Beatles or Bill Haley and the Comets, and people just sit there and say, 'Oh yeah, remember that song?' But you throw on a Barry White, Bonnie Pointer, France Joli record or something like Cher's 'Take Me Home' and, all of the sudden, the 40, 50 and 60 year olds are back in their 20-year-old bodies, and they are back on the dance floor! They will never get tired of this music. It makes people feel young, and it inspires you to get up and dance."

DeSario: "I think that disco was a very strong agent in the breakdown of prejudice. It played a huge role in breaking down barriers between heterosexual and gay people and people of different races. Disco created a new sense of freedom.

"That freedom was especially strong in the gay nightclubs. I remember performing with K.C. in a gay club that was packed. I performed my songs on top of a table! Literally! That was my stage. All these people knew how to celebrate. That's what I always loved about the LGBT community. In the face of everything they had to deal with, they had this great capacity for joy. The atmosphere was very free and loving. It was so much fun just to have that permission to cut loose. I always remember being accepted by the gay community and being very thankful for it. Disco music was an important part of that.

"I came to disco music through the Bee Gees. I was a singer/songwriter—a folk artist. When Barry Gibb, Karl Richardson and Albhy Galuten approached me to do 'Ain't Nothing Gonna Keep Me from You,' I did that song not really identifying it as disco. I chose the song because I liked it. I think in its original form it was about three or four minutes long and only hit the lower portion of the pop chart. I thought that was a shame because everything Barry produced was always hitting the Top Five. And then they cut a longer disco version, and it went wild! I think something in my voice, maybe my vulnerability, touched people. I've had that happen with songs in other genres that I have sung. I have always been able to express some kind of spirituality in my music. I have always tried to hook into the underlying feeling or message in a song.

"In the case of 'Ain't Nothing Gonna Keep Me from You,' it's saying that I love you so much, and I will do anything for love. When you sing something like that with such an inner commitment, I think people respond. It relates to something in them, and that's the beauty of that sort of exchange that happens. I think many disco songs and the vocalists who sang them were able to achieve this connection."

Martin: "Good music will always have value. A good song is a good song, and all or parts of it can always be recycled and used in different formats that will appeal to someone. A lot of what is heard in today's music is 'borrowed' from the past. Disco or dance music, in general, always seems to find a home, no matter what happens or how many years pass. Whether it is in the form of nostalgia or in some sampled form, it will remain part of any culture for those who love to move."

Robbins: "I found disco to be very soulful. In the early days, I considered it to be danceable R&B for the most part. Before disco kind of got that manufactured sound a few years later, the genre had great lyrics, musicians, singers and producers. I loved it—that whole period from 1974 to 1978–79. I think the influence of the gay community on the music also added a lot to it over time. I think it got too big, though, and there was such a demand for disco records that labels like Casablanca, T.K. Records and others were putting out too much material, like 30 or 40 releases a week. I was a DJ at the time, and I was getting all of them. I think it got too intense, and the supply quality weakened in order to keep up with demand. There were always good records, but there were a lot of those mechanical records that just didn't cut it. The genre got watered down, and the bubble burst. But it never went away [from pop culture]—it just became dance music."

Scheer: "There was a traumatic time before the arrival of disco when our president was shot, when Dr. Martin Luther King was shot, when a Kennedy was shot running for office, when we were being drafted for a war that made no sense. We came of age during a reactionary movement, if you will, with intense rock and folk music and heavy lyrics. We believed we had to change the world—a heavy burden on young shoulders. So coming from that turmoil we came into disco, and people started releasing that built-up tension with dancing. We danced away our troubles—it went from this awakening in our minds to an awakening in our bodies. When Studio 54 was in its heyday, it was that moment of time between the pill and AIDS. It was an era where not only gay men and women were shaking it, but heterosexual men were also dancing (something I don't see so much anymore). With her lyrics, Donna Summer gave women permission to do more than dance. Disco brought us a whole new freedom, and I think it will be remembered as something that was capable of being a joyful, higher power in all of us who appreciated it. When a song like 'I Will Survive' played, we were beckoned to the dance floor. We couldn't say no."

Washington: "I didn't know I was listening to disco over the past 35 or 40 years. There are some incredible songs in the genre that I just never realized were actually considered disco. I think this music earned its place just by lasting as long as it has, and the positive reaction so many people have towards it. Its essence still stands today, whether they call it techno, house, nu-disco or dance music. It still has the essence of this genre. If you look at dance moves, there aren't too many today that don't owe something to Michael Jackson. Many contemporary dancers will say that they have been influenced by him. I think the same is true for modern dance music, but today's artists don't acknowledge disco in the same way. Disco was the next phase after the '50s and '60s rock and pop movements. In the '70s, disco moved the country forward, and it has earned a place of respect in pop music history."

Wilson: "Disco's value was the human element, the feeling that it gave people; it's that simple. I really don't think that we have to complicate it—it's not that deep. Disco was a wonderful combination of soul music with a touch of funk and a dash of pop music and that, to me, was an irresistibly infectious combination. This feeling is, of course, a very subjective personal experience. Over the years, as I've toured the world, I have seen for myself that disco really has true value for the millions of people who grew up with this music. For them and for me, there are treasured nostalgic memories attached to this period in music. It brought people together and created a positive ambience and atmosphere. For many, it's the memory of when they heard that first vinyl record that they bought with their own pocket money or the memories that come flooding back of when they think of the love of their life that they met with this music playing in the background. The music generally made people feel good and positive, and it still does today."

How has disco music affected your life?

Causi: "I started in this business in 1979, and I think I have worked in every club in the tri-state area. My career was based in Manhattan, and that was the heartbeat of disco. Every major club known all over the world was in New York—Xenon, Studio 54, the Red Parrot, Regine's, Adam's Apple. Disco was a big part of my life. I lived it and breathed it. It will always be important to me. My goal will always be to make old music sound new and exciting and keep people listening to it!"

DeSario: "I think the people I encountered through disco have affected my life more than the music. I sang a lot of different types of music in my life. I was trained in classical and jazz, and I just love music. I didn't set out to be a disco singer, and I think many of the other vocalists known for the genre can say the same thing. I was there at the right time; people approached me with ideas, and I responded. But it took me a long time to realize that even though what happened wasn't entirely my idea of how my career should have gone, I look back and realize that people listened and danced to my music. And that music was woven into the fabric of their lives. That's fantastic!

"I have a much greater appreciation for disco now than I did at the time. When I was younger, I was obsessed with ambition, and I didn't really stop to consider my career in this genre. Now I am so grateful for everything that's come into my life, and I think it was an honor to have had success in disco."

Scheer: "When I moved to New York from Savannah, Georgia, the disco movement was just bubbling up. I had a job that ended before it started on the set of *Saturday Night Fever*. But when I went to Studio 54 for the first time as a guest, it was just unbelievable. It was like a corridor of joy and freedom. Little did I know I would end up working there and becoming Steve Rubell's assistant. I can truly say that at that particular point, disco was my life—or at least Studio 54 was. When it ended, there was a part of me that was relieved because I needed to get grounded. But 35 years later, when I was approached to do this radio show about Studio 54 with Marc Benecke, I had no idea what a fun project it would be or that disco would once again influence my being. I have discovered that the people involved with Studio 54, disco music and those who participated in the whole movement were not only creative and inspiring forces then, they continue to be today. We not only survived, we thrived!"

Washington: "Speaking from the heart, I'm not sure I fully appreciated disco music until I became involved with Martha Wash. The experience of reading *First Ladies of Disco* was an a-ha moment for me. It was such good music that I enjoyed it, but I didn't pay attention to the label. I had a love for this music and never really knew it. I never put it into a timeline until now. It has really helped me campaign for my clients. Listening to these performers on the radio, dancing to their music, rollerblading to their great songs—I never knew I would be blessed later in life to represent some of the legends."

Wilson: "Disco music gave me a start in life that I never dreamed would be possible. It changed my life on so many levels. My entry into the music business was not planned. My original career plan was to be a graphic designer or an architect because I was very good at art, painting and drawing, etc. I would say the way it all turned out was my fate and purpose."

Alfa Anderson, formerly of Chic
"Le Freak"

"We had to quickly develop musical chemistry because being in the studio with Nile and Nard was sorta like being with two kinder, gentler Ike Turners."—Alfa Anderson

"The world tours made me realize the popularity of our music," says Alfa Anderson, once a prominent vocalist with the astonishingly successful group Chic. "I remember the summer concerts in sport arenas. We did one in San Diego that was a real eye opener. The stadium was filled to capacity with 60,000 concertgoers. Backstage, we were nervous. It was the largest venue we had played to date. My knees were shaking so badly I just knew everyone could hear them. They were so rubbery that I didn't think I could stand. They announced the group, and we entered with the 'Chic Cheer.' For a few seconds we heard nothing. If you've ever played those venues, you know that there is a sound delay. Then it hit us. The wall of sound from 60,000 fans cheering, singing along, screaming—and then the applause! I'm standing on the stage soaking it all in thinking, 'Oh my God, this is real!' That's when it really hit me that I was part of something that was truly magical, something that made people happy. After the performance, we were being driven back to the dressing rooms, but the audience wouldn't stop shouting and chanting, 'Chic, Chic, Chic!' The promoter asked us to come back for an encore!"

It is but one example of the phenomenal encounters with fame that the group enjoyed in the late '70s. An ensemble organized by guitarist Nile Rodgers and bassist Bernard Edwards, Chic achieved astounding commercial success at the height of disco fever. Chic, as their named implied, was the epitome of regal style and elegance. The unparalleled influence and success of songs like "Dance, Dance, Dance," "Le Freak" and "Good Times" was unmatched by any other group of the era. Alfa was there from the start (first as a background singer and then taking the vocal lead) for their multi-year run as one of disco's greatest and most innovative acts.

Anderson goes back to the days when the idea of being a star was still far from her mind. "I was my parents' first child—the alpha child. My father's name was Alfonso," she explains. "So my first name is sort of a combination of those two things. I grew up

Chic (left to right: Bernard Edwards, Alfa Anderson, Luci Martin, Nile Rodgers, Tony Thompson) enjoy good times cavorting for a publicity shot (credited to Bill King) used on the cover of the group's 1979 *Greatest Hits* **LP on Atlantic Records (author's collection).**

in Augusta, Georgia, where music was a part of my life and a part of who I was, right from the very start. We always had a piano in our house, and I composed my first song when I was three years old.

"I remember I broke my father's collapsible ruler and threw the evidence underneath my parents' bed. When mama and daddy asked if I had seen the ruler, I said no. Eventually my father looked under the bed and found the broken ruler. Even when confronted with the evidence, I stuck to my story. 'No daddy, no mama; I did not break that ruler.' But I couldn't keep the truth from coming out. I went to the living room, climbed up on the piano bench, banged on the keys and sang this lyric: 'I broke it.' Bang, bang! 'Yes, I broke it.' Bang, bang, bang! 'And I'm glad I broke it!'

I have many childhood memories of my mother playing the piano and singing. We could always tell what kind of mood she was in by the song she sang. No matter the song, she'd gather us around the piano teaching us to sing—the happy songs, the silly ones and the sad songs—all in harmony. My father couldn't sing though. My mother used to say, 'Your father can't carry a tune in a bucket.' He'd whistle. Ours was a very traditional home, and music was considered a cultural pastime, not something you'd ever consider pursuing as a career. But from the very first, music was in my blood.

"I joined the junior high school band," she continues, "but by the time I made that decision, the only instruments left were the tuba, the trombone, the oboe or the saxophone. I couldn't carry the tuba, the mouthpiece of the trombone stank to heaven, and the oboe required too much work. I settled for the saxophone. I was a horrible player. A honking goose sort of describes my technique. When I went to high school, I decided to continue in the band, but it was not cool to carry a sax, so I opted for the flute. From the flute I switched to the piccolo, which was dainty and small enough to fit in my purse, and it could be heard over all the other instruments in the marching band. Thank you John Philip Sousa! I joined the choir at Paine College and rediscovered my love for singing. We performed in New York one spring, but I never imagined I'd eventually move there and live the life of an artist. When I finished college, my aunt Christine gave me a trip to New York as a graduation present. I enrolled in Teachers College at Columbia University and earned a master's degree in teaching English."

Meanwhile, inspired by the success they had been increasingly enjoying as musicians in a band called New York City ("I'm Doing Fine Now"), Nile Rodgers and Bernard Edwards formed a new group with drummer Tony Thompson. They hired Norma Jean Wright as a lead vocalist and formed the foundation of Chic in 1977. Says Anderson, "I was hired as a lecturer in the Department of Academic Skills at Hunter College of the City University of New York and sang on weekends with Kenny and Everett Brawner, fellow Augustans who had [led and composed music for] a jazz-funk group called Raw Sugar. This led to stints with other bands, and it was at a rehearsal with Lou Courtney (of the Fifth Dimension) that I met some people that would change the direction of my life forever. Fellow background vocalist Ednah Holt [also of the Ritchie Family reformation] introduced me to Fonzi Thornton and Michelle Cobbs.

"That meeting is so vivid in my mind because that's the day I also met Luther Vandross. I walked into the studio and saw this large guy dressed in overalls sitting in a chair. They introduced me, he lifted his head, said hello and immediately put his head back down. I thought he didn't like me, but in those few seconds I must've made an impression on him. He certainly made a lasting impression on me. When he opened his mouth, I heard this magic vocal sound that pulled me in like the pied piper. A few days later, I got a phone call from him. We quickly became friends. I would go to his house where we'd cook, eat, laugh and sing. Meeting Luther Vandross was my introduction to the New York artist community.

"My new friends were not singing as a cultural pastime; they wanted to make music their careers. Luther was fast becoming the king of commercials and background sessions and would often include me in this group of singers. One day, Luther told me that he had a session for us to do. 'Alfa, I have this friend named Nile Rodgers who has a new group called Chic,' he said. 'He wants me to come and put down some background vocals. It's disco music.' I was not enthusiastic. '*Disco?!* Luther, I don't wanna do disco! Are you really gonna do this?' I asked. He said yes and assured me that it would be a lot of fun. So, I reluctantly went to the studio. Luther, David Lasley and I arrived first. Diva Gray and Robin Clark filled out the remaining background vocalists for the Chic debut project that was recorded at Electric Lady Studios in Manhattan. While waiting for the session to begin, I took out papers to grade, Luther ordered food, and David sat quietly, looking like the quintessential hippie, complete with hair down to his butt. We made an unlikely looking trio. As a matter of fact, I later learned that Bernard pulled Nile to the side and questioned him, 'Are you sure these are the singers you want?' Nile replied, 'Trust me!'

"When I first heard the tracks for 'Dance, Dance, Dance' and 'Everybody Dance,' I was hooked. This was something I wanted to be part of. My prayer was answered. Luther and I were asked to provide backing vocals for the first Chic tour. My godson reminds me that, in the early days, Luther and I actually got billing. Luther's mantra was, 'I don't work *for* people, I work *with* people.' Billing was a big deal to him, and because I came in with Luther, I got grandfathered into a lot of perks that I wouldn't have known how to negotiate on my own."

The self-titled debut LP of Chic on Atlantic Records (the original recordings were marketed by Buddah Records, but were quickly shifted to the bigger and more powerful Warner Communications subsidiary) was a nationwide hit. The clubs were the first to catch on to the infectious premiere single, "Dance, Dance, Dance," which held the top spot on the disco chart for weeks and then climbed the pop charts straight to the Top 10. The song was a smash and in constant rotation on DJ turntables for nearly a year. "Everybody Dance," the follow-up single, scored almost as big, and Chic became a phenomenon, though their true identity had yet to be forged. Norma Jean Wright, in her interview for *First Ladies of Disco*, claimed the misleading album artwork featuring two sexy, light-skinned women was an attempt by those marketing the project to coax radio programmers into believing the act's music was intended for a white audience.

Anderson recalls Chic's unique recording sessions and the personalities of her producers with great detail. "We had to quickly develop musical chemistry because being in the studio with Nile and Nard was sorta like being with two kinder, gentler Ike Turners," she laughs. "But Luther made it easy. He was very instrumental in co-crafting the Chic vocal sound. One of the techniques Nile and Bernard used was difficult for me at first, but I learned to work with it. We never heard the songs before we went in to record. We never rehearsed. I didn't even know the name of the songs until I arrived at the studio. 'Just be ready,' they'd say. We would walk into the studio and Bernard would take us aside—mostly Bernard, though sometimes Nile—and they'd still be writing and changing lyrics. He'd teach the song to us. We would take a little time to learn it and then go to the vocal booth and put it down. To learn the notes was one thing, but to really understand the nuances—find the 'Chic-ness'—was something else. During the early days, Luther guided us in that process; later on, Fonzi Thornton did. [Thornton was officially credited with background vocals on only the third Chic album, *Risqué*.] We became a really tight, cohesive vocal unit. Truthfully, I sang a wrong lyric in a couple of my solos, but Nile and Nard liked the results. Spontaneity and passion were more important than correctness. I was always nervous because I had never recorded like that before. We'd usually start on the hook, and once you got that down, the rest was easier. I never did get entirely comfortable with that method. There was always that initial nervousness until I relaxed in it."

To skirt the dreaded sophomore jinx, Chic needed something extraordinary for the group's next LP. No longer hiding in the shadows, the participants were prominently posed on the cover of 1978's *C'est Chic* album, which listed Luther Vandross as a special guest vocalist. From left field came the quirky sound of "Le Freak," the first single released to radio, which vaulted to the number one spot on the charts and ranked as Atlantic Records' biggest selling single. The song, a kind of funky dance-floor cheer, literally had music fans freaking out, and it was an extraordinary, unexpected phenomenon. The album made the Top Five on the pop side and was an international bestseller. There were now three acts that had come to symbolize almost the entire disco music movement, and they were often mentioned in the same sentence by the media: Donna Summer, the Village People and Chic.

Admits Alfa, "For me, 'Le Freak' was the most difficult song to sing under the method I described that Nile and Nard favored. ['Le Freak'] was a duet with Diva Gray. At first, it was hard for me to find the pocket, the rhythm and the Chic vocal pattern to fit that song, but when I relaxed, it all fell into place. I had absolutely no idea 'Le Freak' would be so big. When I heard the playback, I loved it. But who could have predicted the phenomenal success of that track?"

Anderson confirms the story that has been long linked to the creation of "Le Freak." "I don't feel you can separate the song from the era in which it was recorded," she says. "Art really does imitate and amplify life. The '70s was a time when the youth of American wanted to be free. We longed to tear down societal barriers. We were sick and tired of the 'isms.' The '70s was also a time of protest. It was the spirit of protest that prompted Nile and Bernard to write 'Le Freak.' After being denied entrance to the popular Studio 54, they did what musicians did—they poured all that emotion in a song. As Nile tells the story, they were jamming and came up with the lyric, 'fuck you!' Realizing that they had a very hip groove, they worked with the lyric and the 'F.U.' became 'freak out.' It was the right message at the right time." "I Want Your Love," a song supposedly intended for Sister Sledge, became the follow-up crowd pleaser from the *C'est Chic* set, an album that went on to sell well over a million copies.

Chic had entered a new phase of overwhelming popularity, but the extraordinary events and experiences in which Alfa was immersed often whizzed past the singer with little chance for her to take notice. "You know what?" the artist observes. "It was a blur. Things were happening fast and furiously. A few years ago, I was at a George Benson concert and introduced myself. He said, 'I remember you! I will never forget the time we were on the same bill, and you all came out, and I couldn't even go onstage because they were calling for more from you guys!' I laughed to myself because that was one of the stadium gigs where we just tore the roof off the sucka! I believe 'Le Freak' is still the highest-selling single in Atlantic's history. I was so excited and proud to be part of that.

"However, my bubble of enthusiasm burst when speaking to a college girlfriend," she continues. "I told her I had a number one record on the charts. She looked at me and said, 'That's nice, but what are you doing to improve the human condition?' Talk about a reality check! I've since learned that music *does* improve the human condition. If I didn't know it then, I know it now through all the Facebook comments and messages I get from people! Recently, someone came up to me and thanked me for making music that helped get her through her teen years. While touring, you get a chance to see the transformative power of music. Lives were changed because our audience consisted of whites and blacks, gays and straights, all in the mix together, singing along with us and giving us so much love. Here it is 35 years later, and I get the chance to see the timelessness of our music," the singer adds.

Anderson says she had no reason to worry that Chic was being branded as a disco creation at the time. "I didn't object to being classified as a disco act. I got over my earlier prejudice. I had worried that disco was going to displace R&B, and I thought that disco music was static, locked into 122 beats-per-minute and that it took away from artistic freedom. The music of Chic wasn't like that at all and was actually beyond disco. It was totally different from what I was expecting. I don't remember Nile and Nard ever voicing any objection to being classified as disco, but my memory may be a bit fuzzy. I think they started out in R&B and rock. What they may have had an issue with was the fact that they couldn't get a record deal without being categorized. There have always been problems with identity and how people see musicians of color and their ability to play something other than R&B and jazz. Chic certainly shattered any notions about what disco was."

Next up was the groundbreaking album *Risqué*, a monster 1979 release for Chic. Paramount among its many hook-laden compositions was the track "Good Times." From its infectious bass lines to its joyful, summery proclamation of disco's irresistibly euphoric effect, the song was Chic's ultimate moment. The song leapt to the number one spot on the pop charts, drew dancers to the floor in droves and, according to Alfa, exemplified the group at their best. "The words and music of 'Good Times' were infectious, danceable and oh so much fun. That was one of the happiest experiences I had in the studio. We loved it from the first, dancing and singing in the control room even before we went to the vocal booth. People still love 'Good Times.' On the day of the recording, everything clicked—Bernard's great bass solo, Nile's rhythmic guitar, Tony's steady beat on the drums. When we added those slick vocals, we had lift off! It was a group of us that sang it. [The album jacket lists Alfa, Bernard, Fonzi, Luci, Michelle Cobbs and Ullanda McCullough as the vocalists on *Risqu*e.]

"Generally, it's harder to sing unison with a group than it is to sing harmony. Unison requires a cohesive approach to the song. If you don't have that, then you can hear different people. But when it's really in sync, it sounds like one person. The nuances are the same, so you breathe the same, the pitch is the same and the rhythm is the same. The icing on the cake was when we'd come back into the control room and listen to the playback. When the vocals are totally in tune you can actually hear the overtones of an octave. That was the beauty of our vocal approach."

The *Risqué* album cover, featuring the group posed in a black and white photograph wearing Roaring Twenties costumes, was one of the most visually striking of the era. "We didn't have input in the artistic decisions," Alfa says. "The cover was all Nile and Bernard. They liked the Cab Calloway/Great Gatsby era. I think the cover was a throwback to those times. I do get people often identifying me [sitting on a table in a white dress] on that album cover."

It didn't take long for the profound influence of "Good Times" to be noticed by other artists. One of the most famous rap tracks of all time "borrowed" Chic's hit song elements, most notably the Edwards bass line, and managed to become one of the biggest novelty tracks ever, while single-handedly introducing the hip-hop/rap genre to the mainstream. By sampling "Good Times," "Rapper's Delight" by the Sugarhill Gang took a detour off the disco highway and sent urban music in a whole new direction. "We happened to be in England when they released 'Rapper's Delight,'" Anderson recalls. "We found out about it, and Nile and Bernard moved quickly to get the lawyers on that. There was definitely some litigation. The interesting thing was, when we performed 'Good Times' after that, we actually started incorporating the rap in our stage show."

Other artists of the day were also borrowing the Chic sound, albeit legitimately. Among them were Norma Jean Wright, who released her solo set *Norma Jean* in 1978. Sister Sledge set the world on fire in '79 with their stunning hits "We Are Family" and "He's the Greatest Dancer" and, in 1980, Diana Ross was restored as queen of the dance and pop chart throne with her funky, Chic-inspired jams "Upside Down" and "I'm Coming Out." All these tracks enlisted the production talents of Edwards and Rodgers. Says Alfa, "When Norma Jean left the group to pursue her solo career—and there are conflicting versions of how that happened—I was asked to join the group as a lead singer. Naturally, I was thrilled, but I was also nervous about it. Luther, who had served as a good friend and mentor, moved on to pursue a solo career, so this Georgia girl was on her own. There was also an unspoken tension between Luci Martin and me. She had hoped or was promised (another story with conflicting versions) to fill Norma's slot. Nonetheless, we made it work. Norma, Luci and I are developing a project that further explores those tensions and tells the story through our lenses.

"Nile and Bernard's work with other artists didn't necessarily interfere with Chic, but I sure did want to keep a few of those songs for us," Alfa claims. "I sang some of the reference vocals for the Diana Ross album and also sang background. So I would hear some of their productions. I wanted us to keep 'Upside Down' from the Diana project. 'Ooh, that should be our song! You sure you don't wanna save this for us?' I still include 'Upside Down' in a set whenever I can. I was such a Diana fan. When I got the opportunity to meet her, I was awestruck and tongue-tied. Have you ever had one of those moments when you want to say something profound or witty and your brain freezes up? That's how it was for me when I met Diana. So what did I do? I did the next best thing and took the fashionista's approach, complimenting her on her boots. She was wearing these awesome knee high boots to die for. In the end, Diana did not like the Chic-produced album. Neither did Motown. They actually remixed it. That's the version you hear on the radio today. But it's clearly a winner and did much to boost Diana's career."

Though Chic seemed invincible, nearly every act associated with disco took the hit of the strong anti-disco sentiment that was pervasive after a so-called "Disco Demolition" publicity stunt at Chicago's Comiskey Park. Nearly overnight, it became an uphill battle for disco songs to top the chart and Chic, despite their acclaim, was not immune. The release of 1980's *Real People* album, featuring a slightly softer version of the Chic sound, fared poorly. The album cuts barely cracked the dance Top 30, and the tracks were largely ignored on the pop side. Though critically acknowledged to some degree, the subsequent albums *Take It Off* and *Tongue in Chic* saw progressively smaller sales. "It was hard," Alfa remembers. "Nile and Bernard wanted to grow and take the group in a new direction, partly because of the backlash against disco but also to show the versatility of their production. The new direction would've also showcased Luci and me as solo artists. The critical acclaim that Nile and Bernard received for their work with other artists was not given to Chic."

The final Chic album featuring Alfa, ironically called *Believer*, hit store shelves in 1983. The hard and funky single "Give Me the Lovin'" tried to keep pace with changing tastes, but the road for Chic had clearly come to an end. "It seems as if our personal interactions declined with the record sales," says Alfa, her voice softening and her rate of speech slowing. The change in her mood is apparent. "I had no idea that the group was going to disband—I found out in a letter. I think I still have it somewhere. 'As of this date, your services will no longer be required.' It was one of the most painful experiences of my life. I was angry; I was hurt. I was tearful, disbelieving. I felt abandoned. It probably would not have stung so much if I received the message face to face, but a letter—come on guys! In retrospect, I understand the reality of the situation and the business decision they had to make. After all, I wasn't signed to the record company; I was signed to the production company. Production companies have the right to switch personnel whenever they choose. Intellectually, I understood this, but my heart didn't."

Buffering herself from the sudden changes in her life as best she could, Anderson looked at the options before her. "One of the things that made it easier was a call from Luther, who offered me the opportunity to tour with him," recalls the artist. "That cheered me up, and I jumped at the chance. It was a blessing for my bruised ego. I felt safe with Luther. I was offered a few opportunities to go solo, but I had always been a group person. Touring with Luther was a great experience for me. It's like getting a master's degree in performing arts. I continued to grow both professionally and personally. I met my husband, Tinker Barfield, while on tour with Luther. This year will mark 28 years that we've been together."

Nile and Bernard went on to work with and produce other artists, both as a team and separately, including David Bowie, Madonna, the Honeydrippers, Debbie Harry, the Power Station and Duran Duran. In 1992, the duo released a new Chic album (without Alfa) called *Chic-ism*, which yielded a number one hit on the dance chart called "Chic Mystique." In 1996, Bernard Edwards died of pneumonia at age 43.

"That was a call that I never thought I'd get," says Alfa. "At first, I didn't believe it. How could this be? Not Bernard! We hadn't spoken in years, and there were so many things I wanted to say to him, things I needed to say to have closure." In 2003, original member Tony Thompson passed from cancer. "'Oh no! Not another one,' was all I could say. I had spoken with Tony about a year before he passed. He, Norma, Luci and I spent time talking about our time with Chic," she remembers. In 2010, Rodgers told his website followers that he too was diagnosed with cancer. Seemingly undaunted, the producer released an autobiography in 2011 and continues to work today with artists like Adam Lambert and Daft Punk. Daft Punk scored an international Chic-like chart-topper in 2013 with the smash single "Get Lucky," featuring Rodgers and Pharrell Williams.

"Life somehow teaches us that many of the things we obsess about are so not worth it," observes Anderson. "Nile and I had a conversation a few years back with promises of continuing sometime in the future. I had the opportunity to be interviewed for a BBC documentary about his life and work and also for a segment of the *Unsung* show. I look forward to the time when he and I can talk face to face instead of connecting via social media. Maybe I can finally get closure about that part of my life."

Alfa decided to take a very different direction with her life following her disco music career. "It is amazing when I think about it," she asserts. "I've always had this duality in my life—the artist and the educator. A chance meeting backstage at a Luther Vandross concert in my hometown of Augusta planted the seed for me to return to education. This adorable little girl and her brother came backstage to meet me. She told me I was her hero, and she wanted to be just like me when she grew up. I looked at her and could actually see myself reflected in her beautiful, big brown eyes. At that moment, I didn't like what I saw reflected there. I thanked her, but felt compelled to add this: 'The real heroes in your life are your parents and teachers, the people in your community who support your growth and development every day.' It was at that moment that I knew I wanted to go back into education. After Tinker and I left Luther's tour in 1987 (another painful parting), I enrolled in the Bank Street College of Education and earned a second master's degree in School Leadership. I joined the staff of the small New Visions school in Brooklyn and moved through the ranks from teacher to principal. My musical fame meant nothing to me at that time point."

Alfa seems almost amused by her thinking back then. "There was so much pain associated with me and music that I gladly immersed myself into my marriage and into education. I tried to separate those two parts of my life, but how could I? My students found out about my work in the music industry and loved it. The biggest surprise came one year when a senior class representative asked, 'Do you think this year we could march out to 'Good Times' rather than 'Pomp and Circumstance'? It was a very special moment for me, and it was the beginning of bringing my two worlds together publicly. I have such gratitude for all of the experiences that shaped my life. I have no regrets.

"Now that I'm officially retired from the New York City Department of Education, I am singing again and find that I absolutely love, love, love it!" she adds. "I continue to write, record and perform with my husband. [Not long ago], my sons and my husband wrote a song for me called 'Former Lady of Chic.' Today, I proudly proclaim that I am an artist!" The funky track was released in the fall of

"There have always been problems with identity and how people see musicians of color and their ability to play something other than R&B and jazz. Chic certainly shattered any notions about what disco was," says Alfa Anderson in 2013 (courtesy Alfa Anderson).

2013 to great reviews. Alfa also recently reunited with her group mates Norma Jean Wright and Luci Martin as Next Step, and the trio plans to explore the possibilities of bringing their new sound to venues nationwide.

Alfa Anderson's story is one of the most remarkable and important in the annals of disco history, and her contribution to the unfathomable success of Chic places her among the genre's elite. She has experienced the heights of fame that few will ever know, and she looks forward to the adventures that the next part of her life will hold. Though she isn't interested in languishing in the past, she ponders her incredible legacy for a moment and says, "I want to be remembered as someone who never stopped learning, never stopped growing and never stopped loving!"

William "Bubba" Anderson, James "Ajax" Baynard, LA Blacksmith, Tyrone Cox, Mark Lipetz and Phil "Flip" Thomas of Crown Heights Affair
"Dreaming a Dream"

"We didn't like being called a disco group—it was just too limiting to us."—Phil "Flip" Thomas

"We love each and every one of you and hope our affair continues forever," stated Crown Heights Affair, addressing their fans on the back of the 1978 album *Dream World*. Nearly four decades later, the bond between the ensemble and their followers, forged through a series of classic dance and funk tracks, remains as strong as ever. The gentlemen took their moniker by merging Brooklyn's Crown Heights neighborhood with the title of a popular movie of the time (*The Thomas Crown Affair*). They soon found themselves cast as purveyors of a dazzling disco sound that has truly stood the test of time. "Dreaming a Dream," "Dancin'," "You Gave Me Love" and "Galaxy of Love" were their signature hits, but, in one way or another, these musicians are associated with a plethora of classic disco songs performed by a myriad of the genre's greatest stars, from France Joli to Amii Stewart. William "Bubba" Anderson, James "Ajax" Baynard, LA Blacksmith, Tyrone Cox, Phil "Flip" Thomas and Mark Lipetz represent the group during this particular evening's conversation, gathering in a midtown New York office building, the same city where Crown Heights Affair launched their stellar career. Group member Raymond Reid was unable to attend this session as he struggled with complications from cancer. He entered hospice on the very same night, and, sadly, passed just a few days later in late May of 2013.

The group comments on the impermanence of life and the importance of docu-

Crown Heights Affair (left to right: Tyrone Cox, LA Blacksmith, William Anderson, Phil Thomas and James Baynard) looks sharp for a 2013 interview at SiriusXM studios (courtesy Mark Lipetz).

menting their history in some meaningful way. They begin by discussing their early formation. The gentlemen were originally known as Ben Iverson and the Nue Dey Express, a collaboration between Ben Iverson, Mark Lipetz, Donnie Linton and Britt Britton. The group got its start in 1973 and periodically changed its personnel as they began honing a fresh, funky sound. Over the years, the group has consisted of original vocalist Julius Dilligard, Jr. (who sang the original version of "Dreaming a Dream"), vocalist Phil Thomas, keyboardist Howard Young, vocalists/trumpeters James Baynard and Tyrone Cox, vocalist/bassist Lorenzo "Muki" Wilson, vocalist/guitarist William Anderson, vocalist/percussionist Ray Rock, brothers Bert Reid (vocalist/saxophonist, who died of lung cancer in 2004), and the late vocalist/trombonist Raymond Reid. LA Blacksmith, who started his career in the '70s with a band called the New Breed (with Raymond Reid), is the newest member of the group, serving as a vocalist/saxophonist for the past three years. "I started off with the guys at the beginning as a trombone player," recalls LA, "but [the instrument wasn't a good fit for me, and] I got kicked out of the very first group." He laughs. "The trombone was put in the closet after I found my true instrument, the alto sax. But it re-emerged in the mid–'80s when Ray came to my house after falling on some rough times. He was in need of a trombone. I put it in his hands and said, 'Don't let me down.' And he didn't. He used that trombone to make good live music and on some recordings until he couldn't play anymore."

William Anderson stirs up memories of the group's early days. "Donnie Linton, a bass player and later our manager, was really the co-founder of our group," he says. "He started auditions for a new band around 1971. We went through a couple of transitions before we actually became Crown Heights Affair. We did a demo and had a record deal and released our first record called 'I Tried My Best,' but it got messed up by our management and didn't go anywhere. After that, we became known as Crown Heights Affair."

The group landed another deal with RCA Records for a self-titled debut LP in 1974, but the album languished in obscurity. "We had joined RCA and did an instrumental record for them called 'Super Rod,'" recalls Lipetz. "We did shows to promote it at the Apollo, and it started to catch on a bit. The TV show *ABC Sports Spectacular* started playing it, and the song started getting on the radio. The vocal version was never that popular, but the instrumental disco version started crossing over and did pretty well on the R&B chart.

"We wanted to go towards being a jazz-funk band," says Williams, "but RCA wanted to turn us into a soul-disco band, and we were a little rebellious about that."

James Baynard chimes in, "We weren't concerned about being stars when we recorded for RCA; we were concerned about playing really good funk music. We were still in that time right before the disco era at this point, and I think we played some very good stuff. We recorded some great songs in those days, like 'Music Is the World.' I recently heard it on the radio at three in the morning. I listened to how it sounds today, and let me tell you—it really sounded good! I think the DJ mentioned it was Crown Heights Affair, and I wanted to shout, 'Yo, yo, yo, listen to this! We're on the radio!'"

Adds Mark Lipetz, "We had a great album with RCA, but our stuff was never promoted properly. RCA was focused on John Denver, Perry Como and Elvis Presley of course. The Main Ingredient was the only black group they were promoting, and even they didn't do as well as they could have. We were starting to think they just signed us as a tax loss. We did a demo for our next album, which was the song 'Dreaming a Dream,' and nobody at RCA was happy with it. We decided to leave the label, and after we left they started promoting the Hues Corporation's 'Rock the Boat' and acts like that. I always thought they started doing that because they were thinking we might come back with a prejudice suit.

"We were looking for a new record company. [Executives] at A&M Records and a few other labels had turned us down. We connected with Fred Vigorito ('Mr. V'), who was [one of the gentlemen who ran] De-Light Records, and he loved the Crown Heights Affair song 'Leave the Kids Alone' that we did on RCA. So I sat down with him, and he said he wanted us. I brought the idea back to my management partners, and we signed the contract," he says.

The gentlemen seated around the table are quick to jump into the conversation, innocently but frequently speaking over one another with tremendous enthusiasm. James gets the lead and adds, "In between our first and second albums, we were rehearsing, but there was no money coming in. So I was trying to work, to make a living, and Anderson was insisting we had to keep rehearsing five days a week. I was frustrated. We must have done 'Dreaming a Dream' over about 10 times. I never thought the song made much sense. Just before we were about to record it, I got an offer to go to Europe to play with Sam & Dave. I played my trumpet on the 'Dreaming' song, and when I came back from Europe, it was getting airplay. Ironically, Tyrone had joined the group as a trumpet player and was getting the credit, and everyone was saying to me that I missed my big break! I would insist that it was *me* on the record, and they'd all say, 'Yeah, right!'"

The group concurs that they thought the song "Dreaming a Dream" was a bit corny at the time, but club goers and record buyers felt otherwise, embracing its distinctly infectious and funky New York vibe and hustle-inducing energy. The song vaulted to the number one spot on *Billboard*'s disco chart by the summer of 1975, a survey they would see their group name listed on numerous times as the era unfolded. The song was a fixture on the chart for the remainder of the year and made a solid dent on the pop side. "'Dreaming a Dream' wasn't planned to be a disco record exactly," claims Mark, "but the record companies started wanting a three-minute radio version, a disco version that was about five minutes, and then sometimes an extended play as dance music became more and more popular." The single "Every Beat of My Heart," with its catchy hooks, pop-conscious beat and smooth harmonies, took the men right back to the top of the club survey as "Dreaming" began easing off turntables. The song gave them yet another modest pop hit.

Phil says the group resisted being branded as a disco act, even in those early days. "We didn't like being called a disco group—it was just too limiting to us. We actually thought of ourselves as a jazz-funk fusion group. We listened to people like Tower of Power; Blood, Sweat & Tears and Kool & the Gang. It's funny; back then Kool & the Gang was not a disco act, but the label was putting pressure on them to get into this music too. I knew them from Jersey City and Lincoln High School. I remember saying to them that they needed a lead vocalist, and they went out and got J.T. [James "J.T." Taylor]. Once he was in place, they started to get that disco sound."

Mark injects a quick flashback regarding Kool & the Gang, a group that rose to the top of the disco heap a few years later. "We were supposed to be on the *Saturday Night Fever* soundtrack but got bumped for Kool & the Gang's 'Open Sesame.' That was the record company's decision." The others talk amongst themselves about that turn of events and the lost opportunity. Claims Phil, "The gentleman who actually wrote the *Saturday Night Fever* story—his favorite group was Crown Heights Affair, not Kool & the Gang. He told me that himself. But he had no ability to do anything about who the executives picked for the soundtrack."

With 1976's "Dancin'," Crown Heights Affair continued its hot streak on the dance chart. The song reached the disco Top 10 and, like it or not, the group became synonymous with dance music. The gentlemen return to the subject of being classified by a single sound. Baynard insists, "We wanted to do more than disco. The producers always wanted us to do the same rhythm—120 beats per minute. Of course we did do some ballads on our albums, but the labels didn't push anything but the dance music. We didn't have the freedom to just put in a horn solo that we could rehearse and creatively add to the song. The label's philosophy was, 'If you're going to do a solo, you need to do this part here, this part there.' There was a formula they wanted you to stick to. That was all part of the disco thing. It was often a set routine. The music was good, but it could be limiting. I can give you another example. There was a stereotype that all of [the black] groups at the time were interchangeable. We'd meet a girl at a club, and she'd say, 'Oh, you were just here last week.' Meanwhile, it was the Trammps or Tavares that had been there. After a while, we started asking ourselves, 'Is this what we want? Everyone doing the same thing?'"

William pipes in, "We didn't hate disco music; we just hated the categorization."

Thomas acknowledges the support the group had from the gay community, but admits the inroads the group made with the underground culture was a double-edged sword. "Every style of music had drugs or some kind of perceived negativity that could be connected to it," he claims. "There was a stigma back then to being gay or having an alternative lifestyle, and the gay community was really into disco. That was sometimes perceived as a negative. That created another restrictive label you had to deal with being in disco. We played at all the best clubs in New York and around the country. And a lot of them were gay clubs. At the time, the music industry, a lot of the executives—the higher ups—were prejudiced. They had an issue with getting too involved with that culture."

Says James, "Back then, we were in the mix with the gay community, and maybe we were naïve, but we didn't see a blatant problem by appearing at those clubs. It certainly wasn't a problem for us."

Crown Heights Affair had a strong following and fans of both sexes and orientations were never in short supply. James laughs as he remembers, "I'd always run into girls who'd say, 'I have a friend who is dating one of you guys.' Now half the time, mind you, they'd be talking about B.T. Express or Brass Construction. But between the eight of us in the group, we'd have a sizable number of women covered. When we were on the road, a girl might say, 'I wanna meet so and so from your group.' And if he wasn't available, we'd say, 'Well, the rest of us are!'"

Lipetz smiles and claims, "To this day, these guys have groupies that they've had for 35 years!"

As all the gentlemen voice agreement, Phil adds, "We were in London appearing at the Hammersmith Odeon. There was a tall blonde girl that kept coming back trying to meet us. I think she was in transition at that point—you know, a sex change. If I had been more open-minded, I think I would have had a fan for life!" The group lets out a laugh.

Crown Heights Affair was constantly touring during the disco era, and their music was well-received by DJs and dancers, especially in the Northeast. In 1976, the group scored another club smash with "Far Out," off the album *Do It Your Way*, as they continued their De-Lite Records winning streak. Their appeal spread overseas, where the gentlemen's hits "I'm Gonna Love You Forever" and "Dance Lady Dance" began a love affair with the U.K., a country that was especially enthusiastic about their music. As the '70s drew to a close, the gentlemen scored more chart entries in England with the energized, almost ominous sounding "You Gave Me Love" (a major U.S. club hit) and the lighter "Galaxy of Love," the latter cracking the U.K.'s Top 30. The group was often seen on the classic television music shows of the day, including *American Bandstand, Soul Train, Disco '77, Don Kirshner's Rock Concert* and *The Steel Pier*.

Says Mark, "'Galaxy of Love' is like a national anthem in the U.K.!" "They treat us in a whole different way over there. Here in the U.S., people will tell us they like us, but over there, man, they treat you like a king!" adds Baynard. Thomas agrees and says, "We got off a plane in England and almost got the kind of reception the Beatles received! We weren't used to that at all!"

Though creatively successful and widely respected, the financial realities of life in the music industry were frequently on the minds of Crown Heights Affair members, especially in terms of their participation in disco music. Admits Lipetz, "It was very hard to make money from being just on the club charts. If our music hit the top of that chart, it would have to go through the channels and cross over to pop to make any real money. 'Dreaming a Dream' was number one on the disco chart, but unless it crossed over you just couldn't make much."

"De-Lite wasn't getting us the money we could have made," believes James. "They'd release and promote our records on the east coast and then debate about maybe doing the west. I'd have friends out west that would sometimes see our records in the stores, which were a hit on the east coast, and they'd never hear us on the radio. By the time the record company finished [promoting our records to] the east, we'd have to go back into the studio and start recording something new. They could have worked the albums a lot more and done it nationwide."

Mark adds, "There was also often confusion about what we were releasing. The *Dreaming a Dream* LP was released on the east coast and then released on the west coast as *Foxy Lady,* with a different album cover and everything. This was kind of shady."

By late 1979, the United States was embroiled in the burnout effects of a market that had been overrun with disco records. Lipetz observes, "When disco really started in 1974, the whole economy was in very bad shape—especially in New York City. People found that by going to a disco, they had a cheap release from all their stress and problems. They had their fun, bought their drinks, heard great music and went to work the next day. Disco music was almost secondary to it all. The primary thing was to go out and have fun and party all night long. But by the end of the decade, things had changed."

Phil agrees. "There have been some amazing disco songs. 'Turn the Beat Around' by my friend Vicki Sue Robinson—it was a whole different vibe. That was an arresting song—it grabbed you!" Adds Tyrone, "But then everyone and their mom started to have a disco record. The *I Love Lucy* theme was a disco record. The *Star Wars* music was even made into disco. There was a cliché that began to be associated with disco." Mark notes that Meco Monardo, the man behind the disco version of the Star Wars theme, handled the strings on their hit "Every Beat of My Heart."

James adds, "When you had a hit, the record company always wanted the same formula after that. They didn't want to take a chance on anything else. The question is—when do you decide to do something different to create another sound? It's very hard to be on the cutting edge and know when enough is enough on a particular formula."

"Our audience always responded to whatever we did," says Thomas, "because we knew how to tailor it a certain way. But we had producers who'd say, 'Phil, no jazz chords.' Instead of being proud of what we could do, like adding in a jazz element and letting us grow, they couldn't step out of that formula. That's what helped to kill disco."

With a new decade upon them, Crown Heights Affair began to explore options that might expand their influence in the music industry. Disco had survived its crash and began morphing into a new brand form of dance music that was an ideal fit for the production and writing talents of Bert Reid, Raymond Reid and William Anderson. They started working with a stream of notable artists and incorporated the musicianship of their fellow group members into their projects. The gentlemen speak warmly of the Reid brothers, acknowledging the tremendous contributions these gentlemen made to their mutual experience.

Recalls William, "Ray, Bert and I took the initiative as songwriters and producers, but the plan was to have everyone in the group get their turn to branch out. We were all collaborating on each of the new productions we began, and it was a collective effort."

Phil adds, "We delivered our obligations to De-Lite Records, and they wanted us to resign with them. We delivered 10 songs to them for a new album, but they rejected all of them out of hand. That really forced us to take a different direction. Eight of those songs went on to be hits on the charts when we worked with other artists performing them. What we did by developing these other projects was keep each other working."

Says LA, "We had all been playing on a lot of records by other groups like Fatback Band and Brass Construction already, so we had that experience. But William, Ray and Bert were responsible for putting us down on a lot of big hit record records!"

The gentlemen recount some of their memories of working with major dance artists of the early '80s. "'Gonna Get Over You' for France Joli was one of those great songs we did," says Anderson with pride. "She was a very talented vocalist who goes at it and doesn't hold back. I wrote the song with Ray Reid [although the LP lists only Anderson as the writer and Ray as one of the mixers] and Crown Heights Affair provided the music on it. We did a lot of work for Prelude Records." According to Anderson, he was also involved with the productions of 'I Specialize in Love' for Sharon Brown and 'Dyin' to Be Dancing' by Empress.

"It was a pleasure working with Amii Stewart," he recalls. "She was so professional, but it wasn't like it was even work. We were having fun! She took everything to heart! She listened and followed instructions so well. Then you let her do her thing. We knew she had gone to number one with 'Knock on Wood,' but we didn't feel any pressure to try and duplicate that. We were more concerned with the artist singing and being happy with the material. The only downer we had with her album [*I'm Gonna Get Your Love* (1981)] was because of the record label, Handshake Records. It was bad timing. Everything just folded with them, and that project could have gone much further," he says.

Phil adds, "Amii was very respectful and was very reticent about overstepping her boundaries as far as contributing to the process at first. Ray was always telling her, 'Do what you do!'"

Anderson remembers the story behind Taana Gardner's monumental hit "Heartbeat." "That was Ray Reid and Kenton Nix," he says. "Kenton was a banker at the time, and he wanted to do a record. He came to Ray because he had no clue how to do it. Ray called Raymond Rock and I to rehearse in our loft on 30th Street, and we put together the arrangement for 'Heartbeat.' We had Muki Wilson on the bass line. I was originally supposed to be the guitarist, but I wasn't able to make the session."

Says Blacksmith, "Kent had no musical knowledge, but he definitely had the vision to get to the right people and get things done!"

Adds James, "I remember many people were saying 'Heartbeat' was too slow when it was about to come out, but they were wrong. I remember I heard the instrumental track and thought, 'It will never work!'

Denroy Morgan was another success story for the gentlemen, an artist who hit the dance Top 10 in 1981 with a reggae-fused shuffler that caught on big. "Bert Reid handled 'I'll Do Anything for You,'" William says with a playful groan. "I will always remember saying to him, 'That was *our* song that you gave away! That should have been a Crown Heights Affair hit!'"

Baynard also winces at the lost opportunity. "We always had that trademark 'did-it-did-it-dat-dat' sound in our songs. Bert was very good at gimmicks like that. To me, the horns, everything about 'I'll Do Anything for You,' was Crown Heights. If you think about our music, it would have been a fine example of a hit that could have been ours. But he did it with Denroy. I found out Denroy couldn't get a record done properly with his accent and Bert was helping him out. Bert even rapped on that record!"

The group acknowledges the accomplishments of Raymond Reid. Upon his passing, a memorial service saw a wealth of associates, friends and family pay tribute to the depth of the man's humanity. Many called him a creative genius whose love of his family, culture, community, friends and God were all translated into his music. Others noted that Raymond had a gift for seeing the raw talent in musicians and a knack for skillfully developing and coaching new producers, writers and artists. It was further acknowledged that Raymond worked with the Jackie Robinson Center for Physical Culture's afterschool program and taught lower brass horns to the youth of the renowned Jackie Robinson Steppers Marching Band. His passion for working with young people extended to his work at the Jewish Board for Family and Children Services (JBFCS), where he directed therapeutic recreational activities. Reid remained on the staff of the JBFCS until early 2012, when health challenges caused him to take medical leave. Despite his illness, Ray's passion for music never lessened. He and fellow Crown Heights Affair member William Anderson were unrelenting in their efforts to co-produce new songs until his very last days.

Today, the remaining gentlemen of this pioneer group continue to perform and delight fans who still eagerly embrace their disco funk creations. And there are plenty of devotees filling their shows as Crown Heights Affair tours the U.S. and Europe on a regular basis with artists such as Lime, Rochelle Fleming, Fonda Rae and Rose Royce. While they accept and respect their status as legends of disco, something about the genre's name still doesn't sit quite comfortably with them.

"I think a lot of black artists thought that disco was the stick, and we didn't think it was identified with us," says LA. "As Ajax [James] mentioned earlier, it kind of put us in a box. We grew up playing almost everything, and many of us didn't feel like we belonged in a box. Most black artists, musicians like in my original group the New Breed, played a lot of different genres of music, and that's what made us attractive. So to be pigeonholed into one category, we were like, 'Yo, can we get out of this?' We didn't understand the purpose that disco was serving at the time. Today we can look back on the music and say, 'Wow, that solo was really kicking ass,' but we didn't always see it that way at the time."

Whatever awkwardness the term 'disco' may generate for some, there is no questioning the artistry that lay behind the creative efforts of one of the genre's most beloved pioneering groups. Collectively and individually, Crown Heights Affair's members have created an unforgettable musical legacy, which they each ponder for a moment.

Says William, "I'd like Crown Heights Affair to be remembered as music lovers who were inspired by those that came before us. I'd like everyone to remember that we became a big family of musicians for whom music really was the world. And we were very happy guys playing the music we loved!"

"I'd like to think that we left behind something that was considered quality," LA adds with pride, as he adjusts to sit taller in his chair. "Crown Heights Affair was about having a party through good music and having a good time. We were more than a disco group, but we were happy the genre brought us to a point where we were widely recognized across the world."

"We had fun together, we fought together, we travelled together," Mark declares. "We travelled to ungodly places and some really wonderful places. But it was always about the camaraderie and the music. How many groups have been together for nearly 40 years? Crown Heights Affair was like a tree branching out because we were a part of so many other groups and artists. And now the younger generation is working with a lot of our material, so it kind of says a lot about what we were able to do and our legacy."

Tyrone simply says, "I just want to be known as a person who entertained people for as long as I could until I was no longer here. That's it!"

"I want to be known as a person who was so passionate about music that he could perform for the Queen of England and then perform at a local bar in Brownsville!" states James. "I want that passion to be remembered!"

Phil, last to make a statement, adds, "I hope our legacy will be that every man belonging to or associated with Crown Heights Affair will able to take care of his grandchildren and great grandchildren from the money we *should* have gotten for our work. I hate to sound materialistic, but pay us what we were owed!"

The rest of the group loudly responds in unison, "Amen!"

Clare Bathé, formerly of Machine
"There But for the Grace of God Go I"

"When we'd sing the line about no blacks, no Jews and no gays—as we say in the theater, they went up!"—Clare Bathé

In 1979, just when disco music had begun to suffer from a growing reputation as a somewhat frivolous music form, along came Machine. Comprised of Clare Bathé, Jay Stovall, Kevin Nance, Lonnie Ferguson, Melvin Lee and produced by August Darnell (Dr. Buzzard's Original Savannah Band, Kid Creole), the group exploded onto the scene with a high-energy electrical storm called "There But for the Grace of God Go I," turning disco generalities upside down. With its powerhouse arrangement and thought-provoking lyrics referencing the bigotry that was often levied against minorities of the time, Machine stirred up considerable controversy (on the radio and the dance floor). In doing so, they created a disco classic. Bathé, once the group's lead singer and a highly accomplished jazz performer today, takes a moment to recall the impact of her time in the spotlight.

The influence of music was felt early in Clare's life. "I came from St. Louis, Missouri, and my parents sang," she says. "I am the last of seven children, and six of us could sing. We were a very musical family. I grew up in a time when you were encouraged to follow your dreams and, of course, there were several stars that influenced me. Singers like Little Jimmy Scott—one of my favorites—Nancy Wilson, Sarah Vaughan and Gloria Lynne moved me greatly. I tried to emulate them. I sang in church of course. The theater bug bit me while I was in college. When I finally went to New York, I pursued a career in theater while trying to get very lucrative background and jingle work. I met Norma Jean Wright (of Chic) through a guy who was playing bass for a Broadway show. Norma and I formed a friendship and a very strong bond. She introduced me to Nile Rodgers and Bernard Edwards, and I recorded some uncredited background vocals for Chic's first album in 1977. Norma also introduced me to the lead singer of Machine, Jay Stovall, that year. He liked my voice and hired me on the spot."

Bathé recalls, "I had to come back home and settle some family matters and took a job doing summer stock in St. Louis. I was performing with Vincent Price and Michele Lee in *Damn Yankees*. I got the call from Jay that they had taken the group Machine to the next level and they flew me back to New York. I went right into the studio and recorded 'There But for the Grace of God Go I' and flew right back to St. Louis. I can't remember how many takes it took, but we were in and out in a couple of hours. August Darnell produced Machine, but he was not an actual member of the band, and I didn't know him personally. We weren't friends or anything—we didn't socialize in the same circles—and the studio was where I first met him. It was Jay who convinced August I would be perfect for the record. I don't believe August was really sold on the idea at first because he had never heard me. August gave me direction on how he wanted me to sound on the record, and I took the direction very well. I gave him exactly what he wanted. I remember him saying he wanted me to sound like a little girl in the schoolyard going, 'Nah, nah, nah, nah, nah, naaah!' So I pitched my voice very high and he said, 'Jay was right; you're perfect!' I joked with August, saying he produced Cory Daye, Clare Bathé and Fonda Rae!" she laughs. "I eventually moved back to New York and began working with Machine full-time."

"I would have been surprised if we had not been a hit. I joined the group thinking we would really go places," says Machine's lead vocalist Clare Bathé, seen here starting a fire with the number one hit "There But for the Grace of God Go I" (courtesy Clare Bathé).

A message from the group on the back of their self-titled RCA debut album read: "Machine is about truth and facts. We do have messages in our music besides a good beat. So will our followers be about truth." The single "There But for the Grace of God Go I," written by Nance and Darnell, lived up to that claim. It wove impactful lyrics throughout its five-minute beat and guitar frenzy that caught the ear of nearly everyone who heard it. It's the tale of a couple leaving the Bronx for a place free of so-called undesirables. Those who understood the song's lyrical indictment of modern-day discrimination applauded it. It disturbed those who only heard three key words of its lyrics: *blacks*, *Jews* and *gays*. The song blasted into the Top 10 of the dance chart and made serious headway on the pop side. "We were actually hoping the lyrics would be impactful and that people would open their eyes to the prejudices that existed in our country," the artist asserts. "We were counting on it doing exactly what it did. We had an alternate line in the song that changed the controversial reference to one about moving where there's only upper class people. We recorded it both ways, in case the song couldn't be played in every market. I don't remember having to use the alternate version often.

"I can clearly remember where I was when I heard the song come on the radio the first time," she adds. "I was in my apartment in Brooklyn with Jay talking about something and he suddenly goes, '*Shhhhhhhhh!*' The song was playing on the radio station. I realized the song was a hit at that moment. It had a powerful beat and a catchy hook to it. There was something very edgy about the song. I thought it was different because it had a disco-rock sound, and Jay's guitar wasn't a sound you'd usually hear in a disco song. I've heard people say the music appealed to a Caucasian audience more than a black audience because of that rock influence. Jay Stovall was one of the finest rock guitarists ever. I'd rank him just under Jimi Hendrix and slightly above Prince. He was *that* good! In fact, he still is! I remember the record was a big hit, and we got this strange booking at a club in Maryland. It was an all-white, middle-aged audience, but—what's the best way for me to describe the patrons without sounding judgmental? They just seemed to be an audience that liked to drink beer and listen to country & western and rock 'n' roll—let's put it that way. We were singing our hearts out, and they were just *not* having us. Jay, perceptive as he was, went into his bag, and we just knew to follow him. He went into a Jimi Hendrix roll, and the people ended up on their feet cheering!"

Naturally, young people were generally the most appreciative of the all-black group's talents, according to the artist, though she believes the record company may have been courting a more specific audience. "I believe the label felt our music had more appeal to white people, and they really didn't want to put our faces on the album at all. They chose to show a motorcycle with a white leg on it, and a lot of people thought that was my leg—and it absolutely was *not*! My leg would have been much prettier and much sexier," she laughs. "I think it was Jay and another member of the group who balked at that visual, and so the record company ended up putting a small picture of us on the back of the album, but they might as well have just left it off. The music industry today is so different. None of that stuff matters today." The seven-track album, with its distinctive cover credited to photographer Jim Reiher, became one of the more memorable record jackets from the era. The LP yielded one more club hit, "Marisa," with Norma Jean Wright on backing vocals.

One thing was obvious to everyone—gay audiences loved Machine. "I'm sorry—

and I stand by my convictions—but you just can't beat a gay audience! They let you know when they love you!" declares the singer. "I was so pleased and happy to perform for them, and they just gave you so much love in return. They were very instrumental in the success of the song. When we'd sing the line about no blacks, no Jews and no gays … as we say in the theater, *they went up*! They got it! It was like a rally for them. Then that high-energy musical arrangement followed, and it was incredible. Just thinking about all that now, I really appreciated that audience so much. The Paradise Garage, baby—that was *the* club. I'm recalling the pictures and paintings on the walls, so I'm thinking that was thought of as a 'gay' club," she laughs. "Jay walked by me in the club and pushed my jaw closed as I kind of looked at the paintings in shock! When we knew we were going to the Paradise Garage, we were so up for it! I have to tell you a little secret. I've always been an early riser, like 5 a.m., and I've been like that all my life. So whenever we'd do those shows, like at three or four in the morning, I'd always have to take a nap in the afternoon. But if we were performing at the Paradise Garage, I didn't need a nap. I was so up and ready for it! That was a wild but wonderful time. Those were great times!"

Bathé says she can't account for the monetary success their blockbuster song may have enjoyed. "I have no idea where the money that's been made off 'There But for the Grace of God Go I' or the album went. I didn't see a penny of the profits, then or today. It's played all the time. The song went gold, and I never even got the plaque. I wasn't a writer, though, and the recording artists usually don't get anything. You usually only got paid to sing the track. Machine got royalties as a group, but the group is all split up, and if there's anything going to anybody these days, I don't know about it. It's frustrating, but there's nothing I can do about it. It was great being with a major label that took care of everything for you, but you paid for that. They got the big piece of the chicken, and you got the gizzard."

Delivering their record company a worthy follow-up was the next challenge the group faced. "I don't remember the label coming down on us about what we needed to do next, but we pressured ourselves," she recalls. "RCA noticed you because they heard something in your group. As a group, Machine had been honing their craft for a long time, and they were signed by RCA based on that. If there was any pressure from the label to have another hit, I wasn't privy to it. It was just expected you'd get more hits. We just pushed ourselves to try to do the best we could," says Bathé. Machine released the album *Moving On* in 1980. "We had a song on the follow-up album I felt was just as important as 'There But for the Grace of God Go I.' It was called 'Power and Reason.' It was deep!" the artist says, and then she sings the lyrical reference to a Mr. Exx-on 52nd Street. The song, similar in style to their monster hit, made an impression in the clubs during the dicey disco backlash days, but nothing on the LP caught the attention of mainstream music consumers immersed in the flux of the times. Bathé also alleges the record company failed to invest the money they had made from the group's hits into their future development, opting instead to concentrate on other acts.

The disco genre encountered a sizable reversal of fortune, which left the wheels of Machine mired in an almost hopelessly sticky marketplace. But the artist alleges that the excesses of the industry and the personal choices of those in power contributed to the demise of Machine as well. "I think most people expect success," Clare says. "I know

I did. I would have been surprised if we had not been a hit. I joined the group thinking we would really go places. I think it could have gone further. The idea [for Machine] may have been around since I think the late '60s—Jay was a kid in high school when he [started putting a] band together. By the time I was with the group, they had already gone through a couple of incarnations. When Machine started taking off, some of the band members got caught up in the glory and the glam. It was a decadent decade after all. In my opinion, that was the reason the group didn't go farther. I think Machine was their own worst enemy in that regard. There were a lot of disgruntled people in the mix. I started making plans to do different things. I felt they were going in a direction I couldn't vocally accompany. I was surprised we didn't last longer, but we got to where we were, and that was the end of it. The time with Machine had come and gone. We had hit records and a lot of fun, but it was over.

"We were in Argentina when I parted ways with Machine. I didn't leave the band high and dry though. We were all in agreement that I would go back to the States. But as luck would have it, a promoter in Argentina found out I was leaving the group and offered me a job as the opening act for Julio Iglesias' South American tour. I couldn't believe the luck and, of course, I didn't turn it down. When I returned to the States, I became the lead vocalist of the Lionel Hampton Orchestra. Once it was determined that I was going to leave Machine, I remember one of the group members said to me, with a bit of a sneer, 'Enjoy working in your little three-piece jazz band when you get back to New York!' I couldn't help but gloat a bit when I was performing on stage with Mr. Hampton and his *21-piece* orchestra!" she laughs.

"It was an honor to have sung with Basie, Art Blakey, Gerry Mulligan, Joe Williams, Joe Simon and many others. I performed in several Broadway shows. I was a backup singer and dancer for Lena Horne in her Broadway show and on her national tour. I starred in major stage productions in Europe and travelled with my own one-woman show. I was grateful to be a versatile artist. I didn't suffer, but I had mouths to feed. I had to take care of my daughter, my mother and myself. I don't mean to sound holier than thou, because I wasn't perfect either. I did my share of experimenting. But I didn't have time to sit and lick my wounds or put stuff up my nose. I had to get busy! I was grateful that I had a few opportunities and other irons in the fire." Though she didn't work further with August Darnell, she continued recording dance music for a time. Clare was part of the team behind the group Fantasy, who reached number one on the dance chart with the 1980 release "You're Too Late," and she also sang on a number of releases for Tommy Boy Records.

Bathé faces aging in the entertainment world head on. "I once heard someone ask Cher about aging, and she said something like growing old was disgusting and that she hated it. You could see on her face how much she was upset by it. When Tina Turner was asked the same question, she said she loved it and that she was enthralled by every day of living. So, I wondered about the difference. We always have a choice in life to be happy or not. For example, I've done a new CD [*I Met a Man*, released via CD Baby, that features a fusion of smooth jazz and sultry vocals]. I have a much more mature sound now. I used to be able to belt out high A-flats and had the lung capacity to hold it for 64 bars. I don't have those kinds of pipes today. But I do think people will really enjoy the way I sound now. I was a little nervous releasing it, I admit, but I chose to move forward and embrace the future. As it turned out, the project was very well received!" Clare has begun work on another album, *Clare Bathé Sings the Late Great Ladies of Jazz*.

"I played a lot of tennis," she adds. "Now my knees are balking, but I am still playing. I was petite back in days past. I didn't develop what you would call a weight problem until after I was married and started cooking every night for my husband and daughter. My daughter is Ryan Michelle Bathé. She's become a successful actor, starred in the movie *Good Fences* and has been a guest star on many television shows. I don't look shabby today, but things could always be better. I have nothing to prove to anyone, but I want to look good for me. I may need to lose a little weight, but it's for my health, not necessarily about my vanity. I don't allow those pressures into my life now. I also have a computer full of books I've written—romance novels and self-help books—but I haven't tried to get them published yet. Maybe that's next. I'm going to continue to be innovative and open to new things. I'm choosing to be happy, calm and peaceful."

"I'm going to continue to be innovative and open to new things. I'm choosing to be happy, calm and peaceful," insists Clare Bathé, whose current recording career in jazz flourishes (courtesy Clare Bathé).

The artist views the longevity of other disco artists as being a matter of personal choice and, perhaps, a little bit of good fortune. "I think some people are lucky, but it also depends on the artist's attitude. Freda Payne ("Band of Gold"), for example, had that one big hit and managed to parlay it into a long and very successful entertainment career. Norma Jean Wright is still out there performing the music of Chic as well as running her own management company. If you continue to put yourself out there, you can get and hold onto that respect. Otherwise, you fade into the sunset."

When the sun goes down and the rhythm of nightlife beckons, rest assured "There But for the Grace of God Go I" will be playing somewhere, energizing the spirits of dancers and music lovers for decades to come. Meanwhile, Clare Bathé continues to bridge the classic disco legacy of the group Machine with her own enduring sense of forward thinking and creativity. She pauses for several moments to ponder how she'd like her personal accomplishments and those of Machine to be remembered. "I think Machine was one of the only disco-rock bands of the time, and we were avant-garde, breaking new ground. We were thinking and feeling artists who didn't just care about making money from our music, but having an impact on people's lives. I hope people will remember that. I would like to be thought of as a vocalist who sang with compassion, love, commitment and integrity—a singer who participated in the moment and encouraged her audience to do the same. I hope I'm remembered as a good person and as someone who liked to make people feel good!"

Anthony Brooks of Harold Melvin's Blue Notes
"Bad Luck"

"Melvin always had an upbeat philosophy. He never was down."—Anthony Brooks

Harold Melvin and the Blue Notes hold a distinguished position in R&B and dance music history. Not only were they considered soul royalty, these gentlemen were kings of the Philly dance sound that heralded the disco explosion of the mid–'70s. Melvin was born in Philadelphia in 1939 and started out singing doo-wop. By the time he was 18, he had already formed a precursor of the Blue Notes group. Come the early '60s, the Blue Notes (once called the Charlemagnes) were finding success on the R&B charts while regularly undergoing personnel changes. They often toured with a group called the Cadillacs, whose drummer was a young, handsome man named Teddy Pendergrass. Eventually Pendergrass joined the Blue Notes, where his vocal prowess quickly elevated him to the role of lead singer. Strengthened by Teddy's soulful vocals, the group (which, during the course of its history, included Bernie Wilson, David Ebo, Lawrence Brown, Jerry Cummings, Dwight Johnson, Bernard Wilson and Lloyd Parks—the last surviving original member) was signed to producers Kenny Gamble and Leon Huff's Philadelphia International record label in 1972. Harold Melvin and the Blue Notes became the masters of pop-R&B, scoring such massive, irresistible hits as the ballad "If You Don't Know Me by Now" and the proto-disco nugget "The Love I Lost." A duet with Sharon Paige called "Hope That We Can Be Together Soon" in 1975 continued to cement their reputation as the premier soul group of the era.

The Blue Notes added thunder to the storm of disco hits that was building on the musical horizon with their number one smash "Bad Luck," a song that stayed atop the club chart for nearly three months in 1975. The track stayed in active rotation in the clubs for over six months. In his 2004 book, *Joel Whitburn's Hot Dance/Disco 1974–2003*, the author ended up ranking the song as the number one dance/disco hit of all-time. "Where Are All My Friends" and "Tell the World How I Feel About 'Cha Baby" were also dance-floor favorites.

Following an increasing number of conflicts between himself and Harold, Pendergrass left the group to pursue a solo career in 1976, at which time Melvin and his group also departed from the Philadelphia International fold. Harold continued to tour with various incarnations of the group and recorded albums for numerous labels over the next two decades (including ABC Records, which released the disco hit "Hostage" in 1977). A severe auto accident in 1982 resulted in a spinal cord injury that paralyzed Teddy Pendergrass. The singer struggled through the challenges of his condition and continued recording for several years until he passed from respiratory failure in 2010. Following a stroke from which he never fully recovered, Harold Melvin passed away in 1997. Not long afterward, conflicts developed over the ownership of the group's name, which resulted in Harold's wife Ovelia creating Harold Melvin's Blue Notes. This formation of the ensemble, featuring vocalist Anthony Brooks, actively tours today. Brooks speaks of his connection to the iconic Melvin and his group with reverence, respect and affection.

"I started out as an opening act for the Blue Notes around 1970, working in a group called the Wonders in Washington, D.C.," Brooks recalls. "Mr. Melvin said, 'I want y'all to travel with me.' I remember we took a train to New York City, and he picked us up in a limo. He said he wanted to show us the town and then took us to a sound check for a performance we were doing with him that night. We had never done a show with him before. We pulled up in front of a big auditorium, and we went in the back door. He took me out on the stage, and then I truly realized where I was—it was Carnegie Hall. That was my first show with Harold Melvin and the Blue Notes. You can't get no bigger than that! Harold said to me, 'If you can handle this, you can handle anything!' We got standing ovations all night. After that, we were on a roll and it was fabulous. It was phenomenal.

"Harold Melvin was a realist," Anthony says of his mentor, with whom he had many opportunities to work. "He wanted to make sure what you did on stage was real. Melvin always had an upbeat philosophy. He never was down. He would always find the good in everything, no matter what the circumstances. I thought that was a really great trait to have. He was a human being who appreciated folks with talent, and he could really find those people. He was quite gifted at bringing out the best in people. For example, there were times Teddy wasn't that confident about performing. But Harold instilled a sense of confidence in him. He told him he could be one of the greatest singers in the world if he would just believe in it. And Teddy was. I also don't think I ever had a fight or argument with Mr. Melvin. We always had a way of working things out."

During their glory days, the Blue Notes ensemble gradually moved from an R&B force to unstoppable dance-floor masters. The 1975 album *To Be True* placed the group at the forefront of the disco explosion, and Brooks recognizes the significance of the landmark LP. "Some days don't go as well as others," he says, describing the tremendous appeal of the song "Bad Luck," written by McFadden and Whitehead ("Ain't No Stoppin' Us Now") with Victor Carstarphen. "Some days start off good and turn out to be bad. And you gotta accept it and move on. 'Bad Luck' just said, simply, 'every day ain't great,'" Brooks laughs. "But you gotta get through it. Bad luck is just for a short time. You can have it, and you can get over it. And I think people related to that idea. They loved that song. The New Yorkers really loved it because they had problems [with their economy and city] back then.

"As far as disco was concerned, some of the music [of the Blue Notes] was already danceable or moving in that direction," Anthony believes. "McFadden & Whitehead wrote [or contributed to the writing of] a lot of their up-tempo stuff. They were part of 'Wake Up Everybody' and 'Where Are All My Friends.' They always had Harold's back and tried to give him the best product. He loved what they wrote. To this day, we are thankful for what songs they wrote, many of which turned into classics. Disco really started to explode out of these hits—'Bad Luck,' 'Don't Leave Me This Way.' Disco allowed for more longevity and let the group successfully work through that period. Harold Melvin and the Blue Notes made a lot of disco versions, although they weren't all hits. But again, Harold had a knack for recognizing the right material and picking the best talent. Most of the time he was right on the mark."

Thelma Houston covered the group's "Don't Leave Me This Way" and turned it into a stupendous disco classic in 1976. In the process, she earned herself a Grammy. Houston's success wasn't a problem for the Blue Notes according to Brooks. "It was no big deal when Thelma had such a big hit with it. We didn't have that 'player hate' in the old school, like they do today. We didn't waste time with that. If you were out there and got a hit, you were blessed. You know what I mean? You can't be mad when something like that happens. That was the only way to look at it."

During the disco heatwave, Brooks continued to build his friendship with Melvin and was able to see the esteemed artist work his magic for some time. Around the time that Harold Melvin's group was entering a period of instability in 1976, Anthony left show business completely and opted for the security of working for a tractor-trailer company. Late in the '90s, he was approached by Melvin's widow who asked him to become a part of the group she envisioned would carry on Harold's legacy. "[When the new ensemble was formed], she wanted to really establish our credibility angle," he remembers. "She wanted it to be a group that really knew Mr. Melvin. She wanted to re-establish the Blue Notes sound, the steps, the dancing, the personalities. That was her picture, and we brought it to life. We knew what Harold liked and how he worked.

"Mr. Melvin was an astute teacher, especially when it came to the music. We all have been affected by his teaching in one way or another. We all have his instincts. The group presently consists of John Morris, who has been with the Blue Notes about 14 years, Rufus Thorne, Jr., who was with the group since about 1985, and Donnell Gillespie, who has been taking on the role of Teddy Pendergrass. It's a good group, and we click really well. A lot of groups in our age bracket—they kind of just stand around. We actually dance, just like in '70s. There is always a great response to our music from people in our age group as well as young people. Our audience is always very diverse. It's interesting because Harold Melvin's music is known by people of older generations as well as younger people."

Brooks is fully cognizant of the negativity that occasionally surfaces in contemporary discussions about Harold, the Blue Notes, Teddy and the legitimacy of the formations that utilize, in one form or another, the group's original moniker. "Listen," he says assuredly, "I believe in my heart Harold Melvin was put in my life to make me a better man. It really worked. I am a better man as a result of knowing him. After 40 years of being involved with him and his family, I consider myself to be *a part* of his family. Everything that came into play has been incredible. I didn't think I'd ever be back doing his music again, but I'm blessed that I got that opportunity. I can speak about the good side of Harold Melvin instead of all the negativity, which I often hear about.

"In terms of drinking, drugs and such," the artist continues, "it's true Harold had some problems with some of the guys in the group. Everybody has demons. He had to deal with situations like that at a time when recreational drug use was kind of common. However, I should point out that if you *didn't* do things like that, nobody forced you. Marijuana was a big thing. I had asthma, so I couldn't handle that. [Anthony laughs.] I didn't go in for any of that. I was in it for the craft, for the work. I had been through all that when I was in Nashville, and by the time I got with Harold, I was ready to work. I was also running and exercising a lot to be up for those shows. As a matter of fact, I still run and hit the gym. My blood pressure now is as low as it was when I was in high school. You had to be in shape back then, but at my age now, man, you *have* to keep yourself in good condition. About five years ago I had fluid on my heart, and it almost took me out of here. I learned a lot of lessons from that, and I've been blessed to get my health back.

"All that said, I don't think the general public today is affected by the negative comments of a few. When you hear the name Harold Melvin and the Blue Notes, you automatically think of Teddy Pendergrass. The negativity surrounding Teddy or Harold comes from other sources, and when we go onstage, the thoughts about what this one or that one did don't even matter. It was a long time ago. The audience just gives us love—they tell us they love our sound and that they are glad we are continuing to bring it. That's our joy—that we can deliver it, just like Melvin would want it. That's what we concentrate on—anything else we just let roll off our backs," Brooks insists.

Today, Brooks lives in Maryland, not far from where he grew up in Washington, D.C. He remembers not only his musical history within these surroundings, but the civil rights battles he vividly witnessed in 1963—a time that set the stage for the escapism of the swinging '70s. "I was at Dr. Martin Luther King's march on Washington," he recalls. "I remember my mother said I was going no matter how hot it was. I had an opportunity to work with Dr. King on a few demonstrations in Nashville, Tennessee, and Memphis. That was my college life before meeting Mr. Melvin. I went to Tennessee State for a year, and it opened my eyes to a lot of the disparity out there as far as race was concerned. I took that as an education. I met a lot of incredible people in Nashville that I still consider my heroes. Back in those days, we had to be off the street by 11 p.m. or they locked you up. They'd have periodic raids and search your apartment and go through everything that you had. It was an education—besides the one I got from books. I eventually transferred back to Washington to a place called Federal City College. A great school—that's where the music really started to bloom in me. They created this college after the riots to help keep everybody calm. [Because of limitations where black people could teach,] they had a staff you would not have believed—Gil Scott-Heron teaching English, Marion Barry teaching political science; Sam Jones was a basketball coach. It was a very interesting place," claims the singer.

"As far as my experience in show business was concerned, I guess you could say the Blue Notes had no color," he adds. "By that I mean we worked for very varied audiences. We didn't experience the type of racism I experienced when I was in college. It was probably the same way for other entertainers too. Because of what we did, our fame or whatever, we were able to be separate from class structures. But I can tell you—being in college and then learning the entertainment trade, it was pretty hectic."

Through it all, Anthony has tried to keep his life in balance. "Harold taught 'the stage' but he also taught life," he says of his mentor. "I still follow those lessons. He said you have to separate show business from your personal life. Keep your personal life personal, and don't take your work life home with you. Harold would come home to his family, and [my family and I] would all go to Kentucky Fried Chicken with him. When I come home, I'm not a singer; I'm a husband. I have a wonderful wife who works in a hospital, and my kids are in college. You have to make time for family—and I love doing that."

In their highly regarded performances, Harold Melvin's Blue Notes continue to prove there is timeless beauty in the original group's vintage dance music endeavors. These classics have come to be regarded as time-honored gems of the disco pantheon. Anthony takes pride in being a part of that effort, saying, "I want people to remember the music of Harold Melvin and the Blue Notes as stories—stories of everyday life. If you had the blues, you played 'Bad Luck.' If you were missing a lover, you'd listen to 'I Miss You.' I'd like people to remember this music as songs that really meant something. And since Harold's music has been among the most sampled in the history of show business in America, I'm pretty sure his accomplishments will be around for a very long while!"

Ed Cermanski and Robert Upchurch of the Trammps
"Disco Inferno"

"When we recorded 'Disco Inferno,' nobody knew it was going to be the hit that it was, especially after being on the chart and falling off the chart the first time around."—Robert Upchurch

From its energized, cascading, celebratory drum and horn intro to its thundering vocal intensity, the song "Disco Inferno" has all the key elements of a disco classic. It seemed destined to become one of the most iconic hits of the era from the very start. To this day, only a handful of disco evergreens have the historic and influential prowess of the Trammps' signature hit. Long-time keyboardist Ed Cermanski, who came on board in 1975, manages a popular incarnation of the group today (Earl Young oversees the other). Ed joins lead vocalist Robert Upchurch, also a member of the original ensemble since '75, to reminisce about the Trammps' career, which has spanned over 41 years and continues to be a story of determination and artistic pride.

The group got their start in Philadelphia around 1972 with a hefty line-up of musicians and vocalists, many of who had played for Gamble and Huff's Philadelphia International label enterprise. Among them were Jimmy Ellis (on vocals), Harold Doc Wade, Stanley Wade and Earl Young. The Trammps were something of a dual entity, says Ed. "The group was developed out of two competing groups from Philadelphia. Earl Young had one group called the Exceptions with Jimmy Ellis (they had a popular song called 'Down by the Ocean'), and the other featured the Wade brothers called the Volcanoes, who had a hit titled 'Storm Warning.' From merging those groups, the Trammps evolved. There was a Trammps live band and a separate Trammps that featured the studio members. The studio group included Ronnie Baker (bass and vocals), Norman Harris (guitar and vocals) and Earl Young (drums and vocals). They were pretty much the guys driving the group forward. Ron Kersey [a popular keyboard player often referred to as Ron 'Have Mercy' Kersey] was also a key figure and functioned on both levels for a time. Before 1975, there was this large mix of gentlemen who did their work in the studio and in live performances."

Signed to Golden Fleece Records for a time, the group moved to Buddah Records, where they had success with an upbeat version of the Judy Garland classic, "Zing Went the Strings of My Heart" (originally recorded by the group in 1972 and then later remixed by Tom Moulton as a heavily orchestrated early disco production). The song received extensive play in New York nightclubs, putting the group on the map, at least as far as DJs were concerned. The Trammps continued to make their presence known with soulful jams like "Where Do We Go from Here" and the Top 40 pop hit "Hold Back the Night" in 1975.

Robert says, "I had been performing since I was 12 years old and was a solo artist on the Golden Fleece label. Eventually that company folded. [After recording for Buddah Records], the Trammps went over to Atlantic. The people at Atlantic thought my voice would go well with that of the group's lead singer, Jimmy Ellis, and the combination worked well enough to have them sign me on. I began with the group on the *Where the Happy People Go* album."

Ed adds, "I came to be in the Trammps thanks to a friend named Roger Stevens, a trumpet player who was doing studio work at Sigma Sound. He was also part of the live Trammps act. In the spring of '75, Ron Kersey had made the decision he wanted to concentrate on working in the recording studio only, producing and writing. It was good that he did, because that led to 'Disco Inferno,' which he composed with Leroy Green. He was doing work for everybody, including the O'Jays, Michael Jackson and the Spinners. I think almost everything that came out of the Salsoul Orchestra, Kersey played on. Roger introduced me to Ron, and he introduced me to Doc and Earl. I performed for them, and they invited me to join the Trammps. It was great timing too!"

Secure with the Atlantic Records label, the Trammps' reputation for infectious, beat-driven music began to grow. "When I joined the group," Cermanski says, "they had already signed a five-album deal with Atlantic. I don't know how the transition from Buddah to Atlantic took place, but certainly Atlantic was a much bigger and stronger label and it was very advantageous for us to be with them. Before that move, the large body of their work was very melodic music, especially with songs like 'Stop and Think.' I think the Trammps weren't intentionally focusing on disco in the early days, just good songs and some good dance music. The music that was happening at that time was R&B, and it was starting to have a more produced kind of sound. I think eventually the Trammps were labeled as a disco act because the DJs in New York loved their music— it was danceable, had the right beat and so on. The group didn't exactly set out to be a disco act, but they certainly ended up being one of the first and best."

Upchurch says the group had a unique sound that distinguished them from other male ensembles entering the disco market. "Whenever you heard Jimmy Ellis, you knew it was a Trammps song. There was no mistaking who you were listening to," he says. Commenting on Tom Moulton's remix work, he observes, "I think his work put a different light on our songs. I think it enhanced them with a more lavish production. Tom certainly had his little tricks on the board. Our songs were suited for his touch with the melodies, the beat and lyrics."

"By the mid–'70s," says Cermanski, "discos were up and running, and we became identified with the music; that's just what was happening. At that point, our fans were going to discos, and we were getting a lot of gigs at the clubs. So our music started to reflect those themes, like 'That's Where the Happy People Go.'" Lifted from their Atlantic debut LP *Where the Happy People Go* and mixed again by Tom Moulton, the nearly eight-minute track reached the number one spot on *Billboard*'s disco chart and firmly linked the group to the blossoming nightlife scene. "Disco Party," off the same album, also hit the top spot and "Ninety-Nine and a Half" fell just short of making it three in a row. "I don't think the group, after coming in and talking with some of the elder members, ever decided to actually 'go disco,'" conjectures Upchurch. "I think that was more the work of the production team and also because of what was happening with the music scene at the time. I think you can sometimes get pulled into things without it being your intention, and it just happens to work."

"Personally, I'm more of an R&B person," Robert continues. "Disco was okay, and I enjoyed doing it, but if it had been up to me, it probably wouldn't have been my choice for a direction for the group. I didn't think disco was less legitimate than other forms of music; it just wasn't my preference."

Atlantic had their premiere disco recording stars with the Trammps, but Cermanski says it was their live performances in the clubs that earned them a good living and cemented their reputation as great entertainers. "Back in that time period," he says, "most of our income was from live performances. We worked four or five nights a week in New York. New York had so many clubs—in Manhattan, Long Island, Staten Island, the Bronx. You could work virtually every night. We were performing everywhere in '75 and '76. Disco was always popular in Europe, even in the early days. We made our first trips to the Netherlands, the U.K., Germany and Belgium in 1975. The Trammps really stayed afloat in those days because of live gigs. The audiences in New York and Europe both loved to dance. Obviously, there were cultural differences and languages, but people who wanted to go to the clubs and have a good time were the same all over the world. In our experience, the people who loved disco were peaceful; they loved to dance. It was a really good era in music!"

While some disco stars of the period readily identified gay audiences as the group that responded to their music with the most enthusiasm, the Trammps looked at their fans in broader terms. Says Ed, "We never really identified whether anyone in our audience was straight, gay or a Martian. It wasn't something we ever zeroed in on. I know many of the DJs of the time appealed to the gay crowd, but we were appreciative of *any* audience that enjoyed our music. In retrospect, I can say now that some of the clubs did have large gay crowds, and I think that they may very well have been a driving force behind disco and getting the group started. I just didn't know it at the time. I also didn't notice if there was a stronger appeal to say a black or white audience. During the late '70s, we played primarily to white audiences in the New York area, but we also travelled down south and appeared regularly at mostly black clubs. I think we appealed to everyone."

As their hit singles and animated performances fueled their growing success, the Trammps remained a cool and levelheaded ensemble. "Amazingly, you would think it would be hard to manage everybody's ego, creativity and input, but it wasn't," claims Cermanski. "We always had a lot of people on stage, a large crew traveling with us, a couple of buses. These were guys who were with each other almost 24 hours a day. Despite all that closeness, I don't really recall any real major arguments or fights. Everyone got along very well and was professional. It all came very naturally for everyone. We never even had to practice. We learned most of our routines on stage. If it went well, a song or something we did in a show, it was in our repertoire for the next performance. Everyone knew what we had to do. We never had any group members who were prima donnas or who were over-the-top. We got along really darn well together!"

Still recording at Sigma Sound in Philadelphia, the Trammps unleashed the album *Disco Inferno* in 1976. The celebratory title track (another Tom Moulton mix, clocking in at over 10 minutes) was a blistering high-energy indictment of dance floor mayhem. "As I heard it told," Cermanski remembers, "Ron said he had a really cool groove. He put the words together, and it was supposedly inspired by the movie *Towering Inferno*. I think his idea was to put a disco theme around the influence of that movie. Of course, the song wasn't meant to be about burning a building down; it was more about the burning desire to dance!" Though their biggest hit to date on the disco survey, holding the number one position for well over a month, the single "Disco Inferno" only managed to reach the midsection of the pop chart.

Fast-forward two years. The recording was added to the legendary soundtrack of the 1978 mega-hit movie *Saturday Night Fever*, and the game completely changed. "The Trammps had regularly played the 2001 Odyssey club in Brooklyn, where *Saturday Night Fever* was filmed, and they were very popular there. As a matter of fact, the group had actually gotten a trophy for being the best club performers in New York in '77 or '78, around the time when the movie came out. They couldn't do a movie with just the Bee Gees, and New York was the Mecca for disco music. 'Disco Inferno' had already been out and had been a big hit. It added local flavor to the movie and kind of an ambience. The Trammps *were* disco, and it just made sense to feature the song," Ed says.

Recalling the time, Robert adds, "From what I was told, our attorney at the time, David Steinberg, was having lunch with [*Saturday Night Fever* producer] Bob Stigwood. The soundtrack came up in the course of conversation and the suggestion of putting the Trammps on it was discussed. The 2001 club was like a home for the group. We could work there when we couldn't work anywhere else. That club was a hotbed for disco acts at the time and also R&B acts out of Philadelphia, like Blue Magic and artists like that."

The gentlemen vividly recall the astonishing aftershocks of their participation in the film's soundtrack. "Well, it was just a giant boost for us!" Ed says. "The group had been doing well before. I believe they would have continued on an upward trajectory, but when the movie came out it just changed everything! The soundtrack was the biggest selling of its time, so that was a great thing for us. The movie and the soundtrack brought disco music out of the big cities and into suburbia. It spread it out to areas that weren't as exposed to the music as New York was."

"I was surprised John Travolta could dance," Robert chimes in. "To see him dancing to our music in the film was fantastic. It was actually a rush!" "Disco Inferno" returned the group to the pop charts in 1978. The song peaked just shy of the Top 10 and was a Top 20 smash in the U.K. "A song returning to the charts doesn't happen very often in America!" Robert says with pride.

The Trammps won a Grammy for their contribution to the *Saturday Night Fever* LP, a monumental accomplishment for the group. "It was a big shock for us to get a Grammy. We knew the album was nominated, and Earl went out to California to attend the show. The rest of us were doing a live show in Boston at a club called Lucifer's, so we ended up watching the awards on TV. I think everybody, the main players of the group, got their own Grammy, and I guess they all have it on their mantles somewhere!" Cermanski laughs. The *Saturday Night Fever* soundtrack was added to the Library of Congress Recording Registry in March of 2013 for long-term preservation.

Both gentlemen recall the boon to the group's bookings. "We went from billing four or five nights a week to touring 30 cities in 31 days. We did Madison Square Garden and the Superdome with KC and the Sunshine Band. We were getting way more club gigs, but also a lot larger venues like the Garden!" Cermanski says. Robert agrees that the event was a major career highlight. "I remember running out on that stage to a crowd of that size, and it was unbelievable. Crown Heights Affair was also on the bill, and I believe Gloria Gaynor, too. The crowd was excited about what we were singing, and it felt great!"

Atlantic had released their next album, *The Trammps III*, in 1977, and *The Whole World's Dancing* in 1979. Containing more Tom Moulton mixes, expectations were high that these collections would contain another "Disco Inferno." "I think there always is pressure to have a big follow-up hit," Ed says. "They were addressing those issues at a higher level than where I was. I was the keyboard player at the time and wasn't that involved in the politics. But there was always a push to get something as big as 'Disco Inferno.' I think they banked on 'The Night the Lights Went Out' [from *The Trammps III*] as the follow-up song. I think there were some other songs on that album that could have been pretty good songs in the dance genre, like 'People of the World, Rise,' which might have been better to follow up 'Disco Inferno.' But most of us were not involved in those decisions." "The Night the Lights Went Out" capitalized more on a recent New York City blackout than it did the nightlife sensations of their monster hit. Only managing to reach the lower portions of the R&B survey, the more melodic, less ferocious song did manage to score a Top 10 placing on the disco chart. "Soul Bones" (featuring a harmonica solo by Stevie Wonder) off the '79 set was a modest club hit.

Upchurch agrees that pressure for follow-up hits was felt. "We felt it sometimes from the production team, who got their orders from the record company," he says. "You always want to see the public receive your music well. You just don't know what's going to happen. Sometimes you know you have a hit, and other times you just *feel* that you have a hit. When we recorded 'Disco Inferno,' nobody knew it was going to be the hit that it was, especially after being on the chart and falling off the chart the first time around."

The Trammps continued to record with Atlantic for the next few years, scoring a few minor hits on the dance chart like "Hard Rock and Disco." Their final album for the label was the ironically titled *Slipping Out* in 1980. The group recorded an LP for the European market called *This One Is for the Party* on the Dutch label Injection Records in 1984, but thereafter concentrated mostly on touring.

Cermanski and his band mates observed their career slow down. "I think the most difficult thing about being in the music industry is probably similar to what athletes experience when they are towards the end of their playing career," he says. "At some point, your career stops—not because you want it to, but you just can't continue to live and pay the rent from what you're doing. The Trammps almost hit that point and had to take a hiatus every so often. The gigs just weren't there for a time. You have 10, then it drops to five—then you just don't know when the next one is coming. I think that's the hardest part of this business—when you've done extremely well and the bottom falls out."

"A lot of the familiar places we had been able to work just began disappearing," Robert also remembers, "and if it impacts your livelihood, of course you become concerned. Things slowly declined, and you could sense the times were changing. I didn't see the precise moment when the decline actually began, but I felt there was an increasing movement to push disco music out of the way. A lot of people didn't like that type of music. I could also see that there also may have been too much disco music out there. It was too late for the Trammps to try something else, a different type of music. I think if we had ventured into serious R&B, I don't think it would have been received well. Not in light of what the group had already accomplished with disco."

"The rockers in Chicago didn't help either with their stadium record-burning stunt," adds Ed. "For whatever reason, they felt the need to trash disco. Frankly, the albums they were burning probably had more sophisticated music than the stuff they were supporting. Burning disco records, like burning books, is really dirty pool. It was a stunt for them, but I think it was a bad way to voice your opinion about something. It ended up that disco was just called dance music after that, and that's what it was called before it was known as disco. So the stunt didn't really accomplish much. I think another part of the problem was the fact that almost everyone wanted to make a disco record. Ethel Merman, Andy Williams—once that happens you know you've jumped the shark. It gave the haters a reason to say, 'Hey, look at this!' None of that negativity ever happened in Europe. They were very, very loyal fans over all the past decades. The Trammps played constantly over there, especially Holland," he acknowledges.

Ed looks at the positive side of life after the disco boom. "The good stuff—the Donna Summer music, the KC songs, A Taste of Honey, Tavares, Gloria Gaynor—that's still being played today. The climate for disco has gotten better. I think it's begun to sink in that these artists were really good. I think that's where people are at today. The taboo of the '80s and '90s is over, and you count your blessings. Not everyone had that *one* big hit. 'Disco Inferno' has become so iconic over the years that the group continues to work thanks to it. I guess the question is, would we still be working without 'Disco Inferno?' I think we probably would be. Would it have been nice to have a couple more hits the size of that smash? Yes, it absolutely would have made a big difference. But everyone is thankful to have had the one song." "Disco Inferno" has since been heard in everything from movies like *Donnie Brasco*, to episodes of *Friends*, *The Sopranos* and the *So You Think You Can Dance* show. Tina Turner and Cyndi Lauper have also covered the song.

With the passing of time, the Trammps have had to face the inevitable loss of some of their members. Norman Harris, who went onto a remarkable production career at Salsoul working with many of disco's finest performers, passed on in 1987. Ron Kersey left this world in 2005 and tenor Jimmy Ellis passed away most recently in 2012. "The passing of Jimmy was very sad and a tremendous loss," Ed says, his voice revealing the tone of a heavy heart. "He had been doing the live show with us up until about a year or two before he passed. He had dementia for about three or four years, but he still knew every word of every song. When he left us, you realize you don't know how much you'll

(Left to right) Stan Wade, Dave Dixon, Harold Doc Wade and Robert Upchurch currently tour as The Trammps and perform the group's legendary dance classics, including "Disco Inferno" and "Disco Party" (courtesy Donna Upchurch).

miss someone till they are gone. He was one of the best vocalists I have personally had the pleasure of hearing and performing with. It was a blessing for all of us to have known him. We have Robert Upchurch now in the lead spot, who worked next to Jimmy for so long, and he can really convey that energized sound."

"Ellis was the sound of the Trammps—unmistakable," Upchurch says, pausing for a moment to reflect on his lost group mate. He exhales. "He was extraordinary. We came to know him as the man with the golden voice. He was so unique in his way. I don't think anyone in the music field had that sound. Another nickname we had for him was 'Gentleman Jim.' He was always classy, always a perfectionist, always professional. A fantastic guy. It's difficult at times for me to take the lead vocalist role in the group. It was his legacy. It's all of our legacies, but it's his sound that we are trying to reproduce. There is only one Jimmy Ellis, and there won't be another. So now, we just try to help the crowd remember."

"I think we've all slowed down somewhat," Cermanski says, reflecting on the passing of youth. "We're not kids. I know I really enjoy the times I have performing today, being on stage, and I think you come to understand it's a nice thing to still be doing. We've survived the years; we continue to work here and overseas. I think we're a little more reserved than we used to be, but that's the difference between being a young buck out there and a more mature performer. Essentially, we haven't changed in our desire to create the experience we want to bring to our audience."

Robert is equally cognizant of the effects of time. "At this stage of our lives," he says, "we know what we can and cannot do. I think as long as you are aware of those parameters, you will be okay. I am more comfortable with the performing end of life now than I was in the '70s or '80s." The group recently returned to the studio to record a new single called "Chapter One," melding the Trammps of old with a contemporary sound.

It's hard to find anyone who is unable to identify the signature song of the Trammps, a group who defined disco from its inception. True royalty of the genre, the group delivered raw, soulful, masculine harmony and a unique kind of energy to music that became synonymous with the dance floor. Comments Robert, "I'd like people to remember that our music made them smile, took their mind off their troubles, and that we made music that made you want to dance. I hope people associate us with the good times in their lives."

Ed takes a moment and in a strong voice says, "We're proud of 'Disco Inferno,' of course, but we're also proud of all the other material we did. Right back to the first albums, with 'Love Epidemic,' 'Sixty Minute Man,' 'Where Do We Go from Here'—they were melodic, pretty songs with a lot of soul. I hope people will remember that work too. We have always been a party group though, and that's a great legacy. I think the whole group would love it if people look back and say we put on a really great show! That they were really happy when they came to see us! That they didn't ever sit down like at a formal concert—they partied and danced! That they forgot about the nine-to-five or whatever else may have been on their minds. If you think of it that way, maybe the Trammps did a really good thing!"

•••••••••••••••••••••••••••••••••

Sarah Dash
"Sinner Man"

"The moment I hit 'Sinner Man,' the moment that they hear that thump, it's over!"—Sarah Dash

"The universe takes care of you! Faith is the key! It gives you strength; it gives you hope. It doesn't mean that things are over because you are not getting 25 offers a day. It just means the season is over—but then you stay in your season by accepting where you are and surrounding yourself with the people that make you happy and who love you," observes Sarah Dash. She speaks of life nearly 40 years after she was thrust into the limelight as a member of the legendary trio Labelle. As a remarkably powerful vocalist in one of disco's original and most innovative girl groups (whose signature smash "Lady Marmalade" is hailed as an early disco masterpiece), Sarah possessed a unique and profoundly distinctive vocal and song-writing talent that would see her through to a stellar solo career. He classic gospel-soul dance-floor milestone "Sinner Man" became a signature song of the disco genre and just one of many accomplishments for this gifted artist, who has served on the Grammy Board of Directors and whose career continues to flourish today.

"I had my first brush with singing in second grade," she says of her childhood. "I was maybe six or seven years old, and I was humming in class and my teacher ended up putting me in the Thanksgiving Day ceremony for the school—I was the youngest in the school to ever be included. Later on, I was in the youth choir at a church in Trenton, New Jersey. I didn't know whether I was going to be a successful singer or not, but I knew in my mind that I was not going to have a nine to five job. I think by age nine, it was clear as a bell ringing in my ear."

Sarah wasted little time connecting with her musical destiny. She crossed paths with Patricia Holte (who would later take the stage name Patti Labelle) and became part of the earliest formation of the Bluebelles. She recalls, "Patti Labelle and I were teenage high school singers, and we each had our little groups. One of the girls in my group was named Sandra, whose mother worked in a nightclub. During the time she was working there, they would bring in different performers from out-of-town to sing, and she met a manager by the name of Mr. Montague. She asked him if he would listen to her daughter's group. He heard us and liked us, and in the meantime, he was managing another teenage group out of Philadelphia—that was Patti's group called the Ordettes. So that's how I came to meet Patti and Cindy Birdsong [who had replaced Sundray Tucker in the Ordettes]. Nona Hendryx was in another group from Trenton and the Bluebelles formed out of that."

Patti Labelle & the Bluebells hadn't found major commercial success with their recordings until the release of their 1974 LP *Nightbirds* on Epic Records. Now going by the name Labelle, their album reached the U.S. Top 10 in 1975 and sold over a million copies—fueled by its number one juggernaut single, "Lady Marmalade," which ranked among funk-disco's very first blockbusters. "'Lady Marmalade' came about while we were on vacation, and we were on our way to New Orleans," Sarah says. "We were going to a CBS Records convention in California and then heading to New Orleans to record. We went to [artist and songwriter] Bob Crewe's house for dinner, and he was telling us we had to record this song he had written [with Kenny Nolan] and said he thought we would make a million with it. I arrived in California just in time for the convention, and they played the song for me. And I was like, 'This is a hit!' I knew it immediately. They sent it to Allen Toussaint, who was our producer, and the rest is history. It was really one of the first records promoted directly to the clubs.

"'Lady Marmalade' was a different type of sound," Dash observes. "Very rarely did you hear a song break down on record and just have a drum beat—and that what it's got! The chords, piano, everything cut out except the drummer and the bass, and that had not happened on a record up until then to my knowledge—but I don't know everything!" she laughs. "You never had that kind of breakdown—you had never heard that before. To hear females singing those lyrics—I think that contributed to the interest in the song. And also that it was partially sung in French. People were trying to figure out what to make of it! It had the catch—the whole 'gitchiyaya' sound. People loved slang and loved saying things that had a hook to it. So that phrase was coined, and it started showing up on TV and sitcoms, and people were saying you have to get your 'gitchiyaya' on. It was an odd sounding dialect, you know, and I think that is what attributed to most of the interest from the public's perspective."

"Lady Marmalade," fusing R&B, funk, disco and rock, was more than just a startling dance hybrid. Its intriguing lyrical content, swirling in themes of prostitution and the sexual liberation of the '70s, made the song both controversial and irresistible. Like Donna Summer (with "Love to Love You Baby"), Labelle struck pay dirt in this largely uncharted territory of early dance music. Observes Sarah, "On the one hand, we had the nuns in Seattle marching [against] our lack of morals and radio stations running French contests if [listeners] could tell them what we were saying. It was just that kind of time and moment that we happened to come in when America wanted to hear something different. And it's not only in America; it became an international hit as well!

"I thought we were hidden to a certain degree from the conservatives' criticisms, because, again, here we are, coming out singing [the French lyrics], which translate to a bold offer to make love. Who in the world would make a song like that? If we sang those actual words in English, we would have been totally blasted! But the discovery of what we were saying made it more interesting!" the singer conjectures.

"The record was first promoted in France, where they thought we were three black French girls, and then Belgium and then Spain. We were just traveling more and more. There were times you would feel like, 'Oh my God, this *is* happening! This *is* going on!' Gold records! Gold albums! You know, it was finally happening, and we needed to focus on that. Because all those gold records I have on my wall from different countries—when I look at that wall, it gives me strength today. It doesn't make me feel superhuman. It doesn't make me better; it's just a way of being honored for the work," reflects Dash.

The albums *Phoenix* (1975) and *Chameleon* (1976) followed, but took the group away from the funky dance and pop scene in which they had scored so successfully. By 1977, the group was reported to have mutually agreed to split, but Sarah says it was a decision that she hadn't been entirely ready to address. "When the group broke up, I wasn't fully prepared, but I knew I would have to adjust quickly," says the artist. "It was far from over for the young singer. After a period of introspection, she began to reinvent herself and forged her identity as Sarah Dash: solo artist. "One of the things that prepared me to be a solo artist was listening to new songs—and I'm still preparing that way today. In my case, I never stop preparing. Every week I listen to new songs—I write a list of them—even if I don't perform them. This is a habit I have kept since the breakup of the group. I would go and start learning new material and experiencing it. So I ended up going down to a club and worked there with a band and, some way or another, [record producer and TV mogul] Don Kirshner heard about me. He got word that I wasn't signed and called me up and said, 'We are going to take you out kid!' That is how he addressed me; it wasn't anything offensive. That was his nickname for me; he called me 'kid.' And I had many names—they called me 'Inch'; they called me 'Dash'; they called me 'Lady Dash'; they called me 'Lady Sarah.' We started making preparations for songs. He sent me all these songs to learn and, as a result, Don is responsible for the way that I trained and kept my vocals together in learning new material.

"I had one more obligatory engagement at the club I was working at, and he sent [songwriters] Carol George and Rob Hegel to see me. I was singing, 'Who's Watching Me Now,' and I did it in such a way that we funked it up, and they were watching how I moved across the stage and what I was doing and how I was kicking my leg. They liked my moves and said, 'She needs a sinner man,' went home that night and wrote the song 'Sinner Man' by the next morning! By the next afternoon, I had the song sitting in front of me, and I started singing it, and I added that high part to it—it just came out of nowhere. I recorded 'Sinner Man' in one take! So you know it had *something* to it!" she says with fresh enthusiasm in her voice.

Rarely had a singer's first solo effort so magnificently placed her talents on full display or resounded so successfully with the public. "Sinner Man," a rousing, gospel-fused disco journey into vocal abandon, became an instant classic in 1978 and burned its way to the Top 10 of the dance chart. Mixed by Tom Moulton, it quickly became Sarah's signature theme. "The song sure moved me right into disco!" Dash says proudly. "I had to jump right into this new performance lifestyle. I played clubs at four o'clock in the morning. At that time, it was like, 'Wow, look at these amazing clubs!' I had so much fun; I had such a good time! I played a lot of gay discos, a lot of straight discos, the international leather convention—you name it! The fans were so receptive and enthusiastic! You really felt the love! It was just a wonderful time to see and experience this other side of life. There were discos that were large, some were small, and some events were exclusive, private parties. That song just did so much to fire up the audience, and it still is in my show today! The moment I hit 'Sinner Man,' the moment that they hear that thump, it's over!"

From her equally riveting self-titled album debut came another disco hit, "(Come and Take This) Candy from Your Baby," and with it Sarah truly established herself among disco's finest reigning divas of the time. She embraced the music. "Oh my goodness, there were so many great disco songs out there at the time and many I would have loved to have sung. '(You Make Me Feel) Mighty Real'—I love that Sylvester song! What else can I say? I mean, that one to me is truly close to my heart!" says Dash.

The party would abruptly adjourn, at least for a time, as the now infamous disco backlash placed a temporary speed bump in Sarah's path and those of her fellow disco compatriots. The album *Oo-La-La Sarah Dash* followed in 1980 (with Phyllis Hyman providing backup vocals) and despite a moderate disco hit with "Oo-La-La Too Soon," the

Sarah Dash, circa 1980, awash in the energy of Studio 54 (photograph by Charles R. Moniz, used by permission).

effort was mired in the difficulties of the times and faltering label support. The LP *Close Enough*, featuring the rock-tinged track "Paradise," came next in 1981.

With the emergence of hi-NRG music in the early '80s, Sarah found a new home at Marty Blecman's Megatone label, which was churning out many of the era's most popular underground dance anthems (with artists like the immortal Sylvester). Energized dance music auteur Patrick Cowley teamed with Blecman to release Dash's "Low Down Dirty Rhythm" and "Lucky Tonight" in 1983. "I arrived in California to do the two songs, and Sylvester came to the studio," she says. "You can hear Sylvester and I singing together [on "Lucky Tonight"]. Sylvester was the person who had taken over the company, who was mastermind of the whole label at that point, and he later became ill with complications from the AIDS virus that had begun ravaging the community. I was getting ready to do a larger project with Sylvester and Patrick. We were preparing to do a whole album, but then Sylvester [as well as Cowley] got sick, and then I knew he wouldn't be able to come forth with more tracks for me. Sylvester got sick. My mother got sick, and she passed away. It was a difficult time, and I sort of went to the side of the music industry and started to settle down to find myself. I was so heartbroken from [that series of events]. But out of that came some fabulous sounds which people still tell me they enjoy to this day. One night, I was in a club and 'Lucky Tonight' came on. I asked the guy at the door, 'Did y'all know that I was going to be here?' He was like, 'Is that you? *Is that you singing!*'" she chuckles. "Those are the moments that really matter in an artist's time—when a surprise comes and you know someone is paying attention!" Dash's "Lucky Tonight" was a big hit in the clubs, reaching the Top 5 of the dance chart.

Adoration from the gay community was generously bestowed upon the singer, whose history with Labelle was already revered by the culture. "Gay audiences are so heartfelt," she says. "I never thought of playing to a straight audience tonight and a gay audience tomorrow. When I perform, all groups came, and it is still that way today. I'm happy to say I am able to bridge many cultural gaps. But when I hit that song 'Sinner Man,' they are *all* done! No matter what type of person they are!

"You know, my faith really keeps me grounded. It gives me a sense of where I am. So the appreciation I have of every group of people that comes into my life is so valuable to me. Being a preacher's kid, we had all kinds of people coming through our front door, in our home. That filtered down into my life. I tried to be fair and to give everyone an equal opportunity. I really do appreciate all who come into my life," she says.

Dash kept busy in the late '80s and '90s, continuing to perform live at clubs like Sweetwater's in New York. Following session work for other artists, which included a duet with Chic's Nile Rodgers, Sarah recorded briefly for EMI Records and appeared on the Rolling Stones' *Steel Wheels* album in 1989. She reunited with Patti Labelle and Nona Hendryx for the single "Turn It Out" in 1995, which topped the dance chart, and the ladies again teamed up in 2008, under the Labelle moniker, to release the critically acclaimed album *Back to Now*. "I'm Still Here," a soft gospel song that reflects the singer's strong spirituality, was released in 2011. In 2012, Dash returned to the dance floor with the top-selling digital single "Hold On (He'll Be Right There)." Sarah is often called upon to sing at special church functions, where her abilities and spirituality are held in high regard.

She examines her philosophy for managing life as a mature woman. "When I sing, it makes me know that I'm in tune to my spiritual self," the artist observes. "Sometimes we don't listen to our gut, and we allow other people to tell us, or to express to us, how we are supposed to think. With my *Sarah Dash–One Woman* show, I have a support group called 'Team Dash' that is so important to my life. And I learned to look at my team with the confidence to know that they won't lead me wrong. So when I sing a song and I present it, and if the audience receives it, it just makes me feel like the work hasn't been in vain—because it's a spiritual thing to be a performer. It's not following the flavor of the week; it's following what is in your heart!

"Unfortunately, I have been sidelined by different people who would come into my life at different times. But I try not to ever let it set me back. I just try to let my spiritual self develop more. I began to write poetry, started painting again, and I started being more involved by supporting charities and raising funds for homeless people. Music has always been with me throughout my entire evolution."

The singer reflects on an accident a few years back that left her, for a time, in great physical distress. "I was injured at one point, and there were days that I couldn't move at all," she recalls, exhaling with emotions that the event stirs up. "I couldn't walk without the assistance of some kind of prop. I was in a cast from my ankle up to my hip. I was incapacitated for four years, and I couldn't perform. But eventually I began to look for ways to become productive again. I got a call from someone asking me to share my experiences and to offer inspirational talks to others. That led to me start singing inspirational music. All of this revived my motivation. After a setback, the mind expands to another area. And you don't worry about what people might think about it. You change over time. For instance, I don't have a 21-inch waist anymore—but things like that do *not* define me today."

Now that she is well again and actively performing, the artist is able to offer her philosophy for making the most of life. "As you grow older, you begin to truly realize your worth. No amount of money in the world can bring you back your health. So what you do is give yourself the best shot at life you can—by eating healthy and keeping the mind active. And if you happen to be in show business, when things slow down and the people don't come out as much as they used to or the demand is not there, you realize you can *still* do more. You can paint, you can write, you can go and help at a daycare center, a school, or read to the children in the hospital that have cancer. Opportunities are endless. It may not seem like a big deal to you, but it is to those you reach out to.

"When you get older and the demand shifts and goes someplace else, go with the flow. It doesn't diminish who you are. It's just the time you are in. You can't worry about some people saying, 'She's not happening anymore because she isn't at the top of the charts.' That doesn't lessen who you are and shouldn't stop one from doing the things you love. If you are a disco singer, start learning other songs and incorporate other songs into your act, like I do. Listen, I'm not saying that my life is perfect. I know there are certain things I have no control over—I can't do a thing about them. We go through hard times, but that's not a crime. The crime in one's life is to be deceptive. Liars and thieves—those are the bad people. But to have a setback, that's really a *set-up* for a comeback! That's all that is!" she declares.

Upfront, observant and a performer who cuts to the chase, Sarah Dash's esteemed career in music continues to keep the artist reaching towards new achievements. A visionary whose hits became dance-floor staples, she remains a forward-thinking professional. Dash is currently working on a biography and has a schedule of live appearances that would challenge even her youngest contemporaries. She is aware of her important role in the evolution of rock, pop, R&B, jazz and disco music, but she chooses her words carefully when reflecting on her legacy.

"At different times, I have different thoughts about how I'd like to be remembered," she says. "At this moment, I would say I'd like to be thought of as a person who cared, who had compassion, a person who continued to serve and to help others. Not that I was the best person—but I hope people will say I was a kind, generous and considerate person. Everyone who thinks of me is going to remember me differently. Who knows—I may do something tomorrow that may affect the world, and I may be remembered for that! I am sure I will be remembered for my music with Labelle. Our group really revolutionized the industry, and I'm very proud of that. And I hope my legacy as a solo artist will be remembered just as much and that I brought a sense of healing joy through my music that meant something to those who heard me."

"Music has always been with me throughout my entire evolution," says the vocalist, who still performs to sell-out crowds today with her *Sarah Dash—One Woman* show (courtesy Sarah Dash).

• •

John Davis
"Ain't That Enough for You"

"It warms my heart knowing my music made somebody happy for a couple of minutes on a dance floor."—John Davis

The lavish, richly orchestrated productions of John Davis were like colorful, enchanting fairy tales that enveloped dance floors of the disco era. Beautiful compositions, delicious harmonies and conga-fused beats became the artist's trademark, as he weaved booming, soul-stirring audio journeys in discothèques throughout the world. His expertly crafted works collaborating with other celebrated artists of the day rank among the genre's finest, most accomplished musical creations. Famous for early classics such as

"Ain't That Enough for You" with his Monster Orchestra and effervescent, pop-fused tempests (think Diana Ross's "The Boss"), the composer, arranger, singer and musician did it all during disco's hottest days. Davis managed to successfully reinvent himself following the industry downturn but never forgot the uplifting music he loved so deeply. The artist relishes an opportunity to remember his reign as disco's premier maestro.

"I was given a toy clarinet for Christmas as a boy," he recalls of his early days in Philadelphia, "and one September I was finally old enough to get a real clarinet from the school band. So I started taking lessons. I sort of had an aptitude for it and then took on the saxophone. In high school, I met a teacher who started instructing me in music theory. He was very instrumental in lighting a little writing and arranging fire in me, and he taught me a lot. His name was Bob Hamilton. I thought to myself, 'Boy, I really like writing more than playing an instrument.' I started to lean more towards that end of the business. I graduated college with a degree in music composition and went through all my master's work."

From there, John began working professionally in the music industry. Davis is surprisingly quick to identify the moment in those early days when he felt he had truly become a top-shelf player in the game. "I had done a Philly Devotions record called 'I Just Can't Say Goodbye' in 1974," he remembers. "It was on Columbia Records. It was the first time I hit the pop charts with one of my records that I had produced and arranged. When that hit, I sort of felt a bit of acceptance that, jeez, maybe what I'm doing *is* okay. You always question that. You know how much sweat and tears go into these things, and when something like that happens, when it's accepted, it all becomes justifiable. When I saw the record on the charts and heard it on the radio, I said, 'Oh, man, I'm really a bitch!' I'm tellin' ya! Then I produced, arranged and conducted an album out of Philly called *Be Thankful for What You've Got* by William DeVaughn. We sold it to Roxbury Records, and it became a number one R&B record, and it went Top 5 on the pop side. Being so young, I didn't even know what a number one record really meant. But it was a huge recording, and all of a sudden people started calling me. Probably the best phone call I ever had was from Eddie O'Loughlin at Midland Records. He asked me to work with him on the Carol Douglas album *Midnight Love Affair* in 1976. That was right after that I did the album *I'm in Heaven* for Touch of Class."

SAM Records was founded in 1976 and based in New York's Long Island City area. Sam Weiss, who had been involved in music since the mid-'50s, ran the company. The label eventually scored a lucrative distribution deal with Columbia Records at the height of the disco era. Davis crossed paths with Weiss and found a new home for his creativity. "Sam had gotten hold of my Touch of Class record and searched me out. He said, 'God, I just love that record. It's one of the best I've ever heard.' He asked if I thought he and I could do something together. I told him there was a lot of orchestral dance stuff going on with Salsoul and Van McCoy and suggested we take a shot at it. Sam said okay and told me to make a single and we'd see what would happen. One thing led to another, and the song 'Night and Day' by John Davis and the Monster Orchestra came out of that. It turned out to be fairly successful, and we did an album. Sam and I became good buddies after that, and we ended up doing a lot of great things together."

"Night and Day" had been a hit for Fred Astaire in the 1930s. Utilizing the vocal charms of "The Sweethearts of Sigma" (Evette Benton, Carla Benson and Barbara Ingram), Davis incorporated the strings and horns of Don Renaldo and took the song to the Top Five of the disco chart. Davis' debut album of the same name contained more lush orchestrations of Cole Porter tracks mixed with a prominent beat. It also featured his self-penned tune "Tell Me How You Like It."

John had discovered a musical niche that allowed him to paint exciting, danceable musical landscapes. "I felt disco was the right genre for me because, at the time, there weren't a lot of fully orchestrated music forms other than disco," the artist says. "I came into music as a writer-arranger and always wanted to put together a 40-piece orchestra and go crazy. I wanted to try different musical colors and different textures with the instruments. Disco gave me a lot more opportunity to experiment with a bigger group of musicians, and that always appealed to me. Disco was very good for me, and whenever I had the opportunity to beef up a song, I would go in that direction."

The path Davis took led him to become one of the most dependable producers of the classic disco era. His 1977 single, "Up Jumped the Devil," hit the Top Five of the disco chart, and the album of the same name featured all original compositions. Davis supplied lead vocals, arranged, wrote and produced the tracks and even played his trusty flute and sax. In the two years that followed, John hit his stride. "Ain't That Enough for You" gave the artist his highest career ranking on the disco chart when the song reached number four in September of 1978. "For me, it was always about the song. If you could get a hook that will stick in somebody's head, you could hang on the charts forever. People will start walking around singing it for no reason. When you catch something like that, it's really a miracle. Your music has gotten under their skin and becomes part of them. That's a great feeling. It doesn't happen a lot, but boy—when it does, it's nice! There were a couple of songs I recorded that did that. 'Ain't That Enough for You' was certainly one of them. Everyone in New York was into that song. I actually heard people walking down the street singing it, humming it. Talk about the greatest high in the world! Boy, that was it!" he says, his voice filled with fresh excitement.

On *The Monster Strikes Again* LP from 1979, Davis served up one of his most beloved collections. Clubs devoured the hits "Holler," "Love Magic" and "Bourgie, Bourgie," the latter a remake of an Ashford & Simpson track. Davis states, "One of the best things to happen to me was with 'Bourgie, Bourgie,' when Ashford & Simpson sang on the record with me. There really were no lyrics in the original version that they did for Warner Bros. I heard it and thought it could be a really great dance record. I called up Valerie Simpson and asked if they could put some lyrics together for it. It was funny. Nick Ashford came into the studio with all the lyrics on a crumpled up sheet of paper. He was really one of those free spirits. He was a lovely guy, and I am broken-hearted that he's no longer with us. I will always feel that music suffered a major loss when Nick passed, and I will always miss him and his great sense of humor and lovable spirit. I had done some arranging for their records and worked on a Diana Ross album with them [1979's *The Boss*, for which Davis arranged the smash title track]. I also did some work for Valerie's brother, Ray Simpson [who replaced Victor Willis in the group Village People]. So I had a pretty close relationship with them. Nick and Valerie were two of the nicest people I ever met in the business. When they came in and said they would sing 'Bourgie, Bourgie' with me, my heart was in my throat! I'm not a 'singer singer,' but there I was singing next to Ashford & Simpson. It was just crazy. They were—they are—my idols. What came out of it was really magic, and I loved that record."

"Love Magic," released as a single in 1979, was a triumph that has been hailed as Davis' masterpiece by many. Its almost ethereal strings, swirling sense of romance, hypnotic congas, infectious rhythm and neat guitar licks were well-received by DJs and dancers, keeping the track on the club chart for nearly half the year. "I released 'Love Magic' when Rod Stewart and Donna Summer were releasing music with a little more of a rock edge, rather than the big orchestral sound," he says of his ambitious composition. "I felt like I wanted to try something with a little more guitar and funkiness than the big productions I'd been doing. When I wrote 'Love Magic,' at the time, I was actually having a little romance with my wife. We've been married 35 years. She was always inspiring me with song ideas, and I was just real excited about it. 'Love Magic' came out of that. Craig Snyder came in, and we started fooling around with some overblown guitar parts. It was a little different for me stylistically."

Despite his prominence on the dance charts, Davis was not a recognizable face on the club circuit or TV. "I never performed any of these disco hits live," says the artist. "We were going to do Madison Square Garden once with four other groups—groups that were on the disco charts. They booked us, paid me, and I started rehearsing for the show. About two weeks later, they cancelled it. My group was just too big to make it financially feasible to perform live. The Monster Orchestra would have been comprised of about 30 guys. I'm not sure how much my vocalists, the Sweethearts of Sigma, would have wanted to go on the road either. They were too busy in the studio to go on a tour, so I would have had to find some other singers. It was just too big of an operation to do concerts. Nobody, other than that one booking agent, ever approached me to tour anyway, and the record companies didn't push for it. I would visit the clubs up in New York with Sam once in a while and meet with the DJs. I never did that on a radio level though, and the record companies rarely pushed for that either. It was easier to do those promotional things with single artists. One of the features of the Monster Orchestra was that big sound quality, and you can't get that without the proper instrumentation. It really would not have been practical."

The stamp of approval from gay audiences was almost mandatory for success in the disco market, and Davis says his music was no exception to the rule. "It was absolutely true that the gay culture could make your record a hit, and I thought it was great," the artist says. "I was so happy for their support. I felt as far as inhibitions were concerned, I was getting a total feeling from these guys whether my work was good or bad, and I wasn't gonna get any of the business bullshit you'd get from 'yes' men. None of that, 'Yeah, your record is really great!' stuff, whether it was or it wasn't. I found with the gay community, if they liked it, they let you know it. If they didn't like it, they let you know it. I always felt a great deal of honesty from them—a lot more than from the other crowd. I just loved how they had no inhibitions. They just danced and went crazy. It was just a party, and it was wonderful!"

As his reputation for club-ready, commercially successful and artistically polished compositions and productions grew, Davis' opportunities to share his talents with other artists multiplied. He produced numerous classic disco singers of the day and recalls a few of the standouts. Among them was the aforementioned Carol Douglas, for whom he wrote tracks for the *Midnight Love Affair* album and produced and arranged side one of the Grammy-nominated *Burnin'* LP in 1978. "Anytime I think of Carol Douglas," he says, "I think of the sweetest person I ever met. She was so polite and soft-spoken. When she got into the studio to do her vocals, you could ask her to stand on her head, and she would be willing to do it. She was always willing to do whatever it took to make the music the best it could be.

"Eddie O'Loughlin produced the first couple of albums for Carol. He was pretty much autonomous with the vocals before the *Burnin'* album. The only thing I brought into it was a different type of musicality. Eddie was brilliant and had great ideas, but sometimes it's hard for a non-musical person to put their feelings in a musical context that people will understand. Eddie had great ideas, but sometimes he wasn't the best at explaining them. So it would take some time to discuss and get to the bottom of what he was after. But when I went in with Carol, we could really talk it out. Like I'd say, 'This note is a little sharp, and I think it could be a little more legato or smoother at this point'—just little suggestions like that. I think it was a different experience from those Carol had prior with just Eddie at the helm. I can't dispute her work with Eddie though, because she really just sang her butt off with him. Eddie was a super guy—he was Mr. Fun. Everyone would call him 'Crazy Eddie,' in a good way. His track record was amazing. Getting the Grammy nomination was another one of those great moments in life where you get a validation for your work. At that point in my career, the financial rewards were nice, but you want to start looking back on your body of work and start appreciating what it was all about. You wanted to know people appreciated your work for what it was. It wasn't just about making a buck. When the Grammy nomination came up for *Burnin'*, I thought to myself, 'Wow!' The whole industry was at its peak and starting to slide a bit. So getting that nomination with Carol at that point helped make me feel complete.

"Wardell Piper ["Super Sweet," "Captain Boogie"; see *First Ladies of Disco*] was another amazing artist—pure talent. She was probably one of the best singers I ever worked with. I think she got caught up in that whole disconnect between disco and radio. She made some great dance records, but she had a really tough time getting on the radio. If anyone deserved a big hit, she did. Ruth ['Silky'] Waters also stood out for me. We did her record 'Never Gonna Be the Same.' She was a very talented singer, but she was a piece of work. She came from the jazz school—the old school—and sometimes she had a little difficulty jumping into a pop-oriented vocal. She lent herself to the blues side, rather than the cutting edge side. Her record was one of my favorites. Millennium Records signed her on the spot when I played the track for them, but, unfortunately, it got lost in the shuffle."

Davis's work on Diana Ross's "The Boss" has been one of his most celebrated arrangements. The song was a Top 20 pop smash and a number one sensation on the disco chart in 1979. "I remember being called by Ashford and Simpson to do the arrangements for 'The Boss' in New York," John says. "Val, who usually interacted more with me when I did arrangements for them, called and said they were doing Diana. Of course, these things were always done at breakneck speed. Everyone was in a hurry to get this project off the ground. I did not have the pleasure of meeting Ms. Ross at the session, and the reference vocal on my work track had pilot vocals by Nick and Val. But I knew immediately that this was a great song and that it would make some noise commercially.

When I went to New York to record the orchestra, Nick and Val were there and our impressions were very positive when we finished. When I eventually heard the track with Diana's vocals, I knew this was a hit! As always, it was a blast working with Nick and Val!

"I've been the luckiest guy in the world to have had the opportunities I've had to record and work with such great people. It got to the point that I was just so busy that I'd finish a record, turn it in, and the next day I'd be working on the next one. I'd just have to forget about the one I did yesterday. I would follow my stuff on the charts, and thank goodness most of them went that way! I would go crazy in the car if I heard it on the radio, but I really just bounced from one project to another. I didn't have time for the parties and stuff that some of the other guys did. I'd always say I couldn't hang out too late because I had to be in the studio the next day," he confesses.

Save for his work with Ms. Ross, John enjoyed only a modicum of crossover success with most of his disco artists and the Monster Orchestra. But it was of little consequence. "Every label wanted a crossover hit, and when I went into the studio, of course that was always the idea," he admits. "However, my primary goal was to get something on the disco charts, and then it was up to the record company to get it on radio stations. My name and records were well known by DJs. They'd give it a spin, and the record would live and die on its own merits. Radio was a whole different jungle, and I had no control over it. You had to depend on the promotional guys, and there seemed to be a lot of external factors that we had no control over. The promotion guys were walking around with a dozen records in their briefcase every week, taking them to the stations and trying to get airplay.

"I remember the Philly Devotions record came out at the same time as an Earth, Wind & Fire record. I felt that when a promotion person walked into a station with those two records, radio was gonna play Earth, Wind & Fire of course. I needed somebody to go in there with a hammer and say, '*This* is the group we want to break!' But I never got the feeling that I had the full support of some of the labels at the time. I think they were happy to just get the disco hits. If they threw it against the wall and it stuck, great. I never really got crazy about whether my work would succeed on radio because there was nothing I could do about it. I had some noise and buzz over my records, but I never got that massive hit outside the discos—that number one pop record. However, SAM Records sold the Monster Orchestra like crazy. We probably moved a couple hundred thousand albums here in the U.S. In Europe, you could double or triple that amount. So I was able to make a very good living without the crossover success."

Ultimately, despite the great results he achieved with other artists, Davis preferred crafting his distinctive sound for his own satisfaction. "I really enjoyed working for myself the most," he claims. "You had so much more freedom to do whatever you wanted. I did a lot of arranging for people, and loved that, but you'd have to work with producers or artists who may have been thinking something different from what I wanted to do. Occasionally you'd run into a speed bump in the studio, but I never ran into a big problem because, with my training, I was pretty agile. If anyone wanted to change something, it wasn't a big deal, and I was pretty quick at it. Subsequently, that was a pretty good skill to have when I moved to L.A. and started writing TV scores. That was my key to success—being so quick at it."

Scoring the Broadway show *Got Tu Go Disco* was next on Davis' to-do list, and the assignment came just when the rug was pulled from under the genre's dancing feet in

1979. "I was very puzzled by the whole thing," he recalls, "because they did bring in so many different writers for the show. I did a few songs, and another one of the bigger disco writers was involved. The ironic thing was I think the show opened [around the time] when my twins were born. I was going to go to the opening, and my wife went into labor. I never even saw the show! They put all this money and work into it, and it ran for three or four nights. It was so frustrating that it went under so fast. The whole disco backlash may have contributed to that.

"I never saw that disco required any less effort or had any less musicality than other music forms. Perhaps the connection of disco to the gay culture may have had something to do with it. I think they were both pretty much grouped together at that point. The rock 'n' roll purists had also gotten really down on disco. I think there was a lot of envy and anger starting. It's funny. I think when disco died it was really sort of starting to change. I thought, 'Wow, they really buried it prematurely.' Giorgio Moroder was starting to come out with dance music that was more rock-edged and real 'song' songs, rather than songs built on a riff or a groove. They were becoming scarcer. I don't think they gave disco a real chance to develop. Man, they dropped it like a brick. I was in New York at the time. Everyone started going back to his garage to record. It was amazing!

"Bob Reno of Midland Records and I were very close, and we were talking about how bad it was and that nobody could sell any records. Bob said he might go to work out in L.A. He asked me if I ever heard of a guy named Aaron Spelling. Bob was a big music publisher, and Aaron wanted him to run his publishing companies. So Bob invited me to go out there. My family and I moved three months later, I met Aaron, and I started making music for all his shows, like *Hart to Hart*, *Vegas* and *The Love Boat*. I was out in L.A. for pretty close to 20 years doing that," Davis says.

He pauses for a moment to compare his two remarkable careers, one as a celebrated disco maestro and the other as a television soundtrack composer. "There's nothing more satisfying than hearing your record on the radio or walking into a club and seeing people dancing to it and having a great time with it. That was the hallmark for me. On the other hand, as a classically trained composer, all the scores for TV shows I worked on used upbeat, disco-like scores in the background. The car chases and fight scenes especially—like on *CHiPS*. Not many guys out there were experienced enough to do those kinds of tracks. Then the next scene would call for

"I've been the luckiest guy in the world to have had the opportunities I've had to record and work with such great people," admits John Davis, whose stellar career in entertainment extended far beyond his disco music accomplishments (courtesy John Davis).

more of a classical composition. So I really loved that challenge because I got to utilize both sides of my personality—what you might call 'legitimate' side and the crazy dance side. I was able to have both worlds at once."

Davis says he is often nostalgic about the era. "It was a great time in music history. I turn on those SiriusXM disco channels today, and I just go back in time. The music was so well done, and I just don't think it was appreciated the way it should have been. Maybe now people are looking at it and saying, 'That's not junk—that's really good stuff!' A lot of technique, talent, and capability went into it. There weren't too many really shabby records that came out, and people are discovering that now. Look at what is out there today. There are a few good songs, but by and large, I'd take the disco stuff any day. I think, back then, the industry promoted more experimentation. I don't hear that so much today. Now it's just, 'get out there and make a Top 40 hit.' Do what the other guy's doing. So I just play disco, and I enjoy it.

"I do look back on my accomplishments in a way, but I never really thought of it until more recently when I started to see posts online, like on YouTube. I think, for a time, I lost my perspective on how people were really touched by my music. I see it now with the comments people have made and realize it was so much bigger than I appreciated when I was in the middle of it. I am most grateful for it. It warms my heart knowing my music made somebody happy for a couple of minutes on a dance floor."

Life is a bit quieter now for the artist, but he never stops nurturing his creative side. "I'm not sure it's something I do intentionally, but it's always been in my personality that I sort of look to the cutting edge and for something different and innovative. I'm really into computers and electronic music now. I just love constantly going forward, but with a marked admiration for where I've been. I wouldn't be where I am today without that. I also wrote a father-daughter dance song for my daughter's upcoming wedding. After the wedding, I'll post it onto YouTube. I'm working on commercials and some other things, but no big deals. You know how the industry is—if you're out of town for a couple of years, you might as well be dead. I'm okay with that. I've been there, I had it, I loved it, and I wouldn't have changed anything."

John Davis is the very definition of the word artist. It's impossible to measure the amount of positive energy his works have generated over the past several decades. His musical legacy continues to inspire millions of people who appreciate the complexity and beauty of his compositions and arrangements. He sighs in humility when asked how he'd like his work to be remembered. "I'd like to be thought of as somebody who tried to do his best, especially with disco," Davis says earnestly. "I want to be remembered as somebody who, when a John Davis record came on, people went out there and danced their ass off!"

• •

Leonard "Butch" Davis and Joe Harris of Double Exposure

"Ten Percent"

"All you can do is go with what you think sounds good, sounds right, and just hope for the best."—Joe Harris

In 1976, a music trade paper ad placed by the rising new force in disco music, Salsoul Records, boasted the company's all-star team. Among the touted performers were the Salsoul Orchestra, Loleatta Holloway, First Choice, Claudja Barry, Carol Williams, Eddie Holman, Silvetti and the handsome four-man Philly group known as Double Exposure. With songs largely arranged and produced by Norman Harris and composed by a stellar group of writers, the group's debut album, *Ten Percent*, was a sure-fire smash hit. It firmly placed the quartet and the Salsoul label at the forefront of the disco explosion. While their single "Ten Percent" burned its way to the top of the disco chart, Double Exposure, as their name suggested, worked doubly hard to make sure that more than just one side of their talent was seen and heard. The group took as much pride in their R&B offerings as they did in their disco endeavors. Their stylish look, smooth and mesmerizing choreography, intoxicating vocal prowess and uplifting energy fueled their success for several years. All of the original group members (Jimmy Williams, Charles Whittington, Leonard "Butch" Davis and Joe Harris) remain together today (nearly unheard of in the 21st century), with a tight, brotherly bond still felt between them. Leonard and Joe speak for the Double Exposure ensemble on this particular day, vividly recalling the details of their remarkable journey.

Known as United Image during the group's very earliest performing days, the quartet has been singing together since junior high school in Philadelphia. "The Temptations, Imperials, the O'Jays—we all aspired to be like them and go as far as we could. We knew we had some talent, but you don't really know how far you can go at that age," Leonard says. Joe observes, "When we were at John Bartram High School, singing and performing was something that we loved, but it was also kind of like a competition thing with other groups from other neighborhoods. Whoever shined got the girls—you know what I mean? You were always trying to do your best, man. We would go to rock 'n' roll shows—every city had its shows and venues. Like Philly had the Uptown, New York had the Apollo, and we used to go to those shows religiously. The first opportunity we had to be in a talent show—I will never forget it—the headliner was Sam Cooke, along with the Valentinos, Chuck Jackson and Dionne Warwick. We performed after the main show on a Saturday night. Although we didn't know it then, the Valentinos consisted of Bobby Womack and his brothers, and they were managed by Sam Cooke. Man, we used to study those acts and every little thing we could pick up—everything we thought we could do. That's how we learned."

After serving in the military, the guys reunited and began a serious quest to become professional performers. They worked countless hours on what was known as the "chitlin' circuit," a sometimes shady and dangerous string of clubs riddled with occasional shootouts—and, as the gentlemen point out, managers who wouldn't pay. The group rolled with the punches, but these challenging conditions gave them an unmatchable opportunity to learn how to properly entertain an audience. United Image landed a contract with Stax Records and released the single "Love's Creeping Up on Me" under the Enigmatic Productions banner. "It was great getting signed to Stax, but it was heartbreaking when they had problems and folded," says Joe.

"Salsoul was a few years after that," he adds. "We got to Salsoul because of Norman Harris [1947–1987]. He was a producer in Philadelphia [and a purveyor of the Philly disco sound who worked with MFSB, the Trammps and countless others] and an old friend of ours. We had been messing around for a while trying to get something to happen. I was downtown shopping for clothes and walking down the street when I heard someone call my name. I turned around, and it was Norman. He said they were trying to find us, and nobody knew how to locate us. He said, 'I got a deal for you!' Just so happened he had signed a deal with Salsoul to produce some music, and he needed a group. We were in the right place at the right time. We auditioned for the record company and some of their staff writers. The audition went great, and it all began!"

Around this time, the group decided it needed a fresher name. Band members, joking about the look of some recently taken photographs, came up with the idea of being called Double Exposure. The Salsoul creative team, led by Harris, began formulating music for the group that capitalized on the emerging dance frenzy. In early December of 1975, the guys went into Sigma Sound Studios in Philly and laid down the tracks that became the essence of their first album, *Ten Percent*. Says Joe, "When we first auditioned, we had no idea what disco was. We weren't really aware of disco until the record company brought us to New York. When we got there, that's where the whole craze, that whole market and style of music, was exploding, and once we saw what was happening, we knew it was going to be big. When Norman started coming up with our material, when we went in the studio and began recording, this was the start of our connection to disco. This is where the record company took us, and it turned out to be a great success. Everything just worked." Vince Montana, Jr., of the Salsoul Orchestra wrote, arranged and produced a track for the set, "Just Can't Say Hello," and also conducted the orchestra for the cut.

Joe recalls, "'Ten Percent' was the first track we recorded for the album. I remember being in the studio that day, and the label just created a big party atmosphere. They had food, drinks. Everybody was so excited. But it was a lot of work recording that album. We put in a lot of hours. But when we sat back and listened to the finished product, we were really proud of what we had done. Sometimes you were tired, but you pushed yourself because it was what you wanted to do. We had spent years trying to get to this point. We were working with pros, surrounded by people who helped us learn a lot of things. But we really got to hone our craft. Totally different than today, with all the electronics—*we were singing*!" Leonard adds, "When we recorded 'Ten Percent,' we had no idea whether it would hit or not. We just knew it came out good."

"Good" seems an understatement in retrospect. The *Ten Percent* album was a triumph. The title track crossed over to the R&B and pop charts after reaching the number two position on the *Billboard* disco survey for several weeks. "Everyman (Has to Carry His Own Weight)" followed and was a club favorite. The driving rhythm of "My Love Is Free," arranged by Ron Kersey and the third single off the set, proved the group was truly unstoppable in the clubs as it cracked the disco Top 20. Their songs told stories of human interest with an infectiously rhythmic beat that epitomized the soulful side of disco. While the album went gold in the U.S., it also became a smash in Canada, South America, England, South Africa and Kenya. "I believe we had the first 12-inch single for commercial sale with 'Ten Percent,'" claims Joe. Some reports suggest Carol Williams' "More," also on Salsoul, may have been the first. The track was "disco blended" by Walter Gibbons on side A, and Ken Cayre on side B. Salsoul made note of the surprising sales success of the newfound extended-play vinyl single format in music industry publication ads, claiming it was proof "the disco dancer *does* buy records."

"The first time we did a dance music convention, it was also the first time we heard the final mix arrangement of the song 'Ten Percent.' Isn't that right Joe?" asks Leonard. His group mate responds, "Yes! We performed at the first disco music convention ever. It was in New York in January of 1976. When we went on stage—we hadn't even heard the finished product—the finished studio mix of the song. We had only been able to rehearse with the rhythm track. The arrangement on 'Ten Percent' hadn't even been recorded yet. Well, the orchestra was there, and the music starts—the full disco arrangement—and we're like, 'What the heck is that?' We had to just keep going and pay attention. Ron Kersey was directing the orchestra that night, and he knew our moves and signals from way back. He had played with us live in the past and had worked on the album with us. He gave us cues at certain spots in the song so we'd know what to do out there. So we were able to pick it up from him, and that was a tremendous help. After the performance, we felt so bad because we really thought we had messed up. We thought all our choreography was out of sync. We were sitting all depressed in the dressing room, and then everyone came in congratulating us. They said, 'Y'all are great performers!' Man, they loved us! I remember thinking, 'Ain't that something!'

With their single "Ten Percent" a disco smash, Double Exposure (left to right: Jimmy Williams, Joe Harris, Charles Whittington and Leonard "Butch" Davis, seated) became one of Salsoul Records' premier acts (courtesy Joe Harris).

"We loved the songs and worked our own personalities into them, especially when we worked live," Joe adds. "When we worked with the band, we took things in a whole other direction. The combination of disco and R&B just worked for us. We were constantly being booked to do live performances and our formula worked."

Leonard expresses agreement, but acknowledges the group's musical diversity was already beginning to be eclipsed by disco stardom. He observes, "When we performed the up-tempo songs, we were a high energy group. That energy just seemed to fall into place perfectly with disco music. We were very comfortable being on stage, and we had spent a lot of years performing before 'Ten Percent' was ever released. Being on stage was just like being at home for us. Then we had a song, a hit that we loved. It just fell into place. Salsoul was very focused on the disco material, but we were just as great at singing ballads too. Not many people got a chance to see that. We aren't complaining—don't get me wrong—but I think we weren't appreciated for all that we could do."

Joe shares his viewpoint. "We had some great writers," he chimes in. "We had some ideas, and the writers would come to us with songs that kind of matched up with our vision because they knew the group. We would all sit down together and sort through different songs. We were always looking for a mix of high energy and sweet and soulful—you know, ballads. Working with the writers and producers, we had a good marriage with those guys. We always wanted to come up with a hit, but you can't predict a hit. All you can do is go with what you think sounds good, sounds right and just hope for the best. That's just how the business was. But we were pretty confident. We wished Salsoul had worked R&B radio a little more. If you listen to all our material, other than just the up-tempo songs, I think you'd say we did a really good job on the slow stuff. You know, those soul ballads worked well in the clubs with the girls too, and if the women like it—you're in!"

"Overall," he continues, "we weren't that pleased with how Salsoul handled our music. They did a great job with disco, but they did not go and work black radio like they should have. I think we could have gotten a lot more mileage and longevity as a group if they had. We went to a lot of R&B markets through efforts of our own. A perfect example—there was a young woman at Salsoul named Connie who would give me copies of the tracking reports. Every Thursday was tracking day. That's when stations report to the trades what they are playing, and that's how *Billboard* developed its charts. The report would show where a song was played, how often and what rotation it's in. We were getting very positive feedback from the oddest places. On our second album, there was a ballad called 'Perfect Lover' that was number one for a couple of weeks in Omaha, Nebraska. We were shocked! It just turned out to be a place where a good R&B ballad worked. We didn't even know they played music in Omaha, Nebraska! There were a lot of other markets like D.C., Detroit and Atlanta where we performed live, but they weren't aware of our soulful music. There were places our booking agent sent us where our records weren't even on the radio. Then, after they saw us perform live, they started buying our records, and it forced radio stations to start playing us. That's what sold us—our stage show. Salsoul did a great job in New York and the Northeast and overseas. England, South Africa—we were superstars. We had the disco songs, but they just did not work R&B radio here in the States like they could have. I don't know if it was politics or money, but they dropped the ball on that. But listen, I have to say, we had a great deal of success with disco, and I am thankful for the opportunity that we had."

Despite their fame, there is little evidence of egos or solo aspirations having interfered with Double Exposure's group dynamic. "It wasn't hard for us to be a group and keep egos in check. We had been friends and gelled together so well," Leonard says. "I guess if you wanted to compare us to anyone," adds Joe, "I always like to look at the Four Tops. Here were guys that were together till they died. We were like brothers. We had our ups and downs, our disputes and disagreements—like any group of brothers—but we always were able to work it out and move onward. We just celebrated 50 years of singing together, so that ought to tell you something!"

Though their Salsoul affiliation helped make Double Exposure synonymous with the celebrated disco label, interaction with the record company's other stars was infrequent.

"We did a couple of the disco conventions," Joe remembers. "Salsoul flew everybody to one in California. It was us, the Salsoul Orchestra, First Choice, Loleatta Holloway, Eddie Holman. But we didn't get a chance to see or work with many of the artists on the label because everyone was usually on the road. We would cross paths once in a while, but we couldn't even go see them because we were always working too." Leonard adds, "Everyone was with different booking agencies as well, so there just weren't a whole lot of opportunities to meet other performers on the label."

With their success came exposure to management and booking improprieties, which caused a delay in the release of their second Salsoul album, *Four Play*, until early in 1978. The LP was also hindered by a dispute between Allan Felder (co-writer of Eddie Kendricks' "Goin' Up in Smoke" and many of Double Exposure's first hits) and Mr. Harris that resulted in a cessation of collaborations between the two composers. This frustrated the group members who felt the problem was "petty," yet impactful to their career. Despite feeling restricted in their still-binding recording contract with Salsoul and their irritations with the new song material, they persevered. A remake of First Choice's "Newsy Neighbors" was a hit in the clubs, and the gentlemen continued to do their best to cement their reputation as a relevant group.

Their appeal crossed many ethnic and cultural barriers and, as was the case for so many acts that performed disco material, the gay community rallied behind the group's artistry. "The gay underground clubs and audience weren't totally responsible for our success, but they played a large part," Joe asserts. "We worked some gay clubs. They loved the music, and they supported us. We didn't have any problem with that. We were able to work anywhere because of the way we performed and our versatility—our ability to crossover. Gay clubs, black clubs, we were able to work all of them, never had a problem and were always very well received. That's why we were able to perform for a long time. We had a good time in every one of them. Gay people were spending their money to see us perform. They were buying our music. They were partying and having a good time. And we were glad to be a part of the party."

Leonard says, "'My Love Is Free' had a heads up with black audiences, whereas 'Ten Percent' was stronger with white audiences. We made music that would appeal to a lot of different types of people. I remember us playing the Felt Forum in New York to a huge crowd. Every type of person was there! And we were smoking! By smoking, I mean that we were hot! Radio station WBLS was telling everyone they had to get down there and see us. Man, we set that stage on fire!"

Joe jumps in. "Oh yeah! There was a debate as to who was gonna open the show. People were telling the promoters not to let Double Exposure open. If anything, we should be closing or next to last. It was tough for the acts to follow us and keep up the tone and energy we had! We opened first anyway. I'm not trying to brag or anything, but we put it down! Nobody wants to sound big-headed, but you know in your heart when you've done your job. And the audience is sure gonna let you know too!

"We did a lot of shows," he continues, "but I have to say the most interesting place we ever performed, for me, was South Africa. We toured there for about a month in October of 1978. When we were first approached about going there, we initially said no because of Apartheid. It was really viewed as a negative if you went there and were performing only for white people. Then it was brought to our attention that 'My Love Is

Free' went gold in South Africa. It was the brothers and sisters living there that were primarily buying the record. So our attitude changed, and we thought, 'Well, they're trying to support our music and us. If our music is bringing them a little happiness and peacefulness, we got to go!' When we got there, you would have thought the Jackson 5 came to town. It was awesome. We had made a stipulation that we weren't going to perform for any segregated audiences, period. It was like being in the south of this country, say a generation ago. You knew people were subjected to a lot of stuff, but folks still found a way to have a good time. We were so well received—I think it was our personalities and the way we were able to interact with the people. Our audiences were mixed or all black. The brothers and sisters, man, they just loved us. We ended up making a lot of personal friends. We just had a great time. I took tons of pictures of that tour. It was more than an experience—it was an education."

The guys laugh deeply when asked about the women who were interested in more than just their musical talents as they toured the U.S. Leonard gives a sly chuckle and admits, "The groupies were out there, no doubt about that. You could have the pick of the litter if you wanted. Women liked entertainers, and if you were a decent performer, they were at your doorstep. Plus, we were all young and nobody was married. So we had fun!"

Says Joe, "We worked both dance clubs and nightclubs. The nightclubs were more intimate because you had a seated audience. There was an abundance of beautiful women everywhere you went. I met my wife at a club in Brooklyn, a place called Town Hill Two. It used to be one of the top black clubs in the nation. I was in my dressing room with two young ladies. One was combing my hair, and another one was feeding me a drink. The door was open, and I saw this cute little thing walk past the door. When I saw her, I was like, 'I gotta meet her!' I jumped out of the chair, and the other two young ladies knew to stay right there until I came back. I proceeded to meet the young lady in the hallway and introduced myself. Little did I know then I was going to marry this woman years later! That's just one of many stories! The girls coming on to us—it was almost like second nature."

"When we were performing," Leonard adds, "I remember meeting girls who wanted to hook all four of us up. What would happen is a girl would target one of the guys in the group and tell him that she had three other girls that wanted to meet us. We all had fun!"

Joe remembers a potentially wild party opportunity lost because of television appearances on *Disco '77* and *Soul Train*. "We had arrived in L.A. to tape *Soul Train* on a Sunday. When we arrived at the studio in our limo for the taping, it turns out the fellow who was in charge of greeting the artists was an old buddy of Jimmy's. They hadn't seen each other in years. So right away it was a reunion. And right away, we started getting the inside scoop on all the women, all the sexy dancers on *Soul Train*. Had we been able to stay there longer, we would have had one heck of a party! We had to take the red eye to get to Ft. Lauderdale the next day to do *Disco '77*, which was being filmed at 10:30 Monday morning. I was begging and pleading, 'Man, is there any way we can change this date? I wanna stay in California just one more night!' Oh man, you talk about somebody heartbroken. We got into Miami, and we had about an hour and a half to freshen up, shake off the jet lag and get back in a limo. They took us to the club [Pete 'n' Lenny's] on East Commercial Blvd. in Ft. Lauderdale, where the show was filmed."

Leonard laughs at Joe's recollection. "I don't know how he remembers all that stuff! He'll be talking about something that happened and says, 'Don't you remember that such and such happened on Tuesday night, July 4th, 1976, at 8 p.m.?' I don't know how he does that!"

Sex appeal was the focus of the album jacket for Double Exposure's final LP for Salsoul. *Locker Room* was released in the summer of 1979, and its cover, which was designed to play up the forthcoming 1980 Olympics, caused a stir. The front photo of the jacket features the guys dressed in sports gear, while the flip side shows them wearing a good deal less. "If I remember correctly," Joe says, "there was a bunch of females in the photographer's crew, and they kept saying, 'Come on baby, let's see something! Show us something!' So we were like, 'Okay, yeah, here it is! Take a look!' They snapped the picture of us in our jocks and stuff, but I had no idea it was going to be on the album cover," he laughs. Jimmy Fallon poked fun at the album cover for laughs 34 years later on his *Late Night* show in 2013, though the host acknowledged the music sounded pretty good. The thumping single "I Got the Hots for Ya," mixed by Bobby "DJ" Guttadaro, got some spins in the clubs, but the funkier album failed to have the impact or generate the sales of the group's previous efforts.

Joe remembers the frustrations of that time. "We were in the process of recording a fourth album when some business problems came between the producers and Salsoul. It was near the end of our contract. Salsoul wasn't spending time trying to develop their artists. Meanwhile, we were trying to get them to be interested in some new ideas. They were signing other acts, and it seemed like they were just interested in churning out records. For example, First Choice was on the label. We thought it was the perfect opportunity to do a kind of Temptations-Supremes kind of thing. There were ideas both groups had for the project that we wanted to present to Salsoul. They might have worked, and we might have gotten some really classic songs out of it. But they never moved on it. It didn't seem like Salsoul was interested in their artists anymore."

At the same time, the so-called disco backlash was in full swing and artists associated with the genre were pondering their next move. "We weren't that concerned about the disco backlash, because our roots were in R&B," Joe says. "We felt all we really needed was to get out a couple of good new songs. If we did, we thought we'd be okay. But we never got that opportunity. Salsoul just didn't support us. We did some other things, like recording 'After All This Time' for producer Lionel Job (Starpoint) on the Chicago label Gold Coast. But that company ran into financial problems too, and it just never took off. We had a couple of projects going, but they just didn't happen. It's the nature of the business. At that point, everybody got a bit of a stiff back. Everyone just wanted to get [his life] in order. We looked around and wanted to start building a little more financial security for ourselves. Without a hit record, a new one, you couldn't really make a good living. Without a hit, the labels can't sell you, and they won't try. Hit records—that's the bottom line. There was a time, even without a hit, you could work the dance clubs. They'd have live acts on Wednesday and Thursday nights and sometimes on the weekends. Those places started disappearing, and the opportunities just weren't there. All the clubs started focusing on DJs; they weren't bringing in as many live acts. Even though we'd do gigs off and on, everyone just started getting other careers, going to work and just making other things work for them."

Leonard agrees. "When you're viewed as exclusively a disco group, you weren't exposed to the other music markets. The dance clubs started eliminating live acts. Because we were classified as a disco group, we couldn't get to those R&B audiences. On our first album we had a gem of a soul song called 'Just Can't Say Hello.' I personally think that record could have popped, but it wasn't disco."

Joe adds, "This is where Salsoul hurt us by not marketing us more to that R&B market. Had they done that, we might have had more opportunities to work." Though they never officially declared a breakup, Joe became an electrician, Leonard opened a successful plumbing business, Charlie became a physician's assistant and Jimmy Williams became a vocalist with the group the Trammps.

Despite the perceived shortcomings of being branded a disco act, the gentlemen are quick to champion the performers who pioneered it. "I don't think disco has gotten its props," Joe insists. "Personally, I just related to the music as songs—period. A good song is a good song. There were lots of disco songs that crossed over to R&B. Many artists had disco hits that were heard on pop and R&B stations. Many disco artists became superstars; some did not. Some moved into funk music. The concept behind disco was to dance. You still have that. I think there are people who still appreciate disco. You still hear it in the big cities—New York, the gay clubs, revival shows. It's still played. Everything from our era is being sampled. Man, the music from the '70s, *that's the music!* That's what you hear all these rap artists imitating."

With time has also come a newly revived public appreciation for the classic sounds of Double Exposure. The ensemble now reunites regularly to perform. "The last couple of years have been awesome," Joe says eagerly. "One thing you see now that's really great is that most of the people we play for are those who grew up with our music. They're taking their kids and letting them see the artists that they used to jam to. It's very rewarding to see them react so positively!"

"They know every lyric, every groove!" says Leonard with pride, crediting the group's songwriters with helping make their sound so memorable. "We had a really great team of writers. T.G. Conway and the late Allan Felder, who wrote 'Ten Percent' and 'My Love Is Free,' Bunny Sigler, Bruce Hawes, the late Bruce Gray, Vince Montana, Ron Tyson, currently with the Temptations, and the late Ron Kersey. All of these guys helped make Double Exposure."

Double Exposure continues to record new material. They worked with Vincent Montana once again in 2006 on the song "You Are My Everything" and, in 2009, recorded a markedly intoxicating R&B track with producer Bobby Eli called "Soul Recession." By their own admission, they've mellowed a bit with time, and the gentlemen seem very much at ease with life. Middle age appears to have a knack for heightening its population's philosophical side, and the members of Double Exposure seem to be comfortable with theirs. "I have a saying," Joe affirms, "and everybody who knows me, knows it. Take life as easy as possible! That means I'm not worried about nothing! I'm grateful for everything that happened, the experiences. I've been blessed to have experiences that the average person only dreams about. I take things one day at a time, thank God for my health, thank Him for the great things that have happened to me and just enjoy life. Don't worry about nothing—don't let anything get you down! And don't worry about things you can't control anyway! Just keep it going!"

"I spend a lot of time thinking about our lives," Leonard joins in, "the places that the four of us have been to and people we've met. We've had a chance to see how people live. Good and bad. You know, you can take life for granted, but I've grown to appreciate it much more now as I have reached middle age."

In October of 2012, the group was honored by the Legends Promoters of New York and the Borough of Brooklyn for their contributions to the music industry and acknowledged for being together over 50 years. The National R&B Music Society awarded the group a lifetime achievement award in 2013 at a ceremony held in Atlantic City.

If there is one thing the classic "Ten Percent" proved, it's that disco music is enduring. Double Exposure, through demonstrated professionalism, exhilarating vocal skill, a stimulating catalog of great songs and simple, brotherly love, have shown the world the stellar results of putting heart and soul into a musical legacy. Joe and Leonard pause for a moment, contemplating their careers. "Remember us as a good group who gave everyone some really good music. That we always gave a great show and gave 100% on that stage," says Joe. "I hope the people that heard us sing live, at full capacity, really enjoyed what we did!" Leonard says.

•••••••••••••••••••••••••••••

Venus Dodson
"Night Rider"

"There was an eclectic type of rhythm on this LP, and the lyrics of several songs weren't the regular 'I'm dancing, so I don't need to know what they're talking about' brand."—Venus Dodson

"I was always happy that I didn't end up doing 'rubber stamp disco.' I felt disco was challenging, and I enjoyed singing it, but I never got stuck doing lots of the long extended play kind of records. Disco, as a whole, was a good fit for me at the time I did the *Night Rider* album, but I did find other ways for me to create and express myself," says vocalist Venus Dodson of her time as an artist in the disco spotlight. Venus' spirit of independence and sense of integrity helped to make the singer a prominent figure in disco music for a short time, but the artist proved she had more up her sleeve by growing beyond the genre's parameters. A protégé of the legendary dance music producer Patrick Adams, Dodson enjoys her status as a pioneer of disco and is equally satisfied by her contributions to a variety of other music styles. Her desire to develop her artistry in unique musical ways has become a life-long quest.

"I guess we all must start out saying—it seems like we've been singing forever," Dodson chuckles. "I always knew I wanted to sing—it came so naturally. I started in school choirs and put a band together in high school. I went to college, and then the first professional work I had was being a part of the All Platinum label, working for Joe and Sylvia Robinson. She had the big hit 'Pillow Talk.' While there, I met Al Goodman of the Moments and Ray, Goodman & Brown. I did a lot of background vocals, and I wrote a few songs for the Moments and other artists. Al had always told me, 'Singing is great. Writing is better!' He meant that after the singing slows down or it changes, if you've written songs, you could always collect royalties. That was an excellent lesson I learned. I wrote 'Girls,' which was a hit for the Moments, and 'Fascinating, Devastating Man' for Eleanore Mills around 1974. After that, I put a jazz band together and continued performing.

"I was still doing a lot of background work for artists in the mid-to-late '70s, like Disco Tex & His Sex-O-Letts, Major Harris of the Delfonics, and a lot of others. I was even on Herbie Mann's *Super Mann* album. I worked for quite a few people, and I have to admit sometimes it's hard to remember everyone. I recall I did a demo for the song 'Shoot Me (With Your Love),' which was eventually sung by Tasha Thomas. I was introduced to Patrick Adams through Christine Wiltshire, a vocalist in the group Musique ("In the Bush"). I starting singing background for Patrick and writing a few more songs. One day, he called and asked me if I wanted to do an album. Of course I said sure! That's how *Night Rider* came about," she says.

Night Rider, which Dodson refers to as her "adventure in disco," featured background vocals by Bruni Pagan and was released by RFC Records in the United States. The prestigious custom dance label, home of disco stalwarts Change and Gino Soccio, among others, was an offshoot of Warner Bros. Records and formed by executive Ray Caviano, a former A&R man at T.K. Records. A collection of refined R&B, funk and disco, the album featured "Night Rider" as its lead single, which climbed its way to the upper echelons of *Billboard*'s dance chart by the summer of 1979. Jim Burgess ensured a heated response from the clubs by giving the track, which was written by Patrick Adams and Ken Morris, his signature stylish mix. It became an underground sensation.

"Night Rider" brought Venus Dodson to the top of the disco chart back in 1979. "It was really amazing hearing your song played on that dance floor and seeing the dancers' response. The thing that I got from that was the power of it all" (courtesy Venus Dodson).

"I didn't have time to think about it very much," the artist admits. "It wasn't something that we really planned a lot. It was kind of all-of-a sudden. I wrote some material for the album, like the song 'It's My Turn,' and it was all very exciting. It required a lot of studio time, and I got very little sleep. A lot of rehearsing, memorizing lyrics—it was just kind of like a whirlwind. I didn't really have a chance to enjoy it because of the timing. There was just so much to do, and you have to remember I was still singing live with my jazz band at this time. We were working in lower Manhattan doing clubs, weddings, dances and things like that. I guess I just didn't get to really step back and notice everything that was happening."

Still, the song's high chart position and DJs' demand for the single did register on the artist's radar. "'Night Rider' was the track that really took off, and that was the cut that Patrick had sold to the record company as the lead song. It did very well on the dance chart. I felt—how did Tony the Tiger say it? *Grrrrrrreat!* I was really excited. I didn't even know it happened! Someone called me and told me to pick up *Billboard* and *Cashbox* magazines, where I saw it was at the top of the disco chart. That thrilled me! But to be honest, as an artist, you just start thinking about the next job. But I did hope it would take off and that it would catapult me into the musical arena and put me front and center.

"One of the things I liked about 'Night Rider' was that the single *was* disco. That was Patrick's territory. But the album was a mix of R&B and other styles. Coming from a jazz background, you don't want to do anything too trite. So I was able to come at this album in a respectable way and feel good about it. There was an eclectic type of rhythm on this LP, and the lyrics of several songs weren't the regular 'I'm dancing, so I don't need to know what they're talking about' brand," she laughs. "We had songwriters like Leroy Burgess who did 'Shining' and 'Where Are We Headed,' and he was proficient at doing R&B. Songs like 'He Said, She Said' kind of melded R&B, funk and dance. There was a lot of good disco music out there at the time, especially by those who were merging R&B and disco—where they kind of fused that sound together. I really appreciated that style and was glad it was a part of my album. Lyrics are always important—even if you are mindlessly dancing to music like disco. There is always a subconscious response to music and lyrics, and it's another way to manipulate the masses."

Night Rider was especially well received in Italy, and Dodson made her way to the disco-hungry country to promote the album. "It was really something," she says with enthusiasm. "I loved visiting Italy and did some Italian television, including a disco music show and a game show. This, for me, was a wonderful experience. I would say the trip to Italy was the highlight of that time for me, and that's when I began to really appreciate the album and what was happening in my life. The song was very popular there, and I was treated so well. I was doing interviews and [visiting] radio stations, and it felt great that I was getting noticed internationally.

"I think Europeans were, to some degree, more receptive to disco than perhaps their American counterparts, but I also think it was because it *was* American music. At that time, any music coming out of the United States was popular over there. Disco was just a very big deal there. Stateside, I think it did very well, and I got a lot of airplay from DJs. They always appreciated the 'Night Rider' song and were very verbal about it when I would meet them. I performed at Studio 54—they'd play the song, and you'd see people going crazy over it! It was really amazing hearing your song played on that dance floor and seeing the dancers' response. The thing that I got from that was the power of it all. I always felt you had to be careful about what you put out there because you influence so many people. So rather than influence in the worst way with negative or suggestive lyrics, I always thought it was better to put something uplifting and positive out there.

Disco was very sexual and suggestive at times, and of course you had some of that being played. But I was very glad my songs had lyrics that weren't like that, and I had an appearance that didn't just scream 'sex!' My songs weren't explicit, and they left more to the imagination."

One of the most striking album covers of its time, the LP sported an understated, exotic photograph of the singer dressed in a luxurious cloth and carrying a parasol. Says Venus, "I loved the photographer. Eric Stephen Jacobs was his name, and he really worked closely with me. The photo you see on the cover of the album was not the type of image the record company wanted me to do. They wanted something really 'disco diva,' wearing a tight, tight outfit. I decided I wanted to something else. I'm Afro-Centric, but I took the ring out of my nose for the shot. I do have a very small stud there however if you look closely. I felt that when this disco thing passes, I will still be doing music, and I wanted to be seen for who I was (and who I am). That way I'm not fooling the people by giving them one look and then suddenly I'm something else. I wanted a look that would carry over no matter what happened with the album. A girlfriend wrapped me in this beautifully woven cloth, and I had just come back from the Virgin Islands and told the photographer I didn't want a lot make-up. I had really nice color because I had been in the sun a lot. So the photographer did not use foundation. He just used powder, eye make-up, blush and lipstick. And that's how that photo came to be.

"The boys at RFC, Ray Caviano and his brother, were not happy with me. They didn't want that photo used, and I chose it anyway. They called me in and read me the riot act. I almost didn't get to go to Italy because they were so displeased. When the call came from Italy that they wanted me over there, the boys failed to tell me. Actually, a secretary at the label informed me that the Italians were interested in having me promote the album over there. I got the contact information, and I made the call and made it happen. I think the Caviano brothers were trying to punish me because I hadn't given them the album cover they wanted. I have to say it was a shame because the sister who sang 'Knock on Wood,' Amii Stewart, was on the same Italian TV show as I, and she came out dressed in a beautiful Indonesian outfit. I had let management talk me into wearing some disco diva pants and top for this show. I would rather have continued the look I had on the album cover. The more exotic you look, the better shot at longevity you have because you will have made a statement that will stay in the minds of your fans. While in Italy, I had also done an interview at a socialist radio station, and I was pretty pointed about my views on racism and things like that. I think my label was very unhappy about that too," she says, shrugging any concerns about such things aside.

"It was all very petty, and I have to say it took some of the razzle-dazzle off of being in the disco explosion. For whatever reason, they decided not to do a second album. So 'Night Rider' became my little one-hit wonder! My photo choice may have cost me, but it was worth it! I made some wonderful connections in Italy and was able to go back there without the help of Warner Bros. and RFC," she says proudly.

Venus takes a few moments to examine the evolution of disco and the divide she believes separated the genre from black music during the era. "The late '60s and early '70s were a time of great social and political unrest. This seemed to be reflected by the battle weary youth and young adults needing to turn their attention to something much lighter by the mid–'70s. Enter disco. Disco was not a true evolution made from black music, as the claim is often made today. Black music of the time was funk, R&B and jazz-fusion, along with a mix of Brazilian and other Latin rhythms. This had been the natural evolution of our music in the early '70s, and much of it was instrumental. We were listening to the Black Poets, Gil Scott-Heron and other artists, like Chick Corea, Stanley Clarke, Donald Byrd and George Duke. The disco era put many great bands and performers out of work. All the large venues were becoming discos and were ruled by DJs. Don't get me wrong—DJs treated me (and the song 'Night Rider') wonderfully, and I'll never forget that—but I wish there had been more of a balance. Great bands like Kool & the Gang, Ohio Players, Funkadelic and the O'Jays, were locked out unless they made disco music, and the saturation of this genre literally helped kill fusion jazz, which is now watered down and called smooth jazz. Black dance music, not all the European multicultural stuff, was different from disco, and that's why we still continue to create our own music outside of the trends.

"I think disco distracted the people from taking the marginalization of blacks in America seriously and from engaging in lasting change. If we had been asked back in those days—those of us who had nothing to lose because we were not dependent on disco to survive musically—we would have revealed our thoughts on the subject. I think if we had more of a say in the disco era, there would have been a more balanced approach to this music."

Though she may not have been calling all the shots back in the bull market of disco, she is proud that she did things her way. "I guess I was stirring things up in those days," she reflects, "but you have to be true to yourself. You know, in the music industry you are in today and out tomorrow. If you sell your soul, as I watched so many people do, and then the folks in the industry turn on you—you can be left with nothing. This industry is not based on your musical pallet. It's based on your viability at the moment. Are you in the trend; are you happening now? If you don't fit the trend, if you get older, if you change your look, if you have an opinion that's different, if your next song doesn't sell as many copies, whatever—you're out. So you can't base your life on the entertainment world. Now the artistic world is different. There, you *can* have longevity. You can sing jazz forever as long as you can still sit up and sing. I think with disco, as an artist you are—sometimes, perhaps not always—expected to somehow stay young, sleek and sexy, and you have to maintain that energy and look to stay in that genre. Music is what I do for life, and I want to fall off the stool doing it—this is how I want to 'go out' if you will. I needed to sing music that will allow me to do that."

Dodson left New York in 1985 and took up residence in the Virgin Islands, where she still resides today. "I kept my band together the whole time, and I continued performing. I love it in the Virgin Islands. Lots of sea, sand, beautiful flowering trees and sun. You can smell jasmine in the air. It's the real me. I come back to New York every summer, but the islands are my true home. Today, I'm doing world jazz, standards, be-bop—you name it. I do the resorts and hotels on the islands (a one-woman show or with my band, depending on the gig) where I've really gotten to master my art. I'm writing and doing original music and making independent CDs. I'm blessed because I still travel all over, performing in Panama, Germany, Brazil, France, Holland—traveling the world. I'm still here!"

Disco is less a part of her world today. "I don't perform 'Night Rider' or my disco material today," the singer says. "Not that I don't want to. It's just that my audiences aren't usually looking for that kind of music. I certainly wouldn't mind doing a disco review. People from what the kids call 'back in the day' think of me as the disco diva. Yet in a place like Brazil, I'm just 'Venus Dodson performing music.' That's really a lovely thing. I have fond memories of 'Night Rider' and disco, and I expect, as I do more concerts, I can add a song like that into my repertoire. At world music concerts, you can arrange music differently and still do the songs. Take a track like 'Shining'—it translates well into many styles. Because songs like that were funk-disco hybrids, you can do things like that. I just have to get my hands on the sheet music from Patrick Adams—who is still my friend to this day."

Upbeat and comfortable with the variety that comprises her musical repertoire, Venus has an equally positive view of the maturation she's experienced. "I have no problem with aging," she declares. "I am 64 and loving it. Life has been very good to me, and I've been very blessed. I think, for me, moving out of the United States was a big, positive decision. Living in an environment like New York City was not for me. I'm not really big on cities, and I'm really a country type of person. I was like that even when I was doing all the disco stuff, so it was kind of a tug of war for me at the time. I don't like crowds. Music in my life has been so eclectic, and I have never gotten into a rut emotionally or spiritually. With that variety comes inspiration for living. My philosophy, if you want to call it that, has been to be observant about how I live and what I say. When you give your word, you have to mean it. I'm not a Christian, and I haven't been since I was about eight years old, but I pray and I believe in righteousness, honesty, and that if you treat people the way you want to be treated, the one supreme creator is going to take care of you—that whole 'what goes around comes around' concept. I try to remember that I am made in the likeness of God—and it's not only in how I look but how I act. It's a joy to be alive!

"Health is so important too," she adds. "I am recovering from breast cancer, although I won't say *just* recovering. I've been in remission for 19 years, and I am cancer free. I didn't do chemotherapy—I didn't do any of that stuff. I'm still alive after they told

Says Venus Dodson today, "I'm blessed because I still travel all over, performing in Panama, Germany, Brazil, France, Holland—traveling the world. I'm still here!" (photograph by the author).

me I'd be dead within five years," she says, her voice soft and calm as she thinks about the path she's been traveling.

Venus Dodson urgently and euphorically sang of an energized journey into the twilight with her disco classic "Night Rider" and continues to bring that passion to her music and life today. She takes a moment to reflect on her career, saying, "I'm very happy, and I'm at peace. Music has been very good to me—it's been my savior. It allowed me to make choices for myself that were good for me. In turn, I hope that I contributed something to other people's lives. Something that made people feel good—something that they can remember and say they enjoyed. And I hope that they will know I was true to myself the whole time. But hey, for me it's all about longevity. I plan to grow old and be here for quite a while!"

Joy Dorris of Lime
"Your Love"

"You know, for a while I think we were like the house band for Studio 54. That's how often we played there."—Joy Dorris

The true identities of some artists and acts synonymous with classic disco were sometimes shrouded in mystery. Take, by way of example, any of the dozen or so acts that turned out to be pseudonyms for the amazing voice of Jessica Williams, back when disco records were being churned out at a ferocious pace in the late '70s. The seminal disco group Lime is another. The group's first appearances were originally fronted by husband and wife Denis and Denyse LePage, the actual recording vocalists and creators of the duo's hits. Denis LePage (aka Nini Nobless) frankly reveals the details of his experience as part of Lime elsewhere in this book. The LePages delivered quirky and exciting hits, such as "Your Love," "Babe, We're Gonna Love Tonite" and "Unexpected Lovers," and they were consistent chart-toppers. Together, they lent a kind of energized stability to the dance floor during the decidedly unstable post-disco years. Lime bridged the disco of old with the emerging electronic dance sound of the '80s. However, a short time after the group broke internationally, a separate team of performers stepped in to represent Lime on tours. Joy Dorris became the lead female vocalist for that group, appearing on stage as far back as 1983. She candidly relates her unique experience representing the group on the club and venue circuit, which has now spanned decades.

When Joy speaks, one can instantly hear some of the vocal qualities that made this native of Long Island, New York, the perfect candidate to represent the energy of Lime. She is articulate and upbeat with a charm that is utterly disarming. Joy remembers how her journey began. "I had been doing a lot of demo work, modeling and acting in Manhattan, and I got a crazy phone call one day in 1983 from Sy and Eileen Berlin of Red Heart Management," she says. "Unbeknownst to me, they had demo tapes of mine that I had recorded. They literally talked to me for about five minutes and brought out Chris

Marsh. I had no idea who he was or what was going on, and they asked us to stand next to each other. Then they asked us to put our arms around each other, and they said, 'Okay! That works!' They asked us how we felt about leaving for Holland in three weeks to be the live vocalists for the group Lime. I had no clue that there'd been auditions for this or that they had been unable to find the type of vocalists they had been looking for, but apparently we were it.

"We kicked off our very first show at the Saint—October 30th, 1983. The poster said 'The American debut of Lime,'" Dorris reads, looking at the cardboard banner announcement framed on her wall. Though Denis LePage says he performed under the moniker Lime for a number of shows in the U.S. with his wife, the Saint appearance announcement is reasonable evidence that management was anxious to relaunch the act with Joy and Chris. "I think we went to Boston after that and then right to Europe," she adds. "We'd go there for five months at a clip, working non-stop. Crazy! We came back to America, and I don't think I was in my apartment in Manhattan for more than 24 hours when I was back on a plane again to the west coast.

"There was a lot of craziness that went on with the group, resulting in multiple male partners coming on board. *Multiple!* I felt like renaming the group 'Joy and the Boys' because I remember landing in Germany and the Deutsche Grammophon label greeting me saying, 'Hi Joy. Who did you bring with you this time?'" Dorris laughs. "My first partner was Chris—they used to call us the Donny and Marie of disco because we were two blond, wholesome, all-American looking people. Chris was, vocally, a dead-ringer for Denis LePage. You couldn't tell them apart. I also had a very good vocal range and could do Denyse's part where you couldn't tell the difference. When we went out on the road, those were our vocals. We sang live on every show. I think the reason we didn't fall into that Milli Vanilli type of backlash and that we were so accepted by DJs, radio and fans was because we were singing live.

"You know, for a while I think we were like the house band for Studio 54. That's how often we played there. There were some management issues going on, and Chris decided to leave the group. He went to California to pursue acting and from there it was a revolving door. The first replacement came and went in a few months. I remember I then worked with Benjy King for a time, who, in those days, was also the keyboard player for Scandal. He had that same type of Denis LePage vocal style. Then Chris Todd accepted the role, then Mitch Malloy. Mitch and I worked together for quite a while."

Around 1988, Joy decided to leave Lime and almost instantly received an offer to go solo under the name Joy Winter. She secured a recording deal, which resulted in the single "He Said, She Said" on CBS Associated Records and an album called *Frantic Romantic* for Epic Records. Notables such as rising freestyle star Stevie B, Lewis A. Martinee and (then husband) John Luongo produced the tracks, which included a cover of the Lime hit, "You're My Magician." "The Lime thing was starting to be a bit much for me by that time," she admits. "I felt we were starting to lose a little bit of our legitimacy with the partner changes, and I was really excited at the prospect of going out on my own. I signed with CBS Records and just moved on to other things. Some time later, they gave my role in Lime to another singer, but eventually Lime kind of just disbanded."

Roughly nine years ago, as disco started creeping back into vogue, a DJ from a radio station in Miami got in touch with Dorris. "The Hard Rock Hotel down there was

Still performing to enthusiastic crowds, Joy Dorris teams with Rob Hubertz to bring the music of Lime to life today (photographs by the author).

opening a free-standing venue, and they had a one-night disco show planned for their grand opening," she recalls. "They asked if I'd come down to do it. I guess the sun, moon and stars were all aligned, and I said, 'Okay!' We got hold of Benjy King, and we went down and did this huge show with Heatwave, France Joli, Evelyn "Champagne" King—it was just amazing. It was like getting back on a bicycle for Benjy and I. We started getting bombarded with calls to do more, and it snowballed." However, a fall in a New York City subway station resulted in a fatal injury for Benjy that Joy describes as a devastating loss. Rob Hubertz has since been Joy's partner on stage.

The repertoire of Lime songs Joy sings never fails to stir her audiences into a frenzy. She rattles off audience favorites with ease. "'Babe, We're Gonna Love Tonite' gets as big a reaction in Tokyo as it gets in Miami. It's like a disco anthem. 'Your Love' also gets a huge reaction wherever we go. 'Angel Eyes,' no matter if it's a fair or feast or an arena concert, always gets the crowd roaring. 'Unexpected Lovers'—the same thing. I think it was the hooks Denis came up with. He was a genius. If you think about 'Babe, We're Gonna Love Tonite,' it's almost like a nursery rhyme. He came up with the type of melodies and hooks that you almost knew the song before you finished listening to it." Lime continues to tour actively, performing at heavily attended events at premier clubs in the U.S. and throughout the world.

Ironically, Joy says she has never met Denis or Denyse LePage and has never spoken to them directly. "I have nothing but the utmost respect for both of them," says Dorris. "I've met the Canadian label personnel and, of course, the New York executives, but I never did meet Denis or Denyse—nor did any of my onstage partners. I truly respect Denis' genius and think he was ahead of his time with the music he created. Because of those two amazing artists, I have been blessed with so much good fortune.

"During the years, many people or interviewers would ask who were Denis and Denyse LePage. There was a time where some people thought they were our parents! I'm not kidding. We always acknowledged that we were not Denis and Denyse; we always said who they were, and we never tried to hide that fact or deceive anyone. There's so much confusion about who Lime was. It was very frustrating for me when I'd hear or read about someone saying, 'Oh yeah, I worked with Lime three times, and it was never the same group.' I'll be honest with you, one of the reasons I returned to performing as Lime over the past few years was because of a performance I was not a part of in the New York tri-state area, just shortly after I started up again. I started getting postings on my Facebook page asking if that was me on the stage, which it wasn't. The reviews weren't that favorable, and I have to say, feeling protective of the Lime brand, if you will, that sort of drove me to get back out and make sure the name is properly represented. I'm very proud of my association of Lime. While I wasn't in Montreal recording these songs, I feel I am very much a substantial part of Lime's history."

Today (and for a good portion of the past three decades), Joy Dorris has enjoyed the unique honor of representing a musical concept and act that might otherwise have faded into oblivion. She keeps the legacy of Denis and Denyse LePage alive and continues to give new life into this important music. In doing so, she shares in the legacy of Lime and appreciates the opportunity she has been given. She reflects on her uncommon position in life today. "I was sitting having dinner with Martha Wash ("It's Raining Men") recently," says Joy, "and we were commenting on how different things are today. Back then, there was so much pressure and everyone was watching chart positions and worrying about this and that. It's so much fun now. I am so happy to be doing this—it's been such ride.

"As part of Lime," Joy says humbly, "I have had the great fortune of being asked back to many wonderful venues over and over and to have been blessed to be able to help people flash back to those great disco days. My partners and I have been entrusted with delivering the Lime sound to the public and to be the stage personalities that keep it going—and that is an honor."

• •

Bob Esty
"Last Dance"

"I really enjoy hearing [my] records when they get played. There's a great deal of satisfaction in that."—Bob Esty

Bob Esty's musical resume is as impressive as anyone in show business could hope to have, especially when viewed in a disco music context. He's written, produced, arranged and/or sung with the giants of the dance and pop music industry—Streisand, Summer and Cher just to name a few. His work can be found in the records of the Weather Girls, Billy Preston, Brooklyn Dreams, Jean Shy, Thelma Houston, the Pointer Sisters, Raquel

Welch, Roberta Kelly, and even Dusty Springfield and the Beach Boys. Esty's achievements were formidable, but his enthusiasm and innocence during the era of the glitter ball and celebrated dance floors often blinded him to the bitter realities of the recording industry. Yet he is able to tell his story today with great charm, humor and warmth, just a few years after having suffered a minor stroke (which thankfully spared his ability to create, his wonderful storytelling charm, and his detailed memory). Bob Esty shaped some of disco music's most prolific and revered classics, and he eagerly relates the events that led to his reputation for excellence as one of disco's most accomplished legends.

"I was born in Massachusetts," Bob says, "and when I was a young boy, my family and I moved to Baltimore. I was always a precocious child. The church across the alley where we lived had a choir director, Forrest Charles Barrett, and he taught me piano, organ and voice. I would practice every day after school and was deemed talented enough to pursue it. It was the '50s and '60s, and I had a real appreciation of Broadway and the classical composers. I skipped a year in junior high and graduated a year earlier than most students from high school. I was too young to go to college, so I worked in a bank. I enrolled in the Peabody Conservatory of Music, joined the Baltimore Lyric Opera Company and a vocal group called the Baltimore Bach Society that would do classical concerts. At the same time, I started writing musicals, acted and sang. I guess this all led me to my career in professional music."

The stars aligned for Esty as he connected with perhaps the most famous of disco record labels, Casablanca. He built a new friendship with Paul Jabara, a man of Lebanese descent who became one of the label's best-known songwriters, performers and auteurs of disco. "I came to be connected with Casablanca Records through Paul," he says. "I had moved to New York following college in the summer of '69. I met him around 1973. All the things I had done in New York as a pianist and arranger for cabaret shows kind of prepared me for my partnership with Paul. He was doing a musical called *Rachael Lily Rosenbloom (And Don't You Ever Forget It)*, a Robert Stigwood production. Bette Midler had turned down the lead role in the show, and a friend of mine, Ellen Greene, was auditioning for it. I met Paul at the audition, Ellen was hired, and I ended up doing an arrangement for one of the songs in the production.

"I eventually moved to California in 1975," he continues, "where I lived in the guesthouse of my manager. I had begun working for some of the artists he handled, like Sally Kellerman, who I met in New York in 1973. I also worked on a national tour for her. I started playing and arranging for talk shows like *The Tonight Show* and *The Merv Griffin Show* and being a vocal coach."

Esty's career moved into high gear when he crossed paths with a woman he would eventually partner with professionally and creatively. "I met Michele Aller, who was secretary to Studio One disco owner Scott Forbes, and she wanted to audition for me. She was a great performer—a little overweight at the time, but a magnificent singer. She had a wonderful R&B style in spite of the fact she was a white, Jewish woman," Bob chuckles. "She had played a nightclub singer in the Diana Ross film *Lady Sings the Blues*. I loved her, and we started working together. I intended to present her as an act, but we discovered, through osmosis or something, that we were really good at writing together. I hadn't thought of myself as a real writer of music at that time, just an arranger. We did a series of 10 songs that we were going to demo. A young man named David Foster, who looked like a longhaired hippie, listened to our duets, and I wanted him to produce it. David said that I didn't need him and that I should produce it myself. And I guess that's how I became a producer.

"We did end up making Aller & Esty an act. For our first show we opened for Lesley Gore at the Troubadour in West Hollywood and, unbeknownst to us, Dusty Springfield was in the audience and loved our opening song, 'I Found Love with You.' To my amazement, Dusty wanted to record our song. I ended up arranging the track, and it was our first Aller & Esty recorded song.

"Paul Jabara and I collaborated on many things," he continues. "He did a single called 'Yankee Doodle Dandy' in 1976, which was produced by our mutual friend, Ron Dante, and which I arranged. Paul performed it much the way James Cagney had in the movies, and it was really quite a sight to see him sing it. It was also a disco version geared toward the Bicentennial and was really my dance music debut. When Paul performed a single song, it was marvelous. Two songs—it was a bit more of a stretch," he laughs.

Esty recalls his first close encounter with Donna Summer, the artist who went on to define the disco era. "My next record was a song I wrote with Paul Jabara called 'Shut Out,' part of a medley with 'Heaven Is a Disco' in 1977. It was planned to be a duet with Donna Summer. Paul was a friend of Donna's when she was appearing in the German version of the musical *Hair*, and he was in the original American version. They knew each other because the casts often collaborated. I met Donna for the first time when she came over to the house Paul was renting, and we went over this new song. She was so marvelous! When she came in she said, 'I can't stay; I'm going to go shopping.' She'd always say that because she *loved* to go shopping! But she liked the song, and she sat next to me at the piano, and we worked out the middle section of the medley where she had to talk about the other songs that were going to be on the album of the same name for Casablanca Records. The song was arranged to be a disco number. Arthur G. Wright was the producer (with Marc Paul Simon), and he had heard the cassette of my piano arrangement but did the song in a style that was not very 'disco.' I was very disappointed. I wasn't an expert on disco yet, but I always liked dance music and felt it could have been pumped up a bit more. Michele and a few other girls and I sang the backup."

Bob describes the little known chronology of events that followed in the months ahead. "I next worked on 'Last Dance' with Paul. I decided it should be loosely based on the style that Ashford & Simpson had performed on [Diana Ross'] remake of 'Ain't No Mountain High Enough'—a ballad intro. Actually, I decided to go with two ballad sections in the song. That was very unusual, and we didn't know if disco DJs would accept a ballad within the song. It ended up being one of the first disco songs ever to incorporate slow tempo parts. I did the arrangement, and I did the demo with Donna Summer during July of 1977. Giorgio Moroder recorded Donna's vocal just as she had sung the demo, and he banned me from attending the session. Giorgio didn't like the song and didn't really want anything to do with it. It wasn't breathy or high-voiced like 'Love to Love You Baby.' It was a very strong vocal, and that's what I liked about it. She did the vocal in two takes, her usual thing. Take it, or leave it."

"Last Dance" would languish on the shelf for a time before finally being released as part of the 1978 soundtrack to the film *Thank God It's Friday*. It ultimately became a chart-topping smash, peaking at number three on the *Billboard* pop charts. The song was grouped by the publication with "After Dark," "Thank God It's Friday" and "Take It to the Zoo" (Pattie Brooks, Love and Kisses, and Sunshine, respectively) and was number one on the disco chart for six weeks. "Last Dance" became the top disco single of the year and won an Academy Award, a Grammy and a Golden Globe. But before the song was lavished with honors, Esty went to work on Giorgio Moroder's next vision for Donna Summer.

"Giorgio must have thought something of my work on 'Last Dance,'" observes Esty, "because he asked me to arrange Donna's *Once Upon a Time* album in Germany. I was very thrilled by that. He introduced me to a synthesizer studio called Sound Arts in Silver Lake. I basically laid out the whole album there, and it seemed like a Cinderella story to me. So I had to make the songs fit that theme. He didn't say much of anything when the demo tapes were brought to Germany. His place in Munich was in the Arabella Haus (Musicland Studios) and was a compound—sort of a hotel with his studio at the bottom. His offices were on the third floor, and the apartments were above that. I loved being there, but I didn't really get to go anywhere because I was always in the studio.

"I arranged the whole album expect side two," says Esty (although the LP does credit him as arranger on all four sides), "including the Munich Machine rhythm section, strings, horns, over-dubs—and Donna didn't have anything to do with that recording work. Giorgio never came down to the studio, either. I guess he thought I could handle it and was doing a good job, so I just did my own thing. Then Donna came into town after performing in Italy (with Paul Jabara as *her* opening act). She had the cassette of me singing 'la, la, la, la' where the lyrics would go on the entire album. Donna got busy writing lyrics, and she recorded one side a night. Two times through, take it or leave it! All those songs!

"I was, once again, not allowed to go to the vocal sessions, but when I heard the first side late one night, I was confused by this little girl voice she was using. I rushed up to Giorgio's office the next morning and asked him if this recording was sort of a joke. He said (in a German accent), 'No, no. Those are the real vocals. Two times through,'" Esty laughs. "Giorgio said she wanted to be a little girl. Donna also didn't do the whole song in some cases. Sometimes she just stopped—I don't know why. Maybe she was tired and wanted to go shopping," he laughs again. "I had to do the background vocals that filled in the missing parts. By the time she recorded the third and fourth sides, she was sounding like herself.

"Donna was great!" Bob exclaims, his voice exuding a very genuine tone. "Very, very funny and good to work with. She knew everything! She had the best voice I ever worked with. I did think Donna would become big, but I didn't know if disco was going to be able to maintain a mass popularity." Summer's *Once Upon a Time* LP reached the top of the disco chart and stayed in active DJ rotation for almost six months.

Disco music was now roaring through pop culture like a freight train. The movie *Saturday Night Fever* and the success of *Thank God It's Friday's* "Last Dance" had the recording industry scrambling to supply new beats to a disco-hungry marketplace as quickly as possible. No artist, regardless of the genre they had been associated with, could afford to dismiss the possibility of doing a disco record. Esty was quickly scooped up in a whirlwind of dance fever.

"I did a disco track for Andy Williams, 'Love Story,' because he was a great singer, and somebody suggested that I do that song," he remembers. "I found a way to do it, and I loved working with him. He basically copied my guide vocals (I always did guide vocals for everyone in their keys), and I tried to imitate his phrasing. Andy had a strong voice and did it brilliantly. However, I actually turned down doing the same type of thing for Frank Sinatra because I felt he could not relate to disco. By then, Ethel Merman had released a disco album too. I thought, 'If only I had produced that album for her!' They just did Broadway orchestrations with a disco beat, and she sang. Today it's considered campy and delightful to hear, but at the time I thought, 'Why did they do that?' I had also done a Beach Boys disco record ['Here Comes the Night'], and I was starting to see everybody jump on the disco bandwagon."

During the frenzied height of disco mania, Bob took on the challenge of producing an extremely high-profile actress and singer. Cher was a well-established TV star and icon in rock and pop music, not to mention a paparazzi favorite. Like others at the top of their game, she was feeling the pressure by her new label, Casablanca (which had recently signed her), to be heard on the dance floor. Says Esty, "I was at a disco convention in New York, and I hadn't met Cher yet. What happened was Neil Bogart asked me if I could possibly produce another track like 'Last Dance' for Cher—and write it with Michele Aller. I said okay, and we came up with 'Take Me Home,' a song that was kind of unusual because it wasn't very common to hear a woman ask a guy to take her home. Cher was very forceful I thought, and I felt the song could be good for her and kind of a sexy thing.

"I broke my leg just after [we wrote the song] while in the city. The truth is, I was looking for a gay porno theater in the middle of the night, and I had taken my first (and only) Quaalude. I messed around with some drugs back in the day, but I never let it become a self-destructive thing. I had found a somewhat infamous (at the time) gay movie house up around 50th Street, with a neon sign up on the third floor. I wasn't paying attention to where I was walking, and I tripped on a subway grate and went down very hard. I pulled myself up, but I couldn't use my right leg. I needed to sit down, so I ended up going across the street to the theater, paid my $5 and hopped up two flights of stairs—luckily they had a strong banister—and sat down for a while. I was in a great deal of pain. I finally realized I had to leave and took a cab to a friend's place in Greenwich Village. We were going to a brunch that morning, but when I woke up my leg had swelled to three times its normal size! I ultimately carried myself to St. Vincent's [a well-known hospital once located in New York's Village], where I had to spend 10 days recovering from multiple fractures and bone breaks.

"I went home to California, where I was to play 'Take Me Home' for Cher. I was on crutches and had to make my way over to her Beverly Hills Hotel bungalow, where I propped my leg up on the piano and played the song for her. She was a very quiet woman. She liked it, but I have to say she didn't like the idea of doing disco," admits Esty. However, the song revived Cher's career (she'd reinvent herself many more times in the decades to follow), and the song "Take Me Home" ended up selling over a million copies, peaking at number eight on the pop chart and just shy of the top spot on the disco survey.

Esty had successfully helped Cher return to a power position in contemporary music, but says he failed to personally reap the financial benefits others were enjoying from his efforts and hard work. "Cher had originally made an album for Casablanca that their executives had refused," he states. "That's why I was brought in—to save it. Ron Dante was the producer once again. Ultimately, I saved two (of his strongest) cuts on side two of the album, and he made more money than I did! Really, I signed the worst possible record deal. I had three contracts—one for producing, one for being an artist, and one for writing. So they dipped into every account when I did these productions. I had to do the productions they told me to do, and some were successful and some were not. But they never told me about budgets—I just did what I had to do. I had no idea. So basically they would say I owed them money. I was so busy in the studio that I didn't associate with management except for Neil Bogart. So I simply did not know how any of the business really worked. I basically got paid just for playing the piano, thanks to my union contract. I think I ended up getting $15,000 for the LP *Take Me Home*, despite the fact the album was a smash. I was making money and was able to buy a house, but I could have—should have—made much, much more."

Bob expresses more frustration over the difficulties he claims tarnished his extraordinary experiences during the era. "I had done the work on 'Last Dance,'" he alleges, "produced an album for Roberta Kelly, D.C. La Rue, Paul Jabara's tracks, so many things, and I simply didn't pay attention. I just thought I'd be paid automatically. When Paul decided not to credit me for co-writing 'Last Dance'—I wrote the bridge and the hook—he said to me, 'Well, you owe me because I got you into Casablanca.' Nobody knew 'Last Dance' was going to receive an Academy Award, but when he went to receive the Oscar, I wasn't there. I guess he wanted the glory. He always had to be 'on.' And that created sort of a rift between us. We did many things together after that, but it was a rather love-hate relationship. I learned very late that the music industry screws people. But I have to say about Paul (who died in 1992)—I hope there is a musical made about him. He was one of the most endearing, funny and tragic people I ever knew. He was like a shooting star."

Following Cher and Donna Summer's successes, more stars were waiting in line for the Midas touch of Jabara and Esty. "When Paul and I were approached with the idea of working with Barbra Streisand, I said, 'No, I don't want to do that! Please!'" claims Bob. Despite his protests, Streisand's disco debut fell squarely on Esty's shoulders. He laughs a bit as he reminisces about his work with the celebrated actress and singer.

"I had been working with Lesley Ann Warren (we had the same manager). She was a marvelous girl, very high strung and funny, and I loved working with her. She was married at the time to 'hairdresser to the stars' Jon Peters. She had appeared on *The Tonight Show* singing a song I had arranged, and afterwards I had seen her crying and asked her what had happened. Apparently, Jon had berated her about the outfit she wore and was putting her down. So I yelled at Peters, 'Fuck you!' and a lot of other things! The next time I saw Jon was three years later with Barbra Streisand, and I hoped he did not remember that incident!"

Apparently, Peters didn't remember the rant (or, at the very least, regardless of the confrontation, recognized the importance of working with Esty at this juncture).

"Paul Jabara and Bruce Roberts had written a song for Barbra called 'The Main Event' for the movie of the same name, and Jon, the producer, rejected it," Esty says. "Barbra didn't want to have a song in the movie. But when Donna Summer's 'Last Dance' and Cher's 'Take Me Home' hit the airwaves, Peters and the others around Barbra were telling her to just get on the bandwagon. They thought 'The Main Event' could be 'discofied,' and Bob Esty could be the one to do it. Paul was very mad that his original version didn't make the cut, but I re-arranged it and played it for Barbra on the piano at her Malibu Ranch. She was very warm and quite gracious—not at all like the 'difficult' Barbra Streisand I had heard about. I immediately thought, 'Oh, I can work with her!' The first thing she said about the song was, 'Oh, this "extra, extra" lyric. What is that? Who can sing that? I don't like it!' I said, 'Oh, you *can* sing it like this, "Ex-ter-ah–Ex-ter-rah…"' She joyfully responded, 'Oh, maybe I *can* do that!'

"The song had nothing about fighting in it, and it was a boxing movie. It sounded more like the opening of a show about a newspaper stand! Paul and I had written a song called 'Fight,' sort of a parody for the Village People, and it had this great bass line and a call to fight, fight, fight. Well, Barbra loved it. 'That's what I want to do! I'm not doing "The Main Event!"' she insisted! Because Bruce Roberts was sitting behind me, I said I thought I could build a medley between the two songs, and Streisand said if I could work it out, she would consider it. At the studio, I sang the guide vocal for the recording all the way through in her key. She heard it, and, looking at me cross-eyed, said, 'I don't know if I can sing that! You'd have to help me! Direct me!' So I did. It was marvelous directing Barbra because she knows how to be a director and how to be directed." In the summer of 1979, "The Main Event/Fight" peaked at number 13 on *Billboard's* disco chart and crossed over to the number three position on the pop side.

"The 'disco sucks' campaign began after these big hits, so I left Casablanca in 1980," says Esty. "Michele Aller had left the label after we did Cher's second album, *Prisoner*. The album was originally going to be called *Mirror Image*. *Prisoner* came out when the anti-disco movement was heating up and because Cher liked rock 'n' roll. She was going out with Gene Simmons of Kiss at the time, and that's why her pictures on the album have that rock look. So we had to make this disco-esque rock hybrid with the single 'Hell on Wheels.'"

Esty and Aller managed to squeeze out one more effort, the soundtrack to the film *Roller Boogie*. The song 'Love Fire' was sung as a duet on the LP by the duo, which originally had been written for Diana Ross. The late Motown singer Syreeta covered the track on her self-titled 1980 LP. "Syreeta took it as a hand-me-down, using the original arrangement and just slightly changing the song," Bob remembers.

"I know it got Michele real down when they started burning disco records. Luckily, I was able to do more work—two records for Capitol. Columbia Records was also pretty nice to me. For example, I played, produced and arranged 'It's Raining Men' for the Weather Girls. Paul wrote the song with Paul Schaffer in New York, and I worked on it in Los Angeles. But, once again, I never saw a cent of the money that song went on to make," he says with a tone of reluctant acceptance.

"My problem was I didn't have management, and I never connected with anybody else in the business. I talked to lawyers about some of the problems I had experienced, but, at that time, they all really wanted to work for the record companies, and unless you were a major star, they preferred not to handle lawsuits against labels. It meant there would be fewer chances for those attorneys to work for those labels. It wasn't worth it to them. I wasn't the only one screwed—many artists were as well."

Esty says he is still able to take enjoyment from the esteem with which his work is regarded today, despite the difficulties he encountered. "I really enjoy hearing the records when they get played," he admits. "There's a great deal of satisfaction in that. Whenever I write something, it's for somebody else. You have to look at their personality traits and decide what will work for them. Sometimes you hit, and sometimes you miss. It was really all about the lyrics and arrangement style back then. Like with Cher—she was kind of quiet in person, but always laughing when she was with everybody else, so I'd have to create songs that incorporated that personality. You have to always remember what you are singing and what is the message of the song. And I never wanted to write 'faux rhymes.' There are bad rhymes and good rhymes. Today, a lot of music has lyrics that seem like they rhyme, but they really don't. It means you have not spent enough time to actually write the song, or they just write the first thing that comes into their heads and never go back to correct it. Sometimes I also see and hear singers today who just don't connect with their audience—because they don't know how. I tried to make sure that was never the case with my music."

"You have to always remember what you are singing and what is the message of the song," says renowned disco visionary Bob Esty (photograph by Alan Mercer, courtesy Bob Esty).

Esty pauses a moment to think about the artists with whom he's most enjoyed working and chooses to call out a number of men and women he produced in decades past. "Roberta Kelly, Jean Shy, Ava Cherry, D.C. La Rue, Brooklyn Dreams and Taka Boom really stood out for me. And Pattie Brooks as well. I enjoyed working with everyone, but the energy and spirit of the ladies was particularly remarkable. Ava Cherry's *Streetcar Named Desire* LP was recently reissued on CD by Gold Legion (as was Paul Jabara's *Keeping Time* album.) I was lucky to work with so many great people, including Michele Aller and [lyricist] Michael Brooks. If I ever write a book, I'd call it *From Streisand to Stryker!*" he laughs, referencing Jeff Stryker, a porn star from the '90s for whom Esty produced some songs.

Bob's life philosophy is quite simple. "Basically, you have to take everything with a grain of salt," he says. "You have to really stay upbeat and have fun. I've learned not to have fear—just go for it. And if you don't make it, so what?"

The multi-talented artist has worked on and off in Key West, but still calls Los Angeles his home. He is feeling well and maintains a positive attitude. Esty continues to keep his hand in music as he manages through some of the challenges caused by his stroke. "I'm working with an artist named Scott Snapp, who writes 'theatrical pop.'

We've done a CD with a brilliant co-arranger, David Arana. And we are working on another!"

Bob Esty's extraordinary musical legacy helped bring disco to the mainstream, and his songs are among the best-known and biggest sellers of the genre's vast repertoire. He is one of the behind-the-scenes greats, whose bright spirit, energy and sense for irresistible melodies, lyrics and arrangements is palpable in all his masterpieces. As legions of fans admire, applaud and dance to his rhythmic, hook-laden and infectious beats, the creator has a simple wish for his musical estate. Says Bob, "I just want people to have fun with those records and just enjoy them as much as I did creating them."

Jimmie Bo Horne
"Spank"

"All of us were hungry for success, and we all worked together. Nobody had an ego, regardless of how famous you were becoming."—Jimmie Bo Horne

Between 1975 and 1980, Jimmie Bo Horne (often spelled "Jimmy" on recordings), was a staple of the disco charts. He had the kind of voice that mixed masculine soulful prowess with a heated urgency, and it melded remarkably well with the disco productions coming out of Florida (his original stomping ground). Horne soon found himself an integral part of the T.K. Records and KC hit-making machine. His songs, once classified as disco novelties, are regarded today as essentials of the genre. "Gimme Some," "Dance Across the Floor" and the untouchable "Spank" remain irresistible evidence of the artist's flair for feel-good music. A warm-spirited and enthusiastic veteran of the strobe lights, Jimmie recalls his dance-floor days with humor and affection.

Horne settles back in his chair to speak of his beginnings. "I'm a native of West Palm Beach and Riviera Beach, Florida," he says. "I have to claim two places because I was born in West Palm, and my parents later moved to Riviera Beach. I was an only child. In the community I grew up in, everybody had a nickname. Although they knew me as Jimmie Horne, my dad, mom and just about everyone else would call me 'Bo.' It's been this way my whole life. When I got ready to make records, I knew people wouldn't remember Jimmie Horne, but Jimmie 'Bo' Horne might stick. I kept the 'Bo' so people in my community would be aware that I was doing something good musically. In the community that I came out of, the better you did, the more your parents were proud of you. I came from a neighborhood where there was a lot of love. There weren't a lot of rich kids, but, you know, if you got what you needed in life and weren't aware of what you were missing, you were doing all right. People cared about you, and it made you feel rich. I never went without a meal, I had clean clothes, and I went to school. I felt rich. We had segregation back then, but I still felt a lot of love. If you did something good, everyone was proud of you. As a child, when you had older people feeling that way about you, it felt better than anything you can imagine. Later, when they heard my music on the radio, they felt that I had put them on the map. Whether it was a bad or good neighborhood—*sho'nuff was good for me*! Of all the places I've been able to travel in my life because of my music, I can still say there's no place like home!

"My father was a carpenter. He could build anything, and as he was working he'd let me listen to Arthur Prysock, Jackie Wilson, James Brown, Roy Hamilton and all kinds of music. The music influenced me at a very early age. I'd hear their sound and try to duplicate it. The more I listened to it, the more it became a part of me—the more it became like my imaginary friend," claims the artist.

Jimmie's talents were noticed early on. "I got a music scholarship to Bethune-Cookman University in Daytona Beach after I graduated in 1967 from Roosevelt High School. The year before, there was a very a very popular DJ by the name of Joe Fisher (who was the program director at WRBD radio station in Fort Lauderdale), and he liked my voice. He took me to a record company called T.K. Records in Hialeah, Florida, where I spoke to a gentleman named Henry Stone. Henry would become responsible for the original Miami disco and soul sound, later forming T.K. They had Latimore, Betty Wright, George McCrae, Gwen McCrae and many other artists," says Horne.

"T.K. Records became like a dynasty in the Miami area," he says of the emerging disco label. "Mr. Stone had been having hits even before Motown. I was being produced by Willie Clarke, Clarence Reid and Brad Shapiro and was doing R&B music. I was doing well on black radio stations with songs like 'Clean Up Man' in 1972 and 'If We Were Still Together' on the Alston label in 1973. I have to admit, I was opposed to disco at the time. I was a horn man, like you hear in the music of Wilson Pickett and Earth, Wind & Fire. I was kind of locked into that moment and sound. KC (Harry Wayne Casey) used to work in T.K.'s warehouse, and he was in a band. I would work the black clubs and one of the groups I hired was called the Ocean Liner Band. KC was the lead singer of the group. The group wasn't signed to any label back then. At one of these gigs, KC said to me, 'I'm gonna write a song for you someday!' I was like, 'Yeah, right.' Turns out, he not only wrote one song for me, but a lot of my hits. KC's group became known as the Sunshine Band and got signed to T.K.

"Henry wanted to cross me over to pop radio. So I started working with KC, and we released the song 'Gimmie Some,' which went gold in Canada, and then came 'Get Happy.' Next, I remember I recorded 'Dance Across the Floor.' I thought it had a real nice beat, and we were all really enthusiastic about it. Keep in mind, we're young and we're excited because we just knew it would get on the radio. I knew my family and friends would hear it. We knew point blank that we were all part of a winning team because, at this point, T.K. could do no wrong! It felt so good because you were signed to a record company known throughout the world. We had all kinds of cool people working there. We had our brothers like Foxy, Peter Brown and Bobby Caldwell—musical brothers in all colors. It felt like a family, and it made you want to do something great. And when I had records being played on the radio, I would drive 10 blocks out of my way just to listen to them on the air! It was absolutely great working with KC and [his fellow composer] Richard Finch.

"All of us were hungry for success, and we all worked together. Nobody had an ego, regardless of how famous you were becoming. So, if we needed a background vocalist, whoever was in the studio that day would just jump in," he says. "Gimmie Some" and

"Get Happy" took Jimmie to the Top 20 of the disco survey. "Dance Across the Floor" hit the Top 10 of the R&B chart, and the funky, shuffling disco track proved to be a substantial club hit for the artist. The song has been sampled numerous times by several hip-hop artists, including Da Lench Mob and Sadat X.

Despite the frenzy, Jimmie readily admits he dropped the ball with a song that became a monster success for one of his label mates. "KC let me hear the track 'Rock Your Baby,' but I said, 'Oh, I want something more up-tempo,' or something like that, and I turned it down," the artist reluctantly admits. "Well, George McCrae didn't make the same mistake! He said he'd do it, and he did an incredible job with it. *George became disco!* That was the biggest song ever to come out of T.K. It taught me that even when you don't like a record, there are times when an artist should listen to what the producers are saying. Sometimes they can see things that you can't see as an artist. KC was interviewed for the show *Unsung* and told them that he offered the song to another artist who didn't want to do it. I'm that mystery person. He tastefully said 'someone,' and I exhaled a thank-you in relief for sparing my name," he laughs. "I ended up doing a song called 'I Get Lifted,' which KC originally wrote for George."

It wasn't the last time Horne would have misgivings about a track. "I had a song I didn't initially like or want to do that KC produced. It was written by Ronald Louis Smith, Sr., the trumpet player for KC's Sunshine Band, and was called 'Spank.' Ron said it was a song based on slang talk, and I thought it was about hitting somebody. He said it was just a word that meant doing your best. He had to convince me. KC was saying, 'This song is gonna be good for you! Try it Jimmie! You know you turned down "Rock Your Baby!"' I like songs that tell stories, and when I listened to the lyrics, I didn't think it was really saying anything. I didn't think the song would do anything. Well, it was the biggest song I ever had! It was bigger than 'Dance Across the Floor.' It went double gold in South Africa. Man, when I perform that song, you'd think it was Michael Jackson on stage." In 1981, the studio concept group known as Brooklyn Express incorporated the composition "Spank" into their Top-10 disco smash "Sixty-Nine." Ultra Naté also incorporated the "Spank" theme in a remix of her hit, "Release the Pressure," in 1998.

Horne's hits placed him high on the disco chart, while earning him continued attention in the R&B market. The upbeat, hook-laden compositions of Casey and Finch had a sound that worked magic in clubs and on pop radio. He became comfortable with disco and the qualities of the music that were bringing him so much success. "When disco came along," he observes, "the music talked about forgetting your problems. Forget how you don't like your job. Let's do something that's gonna bring happiness tonight. If you're not happy, then let's get down tonight, like K.C. would say. If you felt your life wasn't going right, disco made you feel like partying. If you realized you don't have everything you need, like Bo always said, let's dance across the floor. They took the tempo and boosted it up to the point where you couldn't help but have a good time. It wasn't about falling in love. It was about having a good time.

"Disco was a music form that, whether you were straight or gay, allowed you to be happy and feel accepted. It gave people an opportunity to dance together. For me, it gave me a chance to go to places that I had only read about in history books. I went to countries where people knew all the lyrics of my songs, but couldn't talk to me because they didn't speak English. Yet I'd land at their airport and would be heading to my limo and people would be calling out, 'The "Gimme Some" man!' I would do shows in Germany and other places, and they loved you for the happiness that you brought!"

Horne enjoyed his time in the spotlight immensely. He recalls a few standout events, his voice still exuding enthusiasm. "I went to London with Timmy Thomas ['Why Can't We Live Together'] and George McCrae to do a show around 1977 or '78. 'Dance Across the Floor' and 'Gimme Some' were hot for me and George of course had 'Rock Your Baby.' I felt like I'd really made it when I got to the arena and people were holding up and waving my albums and singles. Doing shows like *American Bandstand* and *The Merv Griffin Show*, *Mike Douglas*, *Dinah Shore* and *Soul Train* made us realize we were really in it! I was in Rome, where Diana Ross filmed *Mahogany*, and it made me feel like, man, I was in a whole other part of the world, and people knew my music! The Italians really went crazy over 'Gimme Some.' It was a rush—that's the exact word for it!" he beams.

"My personal favorite songs are 'If You Want My Love' and 'I Can't Speak.' Those were R&B songs, and I loved them. Someone in London told me if I still had the original 45-rpm single for 'I Can't Speak,' it would be worth about $2,500. I've learned in my older years the significance of keeping a copy of my records, but I never did that during my career unfortunately. It hurt me bad because I started having a lot of people offer me large sums of money for original pressings of some of my records. You get so tied up in your career and getting work and recording your next song that you don't pay any attention to keeping copies of the records. I thank my mom, who took some of my records and hid them. I would ask her for one of her copies because I needed it to rehearse or whatever, and she'd say she didn't want to give it to me. I'd swear I wouldn't lose it. *Bam…. I'd lose it!* Gone!" he laughs.

Basking in his musical triumphs, Horne could not help but observe the excesses of an industry that had blanketed music-making with numerous vices. He says his upbringing kept him from falling into the trap. "When I was growing up, a child didn't have any rights," he says with a mix of affection and acceptance in his voice. "If you were being fed and housed and clothed by someone else, you didn't have any rights. The name of the game in my parents' house was: 'Your name is Jimmie Horne. We call you "Bo." You ain't got no rights. You do what we tell you to do. Don't go out there and mess up this family's name. If you go out there and do the wrong thing and get in trouble, we're gonna kill you!' Not literally of course. That was just a saying, just like when we'd get punished. They'd say, 'This hurts me more than it hurts you!' I never understood that one as a kid," he laughs. "My parents didn't drink or smoke. My parents didn't allow me to be a follower. If I didn't do right, I was gonna get it! And I didn't want to get it! My parents were very strong-minded, and they also had a very strong belt!" he says with a big grin.

"So, when I got to T.K. Records and was having success—and cocaine, heroin and everything else was around me—it was instilled in me that I was a Horne. So I couldn't do that. I'm carrying my family name. Some people would say I must be high because I was performing with so much energy. I'd say I *was* high—on the music! The feeling that you are going to make others feel as happy as you feel—that's the high that doesn't come down. That's what made you want to get back out on that stage," he declares.

The artist was forced to confront issues of racism in his personal and professional life in the '60s and '70s, but he learned to navigate his way through such challenges.

"Race issues were always right there!" the artist says emphatically. "If it were not for T.K. Records and Henry Stone, I'm not sure where I'd be. There would be no Jimmie 'Bo' Horne. This company was one of the rare entertainment organizations in Florida that could see the value of black music. I think of Elvis Presley's records not being played on some radio stations because he was shaking his hips. 'That's black music,' they'd say. Change—remember that word. But when the Colonel came in, he was able to give Elvis the right protection and financial backing—same thing with T.K. and Henry Stone. With racism and segregation, I knew I had to do better to overcome it. My parents would always tell us, 'You've got to be even better than better to get a fair shake!' During my time, I learned that once people heard my music and enjoyed what it did for them, they didn't care if I was blue, green or charcoal black. They didn't care!"

The end of 1979 marked the beginning of the public and media's increasingly negative attitude towards disco, which was felt most acutely in the offices of T.K. Records. The organization encountered financial difficulties that ended with the company being acquired by Roulette Records. "It's the law of life," Jimmie says. "The only thing guaranteed is change. When you've had rock and R&B having their way for a while and then a new music comes along that challenges the status quo, as disco did, some people start shouting, 'This isn't music! This is bubble gum music!' Disco was change, another form of music, an art form that came along. To me, music is like a bus driven by a driver, and each time the bus stops, a new music form gets on and the other music forms have to move to the back. It's change. Nobody ever thought rap and hip-hop would be able to replace R&B. But it did. Remember, before I started working with KC, I wasn't comfortable moving out of R&B. I reacted the same way that some people did to disco because I didn't want to accept change at first. So some people led a revolt against the change that came in and said disco was bad. They were able to stamp out disco for a while here in America, but they couldn't stamp it out in Europe and South America. You can burn records on a baseball field, but it wasn't finished off the way they thought it would be."

Today, Jimmie leads a quieter life. He continues to do shows and maintain his own successful business. "I have two children, Nicole and Jermaine. I have four grandchildren. So I am not without trying moments!" he smiles. "I have the opportunity to have people around me that keep me grounded. I have my manager, Beverly, who was like a daughter to my mother, and I have friends I've had for my entire life. I've been told I'm not the best knife in the drawer, and I'm missing one floor of the elevator ride, but they all keep me in check!" He laughs heartily.

"I lost my mother on January 15, 2011, at 2:15 p.m. I took care of my parents in their later years because they were there for me. I started my own event planning company years ago so I could cater to their needs and still make a living. There were some moments that were difficult running my own business, and if I didn't work, I wouldn't eat. I made a lot of money in the disco era, but I also made a lot of financial mistakes. But those mistakes helped me to get grounded and be where I am right now. I've learned over the years it's not your aptitude that determines your altitude in life. It's your attitude that determines your fortitude in life. My mother and my father let me know the only difference between a good day and a bad day is the way you look at it. That's my philosophy today.

"Success is nothing without the ones you love. I think I heard that in a Diana Ross movie. This, to me, means you need people around you who love you for you. Of course you can get people hanging with you if you're able to do something for them. But if you have people who love you, whether you are up or down, then, believe me, you've got something you'll never be able to get at Walmart or Neiman Marcus—it's priceless. Thanks to that, I've reached a point in my life where it's all right to be me. It's okay to not know all the answers and still be able to learn. I know I'm all right! God has me where He wants me to be."

Jimmie Bo Horne played an important role in establishing the classic Miami disco sound—an integral part of the genre's history. His humor, talent and ease with life have allowed him to come a great distance and be able to look at his legacy with personal satisfaction. "I ask God to bless me so I can be a blessing to others. My late father used to say that when you go out in life, you have to do the best you can. 'Nobody's getting into your grave but you,' he'd say. I want people to remember me as someone who was not only an artist, but a humanitarian. I hope that I've helped other artists and other people and will continue to be able to do that. I hope people will remember me as a performer who opened up his heart on stage with great songs and gave people something real. I want them to say, 'Bo Horne—he was a great disco artist!' 'Bo Horne—he was a hard worker, like James Brown!' 'Bo Horne—I conceived my child listening to his music!'" And with a big laugh he adds, "Man that's gonna be a big tombstone! They better just cremate me!"

Geraldine Hunt
"Can't Fake the Feeling"

"Frankly, we—me, Denis [LePage], Carol Jiani—should all be multi-millionaires for what we turned out. But I don't regret the journey because that was what I was supposed to do on this planet."—Geraldine Hunt

The minute Geraldine Hunt's sizzling voice commands listeners to speak with integrity when whispering words of love in the classic disco firestorm "Can't Fake the Feeling," you know she means business. Born Geraldine Milligan in St. Louis, Missouri, and raised in Chicago, Illinois, Hunt hit the top of the dance charts numerous times with a series of lyrically savvy, hook-saturated crowd-pleasers. Her gritty, dynamic vocals and knack for cut-to-the-chase songwriting helped to make her name synonymous with the genre, especially during the challenging post-disco period of the early '80s (where success in dance music was a hard-fought accomplishment). Hunt, currently a resident of Canada, has a tremendously upbeat personality, marvelous sense of humor and fearless attitude when it comes to approaching life. She shares her memories of being one of disco's premier songstresses and is anxious to convey her personal philosophy of empowerment.

Born at the close of World War II, Hunt says she enjoyed her family life and, despite some of the negative aspects of living where she did, was very happy. "I grew up in a violent neighborhood, and I was the victim of some of it," Geraldine says without hesitation, "but the toughness in life really kicked in when I got into the music business. That's when the disappointments happened—I started out very innocent, thinking the world was my oyster, and then came to realize that there's some real monsters out there. I started out in a time when people could actually realize their dreams if they put in the effort. Ninety percent of my youth was music and a lot of fun, love and family involvement. We weren't the Rockefellers, but I had a nice base for me to end up being a writer, publisher and singer.

"When I was very young, I remember seeing the movie *Showboat*. At the time, the tickets must have been about 10 cents. I came from a musical family, and we could remember the songs easily and come home and sing them together. I remember thinking about all the characters in the movie, and I thought, 'Well I like that. That's what I'll do with my life.' I didn't think anything was beyond my reach, and if I thought of something, I just did it. I internalized it, and that's what ended up happening."

After changing her name to Hunt, she started recording in the early '60s on labels like Roulette Records. By the early '70s, she had scored a few R&B hits, including the song "You and I," a duet with Charlie Hodges. "When I was younger, I had been robbed in my Chicago neighborhood, and someone tried to rape me, and that got me thinking that it was time to go," the singer reveals. "I had some success recording, including a remake of the Four Tops' 'Baby, I Need Your Loving.' So, as a result, I happened to get on one of those military entertainment tours. I went on a gig that I thought I was going to just involve traveling to somewhere in Mississippi. Well, the tour took me to New York and New Jersey, and then somehow we ended up in Canada. While we were there, the military base we were going to visit closed, and the booking agent offered to get us some other gigs in the area until we could make our way back home. When I got to Quebec—and mind you, I had a home and a mortgage in Chicago—and went through their towns and met their people, I said I was never going to go back to America. Never! I set out to make sure that happened. I fell in love with Quebec, and I found French Canadians to be lovely people."

Hunt's first album cultivated in the Canadian disco scene was called *Sweet Honesty*, released in 1978. Produced and mixed by Tony Green (who later launched France Joli), it was a modest success on the club circuit and featured arrangements and keyboards by Denis LePage. She recalls its origins. "When I recorded this album, Canada already had quite a few notable artists—like Gino Vannelli—that were holding it together for this country. I was touring with Alma Faye Brooks, and we were backup singers for a French-speaking artist named Boule Noire. We were opening for people like Donna Summer. A label got the idea of recording Alma and I separately. Alma was able to speak French, but here I was singing in the language and everybody started thinking I was French. I was like, 'Oh my God, what am I gonna do?' I wasn't fluent in French. That's when I decided I was gonna save my money and write songs on the road with my musicians until I had enough money to go into the top studio here. I did a skeleton of each of the tunes as we would come up with them. Of course, then I had to find a record label.

"I was accumulating these cuts and got a call from the recording studio [that was holding the tapes], and they said if I didn't claim my tracks in 30 days, they'd erase all my stuff. Mind you, I had already spent about $1,800 from the start and couldn't afford to lose that investment." Geraldine says at this point she managed to get Tony Green's label, TGO Records, interested in releasing her tracks. "Then we brought in Denis LePage, and the *Sweet Honesty* LP took off from there," she says.

"I didn't set out to do disco music," confesses Hunt. "Again, I came up at a time when lyrics meant something, and the performance was very important. There weren't a whole lot of musical categories until the [music industry] criminals set it up that way, so they could create and control different charts. Everybody used to just do his or her own thing without being categorized. Now, if you vote for music awards, it's like going through the big yellow telephone book with all the categories and genres. It's ridiculous. For me, I started out to make the music that was in me. I wasn't trying to find hooks or worrying about whether it was called disco or not. I was just trying to make sure my story was clear and helpful to the person who was listening. Music is medicine—it's spiritual, and it has healing powers. It was helpful stuff. You tried to make sure you didn't sing off key. That was it. The criminals came in and tried to define what's R&B, what's rock, all of that. So now look at what have—it's a mess. I can't remember what anybody sings today.

"Recording my music in Canada was wonderful," she says enthusiastically. "There was so much energy going on. It was like we couldn't do anything wrong. I had a 13-year-old son at the time, Freddie James, who was Michael Jackson's double. He had done *Soul Train* when we were in Chicago. Tony Green and I had started to produce him, and we had some hits [notably 'Get Up and Boogie' and 'Hollywood' in 1979]. Being a mother, of course I wanted the best for my son. I always felt that if his success were ever to end, he should have something to show for it. It was wonderful working with Tony and he always respected me and thought I was amazing and I loved him for that. But then he signed France Joli and when we got to that point we had to end that partnership. I communicate with Denyse LePage [Denis LePage of Lime's former wife and partner] even now, but I haven't seen Denis in a while. But my God, what a talent he was. He was heavenly. He knew all the people we needed to get in order to achieve that sound. He was the foundation for almost everything great in dance music that came out of Canada at that time.

"Frankly, we—me, Denis, Carol Jiani—should all be multi-millionaires for what we turned out. But I don't regret the journey because that was what I was supposed to do on this planet. The plan has unfolded very well, and I'm just riding the wave. I don't know what happened to the people who stole money from the profits of our records, who did this or that, but it's okay. The journey was the most exciting part. I never made any of these records thinking, 'Oh, that's gonna be a hit and make me rich!' I was doing what came natural, and it was a party. That was the exciting part for me—not the people coming at me from labels and worrying about when it was gonna be released and all that nonsense."

Geraldine had still more to offer, and in 1980 she managed to exceed expectations raised by her debut LP. She unleashed the smash album *No Way*, which was produced by Mike Pabon Austin and largely arranged by Peter Dowse. The collection, released through Prism Records in the United States, featured six tracks that were mostly co-written by the artist (with Mr. Dowse and others). The fiery lead single from the set, "Can't Fake the Feeling," had already been causing a worldwide stir on the underground and club circuit for months. The song's infectiously rolling rhythm and electrifying guitar riffs melded beautifully with Hunt's vocal authority and created a powerful energy that dancers found irresistible. Though making only modest inroads on the American R&B and pop charts, the song leap-frogged its way to the number one spot on the *Billboard* disco chart and didn't budge from that position for seven weeks.

"I was flabbergasted when it hit number one. I mean, come on now! I came into New York on a Greyhound bus. Then there was a long limousine waiting when I arrived, and everybody on the bus was looking and wondering who was gonna get into that. Then they came and got me and put me in there! I started doing a lot of clubs—amazing places like the Paradise Garage.

"Like I said, I'd had some success before getting involved with disco," she adds, "so I kind of had a bit of understanding about the attention. I'd been on the road with the Temptations, Donny Hathaway and Brasil '66 [Sergio Mendes], so this was sort of just a continuance of that experience. But it was fun. The most exciting thing about it was designing costumes that were so outrageous. Remember Amii Stewart? Her 'Knock on Wood' outfit was amazing. I never met her, but I loved that costume. The headdress was like a ram's head or something on her. Those were great days. That's what people were waiting for—the excitement of things like that. It was a very social time on the planet."

Geraldine, the mother of three children, passed her talents onto members of her family. Her son, Freddy James, was bursting with charisma from an early age. "I always took my kids and my mother with me wherever I toured or performed," says the artist. "My son Freddie was backstage with me, and he was very animated as a child. I was carrying my second child and would perform up until six or seven months into my pregnancy. During one of these shows, something happened when I was on stage, and the baby moved in a crazy way in my stomach while I was doing a song, disrupting my performance. René Angélil (Celine Dion's future husband) was backstage and saw what was happening, and—I don't know—he pushed Freddie out on the stage to distract the people. He slid out on the stage like Fred Astaire, and he started doing 'the robot' dance. The people went crazy! That was Freddie's introduction to show business. After that, it was easy to introduce him. It was unbelievable when he started to have hit records."

Hunt claims she never let fame or success get into her head or those of her kids. The artist says she made conscious choices to stay grounded throughout her journey. "The decisions we made in my career and Freddie's probably saved our lives," she insists. "They weren't always the ones I maybe thought I should have made. But in the end, as we stand here now, I think the right decisions were made. You know, there was a time we were making good money, but we'd still stay in a modest hotel. It wasn't the price of the expensive hotels that was a problem; we just felt comfortable in simpler surroundings. I still think that fancy stuff like that isn't necessary. I think being simpler, more conservative, makes it easier for me to be more compassionate about my brothers and sisters on this planet."

As the '80s progressed, Geraldine Hunt had still another trick up her sleeve. She and son Freddie partnered to produce the singer's daughter, Rosalind, who was teamed with a French girl named Lyn Cullerier. They became known as Cheri. The result of this collaboration was "Murphy's Law," which reached the number one spot on the dance chart and managed to be a sizeable U.S. pop hit in 1982. The clever lyrics and novelty, almost chipmunk-esque voices that were incorporated into the track added to the left-field charm of the hit. Singer Amy Roslyn replaced Cullerier on the rest of Cheri's recorded output, which included the club hits "Give It to Me Baby" and "Working Girl." "I had gotten into some trouble, some legal problems, with a few of my record labels," admits Hunt. "It was a real mess. I was basically put on suspension, and I wasn't allowed to record for anybody. Okay, I thought, no problem. I looked at my daughter Roz and Lyn Cullerier, and I got an idea. I tried it out on them, and it worked. The song was 'Murphy's Law.' I got a distribution company here to handle it, and Venture Records in the U.S. picked it up. My record label was shocked, thinking I was the voice recorded on it—

"Do anything and everything you want, but cause no harm," advises Geraldine Hunt. Inset photo shows son Freddie James, Geraldine Hunt and daughter Rosalind (who was once part of the duo Cheri) as a modern family today (courtesy Geraldine Hunt).

they didn't know I had a daughter. They were quite surprised I managed to do something without them—like sneaking out on a Saturday night and then returning to jail. That was how Roz's career got launched. We did some more tracks together, and it was fun. I was somewhat surprised by the success we had with it."

Geraldine identifies the qualities of her music that resonated so strongly with audiences, especially her gay fans. "I love gay people," she declares. "I grew up with gay people, and I have many who are in my life and are important to me. We are all one on this planet. So I tried to make sure my lyrics didn't isolate anyone and didn't say 'he' or 'she.' I tried to make sure my messages were simple—lyrics that had a beginning, middle and an end. I wanted my music to be useful like the music I grew up with. You could sing along with my lyrics, and the songs had a groove that was compatible with your heartbeat. If you played my songs in your car, they kind of rolled with the car too. All of those things were important—the feel of the track, the sincerity, the energy. Let's face it, I wasn't Celine Dion or Whitney, but I always tried to go straight to the heart of the matter and never to eliminate anybody."

Throughout the years, Hunt has tried to balance her career and music with her spiritual side. An avid follower of the ideas professed by Dolores Cannon (*The Three Waves of Volunteers and the New Earth*), the artist continuously seeks to forge her path on this planet with kindness and integrity. "I always try to keep my philosophy in focus," she says. "God knows we are supposed to be evolving. If I talk to you next week, your opinions should have changed. Everybody should be evolving and be responsible for the consequences of themselves and what they do. That is my philosophy—to evolve. Do anything and everything you want, but cause no harm." As Geraldine progresses on her personal journey, she also manages to enjoy some time in the studio, most recently recording a soulful track ("How Could You Do This") for *The Lovetown Allstars* album in 2013.

With enticing compositions, infectious beats and her distinctive vocal style, Geraldine Hunt has earned an honorable place in disco history. Encouraging listeners never to fake the feeling, her gutsy vocal style lent an air of authenticity to her ferocious musical material (at a time when dance floors needed that vital infusion). The artist is proud of the accomplishments that she and her family have achieved. Says Geraldine, "I would like people to remember the content, the delivery and the youthfulness of my music—the comfort and happiness that it brought them. Don't worry; we are going to dance and continue to dance in the streets—there will not be an ending!"

Carol Jiani
"Hit'n Run Lover"

"I am totally blessed to have 'Hit'n Run Lover' as my signature song, and I never get tired of it. It has kept me working, and I could sing that song even if I was in a coma!"—Carol Jiani

Uchenna Ikejiani may not be familiar to most disco enthusiasts, but mention her stage name, Carol Jiani, and the next words you're sure to hear are: "Hit'n Run Lover!" It's no wonder the connection is made so quickly. Written by Sandy Wilbur, arranged by Denis LePage, and produced by Joe La Greca (the latter two gentlemen the creative forces behind Lime's "Babe, We're Gonna Love Tonite," "Your Love," "Guilty," and many other Canadian dance classics), the track became an international sensation in 1981. It charged up *Billboard*'s disco chart to reach the number four spot and stayed in active club rotation for over half the year. "It was a happy, uplifting song, and I put my all into working on it! I am who I am today because of that song and that era. I am so lucky to have been a part of that movement indeed," says Carol, some 33 years later. Nearly as busy churning out dance music today as she was at the peak of her high-energy career, the singer enjoys looking back at the song that took clubland by storm.

Jiani describes her exploits in disco stardom with affection. It was a journey that began on the continent of Africa. "I was born in Nigeria," she says, "and had an amazingly privileged background. Both parents were in the medical profession. My dad was a pathologist surrounded by the best of everything, including access to a high profile, A-list of Nigerian musicians. My dad would throw grand parties and invite these artists to perform with bands, and I would hide and listen to them play instead of going to bed. I guess this was the beginning of my interest in music—it got into my bones in the end!" she laughs. "My dad worked closely with the leader of the Biafran War, and eventually that meant we were in danger as a family. He was a wanted man because of this, and we had to escape to Canada as landed immigrants."

Carol's exodus to Canada in the mid–'70s led her to studies at Concordia University in Montreal, where daydreams of being a singer grew increasingly vivid. "I think I was born a snob," she chuckles, "a drama queen! I guess I felt singing was a gift inside of me, so I thought it was possible I could be a success at it. I met my first producer, Joe La Greca, at the university when he came to visit [a fellow musician], and he gave me his card. I went to see him after that to talk. Some have called that meeting an audition, but it wasn't. I just went to discuss his plans. However, there was something bigger coming—my introduction to [the creators of the group] Lime." After honing her skills on some quick recordings under her original name, Jiani was poised to hit it big.

"The disco scene and the clubs in those days were fantastic. From the university we would go out to the clubs—the good old days when everyone, including me, would jump on those great speakers, dancing to the music, pretending that we were the artists performing. I was ready for disco. I remember everything that happened! Glenn LaRusso from Salsoul Records [who persuaded the artist to change her name to the more American-friendly Carol Jiani] played the song 'Hit'n Run Lover,' written by Sandy Wilbur, to producer Joe La Greca and the [Matra] label in Canada and said that this song would be great for me. Joe then told me he had a song and that he would make me a star. I was so excited," Carol recalls.

"We laid the vocals down in the living room that belonged to the amazing group Lime [husband and wife team Denis and Denyse LePage]—overlooking a fish tank! No one really knows this story! We recorded the vocals in their living room for that single, and we recorded the album later at the studio in Morin Heights, near Montreal. I know it sounds amazing, but that was where it all happened. They were an incredible team to work with. Legends! Can you imagine me with the group Lime? Denis was an absolute genius! Those strings, those cowbells in the intro, the whole arrangement—he was a wizard on keyboards! I had the most amazing time of my life. They were all amazing to work with, especially in the real recording studios. The passion was intense! The music was a powerful tool, and everything was uplifting. We were creative, we took our time, and we loved what we were doing. We knew it was going to be an instant hit!"

It was. "Hit'n Run Lover," with its swirling, lush orchestration and Motown-like analogies to bad intersections and speedy getaways in the middle of the night, was an unstoppable hit in the U.S. and Europe. It was an important recording and groundbreaking underground success that carefully bridged old school disco with the emerging high-energy sound coming out of Canada and England. Distributed in Canada under the Matra label, Ariola Records handled it on the U.S. side (though the company folded shortly after releasing their 12-inch version). Originally released with a running time of just over nine minutes, Matra released a slightly longer "MDR" version and followed it with a slightly shorter remix by Michel Simard (sometimes listed as Michael Simard). San Francisco's Moby Dick Records jumped in the game and released an even more elaborate remix by label owner Bill Motley, Craig Morey, W. *Michael Lewis* (of Rinder & Lewis) and "Trip" Ringwald.

Arranged by Denis LePage, the track had all of his trademark audio hallmarks. Now known as Nini Nobless, the gender-bending innovator recalls the origins of "Hit'n Run Lover." "It was great working with artists like Carol Jiani," says Nobless. "Carol is a great girl, a very classy person. Many people think I wrote 'Hit'n Run Lover,' but it was actually written by a woman named Sandy Wilbur. I met her in New York. She was living in Lake Placid, and she had a steady gig with MCA, as I recall. They had several floors at a commercial building in Manhattan. They had many offices and a studio that had a piano in it. They had several work-for-hire writers who would sit there playing the piano, writing songs like a nine to five job." Joe La Greca met with Sandy, who played [the song] and sang it. "I said, 'Fuck, that's a hit record!'" claims Nobless.

"[Joe] said he had a black singer from Nigeria that he had in mind for it," adds Nini. "Sandy gave him a cassette recording of the song right there, and Joe signed the papers to buy it. Joe took the cassette to my house back in Canada, and we recorded our tracks. Joe was a big influence with the Latin feel that's in the song. He always insisted on that, and I could play any style." For the production, La Greca had LePage hire a saxophone player and a drummer, and Denis played the piano and the bass line on the Moog. LePage arranged the song and did all the rest that was required to fashion it into a smash hit.

"Carol came in to sing, and she was very professional," adds Nobless. "She had a very strong voice. We actually recorded off the living room, in a room adjacent to the living room, so that the speakers wouldn't leak into the microphone. She was in that area all by herself, and I was in the living room with the eight-track, recording her voice over the tracks I had recorded. It came out great. The song took off like fucking crazy!"

"Hit'n Run Lover" caught on with the gay underground clubs first, pulling Fire Island partiers onto the dance floor in droves that summer, and, as word spread, the track crossed over to the national disco charts. "It sold so many copies!" Carol claims with excitement still in her voice. "It went to number one in France and was a hit in many, many countries. It went gold in Canada, and it is still selling today. It's been remixed almost every single year since 1981. I knew that I had arrived when I performed the song at Studio 54 and when I was presented with my gold records. I toured so many places. I guess the only thing bad about the experience was leaving fans after performing and moving on to the next show. I'd always want to stay longer with my new found families!"

The album *Hit'n Run Lover* quickly went into production, and the results were stellar. Featuring several tracks written by Wilbur, including "High Cost of Loving" and "The Woman in Me," the LP had a distinctively heavy beat sound that became the signature of LePage and La Greca productions. DJs jumped on nearly everything the platter offered. Aside from the monumental title track, the dynamic Pete Bellotte/Sylvester Levay composition "Mercy" was the clear favorite, sending Jiani back onto the disco charts. Says Jiani, "Although 'Hit'n Run Lover' is the big classic, lots of DJs tell me they love 'Mercy.' The fact that it was written by the same team [that had written hits for] Donna Summer was a great bonus too. It is still requested today when I perform. I was really lucky to get this song as well." "Mercy" had a zippier orchestration than its predecessor, and that thick Canadian disco flavor sounded magnificent booming in the clubs, where Jiani dominated the summer and fall seasons.

Now a force to be reckoned with, Carol began touring everywhere. "I think the best time or event of my career was when I performed at Studio 54," she recalls. "The only way I can describe it was that it was like the Garden of Eden, where everyone was free and happy. I travelled, sometimes with fans, in limousines all the way from Chicago to New York. The most amazing thing happened to me one night when I went to the Copa in Fort Lauderdale and, my God,

"I knew that I had arrived when I performed the song at Studio 54," says singer Carol Jiani, whose "Hit'n Run Lover" single was an international smash in 1981 (courtesy Carol Jiani).

Sylvester walked past me, brushed by me, and said, "So you're Carol Jiani!" He knew who I was! I will never forget that! He was a wild and an amazing artist. He is so missed.

"I am totally blessed to have 'Hit'n Run Lover' as my signature song, and I never get tired of it. It has kept me working, and I could sing that song even if I was in a coma!" she laughs. "It brings back great memories when we were all having fun—back when they had great melodies. You knew what songs were coming on within a second of hearing the first riff!" Carol cites Sylvester's "You Make Me Feel (Mighty Real)" and Vicki Sue Robinson's "Turn the Beat Around" as two disco era classics with that distinctive sound and hits she would have liked to have been given an opportunity to record.

Coming up with a follow-up as impactful as her remarkable debut would be tough. Utilizing the same production crew, the album *Ask Me* was released by Matra in 1982. The title track, a remake of the Barbara Roy/Ecstasy, Passion & Pain '70s disco hit, was favored in the clubs, but the excitement that had been generated by "Lover" was in shorter supply. The pressure of having a worthy successor to "Hit'n Run Lover" didn't faze Jiani much. "God, I was so young and having too much fun to worry about anything like chart positions," she claims. "I didn't think about it too much; I was just having fun with the music. I guess in the back of one's mind you always want that follow-up hit, but, then again, I was too busy working and enjoying making music to worry about it really. It is great, though, to have a hit in the clubs—that meant you would keep working.

I was lucky! I had a classic to fall back on always. I was lucky that in America the clubs were really kind to me. They were so important for breaking the songs in those days." Another single called "X-Rated" was released, and it kept interest in her sophomore project simmering for a while longer.

It's a bit inaccurate to imply that Jiani missed out on a second blockbuster. Late in 1981, an unknown artist named "Suzy Q" was credited as the vocalist of a tremendous disco hit called "Get on Up Do It Again," a Top Five smash single on the dance chart released in the U.S. on Atlantic Records. As the quirky, funky track was packing floors, three different vocalists were reportedly recruited to handle various Suzy Q live appearances (notably Michelle Mills, who recorded the album material and re-recorded the single as "Get on Up *and* Do It Again"). Carol asserts she was the actual vocalist on the original version, "Get on Up Do It Again."

"George Cucuzzella's [of Unidisc/Matra Records] brother, Jerry Cucuzzella, brought me to the studio with his team, and I sang 'Get on Up Do It Again,' almost as it was being written. Making a long diva story short, it was released on Atlantic Records and became a hit in America. For some reason, another singer was hired to tour using my vocals, etc. I was so young then. That would never happen to me today, and I would know better than to let it happen. The story was that I was under contract [she laughs] with Matra, and they wanted me to concentrate on 'Hit'n Run Lover.' Somebody get me the wine, please!" she smirks, with a touch of annoyance in her voice. "Okay, breathing deeply, but hey, it was another hit with my vocals. I should have been credited and wish it had gone out under my name. Are you ready for this for madness? I re-recorded it again with the same producer many years later! That's bliss dear!" Carol smiles.

The worldwide gay community proved to be loyal followers of the artist's high-energy sound, and members of this eclectic population were among the first record buyers to recognize the potential of her releases in the early '80s. They still support her work today, and Carol acknowledges this significant part of her fan base. "It is amazing being supported by so many gay fans. I never ever thought anything of anything, if that makes sense. All I saw was that I was having fun. It was only later on over the years that people started to use the label 'gay' and say to me that I had a large gay following. To tell you the truth, it has never bothered me; I never wished it were different. It would be like asking if I am bothered that I am black!" she laughs. "I have the best following—period. If it were not for the gay community, I would not be who I am today. We are all equal and all God's children—brothers and sisters—and we must look after each other!"

She certainly gave her fans plenty of material to enjoy. Following her breakthrough success, Carol delivered a string of notable club hits. She released an EP in 1984 called *Dancing in the Rain*, another project by La Greca. The single "Touch and Go Lover" was derivative of "Hit'n Run Lover" only in name and bubbled with a uniquely punchy drive that sparked the dance floor (thanks to a sharp mix by Shep Pettibone). Her rendition of the Thelma Houston nugget "Don't Leave Me This Way" caused a strong buzz as well. The artist's partnership with her Canadian crew ended following this release, and Carol made her way to England to work with Ian Levine and Fiachra Trench (who had scored a monster hit with Evelyn Thomas' "High Energy"). She recorded the songs "Vanity" and "Turning My Back and Walking Away."

"It was not risky to leave the Canadian team," Carol observes. "Everybody moved on. I came to England because my mum was based here and was ill, so I looked after her until her death in 2007. Ian was responsible for signing me to a major label in 1987—MCA Records in the U.K. [with "Such a Joy Honey"]. Mr. Levine was a genius too; he knew his stuff! He was an amazing DJ and a great man to work with in the studio, my favorite place to be."

Throughout the late '80s and '90s, Carol enjoyed numerous club hits, including a successful 1988 U.K. remix of "Hit'n Run Lover," a retake of the Rose Royce classic "Car Wash," and even the 1995 song "Superstar," a re-teaming with the LePage and La Greca duo. As for recording in the modern day, she admits, "I loved the good old days the best really, but technology has made it easier today. But you cannot beat live instrumentation. I think artists were happier in those days too!"

In the 21st century, Jiani scored a dance hit with a remake of Jocelyn Brown's "Somebody Else's Guy" and gave an infectious performance on a revisit of Company B's mainstay, "Fascinated." In 2011, she had a major hit on the digital front with a new track called "No More" and, you guessed it, an update of "Hit'n Run Lover." 2013 saw the release of the dance single "Putting a Brave Face On," and most recently she provided guest vocals on "Hold That Sucker Down" by Jason Parker meets Maxwell.

She laughs about one of the more explicit digital tracks of her recent recording career. "One day we were recording with Ian Levine and the late Clive Scott from the group Jigsaw at his studio. We were recording a song called 'Everybody Funk Now.' So messing about as you do in the studios sometimes, I was tired, and I changed it to 'Everybody Fuck Now.' Good Lord, I would record almost anything for publicity—good or bad, it is all publicity. Hey, we are all human, and we get carried away sometimes. But I am cautious now of certain lyrics. That was a just a diva moment," she laughs, "naughty moi!"

Her success in the recording industry has been tempered with more than her share of lost monies and unfortunate experiences with managers of questionable integrity, but she takes it all in her stride. "I think when you're young and do not understand the business side and don't have someone to guide you, it's inevitable that you will get ripped off. It has happened to most of us, and it is still happening today. I remained focused and kept moving on—and I am still working today. [Because of 'Hit'n Run Lover'], I am making double what the enemy took from me. A classic can never be taken from you, so you come to terms [with injustices] and move on," she calmly says.

Her tone revives a bit when she speaks about the passionate connection she has today with life, music and her personal philosophies. "Music for me has always been a powerful tool, but it wasn't always easy. Leaving my mum every weekend, after spending the day caring for her, was the worst. Especially when I'd have to then go on stage and do the diva business. It was very hard. However, music took me to a different level when I lost my mum," she states. "I enjoy using music to reach the masses to help get things back as they were. [My goal is to] reach out to the youth, to get the melodies back in music, and, most of all, give back to those in need. That is what moves me.

"For example, I fight for better standards of living in Africa. I have lost so many friends in the business to AIDS, so, every World AIDS Day, I campaign and help raise more funds to support those in need. There is so much stigma still surrounding those with HIV and this must stop. I'm also focusing on Nigeria and raising funds for the

'Carol Jiani Medical Mobile Clinic for Nigeria.' We need this to go into the villages of Nigeria and treat the poor that cannot afford medical care and treatment. A great cause saving lives—and everyone deserves the very best possible medical care. Without health, we have nothing. So that is my focus!" In 2013, Jiani went so far as to auction off her gold single award for the track "The Woman in Me" to raise money for her cause.

"As for who I am today, well, I try to stay happy. My vocals have matured through my experiences in life, like losing my mother. I really put my all into my vocal work now. In some ways I haven't changed—I am still as humble as ever! [I stopped counting birthdays] at 25—that is how old I am—and how old I will always be!" she chuckles. "And guess what—red wine works for me! I control it though; it does not control me! I am careful about that sort of thing. I think it is because my parents were strict medical doctors who warned me to stay away from drugs. Plus, I have no interest in them. I stick with having red wine and a few spirits. I would also love to get back to acting, especially 'Nollywood Films'—movies made in and for Nigeria. Oh, and I am a frustrated florist! I am serious. I love flowers, dear! Just let me arrange those flowers at a wedding and perform afterward," she laughs heartily.

Carol Jiani is one of those rare, gifted vocalists who helped define the changing sound of disco in the early '80s and, in the process, created a masterpiece with "Hit'n Run Lover." As the song enjoys a revered place in the pantheon of dance classics, the artist ponders her personal legacy. "I really want to be remembered as someone that brought joy to the dance floors and the world and someone who set a new standard— someone who walked and worked with giants in the genre and in the music business. I'd like to be remembered as an artist that made a difference and gave back to society. I will always be grateful to the DJs, radio stations and clubs that played my music, the producers I worked with—well, the list is so vast. Most importantly, I want to be remembered as someone who always appreciated her fans. I must say it again—if it were not for them, I would not be who I am. Love is the principal thing!"

Janice Marie Johnson, formerly of A Taste of Honey
"Boogie Oogie Oogie"

"I think there are no mistakes in the universe, and it happened just the way it was supposed to."—Janice Marie Johnson

"I am proud to be called disco! Disco was an era of music that brought joy to everyone. There was no color line with this music. The other genres separated people, but with disco, everyone came together. It was almost like a civil rights movement, where it didn't matter what your color or sexual preference was. We all partied together. Disco played a very important role in America's musical history," says Janice Marie Johnson. She's come a long way since the days when her group, A Taste of Honey, sent dancers charging in droves onto nightclub floors with just the first plucks of the bass strings from their monumental hit "Boogie Oogie Oogie." The group won the Grammy award in 1979 for Best New Artist, but it was just one of many highs (and a few lows) the artist experienced during this tumultuous era. Though always anxious to remind the world that A Taste of Honey was never solely defined by any one sound or hit, Janice warmly embraces her disco heritage and shares some of her memories of life in dance and pop music's fast lane.

Johnson first formed A Taste of Honey with longtime friend Perry Kibble in Los Angeles during the early '70s. According to the artist, the band's name was not directly derived from a movie or song title, but was actually the idea of a fellow musician she remembers being named "Smokey" (from a small band with whom she was briefly connected). Perry and Janice quickly went to work honing their craft. "I would play bass, and he would play keyboards," Johnson recalls. "I have to admit, I did not know a lot about the instrument. But he taught me, and we played around town for about six months doing local talent shows. After a while, I told Perry we really needed a guitar player and that I had the perfect girl—Carlita Dorhan, who was a member of my earlier singing group called Soundstage #1, the predecessor to A Taste of Honey. He thought it was a great idea, but the catch was, it turned out, she didn't know how to play guitar. Perry knew how to play most any instrument really well, so he taught her how to play it." Though the group would change some personnel over the following years, they continued to grow and eventually connected with the Department of Defense, performing on USO tours.

"When Carlita announced she was going to quit the group," says Janice, "the search began for a new guitar player. Carlita agreed to stay with us until we found a replacement for her. I had met Hazel Payne, who was performing in another band. She was content in that group, but I kept trying to coax her to join ours. We were becoming pretty successful as a local band, and eventually, I believe sometime late in 1975, Carlita left, and Hazel joined us. Hazel was used to being in the background, but when she joined us she just rose to the occasion. We had our routines, and we needed to sing and play our instruments at the same time, and she picked it up on that immediately. Well, we finally had our complete band—two females, drums, guitar, bass and keyboards. We became the house band for the Etcetera Club in Los Angeles, where we were discovered by Capitol Records."

Johnson's path soon caught up with the explosion of disco music that had engulfed the country. The group's 1978 self-titled debut album scored a stunning number one dance and R&B smash with the infectious, bass-fused single "Boogie Oogie Oogie," a song that would reportedly go on to sell over two million copies. The track, written by Perry and Janice, bumped Frankie Valli's "Grease" out of *Billboard*'s top spot on the singles chart and gave the group its breakthrough signature pop hit.

"'Boogie Oogie Oogie' came about while we were performing at a military base, as I recall," states Johnson. "I think we may have already had our record deal and were in the studio working on the album. 'Boogie Oogie Oogie' was one of the last songs added to that album. We had a show at March Air Force Base for which we learned all the Top 40 songs. Well, we got on the stage and were playing these hits, and nobody was dancing. It didn't dawn on me that the audience might have been somewhat mesmerized

"We were formed long before disco started; we didn't come along to jump on the bandwagon," says Janice Marie Johnson (far right), seen here with A Taste of Honey bandmates Carlita Dorhan and Perry Kibble in the early '70s (courtesy Janice Marie Johnson).

that two females were leading our band. I was thinking we worked so hard to learn all these new hits, and all the crowd was doing was staring at us." Janice stands and recreates the moment that she was inspired to stir up her stoic audience. She places her hand on her hip (imitating the authoritative stance she had taken with the crowd), shakes her index finger disapprovingly, and recites the lyrics, word-for-word, that kick off her famous song. "Little did I know I had just created the entire first verse of our hit song, 'Boogie Oogie Oogie.' They all got up and danced!" she says with satisfaction.

"It was a good thing I had recorded the audio of the show that night. I got back to the motel—I won't say hotel—and was listening to the audio. I heard all the people jumping to the dance floor, and I started playing with a bass line. I called Perry, who was the co-writer, and told him I thought I was onto something and told him to come over to my room. He listened to my idea, and he thought I had something too. Perry started putting an arrangement to it, and that's how the song came to be. I remember we were in the studio recording it, and as they were tweaking the sound in another room, I just started jamming and playing the intro bass line. They had already pressed the record button in the other room and told me, 'Do that intro again Janice!' I didn't know what I had really done, so they hit playback and said, 'This is what you did—do that again!' So that's how the bass intro came about. I remember I was just getting over a cold, and I had a little rasp in my voice. After I sang it down, I asked to do it again. They said, 'No, we want that.' That scratch vocal is the only vocal that exists on the master. One shot—one time!"

Almost overnight, lead singers Janice and Hazel became disco's premiere super female duo. "We used to visit the discos after we'd finish our gigs at Etcetera. We knew about the music, but we were never 'disco' in our minds. We performed a variety of music," explains Johnson. "But now that we were being branded as disco stars—I hated it. We were a show band, and we were trying to get ourselves to the showrooms of Vegas. Disco wasn't going to get you there back then. We just had in our heads that if you get to Vegas, you've made it. We didn't realize that if you get to the top of the *Billboard* chart, maybe that meant you've made it too!" she laughs. "We felt the name disco was very limiting, and we felt it was unfair because we were doing so well on the pop chart. But they didn't call us pop artists. They didn't call us R&B artists when we topped the R&B chart. Even when 'Sukiyaki' hit the top of the Easy Listening chart, they still called us disco.

"'Boogie Oogie Oogie' was just meant to be an up-tempo song," the artist insists. "Back then, anything up-tempo was considered disco. Yes, it was a danceable song, but were we trying to do a disco arrangement? I don't think so. There were groups back then that were formed to *be* disco. We were formed long before disco started; we didn't come along to jump on the bandwagon. I don't think it's a disco song, but I do have a different attitude about calling it disco today. Now I say, 'Call it whatever you want; just call!'"

Reaching the top of the charts opened a whole new world for Johnson and much of it was challenging. "Let me tell you a story about being number one on the *Billboard* charts," she says knowingly. "I was on the road somewhere, and I got a call from Larkin Arnold, the A&R executive who signed A Taste of Honey to Capitol Records. (He was also the one who told me to change the name of 'Boogie Oogie Oogie' because it was too elementary, and he was also the one who told me to take the braids out of my hair because it was too ethnic.) He was so excited and told me, 'Janice, you're number one on *Billboard*!' I said, 'Great! That's fantastic. Tell me one thing—what's *Billboard*?'

"We're just out of doing small club gigs and burst into this whole other arena, which we were not prepared for—especially in regard to our roadies and technical crew, who were used to handling small nightclubs. We lost so much equipment because they couldn't handle the change in caliber. We went from working at small clubs to opening for the Commodores, who, at that time, were a major act. I remember we were on a show with them, LTD, and Con Funk Shun. There was drama going on within the group because we didn't have management, and everybody had their own idea of what we should be doing next.

"I think there are no mistakes in the universe and it happened just the way it was supposed to," she continues. "It might have been better to climb the ranks slowly, but if you go too slow you can lose your momentum. Who's to say? I was so naïve though—not realizing all your songs don't get to number 1. We were very selective and I remember somebody from a publishing company had presented a song to us called 'Boogie Wonderland,' which we turned down. Not that we would have done it the way Earth, Wind & Fire and the Emotions did it, but I'm sure we could have put together a nice little version of it. But we said, 'Oh no, we're a self-contained group. We write the songs we do.'"

Johnson, though new to the ways of the recording industry, was savvy enough to retain the publishing rights on her compositions. "I was one of the lucky ones," she admits. "A lot of people did not secure their publishing and didn't know to ask. I had a few people pull on my coattails along the way about a few things, and I'm thankful for that. A young man from the group Rufus & Chaka Khan, André Fischer, was going through some issues at the time, and he let me know a few things about contracts and things like that. I didn't know a lot, but I knew about publishing."

The group's highly anticipated follow-up album, *Another Taste*, followed in 1979, yielding the single "Do It Good." Though a popular track in the clubs, the song didn't enjoy significant crossover success. Janice says the pressure to have another hit was felt, mostly because of the departure of Larkin Arnold from Capitol Records. "We weren't represented anymore. Larkin had left Capitol after signing a lot of successful artists for them, and he went over to Epic Records because it was time for him to climb his ladder. Meanwhile, we were dangling on ours. The people that came in afterwards couldn't decide on the next record, and we were lost for quite a while. Our second album only sold about 450,000 copies, which today would be a great success, but then—not so much. I remember being upset with Capitol that they couldn't push it another 50,000 units. [The public was] burning disco records, and I felt we were in jeopardy of being let go from the label. To be classified as disco was almost a death sentence. There was a lot of pressure to come up with another hit, but I was too busy trying to keep my head on straight. Everyone in the group had their own ideas about the music and management, and that's the problem when you have a group. We had four different personalities and opinions. That's why we ended up having a third album without the guys."

Twice as Sweet was released in 1980, and though the set contained funky dance material, like the club hit "Rescue Me," it was Johnson's choice of the ballad "Sukiyaki" that brought the group back to the top of the pop charts and the R&B survey, where it reached number one. "It showed that we were more than disco, which was important. There was a time I didn't even realize artists could sing other people's material because we had always written our own. But when I realized this was an option, I immediately thought of 'Sukiyaki.' [The version by Kyu Sakamoto in 1963] was the first 7-inch record I ever bought. I visualized how it could be done. By the time of our third album, Dr.

Cecil Hale was over at Capitol (and was our new executive producer), and I invited him over to my house to hear my arrangement idea. I played it for him, and he said, 'Absolutely not! Black people don't want to hear Japanese music.' I was stunned and so sure he would like it. I looked at him and said, 'Last time I looked in the mirror, I'm black, and I want to hear it!'" she laughs. "He was strictly an R&B guy. George Duke was our producer for the album, and he thought we could do a kind of up-tempo version of it. I said no and that I wanted it as a love ballad, which is how it was done. He did a fantastic arrangement for it.

"George did an interview later on that's on YouTube, and he tells how important that song was to his career. He wasn't as well known at the time he worked with us, and he was very nervous about producing A Taste of Honey. But 'Sukiyaki' was such a hit that it made his phone ring as a producer, and he gives me the credit for being persistent about that song. Radio had everything to do with the song being a hit—they pulled it off the album. So, finally, Capitol Records got on board and put the song out as a single."

In 1982, A Taste of Honey released their final album, *Ladies of the Eighties*, which scored a modest hit with "I'll Try Something New," again favoring the Asian flavor of "Sukiyaki." In 1985, a remix of their classic "Boogie Oogie Oogie" found favor in the U.K., but by then the group had largely faded from view. "A Taste of Honey never really ended," says the singer. "I formed the band in 1971, and I've never played in any other. When Hazel quit in 1983 to follow her own dream, I was kind of a lost soul. The record company had some kind of a deficit against A Taste of Honey, and all of the bills were being directed to me. Capital just kept adding their bills to our artist royalty deficit. It was crazy, and I needed a break. I didn't want to put out a solo record [*One Taste of Honey* in 1984] because all I ever knew was the group dynamic of A Taste of Honey. But Capitol put the album out, and it did make a little noise. However, there were a lot of problems with the promotion of it and all sorts of drama going on there. All politics. By then, not only was there the A Taste of Honey deficit, there was an additional deficit for the *One Taste of Honey* LP. Capitol Records directed all deficits to me, while everyone else was living their lives.

"I eventually filed bankruptcy and started doing other kinds of work—including being a limo driver. While waiting for clients who were partying and such, I would work on a toy designing business I wanted to start. People thought I was crazy, but they didn't understand how annoyed I was by the politics of the music industry at this point. Driving the limo, I was pretty much incognito. I had on my hat and dark shades. I had a few crazy experiences. I was good at it because I've been in both seats of the limo. I did a 24-hour run with a group of guys who wanted to go all over—Vegas, Big Bear, Santa Monica –and I decided to call in for a relief driver because I was just too tired to go on. Turns out the group of guys pulled some kind of robbery after I left and got caught. Everyone, including the relief driver (who was innocent), was arrested. That could have been me! Yeah, I had a lot of experiences—that's not even the half of it!" she laughs.

"I kept up with my toy work and finally caught a break. I intercepted a toy company executive at an airport—I knew he was flying out after a toy convention in the area the day before—and I laid out my line of products on the floor in front of him as he was catching his plane. Right then and there he agreed to give me a toy designer deal. I had my own brand and everything—Soft Sounds by Janice Marie," she says proudly.

"When all the great bass players of the world are playing your bass line—*wow!*" says Janice Marie Johnson, reflecting on the legacy of her hit "Boogie Oogie Oogie" (photograph by Michael O'Connor, courtesy Janice Marie Johnson).

Janice continues to sing live as A Taste of Honey. She released CD music projects called *Hiatus of the Heart* and *Until the Eagle Falls* in the first years of the 21st century and is working on newly recorded material. As a woman of Stockbridge-Munsee-Mohican heritage, she is the recipient of many awards from Native American organizations for her musical work. Johnson has energy and drive to spare and is extremely comfortable with where she is in life.

"There is nothing wrong with aging," she insists. "If you are blessed, you will age. To still be here and to be able to take advantage of opportunities—that's nothing but God at work. I know a lot of people that have allowed themselves to get a little out of shape and have a few problems with aging, but you have to work at it. I work out two or three times a week. If it were easy, then everyone would do it. That's what makes you special—the fact that you can rise to the occasion. Sugar is my weakness. However, I bite down on an apple before I hit that chocolate cake! Mentally, the energy you put out is what you get back. So if you stay positive, you attract positive things to you. Who wants to be around negative energy? If you can take positive actions and help others—how hard is that to do? If you try, you will continue to be blessed."

The members of A Taste of Honey have the distinction of being the celebrated voices and musicians behind one of disco's greatest hits. "Boogie Oogie Oogie" remains one of the genre's most important contributions to pop music, and Janice is proud of her work. "When you do the concerts and everybody is singing your words, it's amazing," she says, her voice filled with warmth. "When all the great bass players of the world are playing your bass line—*wow*! I found out the bass line is part of the curriculum at a college out here on the west coast, and the school administrator told me that all enrolled bass players are required to learn my bass line from 'Boogie.' I've been told I have also inspired many women.

"As far as Janice Marie Johnson goes, I just want to be remembered as an incredible mom," she chuckles. "The music is great, but it's not what is most important to me. My family, my friends—they are the most important things to me. They were there with me when things were up and things were down. If people can just remember that I was here, I would be grateful. The music will live on long past my time, and I am very grateful for that. I was blessed that I was able to put something to pen and paper that will go on after me. I can't ask for anything more than that."

•••••••••••••••••••••••••••••

France Joli
"Come to Me"

"Once you have a song go up the dance charts and cross over to pop, it's a whole different ball game."—France Joli

Canadian France Joli caused an absolute sensation when she crossed from club charts to the pop charts during the height of '70s disco fever. Disco music was at its hippest and approaching its pinnacle as the sultry-looking young blonde star became a fresh new face on the scene. Though merely 16 years old at the time, Joli had a voice that pulsated with remarkable maturity and emotion. Her first and biggest hit, the Top 20 classic "Come to Me," resonated as much with girls and guys charging to club dance floors in the cities and suburbs of middle America as it did with the gay underground that first embraced the singer's innocent charisma. In Europe, her charms were equally appreciated. Once radio caught on, her horizon seemed limitless. Today, France acknowledges both the astonishing thrill ride disco stardom created as well as the challenges that came with achieving fame at such a young age.

Joli was born in Montreal, Canada, and wasted no time displaying a predilection for entertainment. "I started singing when I was very, very young—before I even started to talk. As the years went by, by the age of four, I was saying to my mom, 'I want to be an international star!'" France laughs, adding that she spoke only French during early childhood. "To this day, I don't even know how I understood the word 'international,' but that's what I kept saying. I wanted to be a singer, and I had a mother that loved show business and music. My grandmother was an opera singer—not that she was famous, but she had the talent—so the love of music was in my family. My mom started having me do some amateur shows here in Montreal and tried to get me some exposure."

By about the age of 13, Joli was signed with her first manager, a gentleman named Lee Gagnon, who was focused on refining the young girl's charms in preparation for a full-on show business career. "He was amazing," she says. "He groomed me and taught me so much—how to wear high heels, how to stand properly. He enrolled me in ballet classes and sent me to live with an English-speaking family so I could learn how to properly speak the language. All these activities felt normal to me. I knew I was investing time in something that would help me with what I wanted to do later on. He got me singing on a few jingles, but my mom and I wanted more. So we started shopping around for a manager or a producer, and finally we met someone who introduced us to Tony Green."

The young singer's relationship with writer-producer Tony Green was inspired from the outset. He was well aware of her fondness for Barbra Streisand recordings and quickly recognized her remarkable ability to convey the sentiment of torch songs. So impressed was he with her vocal prowess that Green immediately went to work creating an original song for the young singer. "Three days later 'Come to Me' was written and handed to me," she recalls. "It was quite amazing! He called me and said he had a song made especially for me and wanted me to hear it. He played it on a guitar for me. I still have that recording because he gave me the tape so that I could practice the song at home. I remember thinking the melody sounded like it *was* truly tailor-made for me. I felt that it was meant for me. I was so thrilled about the song. I had to practice it, take it step by step, but during that time I never imagined that the song was going to make *Billboard's* Top 20. Going into the studio with Tony was already so surreal and wonderful for me at that age that I never even thought of hitting the charts with it.

"My experience in the studio made me really feel like a little girl. Well, I *was* a young girl, but it made me feel even younger because I felt vulnerable. It was my first time interpreting something that really was an original song and important to me. In the end, what you are hearing on this record is all about vulnerability and the will to succeed. It's all in there. It wasn't hard for me to convey those emotions because it was all so exciting for me at the time, and I wanted the song to sound real. I'm going to tell you a little secret. When I was very young, like about seven, I used to put 45s on a record player, and I would look at myself in the mirror and mimic the song. I think we even have some Super 8 films of this. My mom would tell me she was amazed that I could mimic the expression of the song despite being too young to understand the lyrics. But they were all love songs, torch songs. So I believe it's a gift I had, and it carried me through my adult life. Later, of course, as an adult you draw on your own emotions and maturity. I think that ability made me able to sing 'Come to Me' in an authentic way," France explains.

The unique qualities of the song were enhanced by the presence of Green, who performed the grittier, rock-tinged male vocal heard midway through the track. "Tony Green wrote a male part for 'Come to Me,'" recalls France, "and he decided to sing it. When he came to me with this song and the others we did, I had this complete trust in him, and when he said there'd be some male vocals in the song—for me it made sense. It made sense that his writing and artistry would include his voice on the record, and I was totally pleased with that. I thought it was a great touch."

Three other extended songs were prepared for the 1979 self-titled debut album (that was recorded in Montreal), and all were written, arranged and produced by Green (who also had a sizeable club hit at the same time with the youthful Freddie James' "Get Up & Boogie" and "Hollywood"). The album was shopped to major U.S. labels like Warner Bros. and Columbia, but a deal was eventually signed with the rising independent folks at Prelude Records, who had begun having a strong presence in the dance music market. The label first promoted the single "Come to Me" to gay audiences. The gay contingent was, unquestionably, an essential barometer of what would and would not make it in disco.

France Joli heats up the crowd on Fire Island as her hit song "Come to Me" begins its breakout journey to the top of the disco charts (photograph by Charles R. Moniz, used by permission).

Joli observes, "I believe that 'Come to Me' was jump-started by the LGBT (Lesbian-Gay-Bisexual-Transgender) community. I have no doubt about that! My first American performance of 'Come to Me'—actually, my first public performance of the song *ever*—was on Fire Island on July 7, 1979, in front of 5,000 gay men, plus a few of their straight friends, at a benefit that has become infamously known as 'Beach '79.' Donna Summer was supposed to perform that night but had to bow out at the last minute. My record company heard about her cancellation and saw an opportunity. It was my first time performing in front of the gay community, and it was quite wild and eye opening! Imagine so many men cheering you on when basically your record isn't even out yet—it's just playing in the clubs. I'm not going to ever say that it was *only* the gay crowd that loved 'Come to Me'; the straight response was tremendous too. Performing in front of gay and straight crowds is equally amazing, but the gay community unquestionably put me on the map. The relationship I have with the LGBT community will always be there, and they have been very loyal to me—and I have been very loyal to them!" Joli's appearance on Fire Island that summer, blonde hair and white dress blowing in the ocean breezes, created a strikingly memorable visual to accompany the beat and electrifying vocal work the artist had unleashed upon the party-happy community.

The stirring, infectiously rhythmic single "Come to Me" vaulted to the number one position on *Billboard*'s disco chart thanks, in part, to rapid, widespread DJ play at the likes of Studio 54 and other major dance clubs. The combination of her youthful age, beautiful appearance and an irresistible song generated a wave of media attention. The singer was soon seen on television mainstays of the day like *The Merv Griffin Show*, Dinah Shore's show, Bob Hope specials, *Good Morning America* and *The Midnight Special*. The song quickly started climbing the all-important U.S. pop charts, peaking at number 15. Joli began an extensive tour that took her all across America, Canada and Europe, where the song was enjoying great popularity in—you guessed it—France.

"Once you have a song go up the dance charts and cross over to pop," she claims, "it's a whole different ball game. I remember when it crossed over, I had been performing it at clubs and such. Then it started getting radio airplay. It was on WKTU and WBLS in New York. Once that happens, the song just starts taking you all over the world. It's really quite remarkable what happens."

At the time, the artist had no hesitation about being branded a rising disco music star. "Disco was handed to me on a silver platter," she says. "When I was 15, having listened to so much Barbra Streisand and so many ballads, I had been leaning towards being a torch singer. But when 'Come to Me' came along, it really opened up my horizon. I really felt it *was* a torch song—one with a disco beat. It suited me so well. It pleased me. For me, to go into disco music was very hip, and yet it was a song I could actually sing with all of my heart. It was a perfect situation for me. And I loved disco back then. I loved dancing. I knew all the dance records by Donna Summer, the Bee Gees, KC and the Sunshine Band, and all of the other great artists of that era. Disco was a great avenue for me!

"It was euphoric when I saw the song climbing the *Billboard* charts, and I remember having this great feeling about it. But I was also telling my mom, 'This is too beautiful; this is too amazing for this to happen. Something bad has to happen because this is so big.' It was almost like it was too good to be happening to *me* and especially at such a young age. My mom would say, 'Don't say that!'" she laughs, "but it was *that* surreal to me."

France pauses. She begins thinking about the blur that became her young life at the height of her fame. "When you are so young and surrounded by people in the business, you just go through the motions and don't even think for yourself. You have a show—you go. You have an appointment—you go. You're just in that wave, and the ocean is taking you and you just do what you have to do. There were times when I got so busy and so involved in everything that I just lost those moments. They just went right past me because I was so tired or so distracted. Some people have asked me if I remember doing this or that, and I just don't. It's today that I most appreciate the success I had back then."

By the time Joli's second album, *Tonight*, was ready for release by Prelude, the media war cry against disco and public exhaustion with the genre was in full swing. The pressure was on Joli and her management to address the situation. Produced and largely written again by Green, the LP attempted to find a balance by mixing rock, light sounds and dance. A ballad, "This Time (I'm Giving All I've Got)" was chosen as a single in an attempt to appeal to the changing preferences of the pop charts, but the mainstream failed to notice it. France's fan base in the clubs provided some consolation by remaining highly receptive to the artist's energized work, and the soaring, majestic single "Heart to Break the Heart" (now considered a classic, just like her debut single) and its companion track, "Feel Like Dancing," brought the singer back to the Top Five of the dance chart.

Despite this qualified success, it was a difficult time for Joli. She observes, "At the time of my second album, the disco backlash had occurred, and I actually went into a little bit of a panic. 'Come to Me' was a disco song, disco had started to fade from the mainstream, and I was recognized as a disco singer. I had to come up with something that was going to be pleasing to the audience I had attracted and that would also address the changes that were going on with music. They want more of the same, but yet they *don't* want the same. It was extremely hard and frustrating. I think a lot of artists went through this. Look at Sheena Easton back then. She had that massive hit 'Morning Train.' People expected her to keep delivering songs like that. The expectations of the fans and the public can really limit you as an artist. You can't keep re-doing 'Come to Me.' You can't keep recreating the same song with the same vibe and magic. I think that's when a lot of artists start making mistakes by trying to do the same thing over and over. Ultimately we fail because we do it out of fear. You're fearful that if you go into another genre or do something a little different, your fans will reject you."

Still signed with Prelude, Joli parted ways with Tony Green and teamed with producers William Anderson and Ray Reid of the group Crown Heights Affair in 1981. As funk and more soulful dance sounds dominated the landscape, she released the album *Now*, which incorporated these trends. The single "Gonna Get over You" was an intoxicating blend of funky disco and stylish arrangements with more of the yearning, passionate vocal sound Joli had branded. The clubs responded almost immediately, sending the song to the number two position on *Billboard*'s club chart in the summer of that year. The pop charts, however, remained unimpressed.

"I always felt the potential of 'Gonna Get over You'—if it had been given the proper push and I had the right record company at this point—I think it would have been a number one pop hit," France conjectures. "It was well-produced and was special because it was an R&B/funk song sung by a white singer, singing it in a different way than a black woman might have. The combination was amazing, and I was told by many record company executives that, with proper promotion, this song could have been bigger than 'Come to Me.'"

"Prelude Records was a small but important dance music label, and that worked to my advantage for 'Come to Me.' I got the attention I needed initially from a small label. If I had been with a bigger record company at the beginning—and I was offered deals by many—the attention I received might not have been as focused. Could have been, would have been, should have been—who knows? Once an artist reaches a certain level of popularity and has hit the *Billboard* charts, the truth is you need money to keep the momentum going and to pay for good promotion. That's where Prelude Records faltered with my follow-up albums and 'Gonna Get over You.' I think they were so thrilled with the success of 'Come to Me,' they didn't promote the other two albums because they thought they could ride on the name alone. It wasn't enough. That's my opinion; it's not necessarily the truth. We'll probably never know the truth, but I believe had they invested more time and money, I might have moved onto the next level," she says.

Despite the crossover success that was eluding her, Joli remained a very hot commodity in New York City. Ironically, her realization that her public and the media still adored her also ignited an insecurity that became increasingly difficult to manage. "I did Radio City Music Hall for a week, and that's when I realized how big my name and music still were, how my career was still thriving. But that light bulb going off in my head also marked my becoming extremely nervous and overly cautious. You know, when you're young you usually just go along without fear. Initially I did that—I just went for it. But when I did Radio City and they were calling me 'The Baby Girl of New York City,' I started to really feel the pressure. I was being very cautious, and it became very important that I live up to the expectations of others—and exceed them. I had to be better and better. I started worrying about what my next move would be. Oh my God, it was so hard. Along the way, you make mistakes while trying to move forward. These decisions—although I was not alone and can't say I fully made any of my own decisions—were often made out of fear instead of out of love and being creative. It started to make a big difference."

In 1983, talent managers, whose organization jointly represented the emerging icon Madonna and superstar Michael Jackson, approached Joli. Through that arrangement, she scored a two-album deal with a major label—Epic Records. The stars seemed to favor Joli when Donna Summer's former producers, Giorgio Moroder and Pete Bellotte, were brought in to helm the first set, *Attitude*. Ritchie Zito handled many of the arrangements on the LP, and one track, "Dumb Blonde," was co-written by Daniel Vaillancourt, a childhood friend who has been very close to Joli for more than three decades (and who manages her today). Despite appearances on shows like *Solid Gold*, the melodically perky single "Girl in the '80s" and subsequent album material failed to move the artist into the new wave-electronic zone that had become fashionable in the post-disco era.

"I was thrilled when Epic suggested I work with Giorgio Moroder and Pete Bellotte," Joli says of the legendary producers. "They were amazingly talented people. But, again, I was going with the flow. I had my ideas about what I wanted to do, but I decided to listen to the professionals I was working with as to what road I should be taking—instead of listening to my own heart and inspiration—finding the sound I should have. For the *Attitude* album, I went somewhere that wasn't me. It wasn't me at all.

"Giorgio was not very present through the making of this album. He had a say in it as the executive producer, but it was more the work of Pete Bellotte and Richie Zito. In any case, whether it did or didn't miss the mark, it's not a bad thing to have those gentlemen on your resume. Some people loved it, but don't think it was reflective of who I was as an artist. I don't regret it, because it was part of my journey. They were the cream of the crop as far as professionals, but the music wasn't something I gelled with. I went through the motions, and I did it." The clubs tried to warm up to her new album and the competent soul-dance follow up LP, 1985's *Witch of Love* (produced by George Duke and her final set for Epic), but the commercial magic so essential to continued progression seemed to have been lost.

Joli expresses no regrets about the direction her career has taken since her auspicious debut. "Even without the crossover hits after 'Come to Me,' I was blessed to be able to make a living, and I still do," she says. "I never needed to work nine to five. I have great respect for that, but I didn't need to do it, which is pretty amazing when you think about it. That said, having been in show business my whole life, I did feel I needed to understand what most other people do for a living and how hard it is to make a buck. So I decided to get some experience with that and applied for a position at a courier company in Montreal. This was more than a decade ago. I took a nine to five job for a year because I felt I needed to understand how the world really works and to appreciate my freedom more. It was an extremely good and grounding experience for me. I worked under my real name, France Joli—which is not a stage name—and so some of the people knew who I was. But that was part of the experience. It was humbling and required me to put my ego aside, and it was something I wanted to do. It helped me understand how hard people have to work to get through life. And on more than one occasion, colleagues who also happened to be fans would come to me—pun entirely intended—during my lunch break and ask me to autograph an album or a photo. It was a juxtaposition of experiences that, again, was humbling—and more than just a little bit funny. I am very happy I lived through that."

"I'm very content today with having done my part to make my life and career as good as they can be, and I am very proud of that," says Canadian France Joli, who continues to headline sell-out shows in several countries (photograph by Millie Aguilar, courtesy France Joli).

Joli looks back on disco today with a strong regard for the genre, while acknowledging it didn't always create a perfect balance. "I loved disco music, and, yes, it did utilize my vocals well on many songs. But I'm not always sure I used my talents to their full capacity in the genre. There are some songs in disco where you can really show your ability, but I have to say there's nothing like a torch ballad for proving your full depth as a singer. Some disco singers are probably not as appreciated as they should be today because the music didn't always lend itself to showcasing their superior vocal talent. I am proud of my label as a disco singer though, and I continue to wear it with honor. My God, disco took me all around the world and made me grow as a human being. I've met so many beautiful and interesting people because of it. Why should I be anything less than proud of it?"

Joli has evolved into a more introspective person over the years, one at peace with the path she has been traveling and pleased with the philosophical growth she's made along the way. "You do what you have to do in order to achieve your goals. The rest is up to a higher power, not me," she believes. "You know, sometimes you just have to let go. When you've given your soul to something, sometimes you just have to step back and see where it goes. I'm very content today with having done my part to make my life and career as good as they can be, and I am very proud of that. I'm not religious, but I'm spiritual. I believe in that higher power, the power of the universe, the power of positive energy, the power of love. I'm here to experience my life the best way I can with the skills I have, and I believe there's a reason that certain people are put on my path. That said, there's a learning process that happens too. When hurtful things happen, I believe it's so you can learn about yourself and deal with unresolved issues you have and grow. I think the main thing in my life right now is to appreciate and love myself. I have lived a good portion of my life not doing that, and now I believe that the key to happiness is fulfilling your own needs and not worrying about the expectations of others. Love and respect yourself and you will love and respect others, thereby earning the respect and love of others—famous triangle."

The artist has also come to embrace the physicality of being a performer. She sometimes struggles with weight issues and the realities of being in the spotlight. "The opinions of others don't matter as much today as they once did. The struggle I went through to stay thin when I was younger, to look as good as possible, was so important back then. The industry, my mother included, taught me to be my own worst critic when it came to my personal appearance. I now know that that was misguided. It really pushes away who you really are. I'll tell you one thing—when you are young and you're striving to be sexy—and I get why the business forces that on you—it comes with a cost. In my case, I veered toward obsessing about my physical appearance more than about anything else. How I looked became who I was. The demands to stay thin skewed my sense of values. People who were very close to me withheld unconditional love if and when I gained weight. That hurt. And I think in some unconscious way, it made me act out toward both ends of the spectrum. I've suffered through both bulimia and anorexia. My sense of self-worth was tied to how light I measured on the scale. It's no wonder I have a problematic relationship with food today, at the age of 50. I'm obviously still struggling with it, and I take it day by day. I may not weigh what I did at 16—so few of us do.

"Today I am honestly thankful that I've had to struggle with weight issues because I believe it's helped me become a better person. I don't look at myself and bemoan how I've lost my hourglass figure. I look at what I've gained in depth as a human being. I do wish I were thinner. But today it's more about health than about vanity and ego. I'll never again look like I did at 16. And let me tell you, it's unfair for people, for fans, for myself to demand that of me. It's tough going on stage and knowing that some people can be judgmental, but it's not going to stop me from performing, from doing what I love. All I can say is I'm working on it slowly but surely, on my own terms. I'll get there—in my own time. And I'll do it for myself, not for anyone else."

Indeed, Joli still loves to perform her old hits. But she also loves creating new ones. In 2012 she released a joyous, hook-laden new digital single, "Hallelujah," that is a dance cover of an iconic ballad by fellow Canadian singer-songwriter-producer Leonard Cohen. Joli shot a video for it in the high desert of Southern California and released a limited edition CD of remixes courtesy of DJs Julian Marsh, Twisted Dee and Joel Dickinson. The song was a club and fan success and brought to light the undiminished talent and vocal electricity of a singer whose power today may actually exceed that of her earlier career. She tours regularly on the disco circuit, and her club bookings have yet to slow down. In addition to performing in very familiar territories like New York, New Jersey and Florida, the last 12 months have seen her regale sold-out crowds at the White Party in Palm Springs, Southern Decadence in New Orleans and Carnival Week in Provincetown—but to name three very popular events. She has also appeared off-Broadway in the hit *My Big Fat Gay Wedding*.

When watching France Joli perform her hits on stage today and the euphoric, jubilant response of her ecstatic audiences, it is clear that neither time nor maturity have had any negative impact on the artist's power. One of disco's finest and most positive-minded ambassadors, Joli speaks slowly and carefully about her legacy. "When I express how much I love and appreciate my fans," she says, as emotion cuts off her breath momentarily, "I hope that they really get the message. I hope they understand how truly important their support has been. My fans have made me who I am and have given me the life I lead. They *are* the most important part of my career. Without them, I wouldn't be part of this book. My voice would have long ago been silenced."

•••••••••••••••••••••••••••••••

Randy Jones, formerly of Village People
"Y.M.C.A."

"I understood we were going into people's family experiences, and I knew we were doing it with songs like 'Macho Man,' 'Y.M.C.A.' and 'In the Navy.'"—Randy Jones

What were the odds that a group of virile, lusty-looking males depicting America's vision of masculine stereotypes—a cop, a Native American, a soldier, a leather man, a construction worker and a cowboy—would take over the pop charts in the United States and command the dance floors of the late '70s? Turns out—pretty darn good! The Village People, conceived by producers Jacques Morali and Henri Belolo (who had enjoyed great success with their female group, the Ritchie Family) took Victor Willis (replaced by Ray Simpson in 1979), Felipe Rose, Alex Briley, Glenn Hughes, David Hodo and Randy Jones and made these attractive and dynamic gentlemen superstars. Their disco hits, including "Macho Man," "Go West," "In the Navy" and "Y.M.C.A.," became iconic party anthems and monstrous hits for the Casablanca Records label, selling as many as 100 million units worldwide, according to some reports. For Randy Jones, the journey has been extraordinary, and he articulately relates many of his adventures with humor and affection.

"I attended the University of North Carolina in Chapel Hill," says Jones, "where I studied theater, film, television and communications. I went on from there to study choreography and dance at the University of North Carolina School of the Arts in Winston-Salem and went to New York in 1975. I had been working professionally for a while and had my Equity and AFTRA [American Federation of Television and Radio Artists] cards and was able to join the Screen Actors Guild. I came to New York to find work in musical theater—that's what I wanted to do. I connected with what I like to call the original 'Girls Gone Wild'—Grace Jones, Jerry Hall, Janice Dickinson—all glamorous models at the time. I was doing modeling and traveled around quite a bit with them. Grace got a record deal in 1976, and her first LP was called *Portfolio*. I appeared in the first act she did to promote that album. There weren't many artists out there performing their dance hits in the clubs. Grace was one of the first to bring a progressive performance into the clubs, and another gentleman and I worked with her in that act.

"Two lessons I learned from Grace—don't work without fog and don't work without a good light. I remember she entered on a motorcycle. At one point, when she did the song 'I Need a Man,' about all I was wearing was a leather pouch over my family jewels and a chain up the crack of my ass and around my waist. The chain was cold! That's how I got started," he laughs. "I didn't go to Broadway, but I was lucky enough to work with Grace as an early pioneer of disco performance art."

Randy says producers Jacques Morali and Henri Belolo saw him with Grace and approached him after a show at a *Billboard Disco Forum* event. "I think they came up to me after that performance," he recalls, "and of course I'm standing there at two o'clock in the morning with this leather jock strap on. In heavy French accents, they said they liked the way I moved and looked. They asked me if I could sing because they had an idea for a group that they wanted me to be a part of. I said, 'That's very nice, and I'd like to talk to you more about it, but can we do it in daylight, in a real office?' Well, I did meet with them, and we came to an agreement, and that's how I became a part of the group. I had gone to see them wearing the kind of the clothing style I would have worn in North Carolina—boots, jeans, a western shirt. I don't think I was wearing a cowboy hat though. I guess I ended up bringing that visual, and that's why I became the cowboy in the Village People. That was in late summer of 1977."

Village People's self-titled debut album was an underground hit on Casablanca Records, favored among the gay culture out on Fire Island and in New York City's Greenwich Village. The album cuts, including "Fire Island," "In Hollywood (Everybody Is a Star) and "San Francisco (You've Got Me)," featuring lead vocals by Victor Willis, reached the top spot on *Billboard*'s disco chart late in the summer of 1977. The songs remained a fixture on DJ playlists for the rest of the year. "They used all models on the cover of that album. I think Felipe was the only member of the group actually seen on it. That album sold more than 100,000 copies, primarily in Latin, black and gay markets. There was a great preponderance of gay DJs at the time, and they really picked up on what that music was about and how people responded to it," observes Jones.

"When it came time for Neil Bogart [president of Casablanca Records] to do a second Village People album," Jones continues, "he insisted that Henri and Jacques have a group that was a solid performing entity that could support Neil's vision. Neil was about making hits. He had Donna Summer, and he knew he was going to crank out the hits as fast as his producers could deliver them. But he knew he couldn't do it unless he had a live, breathing, sweating, bleeding performance entity to sell those songs. It was one thing to have a hit song in a club, like producers Cerrone and Alec R. Costandinos, but not many producers had the performers to back up the concept. Jacques and Henri had to quickly put the Village People together. I had a musical theater background, and so

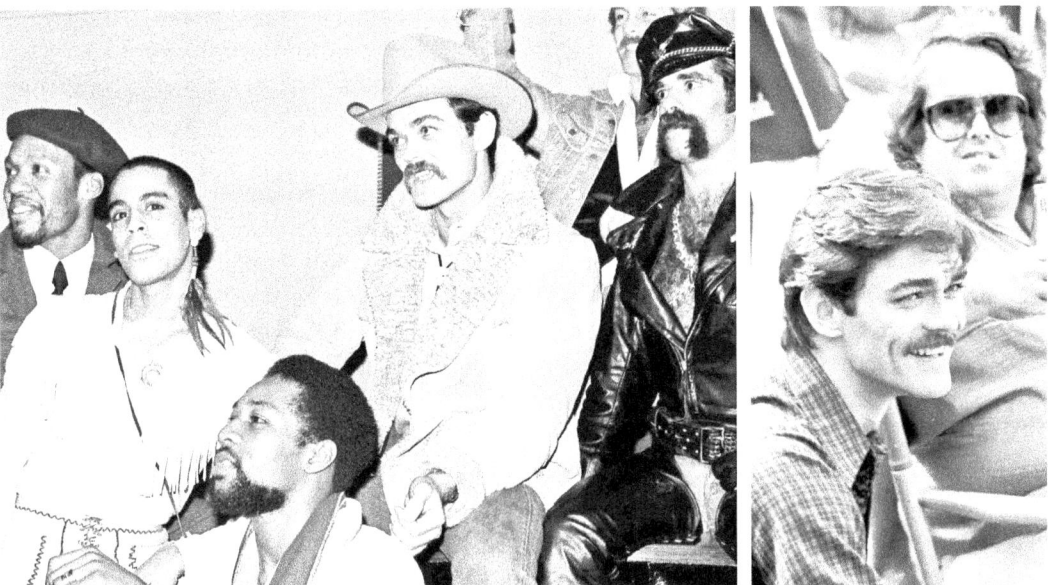

Left: The Village People (left to right: Alex Briley, Felipe Rose, Victor Willis, Randy Jones, David Hodo, Glenn Hughes) brace for stardom in 1978. *Right:* Randy Jones with *Can't Stop The Music* producer Alan Carr (photographs by Charles R. Moniz, used by permission).

did David and Victor. I think Alex certainly had recording experience. I'm not sure of Glenn's background or training, but he had that great look and a wonderful voice."

Randy remembers his producers well. "The partnership of Henri Belolo and Jacques Morali was unique," he states. "Henri, being our manager and executive producer, was also a co-lyricist. His remarkable skills at music management and creating business deals around the world made Village People the success that it was. With Henri handling the business affairs, Jacques was in the studio nearly all the time. We had a great studio band out of Philadelphia called Gypsy Lane, and I believe they had also been the band for all of the work Jacques and Henri had done for the Ritchie Family out of Sigma Sound.

"Jacques was very demanding—definitely not a patient person," he recalls. "I think he could have been a lot more understanding and considerate with the guys in the group. I had never been in a recording studio before. I think some of the other guys might have been in the studio before, but I was very intimidated by all of it. Here I was with a [producer] who had supposedly written all of these songs, his English was hard to understand, he was really impatient and, you know, if you are new to the process, it takes a while for you to be able to hear your own voice outside of your own head. Like the way your voice sounds in your head is one thing, but on a tape it sounds different. It was difficult to make changes and get refined and sophisticated and to learn the craft. I will say there was some pressure to quickly learn what it takes to be a recording artist. I don't think it was until sometime during the recording of the *Macho Man* album that I finally got the hang of what I was doing."

The *Macho Man* LP and single brought the group mainstream attention by early 1978. Towards the end of the year, the group's next album release, *Cruisin'*, had reached the *Billboard* Top 10, and the single "Y.M.C.A." had become a gargantuan nationwide anthem, ultimately ending up as one of disco's most famous songs. The *Go West* set followed in 1979 and yielded another smash, "In the Navy." Once favorites of the underground gay dance club circuit, Village People were now the darlings of mainstream pop culture. Whispers about some of the group members' sexuality no longer seemed relevant to the general public.

"We did not go at this as being a gay group," Jones insists. "In my mind, it was just like—here we are. Stonewall had taken place in 1969, said to be the beginning of the gay revolution, and yet by the '70s, everybody in America still thought anyone who was gay was a drag queen. I knew that wasn't right. Gay men started reclaiming masculine images like a cowboy, construction worker, soldier, cop, and leather man for themselves. It happened in sort of a role-playing way. I realized from my education that the Hollywood film industry had already done most of the heavy lifting. They had made and sold films with those same images of masculinity and created heroes and villains out of them all around the world. The Village People simply took those images a step further. But we knew we couldn't take the songs we were singing and sell them without having some kind of sense of humor about it. I think we had a touch of comedy in our act that combined with the choreography of great soul acts like the Spinners, the Four Tops and the Temptations. Plus, we added a hint of sly, subtle communication with the audience. Not to mention the fact that we had real cute butts—and whether you were a man or a woman, we were fun to watch," he laughs. "The fact that the six of us got the humor, that we were attractive and had youthful energy, combined perfectly with some of the best-crafted, yet deceptively simple pop songs that were written in the last half of the 20th century. Village People were a smashing success. Especially when we performed live."

Randy says these dream-like days in the spotlight were remarkable. "I was thrilled just to have a job," he laughs heartily. "I originally had been hoping to collect enough weeks on the job so that I could collect unemployment if I needed to. But Village People took off like a rocket. From the moment I signed with the group, I never had to collect unemployment—*ever*! It was the most golden decision I ever made in my life as a professional. Those first four years—I never worked harder in my entire life. In retrospect, I honestly don't believe it would have been possible if Henri Belolo hadn't guided it and overseen it and made decisions I'm sure we probably didn't even know about. Without all these people in place, like Neil Bogart and Jacques, Henri—and had my band of brothers and I not been young with energy and the ability to recover and to stay up all night with two hours of sleep, day after day—I don't think it could have happened the same way.

"I'll tell you, for a long time I never heard the word 'no.' Oh my gosh, the television shows we did with Merv Griffin, Hugh Hefner, Dick Clark, Bob Hope, Don Kirshner—they were like our five godfathers. They were the kings of television, and they were responsible for getting us into people's homes. Achieving that kind of penetration into pop culture was incredible. They got what we were selling and the appeal of who we were, and they gave us the platform to go into people's homes—into that box in everyone's living room. I understood we were going into people's family experiences, and I knew we were doing it with songs like 'Macho Man,' 'Y.M.C.A.' and 'In the Navy.' On the surface they appeared to be silly, silly songs, but they were irresistible. We would go in with the sharpest scalpel in the drawer and be able to make a tiny incision right above the heart of anyone in our audience that was the least bit receptive. We were able to give them a new impression to replace whatever old demons they had and a new way to look at concepts they thought they knew everything about. Three minutes later, a viewer's perspective could be changed, even if just by a millimeter. We had a positive impact on how people viewed gay men."

By 1980, the tide had turned against disco, and the timing couldn't have been worse for the release of *Can't Stop the Music*, a feature film directed by Nancy Walker based on the group's exploits. The film, starring Bruce Jenner and Valerie Perrine, was a critical and box-office bomb in the U.S. "We had met Allan Carr, the film's producer, all the way back in 1978," the artist remembers. "We had a big dinner that year at an upscale restaurant in L.A. on Sunset Blvd., and Allan stood up and said, 'We are going to make a movie about the rise of the Village People.' The development of it went on and on. We went on a world tour that went all the way through to 1980. We'd take a few months off and film in L.A.—I remember I stayed at Joan Collins' house for weeks at a time. You have to keep in mind that when the whole disco record burning event took place, we were still playing stadiums and arenas with 30, 40, 50,000 people—sold out shows at Madison Square Garden, Hollywood Bowl and the Greek. Here we are doing very well and not because we were a disco act. We were a pop act, and we had a pop-rock edge to our show, believe it or not. People always associate us with disco, but we appealed to a wide variety of people with all kinds of musical tastes. But eventually, the storm against disco really hit us in the face. And I think one of the problems was Allan came out with the film one year late. If he had released the film in June of 1979 instead of June of 1980, I think it would have been a hit."

The group released the *Live and Sleazy* album at nearly the same time as the soundtrack for the unsuccessful film and neither fared well. "We did the tour for the film, and by the end of 1980, I was thoroughly exhausted," Jones admits. "By then, I believe Neil Bogart had sold off his remaining shares of the Casablanca company to Polygram. So he was no longer with the label. Henri, who also had an agreement with Casablanca, had a clause that if Bogart ever left the company, he and the Village People had the option to leave as well. Everybody was exhausted, unenthused and getting cold feet. We had a meeting by the end of 1980 and everyone was saying people were tired of us.

"Management was going to discard all of the images we had personified, and they were going to go with a new wave look to reflect the trend towards the New Romantic Movement coming out of Europe with Steve Strange, Adam and the Ants and artists like that. I looked at everybody, all the guys in the group, and you would think I had contracted the bubonic plague when I said, 'Are you guys kidding me? How many millions of dollars and years have we spent to create an audience for the images we have been developing? Do you seriously think it will be successful if you take all of that and crumple it up, throw it in the trash, put on all new trendy outfits and paint your faces so that you are no longer recognizable? You are putting yourself in a position where you can be easily replaced by anyone who buys the Village People name.'

"I told them this made no sense, and I'd rather leave. I was worn out and miserable, so I made myself miserable to be around. I couldn't go on in good faith. The deal had come through to record with RCA, and that's when I left. It seemed Village People was a team on which I could no longer play. It was sad for me. That's when the album *Renaissance* came out. It was not successful."

The Village People continued to work, especially overseas, undergoing several changes in personnel. But demand for the group had severely tapered off. A single called "Sex over the Phone" and a megamix of their earlier hits garnered some attention in Europe (especially France) in the mid–'80s, but the group largely floundered and eventually faded from the public eye for several years. Says Randy, "In the early '80s, one of the first solo singles I did after leaving Village People was a cover of Roy Orbison's 'Oh, Pretty Woman.' My pal, Dan Hartman ['Instant Replay,' 'Relight My Fire'], came into the studio and helped me create the background voices for my recording. Later on in '84, Dan was writing a song demo for the upcoming *Rocky IV* film. He told me he wanted me to help with some backgrounds and to help give the song a Village People kinda feel. So in the time-honored quid pro quo tradition, I trundled up to his incredible studio in Westport, Connecticut, and got busy. Today, I'm willing to wager that if you close your eyes and listen to 'Living in America,' it does, indeed, sound like a Village People song—with a lead vocal sung by James Brown!"

At the same time, Randy says he got the idea to reunite the Village People as he began to hear a sound that resembled disco music returning to the limelight. "All the stuff I was hearing by Madonna and other artists sounded like disco to me by the mid–'80s; they were just calling it dance music. I was seeing reunion tours working for artists like the Monkees. I contacted the last agent we had and discussed the possibility of reuniting the group. He called David Fishof, who was responsible for the highly successful Monkees Reunion Tour (1986) and the *Dirty Dancing Live* tour (1988). The first thing Fishof asked of me was, 'How do all the other guys look?'

"I honestly had not been face to face with the guys in Village People since '81, so the first test would be to assemble all the guys in the same room and see how everybody would respond to the idea. I wanted to eyeball the guys before this meeting, so I invited them to my birthday party. They were all doing their own things, like bartending, office work and stuff like that. Well, they liked the reunion concept, but the guys all insisted that they would have to be paid enough so they would not have to maintain other jobs. With the help of David Fishof and his office as management, we reached out to a promoter, and we arranged a six-week tour of Australia with a 50% payment upfront. That paid for the guys' salaries to start rehearsing, and that began our comeback. Village People have continued to perform non-stop since 1987. We were able to create a corporation to organize our business interests called Sixuvus, which enabled all the guys to get on solid and secure financial footing and to get good health insurance coverage," he says with pride.

"I stayed with the group until 1991, when I could bear it no longer," he laughs. "I'm just kidding when I say that, but by that time I really had to analyze whether or not I wanted to keep being away from my relationship, from my life partner. I withdrew from the Village People and became a solo artist, which makes it easier for me to choose show dates and make my own schedule. The other guys didn't have the same type of home life and a partner like I did, and by that time, I needed to spend time with him. By the way, we got married September 13, 2013. His name is Will Grega, and we've been together nearly 30 years! Once again, I made the right decision," he says most confidently. Jones has enjoyed numerous hits on the club circuit in recent years with singles like "New York City Boy," "Your Disco Needs You," and a recent remake of Yvonne Elliman's nugget, "If I Can't Have You." Praeger Press/Greenwood Publishing released Jones' book, *Macho Man*, in 2008, co-authored by Mark Bego.

The former singer takes a grounded approach when looking at his history in entertainment. "My time with Henri Belolo and Jacques Morali was a phenomenal learning experience," he says sincerely. "You know, even an experience that may be considered rather dire to another—I tend to instinctively re-frame it so that I am looking at it in a more positive way. Yes, it could be difficult working with Jacques, but what I decided to do was to learn from it. I learned a lot—how to *not* treat people, how to be more respectful, how to sometimes shut the hell up and not be defensive when criticism comes my way.

"My education gave me a sense of professionalism, and because of that, I was able to take this situation—being hired as an entertainer, a recording artist and a performer—and do my very best, what I was trained to do. Jacques and Henri were trying, in their own way, to get something from the people they hired. It wasn't like we were at war with each other—we were just trying to make the mission happen and create the product. I knew if I had trouble with the communication, I would have to be the one to try harder to understand. In that process, I found I earned a master's degree, if not a doctorate, in the recording and entertainment industry. If I had not known this family of people—Henri, Jacques, Felipe, David, Alex, Glenn and Victor—my life might not be the way it is today. And I love my life today. I've learned that having a good, positive attitude helps you maintain—a good, positive attitude."

Leather man Glenn Hughes passed away in 2001, but the Village People continue to tour today (again, with a few new members). The extraordinary and indelible imprint left by this unique ensemble and its premier cowboy remains testimony to the power and reach of classic disco music. The group helped to shatter conventional attitudes about gay culture in America, and, in the process, reigned supreme at the height of this remarkable period in music history. The unprecedented success of the Village People owes as much to the energy and creative participation of its members as it does to the producers who hired these gentlemen to give their vision life.

"My education gave me a sense of professionalism, and because of that I was able to take this situation—being hired as an entertainer, a recording artist and a performer—and do my very best, what I was trained to do," says Randy Jones today (photograph by Sunny Bak, courtesy Randy Jones).

Randy Jones wouldn't change a thing. "I hope people will remember us with a smile," he says, following a momentary pause. "Listening to our songs and the mention of the words 'Village People' still make people smile. What could be more satisfying than knowing one's performance antics onstage, on film, in video and in songs make people grin, guffaw or even make them point and laugh. Because you know what? From the very beginning, I was in it for the laughs. My goal was and *is* to sing a song so people can have a good time. So with that, I will leave you with a wink, a wiggle and a wave! Good night, nurse!"

Shirley Jones, formerly of the Jones Girls
"You Gonna Make Me Love Somebody Else"

"To tell you the truth, we would close our eyes when they'd put the record on and nervously hope and pray somebody would get up and dance."—Shirley Jones

Brenda, Valorie and Shirley Jones established themselves as a dynamic trio with the ability to weave stunning harmonies long before disco music put them front and center. Born in Detroit, they had been backup singers for the likes of Lou Rawls, Teddy Pendergrass, Aretha Franklin, Diana Ross, Cher and countless other stars. As their journey evolved, they built themselves an impeccable musical reputation that eventually caught the attention of famed Philly soul pioneer producers Kenneth Gamble and Leon Huff. From there, the girls exploded onto the disco scene, ironically with a song that was a rather slow burn—"You Gonna Make Me Love Somebody Else." Still, it managed to soar to the upper regions of the disco and R&B charts in the early summer of 1979. Shirley Jones remembers well the details of those electrifying days and fondly looks back on the unusual journey her sisters and she shared as one of pop, R&B and disco's most respected girl groups.

"My mother, Mary Frazier Jones, was the first black gospel singer that RCA Records signed," Shirley says with family pride. "They signed my mom the same day they signed Little Richard to their rock 'n' roll division. As my mom found out my sisters Brenda, Valorie and I could sing (all three of us were only a year and a few months apart), we became Mary Frazier Jones and the Jones Sisters. We were her backup singers and started singing in the regional areas of Detroit, Chicago, Toledo and places like that. My sisters and I also studied piano for about ten years.

"People started really loving our harmonies. When I was maybe 11 or 12, some folks at a company called Fortune Records wanted us to come into their studios to record. It was secular music, but it was cute and exciting and my mom allowed us to do it. We put out a little local record and the production team of Holland-Dozier-Holland heard it and got in touch with our mother. We started doing backgrounds for them, and they put out a couple more regional records with us. By the time I was 15, Curtis Mayfield had heard us, and we went to Chicago, where he signed us to his Curtom Records. My mother was with us the entire time, and she never left my side until I was about 18. We put out a few more small singles with Curtis, and by the time I finished college, we had become fairly well known. We started performing at nightclubs in the Chicago and Detroit area and working with many major artists," she says. By the time the sisters started releasing records on the Curtom label, they were known as the Jones Girls.

Jones is able to identify the quality she and her sisters possessed that set them apart. "My mother trained us so well," she is quick to admit. "We would train for hours and hours before and after we became the Jones Girls, and we became the premiere backup group. Because of the fact that we were so close in our ages, we had this unique tonality in our voices and were so quick to handle the work, we started to become in demand. We were also very creative—we developed many of those special harmonies that sounded so good behind the artists we worked with. I only wish I knew then what I know now about getting a financial piece of the song for doing something like that. It would be a much different picture for us today if we had realized it."

The Jones Girls found themselves in the studio more often than out, backing some of the most prestigious artists in the business. Ironically, they rarely met stars like Diana Ross while recording. She recalls, "Other than a live album we did with Diana, our recording work was always done separately from her. It wasn't difficult at all to work that way. Back in the day, it was always kind of separate. They would call us in to do our part, and the lead vocal would actually be a 'dummy lead' until the real artist, be it Diana, Aretha, Helen Reddy, Cher, would actually come in to do their work. We were never all together with the featured artist. One thing that I loved about our contract with Diana was when we ultimately became her background singers, we would work six or seven months out of the year with her. But she also let us make money by recording with others. She recognized we were making a living as background singers. I'm forever grateful to her for that because she was paying us very well, and a lot of artists did not allow their background singers to do anything with anybody else. She always believed in our talent and wanted us to be making a good living."

The disco era was now in full swing, and the Jones Girls' delicious harmonies were ideal for the lush and swirling productions starting to make their mark on dance floors in Europe and the United States. The girls served up stellar backup vocals on Linda Clifford's *If My Friends Could See Me Now* album on the Curtom label in 1978. "By the time we worked with Linda Clifford," says Jones, "we were pros. At that point, we liked disco, and it was just becoming the rage. We had also just done a Le Pamplemousse album. My mom was a little concerned because of some of the elements that seemed to go along with disco—the sex and drugs that were prevalent. We always tried to keep things professional at work, and if we were hired for anybody, we would get into the song, rehearse and just go with it—and nothing else. Then there were the TV shows where we appeared with Stephanie Mills, Sylvester and lots of dance music stars."

Inevitably, the time arrived for the girls to step into the limelight. Shirley remembers, "After about seven or eight months of working with Diana, who was *the* icon, *the* woman, she came to us and said, 'You guys are too good to be singing just background for me or anyone. I make a lot of costume changes and during one of these changes I want you to pick out a song, and I'm gonna call you out, and I want you to perform it.' As it turned out (we were at the Shubert Theater in Philadelphia), she called us out to do the song and producers Kenny Gamble and Leon Huff were out in the audience. They came backstage and told us we were terrific and asked if we were signed with anyone, which we were not. It was about a week or so later, maybe even less than that, when they sent us a contract. We didn't know anything, and people were telling us we needed an attorney to look at this contract. But we didn't worry that much about that, and within a month they had flown us from where we were living in California back to Philadelphia to do our first album."

Gamble and Huff's Philadelphia International Records was enjoying a solid hit streak in soul music, rivaling the success of Motown with hits like "For the Love of Money" and "Love Train" by the O'Jays and MFSB's "TSOP (The Sound of Philadelphia)," a group comprised of the label's in-house studio musicians. The label also scored a major disco hit with McFadden & Whitehead's "Ain't No Stoppin' Us Now" in 1979. "One thing I can say about Gamble and Huff was that working at their studios—it was like a school. Everybody had little rooms that were set up like classrooms. We had apartments where we could cook and do our thing for the two or three months it took to do each album. Every day we had a schedule; we'd listen to songs with them, and we would choose which ones we should do. We'd record maybe 15 to 18 songs for an album, and then we'd meet with them again and decide which eight or 10 would actually make it to the album," she says.

Jones describes the long hours required to make their much-anticipated self-titled debut album in 1979. "Being in the studio back in the day," she says, "there was no Pro Tunes, no technology like they have now. I think that's one of the biggest differences between an old school artist and a contemporary artist. Sometimes we'd be in the studio till four or five o'clock in the morning, and sometimes they wanted two or three background tracks, and you'd have to do it the same exact way each time. That could be very difficult—I mean, you couldn't even breathe out of place. It trained artists like my sisters and I to be able to duplicate your own self. My sister Valorie, God bless her soul, was born with perfect pitch. She was the culprit that would force us to stay in the studio so late because she was the one who would say to us, even over the producers, 'No, that's too sharp,' or 'That sounds flat; you need to hit the note this way.' She'd say that mostly to me," Jones laughs. "But it really taught me a lot about singing and performing because it trained you not to depend on electronics to do things with your voice. If you have a God-given talent, you know what to do with your voice even if the electronics shut off. Today's artists are too dependent on technology to take their voices up to perfect pitch and the right note instead of having to do it with their own skill themselves."

The smash hit from the set, "You Gonna Make Me Love Somebody Else," was a Gamble and Huff composition, and Shirley says it was always a standout. "Of course they would always push one of their songs to be the first single," she smiles. The song had the same slow, sensual bass line that would make Herb Alpert's hit "Rise" shuffle its way to the top of the disco and pop charts a few months later. While the Jones Girls didn't go the full distance, their lush harmonies helped make their track one of the first major slow-groove smash hits of the genre. The song reached number 12 on the disco chart, the Top 10 of the R&B chart and cracked the pop Top 40.

"We were absolutely stunned!" the artist exclaims. "At the time 'You Gonna Make

Me Love Somebody Else' first came out, the disco thing was in full swing, and we were still doing backups and touring with groups like the O'Jays. When we would sing the song, people would go crazy! Then we started going to the clubs on promotion tours expressly for the song. Now, keep in mind the song was quite a bit slower than the typical disco record. It had that tremendous bass line, but it was slower. To tell you the truth, we would close our eyes when they'd put the record on and nervously hope and pray somebody would get up and dance. We used to say to Kenny, 'This is not a disco song! Why are we doing clubs?' He told us to trust him and not worry about it. Well, sure enough, it did hit big in the nightclubs and became a really huge disco-R&B hit! To this day, it's the song I close with—that and maybe 'Nights over Egypt.' Those are the two songs most identified with the Jones Girls."

At the time, however, the girls weren't entirely at ease with their newfound spotlight on the dance floor. "When we started doing the clubs like Studio 54, we were hesitating," she admits. "First, we were surprised that song had the right kind of groove to become a disco hit. But it did, and we became a favorite of all those famous nightspots in New York. We'd do them late at night, especially in the gay scene, and to this day we have a lot of fans that remember us from those New York performances. Because we came from a very religious background, the gay environment was kind of shocking to my sisters and me. The type of dancing, the drugs, men dancing with men—it was really, really wild. All these years later, I have a whole different view on all of that, but back then it was very difficult for us and scary. But performing in these clubs was something we had decided to do because of our love of music, and this was the business we were in.

"The clubs were packed with people—I can close my eyes now and see how they reacted to us and how they loved some of our songs. We were confused because we didn't grow up with any of this gay culture. As I said, we came from a very religious background, and we had a lot of questions. But we just accepted the love they were giving us. I think that's what we were ultimately supposed to do. Today, we are still going through issues about whether marriage should be between a man and a woman only, and I'm so glad this country is starting to realize that love is love and whoever wants to be together *should* be together. It's all come a long way, and so has my thinking.

"To this day, some of my closest friends are gay individuals, and I feel like they are my sisters or brothers. Back in the day, we didn't understand it, but I'm glad we were involved in it because it introduced me to so many people like Sylvester, who was simply amazing, and other artists who were gay. My thing is—people are people, and we are all God's children, and God does not make mistakes. That's my feeling today. I've come a long way from my early days in disco," Shirley says with a tone of satisfaction.

There was room on the disco scene for many female ensembles during the era, according to Jones. "We didn't feel any competition with other girl groups. We didn't know the Three Degrees or some of the others, but we knew Sister Sledge, the Pointer Sisters and the Emotions. We were all friends. But people in the media and those who were into gossip would try to say we were rivals when, actually, we were very supportive of each other. I don't recall any backstabbing or trying to get over on each other. I was always very happy for the success all these groups had. We actually would go to each other's' shows, and even though I never got to know any of them really, really well, you could always just feel that the vibe was good."

The artist pauses a moment to think about her experience with Philadelphia International and the group's primary producers. "Things always could have been better. But I have to say, Gamble and Huff treated us very well, and there were times where we also thought we were being paid very well. We didn't always realize that some of the gifts we were receiving were being charged back to us. Had I know that, I probably would never have accepted them. And today, if I write a song, I know enough to make sure I get the proper publishing on it as a co-writer. I think if Gamble and Huff or Berry Gordy and people like that had been more willing to share that information with up and coming artists like we were at that time, well, I would just say we would probably be much better off financially. Back in the day, it was kind of like every man for himself, and if you didn't know it, shame on you. I learned a lot. I can assure you that wouldn't happen today."

The Jones Girls' success led to more hits, including 1980's "I Just Love the Man" from the *At Peace with Woman* album and "Nights Over Egypt," taken from the album *Get As Much Love As You Can* in 1981. Subsequent albums failed to keep them high on the charts, but the girls were extremely popular in live shows, and they continued to tour worldwide. Says Jones, "One of the highlights for us was appearing at the Dominion Theatre in London for three sold-out shows in the early '90s. My mom and my godmother got on stage with us, and we performed together. My mom turned it out! We went back to the days of the Jones Sisters, and every time I go to London, people remind me of that phenomenal performance. I wish they had videotaped the show. There were so many highlights for us over the years, like the west coast shows we did with Michael Jackson and the Jacksons, Luther Vandross—so many great artists. In the disco era, it was amazing performing with Sylvester, the Weather Girls and Stephanie Mills."

As time moved on, the girls went their separate ways. "In the early '80s, Valorie decided she wanted to try college and got kind of tired of performing. She was quite shy and never really wanted to do the group thing, but she did it for the sake of the family," Shirley says. "Then Brenda got married and moved to Atlanta. It just so happened that around late in 1985, Mr. Gamble called me again and asked what I was doing. I said I was singing here and there and things had cooled off. He asked me if I wanted to do a solo project, and that sounded really good to me. I flew back to Philadelphia, and I recorded *Always in the Mood*." Jones' solo debut was a well-received album that cracked the R&B Top 10.

"I then took some time off to be with my family," she recalls. "My mom passed in 2006, and the pain of losing her prompted me to get back into the business. Music is a passion for me, and so I did an album a few years ago called *Feels Like Heaven*. It was more jazz-oriented music, and it did quite well. But now I'm going back to my roots, and I recently recorded a remake of 'I'm at Your Mercy' (a song I had done with the Jones Girls). It's a duet with a young singer named Macy, who is a wonderful southern soul artist. I'm working on the album, which is called *Perennial*. I like the [album's name]—coming back year after year after year, just as vibrant as the year before.

"My philosophy is to enjoy life as much as possible, treat everyone as I would like to be treated and to accept changes in society and just go with the flow," says Shirley about life today. "When Val passed in December of 2001, it devastated all of us. In 2006, when my mom passed, I was crushed. My mom was my rock and foundation, and I didn't know if I could go on without her. But I knew that, more than anything, she would want me to continue singing. I had a personal assistant who was like a sister to all of us who had adopted two children. They were like *our* kids. They were my godchildren. She passed away in 2007, and the State was trying to place them with another family. So, I wasn't about to let that happen, and I raised them, keeping me here in Atlanta a while longer. I've been blessed, and now that they are of age, I can get back to what I wanted to do for myself." Shirley reports her sister Brenda is spending time with her family and grandchild, out of the spotlight for the time being.

With their scintillating harmonies, the Jones Girls added class and sophistication to the disco genre. Both as backup singers and stars performing directly under the disco ball, the group remains one of dance and R&B's most cherished performers. "I hope that we made music that made people smile, made them happy and took them away from their personal challenges that they were going through," says Shirley. "I'd like them to have heard our music and said to themselves, 'Okay, I can get through this.' That was how we all felt before we'd go out and perform. That was always our goal, our mission. And that's why I am back out performing today. When I see the smiles and realize that the audience wants to see me, that they came out to hear 'You Gonna Make Me Love Somebody Else' again, it's wonderful. It reminds them of a time when things were a lot happier—and that's what keeps me going."

My philosophy is to enjoy life as much as possible [and] treat everyone as I would like to be treated," says Shirley Jones today (courtesy Shirley Jones).

Denis LePage/Nini Nobless, formerly of Lime

"Babe, We're Gonna Love Tonite"

"It was so much fun working in those days with 30-piece orchestras. Everyone was working, not kooked up someplace with fucking machines and computers and all these Internet gangsters."—Nini Nobless

As the creative genius behind the enormously popular duo Lime ("Your Love," "Babe, We're Gonna Love Tonite," "Come and Get Your Love") and the composer and arranger of dozens of smash hits that came out of Canada during and after the crash of the classic disco era, Denis LePage became one of the genre's most important and revered figures. In many respects a Picasso of musical composition, his craftsmanship generated a distinctive sound that injected new elements of creativity into the dance genre. LePage helped to place Canada firmly on the dance music map as a prime source of cutting edge club material. His music literally helped to rescue and redefine disco in the early '80s. That was then. Denis LePage has evolved since those days, and though he's now largely out of the spotlight he continues to reinvent his art—and his identity. *He* is now a living as a *she*, an in-process transgender known as Nini Nobless. The artist is a boiling pot of ideas, bubbling over with rapid-fire thoughts, observations and opinions about nearly every imaginable subject. Along with jubilation in her voice, there's the sound of disappointment, perhaps even some bitterness, relative to the tribulations she's encountered on her path to transformation. But one thing is certain—she is a survivor with a flair for brilliance and a life-loving person who has no intention of ever giving up.

"I'm 64, and in my sixth year of hormone therapy—a sex change. It's really something serious," Nini explains. "The change in my body is dramatic. I look like a girl now. My doctor suggested this change. I was born a hermaphrodite, and it's been a problem all my life. But now, with the hormone treatment, it's better. I'd rather be feminine looking than male looking. Some people aren't happy with it, but it's not their life. A lot of people are offended by it, or they want me to stay the same and keep promoting the old [music]. But there really isn't enough work out there to keep me involved in it or make me willing to stay as a man. I'm coming out very strongly with my new records with the way I am now. I'm a living person and a living musician, and I continue to pursue my career. I'm not going to dwell on my past for the rest of my life."

Nobless takes pride in her natural musical talent, education and the early accomplishments that led to a recording career. "I am a highly educated musician," she says proudly. "I had a master's degree at 18, a gold medal in music dictation from a conservatory, and I am an undergraduate PhD from Concordia University. I know how to play and write. I have eight years of private studies, and I don't know how many years with private teachers. If I had studied medicine, I would have been a multi-millionaire. I studied music instead. I used to take it all in good stride in the '80s, and I was respected. Now I'm kind of on the streets—well, a three-and-half-room apartment anyway—with not a lot of anything, and they steal what music I make.

"I started playing a harmonica when I was five. My aunt Helen gave me my first piano lesson when I was 11," she recalls. "My father bought an upright piano, and she showed me what a C-major was after I saw it noted on something and started asking about it. I just developed this connection with music. I had been playing dance halls in Canada since the '60s, so I was always involved with making people dance with my music. At the age of 13, I did my first album with a group called the Stringers. By the time I was 18 or 19, I was already playing the piano on a lot of recording sessions here in Montreal.

"Some of the arrangers were getting older or moving away, and some producers started asking me if I'd like to write out scores and such. I started arranging, conducting and playing for some of the bigger French-speaking artists here, and things started going very well. I built a reputation. I had also been doing a lot of jazz-fusion work, kind of like the music of Weather Report or Jaco Pastorius. I played five instruments and was the busiest trumpet player and arranger in Canada for years. Then, one of my bigger clients suggested I record an album, and some of it was exported to New York and apparently did very well. It was called *Le Pouls* (*The Pulse*), and it had kind of funky rock-jazz vibe. I was one of the first Canadians to work with synthesizers, like Moog and things like that. We had a lot of that sound on the record. Two guys from a New York label drove all the way up to Montreal and told me they wanted to sign me. I started a label with them in the mid-'70s called Pyramid Records."

As the decade progressed, LePage became a well-known musician who would go out on the road with major stars in the provinces of Canada. "I knew a guitar player who was an unbelievable musician. He was a virtuoso of the guitar, a country artist—just incredible! He had a studio with an associate named Bill Hill, and they used to hire me to play piano on his country sessions. One day, Bill said that George Cucuzzella, [a major executive] from Unidisc Records, wanted to meet me. George showed up at the studio, and we had a handshake. He was a hip guy, a very thin guy and a spiffy dresser. He smoked a lot of cigarettes. He had a whole bunch of projects he wanted me to do. The Erotic Drum Band was one. I did 'Plug Me to Death,' which made it to number one in *Cashbox* magazine. I did it all by myself with a Moog. I did it as a phantom writer because someone else signed the copyright. [Producing and writing credits were given to Peter Di Milo on the release by Prism Records in the U.S.] I didn't know in those days. I worked two afternoons in the studio, and they gave me $1500 cash for that. It was great for me. Two days of work, $750 a day—for 1978, that was good enough for me!

"I did a lot of other tracks for people who worked for George, like Peter Di Milo, but it took a while for things to really start up," Nini remembers. "One day, an associate of George's named Joe La Greca showed up at my door with a copy of *Cashbox*, and he asked me, 'Hey, do you want to make another [hit]?' I said okay. He said, 'This time we are going to do it with a big orchestra, and I'll give you the writing credit. You can sign it.' I said, 'Sure, anything you say!' He drew up a union contract, and everything was legit. Joe was a very nice man, a sweet guy. Anyway, we went to work, and I did everything [for this new song] on paper. I scored it.

"I don't even need a keyboard to write a chart. I hear everything in my head and, bang, I write it out, you know? We hired the musicians and went into the studio, and we recorded an album. We did this instrumental track called 'The Break,' which I didn't know would become a monster hit. I was not the artist. It was credited to a black artist [Jimmy Ray] and the concept group was called Kat Mandu. Everything went good. Joe took the master to Philadelphia, where it was mixed, and when I heard the 12-inch single, I was like, 'Wow! This is really something!' That was really my last job with the George Cuccuzzella entourage for a while because nothing else really took off." (In this conversation, LePage fails to acknowledge his arrangement and production skill contributions on other disco classics, like Freddie James' "Get Up and Boogie," released with great success around this same period.)

As the years passed, Denis maintained an outwardly heterosexual lifestyle, was married to his partner Denyse and began formulating ways to stay in the mix. What he came up with would completely revolutionize dance music. Says Nobless, "I went about a year without work. I had money aside, just enough to get by and keep my house. My mother died and left me $30,000 and the same amount for my brother and sister. I went out and bought an eight-track reel-to-reel tape recorder, a board, some microphones and some nice JBL speakers. I had a big house—it had 14 rooms, and the room I used for a studio was huge. That house was all made of wood, cedar, and was built in 1840. It was an historical house that Denyse and I bought in 1978, and it cost about $30,000. [All my new equipment] fit in there.

"I had no work, so I started recording my own songs. My brother had a set of drums, and I played them and created some loops. I had decent demos and called up Joe La Greca and gave him a cassette of the stuff I had recorded. I asked him to give it a listen. He came back with a deal, saying, 'Let's do it!' We hired some better players and did everything properly at my studio and began working on the song 'Your Love' by Lime [sung by Denis and his wife Denyse]. Joe came up with that name for the group. I started a label with him and did some test pressings of the song. Radio stations here flipped, saying, 'Wow, what's that?' Joey—he was a good salesman. He'd say, 'Oh, it's Edgar Winter with Diana Ross!' It was a white 12-inch record with no name on it, and the guys at the radio station thought it was a bootleg. They bought the story!" Nini laughs.

"The DJs on the radio were afraid to play it and say who it was in case it really wasn't Edgar Winter and Diana Ross. Finally, one guy at a radio station realized it was Denis LePage with his wife and said, 'It's fucking good anyway!' They started playing the shit out of it, and Joey and I went to George Cucuzzella and told him to sign up my wife and I as artists, and that's what started up Lime. It wasn't long before American labels were interested in it. Joey was in New York, and he came back with a deal. At that time, it was really complex because we struck a deal with Lenny Fichtelberg [of Prism Records]. He had an office near Spanish Harlem, and he was a good guy. But meanwhile, Cucuzzella was selling the Canadian version, exporting 'Your Love' to stores in New York. Lenny called me up and told me to tell George he had to stop doing this because Prism had the [U.S.] rights. Man, I didn't have time to play a note because I was always on the phone like a businessman."

Lime became a sensation and the hottest flavor on the emerging high-energy music menu. The dual track smash "Your Love"/"You're My Magician," featuring an irresistible beat, a hook-fused melody and the raspy voice of Denis melding with the sweet, ultra-high pitched vocals of Denyse, went straight to the number one spot on the *Billboard* disco/dance chart. In the U.S., Prism released the *Your Love* album, which was followed by a string of LP's (usually featuring unique and colorfully illustrated cover artwork) and a succession of hit single follow-ups. They included "Babe, We're Gonna Love Tonite," "Wake Dream," "Angel Eyes" and "Guilty." "Lime ended up being on the WEA label in Europe and was licensed to major labels everywhere around the world," Nini claims with pride.

"We did really well. I think we had five songs top the *Billboard* magazine disco sales chart. I would write all our songs out, and within three or four days, my wife and I would know them by heart. We recorded everything in our house—it's true. I bought a 16-track reel-to-reel, and they were really expensive but very good machines. Our studio had a very high ceiling and a kind of natural bass trap because there was a staircase behind the board. All the base frequencies rolled up to the second floor. It was as good as an RCA studio."

Nobless describes the formula for success he and Denyse so expertly crafted. "In those days, I was not a PhD. I don't use the same techniques today that I did to write songs back then. In those days, I would come up with a good groove on the keyboard, good chord progressions and a good beat. Then I would improvise over it. [Nini starts singing some Lime song lyrics in her familiar masculine voice.] Sometimes I would stagger a hook line, like on 'Babe, We're Gonna Love Tonite.' [Again, she sings the song's chorus.] Denyse found the harmony part. It was a lot of trial and error to achieve a melody. But, you know, by the time we had a melody, there were so many things to do we'd have to jot it down on our manuscript so we wouldn't forget it. Denyse was a sight-reader like me, and we'd rehearse it and record it. By the time we got to 'Unexpected Lovers,' we really had to use a manuscript, which she didn't like doing. She would want to change a note or a word, and it was rough at times. Working together wasn't always easy during the evolution of Lime.

"From 'Your Love' to the end, it was a steady evolution of synthesizers and new machines," Nini says. "I'd buy the latest machines the minute they came out. With 'Guilty' and 'Angel Eyes,' I was the first guy to synchronize a Roland TR-808 drum machine, the sequencer in it, to a tape recorder and play the sync back into the drum machine. Then the drum machine would be in sync, and the song would sound like it was computerized. It was a lot of work. Sometimes the machines wouldn't synchronize properly, and you'd have to start over. But in the end, the sessions became totally electronic and way ahead of their time. I didn't really like my singing, but my fans did, and they come first I guess," she says.

According to the composer, the husband and wife team initially toured as Lime, but Nobless claims it wasn't something she relished. "We played the Underground and all the Backstreet clubs. When we did the Funhouse in New York in 1981, there were 10,000 people there. We had to do two shows, 5,000 people at each one. I couldn't even cross the street to buy a toothbrush at the drug store without a police escort. People would mob me. We went all the way down to Central America. But, eventually, the [label executives] didn't want us to do tours because they said we were too old looking. Denyse and I also were not dancers. I don't really know why it happened, but I did authorize other performers to go out as Lime. They were pressuring me to let others represent us. But to tell you the truth, going out on the road wasn't that much fun in those days anyway.

"We did a tour for an ex-boxing promoter. It was a $20,000 tour, and we came back with two grand. You'd play for $500 or $1000, and you'd stay at a nice hotel, but it wasn't easy. It was a very tough scene and very hard on us. But you had to promote the records. We had to do what we were told or else. There were a lot of drugs around. Disco *was* cocaine. Man, one time the road manager almost killed us in a car accident. He was drunk all the time. It was insane. You get tired of all that!"

Tom Hayden picked up Lime for distribution on his TSR Records label in the mid–'80s. He recalls the experience of marketing the product in the U.S. "We never dealt directly with Denis, who was such a talented producer and had a string of gigantic hits," says Hayden. "We were dealing with Larry Spier Music out in New York, the publisher on much of Lime's work. I believe [Spier] also booked the groups that would go out and perform. The funny thing was, I think at one time there were four different Lime groups touring the country with different performers, but the performance money was all being funneled through this company in New York. It was my understanding they had a contract with Denis and Denyse LePage to have these groups go out and say they were Lime. It was like the wildest thing I'd ever seen—it was like Milli Vanilli four times over.

"TSR had two really good-looking people performing as Lime. I can't remember their names, but they were great dancers and singers and could sing live over the tracks and you would never know the difference. We got them on *Solid Gold*, *The Merv Griffin Show* and a bunch of TV shows. They were acting as Lime for the two or three years we had a licensing agreement. There were some weekends where we had them booked at like three or four different clubs on the same night in places like Miami and Ft. Lauderdale. They could end up making $10,000 a night or more." [Hayden and Nobless may be referring to the team that included Joy Dorris. Dorris has been performing as the female half of Lime since approximately 1983, although her male counterparts have changed over the years. See the Joy Dorris chapter.]

Hayden discusses the difficulties he experienced with Lime's Canadian label, not unlike those mentioned earlier by Nobless. "We always had—let's say—rather strange dealings with George Cucuzzella at Unidisc," he admits with some hesitation, as he carefully chooses his words. "I will say he was a good record guy with a great ear. He came to us in 1985 saying they wanted to revive Lime in the U.S. after a couple of releases that hadn't been as big as they wanted. They brought us our first Lime single release, 'Unexpected Lovers,' and we absolutely loved it. We were very excited by it and put a big Lime on the 12-inch cover jacket [graphics by Ron Wong] to get the name across and re-launch the group. It just exploded and made it to the top of the charts.

"The single got to be so big that there grew a strong demand for an LP. We contacted George and asked for an album immediately. We could get big advance sales if we could get it out in a hurry. But what happened was he ended up putting out the *Unexpected Lovers* album out in Canada and trans-shipped them into the States without giving them to us. We had a contract for them in the United States. I ended up getting pretty pissed and flew someone up to Canada, and this person waited in George's office until he gave us the master tapes. Within a week we had the album out. [Cucuzzella] had been in the business for a long time, and I guess he wanted to try to make the money from all ends. But it was bad for us because we had paid a hefty advance at the time (considering it was disco music), and we lost those initial sales. I wouldn't be surprised if he had sold 15 or 20,000 units before we were able to put it out ourselves. The album still did okay, but it probably would have been much bigger for us if we had gotten the advance sales we were entitled to. We could have publicized those sales and gotten Lime a higher chart position."

As Lime commerce progressed, Nobless concedes that his marriage was stressed beyond repair. "The business overruled our marriage for sure," she says with a tone that still has a touch of exhaustion to it. "The success got so big, and the ASCAP checks were like $100- 200,000 a year. In the early '80s, that was good money. But the business killed our marriage—that and my feminism—got in the way. The last few years of Lime were not very pleasant. [Denyse and I] were always in conflict. It got out of hand. I felt like I was becoming a slave, and it really was killing the act."

Finances were also a problem, alleges the artist. "I was the biggest selling artist in Canada for a period during the '80s," Nobless claims. "I got some money for writing back then, but I never got my percentages for sales. I went to court over that too. It cost me 50 or 60 grand, and I lost. I think I made about $900,000 over a 20-year basis with Lime." Nini says the last $200,000 of that amount came from the fairly recent sale of the rights to his music to the Unidisc label in Canada.

Prior to and throughout the success of Lime, LePage was commissioned to compose, arrange and write songs for a number of Canadian artists or acts in the early '80s. Many of these creations were tremendous successes in the U.S. Among the names benefiting from LePage's midas touch were France Joli (producer Tony Green hired Denis to arrange the strings and horns on her *Tonight* album), Carol Jiani ("Hit'n Run Lover"), Christopher (Chris) Mills, ("Love Triangle" and "Cold Turkey"), Voggue ("Dancin' the Night Away," originally a project intended for Denyse), Diva ("Double Trouble") and Mother F ("Hot Wax"). "As a studio person, sometimes I was kept from knowing who the artist was," says Nini. "Often, I was served a rough demo on cassette or reel-to-reel and usually it was the writer's voice on it. Like with 'Hit'n Run Lover.' The writer, Sandy Wilbur, sang that herself [before LePage recorded Jiani's vocals]. Tony Green, George Cucuzzella and Joe La Greca were my biggest clients."

Nini suddenly gets overwhelmed with emotion as she remembers those days. "It brings back so many memories. It was so much fun working in those days with 30-piece orchestras. Everyone was working, not kooked up someplace with fucking machines and computers and all these Internet gangsters. The world is not as nice as it used to be. Don't mind me being so emotional," she apologizes.

Nobless thinks about the influences that led her to compose and arrange such dance masterpieces. "My music had a lot of those Isaac Hayes feel-good kinds of chord changes," she observes. "Even the hook line on 'Babe, We're Gonna Love Tonite' I kind of borrowed from Sly and the Family Stone. I was listening to Isaac and Marvin Gaye back then. I was a big fan of Sharon Redd ["In the Name of Love," "Beat the Street"] too. In those days, we were infusing a little bit of seriousness into dance music. We were infusing a little contemporary jazz into the sound with a mix of rhythm and blues to come up with some good tunes. That's where I was getting my inspiration. It was fun. Being active that much, so busy making music that people seemed to love, was very pleasant. Today, I play and sequence everything myself. There isn't a musician community up here [in Canada] like there was back then, hanging out together. Those days are over. Now we're all locked up, stuck in our little dens until someone comes along and walks off with our master tapes. I have two criminal cases going right now. Someday, it will all be okay but it's not at all like it once was."

LePage stayed connected to the Lime concept all the way through 2002, when the last official album, *Love Fury*, was released. "I hired other girls to record the female vocals over time. They remixed the *Love Fury* album, and I didn't like it very much. When it came out, it did very well though. I didn't see any ASCAP money or airplay money from it. I got into a fight with Cucuzzella afterward. Not a physical fight—a conflict of interest. He said the business was over, and he did that album for me as a favor. He didn't renew my contract. Well, he ended up getting it all because I sold *Love Fury* to him as part of my catalog, which all went to Unidisc. What are you gonna do? I owed taxes. I wasn't in the street, but it was hard, and I needed the money. I was divorced from Denyse; I had a secretary that I had to pay every week. Being a recording artist is a business, and you can't do it alone. People always think being a recording artist, you're always drinking champagne and laughing. But that's not true. I didn't get a lot of work after that. People think that because you were a star at one time, you are a multi-millionaire now, and you don't need to work. I never got my proper royalties for Lime. Right now, I should have about two million in the bank. What can I tell you?"

The artist says she dealt with and conquered addictions that arose from what she describes as a grueling schedule and pressure that became overwhelming. "I had started to arrange a lot of records, and it was hard—a lot of work putting together the strings, horns, you know," Nini admits. "Sometimes we had just a week to arrange seven hits. They had to be good to be big sellers, or we didn't work. We had to coordinate a 30-piece orchestra and make sure all the union contracts were in order. The producer would pay the fees, but I had the responsibility of getting all these people together. We'd have to stay up all night and work for three, four, five days. The problem is when you take substances to cope and you don't have time to recuperate, you need more. Then the phone would ring, and they'd tell me I was doing a Lime show in Mexico City tomorrow. Then I had to go to Atlanta and Miami, then the Fun House in New York, then a TV show. You had to do something or you'd fall flat on your face! I went into private therapy with medical doctors several years ago, which involved physical and psychological treatment, and it worked. I haven't had a problem with [substance abuse] since then."

Afterward, Nobless began a process of introspection that led to her decision to live as a female and produce new music that is both a combination of her disco past and today's contemporary technology. She says, "In 2003, I started wearing nylons and dresses and wigs. I'm a good-looking she-male, and there are many of us. I'm also a recording artist. My album covers as Nini Nobless are kind of kinky, for those 18 years and older, and I'm having fun with this. My new music is a lot of fun to listen to. It's real music. I'm not a DJ that puts this and that together. I play every note. As Nini Nobless, I was delivering three albums a year, no drugs or anything! I'd love to go up on a stage and play my new music for everyone and have some fun. I think it's time for the world to realize there are a lot of us trannies out there. We're basically girls. I can't dress like a guy anymore. I have boobs bigger than Marilyn Monroe's. I always try to wear nice clothes and look great.

"It's my own little world, my sanctuary, where I've found peace of mind," she says most sincerely. "Even when people batter me, I can still sit at my keyboard and write a hit. I can put on my eye shadow, a nice dress and write a great song. I know people have prejudices and look at people like me as if we are strange. I sometimes wonder if they ever look at themselves, with their fat bellies and their bald heads, and see anything strange.

"I'm gonna keep going forward. Some of my mentors were people like Miles Davis, and he kept playing until he died. He never dwelled on the past. He kept coming up with new things, and I believe artists should be that way. Art is a living thing and like any living organism, it has to keep flourishing. There are a lot of people that were mistreated in disco. Once the companies made their money, they didn't need us anymore. But you have to keep moving on."

There is clearly frustration in Nobless' voice. "Here in Canada, it's too much trouble to operate your own record label," she insists. "The internet is a big, big problem because many of those companies that upload my music aren't honest. Once I sign off my music to one of these companies, I feel like it's in the hands of gangsters. I released some music to a company here in Quebec, and they have already done some underhanded things and treated me very badly, forcing me to go to the police. I have investigations going, but it's difficult because you need lawyers, and, to be honest, I just don't have the money. I'm semi-retired and getting along on the welfare and a small government pension. I'm getting by every month. Really, all I have is my apartment and recording equipment. Sometimes Canada seems like a third world country to me. The music business in Canada is a bit of a racket. The people who handle music here are often involved in drugs, gambling, and prostitution—you name it. I guess it was the same with the disco labels in the U.S. back then, too. I'm sure they weren't always honest either."

Nini's current albums contain dance beats and vocals strongly reminiscent of the artist's work with Lime (with a twist of electronica). Tracks such as "All Night Long," "Love Station," and "Loly Pop" are feverish and dance-floor-ready concoctions, while curious songs like "Tranny Love" and "A 1000 Times a Woman" reflect Nobless' fascination with the culture she has come to embrace. She continues to be an exceptionally experimental composer with few boundaries.

She admits, "I would still love to be signed to a good U.S. label. I don't feel like they want or need us up here, but they don't want us to leave either. What the fuck can I do? Let me tell you, welfare is no fun. Someday it will be all right, and I'll get these problems worked out, but it's not at all like it once was. Maybe one day I'll get to record 'Babe, We're Gonna Love Tonight' with Lady Gaga. I'm a big fan of hers. 'Poker Face' is a masterpiece—it's beautiful. Her voice is unbelievable. She's really good! She's better than Britney Spears, man; she's better than Madonna. She's a great musician, and I think she's a good person." Nobless recently reconnected with his glory-days associate Joe La Greca, and the duo is said to be currently mulling over opportunities to create new, commercially oriented dance music. Time will tell.

Though disco music often fails to receive its props in pop culture history, few could argue that Denis LePage/Nini Nobless was a dazzling innovator of this art form. Like her infectious, irresistible dance music compositions, Nobless defies easy categorization. While perhaps underappreciated in the challenging circumstances she lives in today, there is an untold population in every corner of the globe that has been moved and energized by her remarkable creations. Nini is cognizant of her rich history and that, for a time (as Denis LePage), she helped make Montreal an epicenter of dance music activity. But she isn't likely to bask in the glow of old reviews.

"I want to be remembered as a good recording artist for sure, and I'm very proud of what I did musically. I wasn't a medical doctor, but I knew how to make someone feel better listening to one of my songs, you know? I don't think there are any bad notes in my music; everything was well founded, and it's fun to listen to. People enjoyed dancing and partying to it," she says.

She takes the longest pause of our rapid-fire conversation, then adds, with a touch of humor, "Truthfully, I wanna be remembered as a lady-boy porno musician!" Amusing as her statement may sound, it's clear she is on a serious quest to remain true to her new identity.

"In the '80s, I was labeled as being gay or bisexual. People had a hunch that's the kind of person I was. But nobody discussed the tranny issue—effeminate men who dressed like women were called transvestites or cross-dressers. Things have changed since then. I am a registered she-male in Canada now. We are kind of protected here. It's kind of like having a panda bear in your zoo. [She laughs.] My mission as a tranny is very important to me, and I hope that will be remembered. I am glad my transformation will be known through this book. Boy George was out there. He wasn't into having a sex change, but he was very feminine. Listen, Beethoven and Hayden were also feminine. They wore make-up, high-heels, stockings. I want to be remembered for wearing my wigs and eye shadow and lipstick and talking Estrogen! I am really proud to be a transgender woman! That's the way it is—and you cannot achieve an understanding of me as a musician without understanding and accepting that side of me."

••••••••••••••••••••••••••••••

Robbie Leslie
Studio 54 DJ

"There were singers you could bank on, and in many ways they were like Hollywood stars. There are so many parallels between movie people and disco artists."—Robbie Leslie

"I go to other countries, and some of the people I meet literally want to kiss my hand because I was a DJ at Studio 54. It's amazing! In a way I'm a bit amused by it, but I appreciate it and count my lucky stars I worked there," says Robbie Leslie of spinning vinyl in disco's most celebrated club at the height of the genre's popularity. The famed disc jockey, now residing in Florida, was born in Maine in the mid-'50s. He embarked on a journey that would lead him to become one of disco's most acclaimed masters of the turntable and whose gigs at 54, the Saint, Palladium, 12 West, and other gargantuan nightlife hubs became the stuff of legend. The link between dance music and the DJ grew increasingly strong as the genre evolved, and Robbie Leslie was there through all of it, selling those beats to packed dance floors from the very beginning.

"When I was a child, I lived in a home that really had no music," Leslie recalls. "My parents married during World War II, and they danced to swing bands and such, but by the time I came along—I was the last born—there wasn't a lot of music in the house. My first exposure to pop music came when I got my first car and started listening to it on the radio. It wasn't much of a stretch to say that there was a lot of Philadelphia soul music that crossed over to pop when I was in high school. That was the stuff that resonated for me. Aretha Franklin was a huge favorite of mine when I was coming up. I came out in 1973, and that was the first time I ever went to a club. They were playing that danceable R&B music, what you might call proto-disco. As I started socializing more in my teens, becoming sort of a club kid, I was pretty much limited to nightclubs and bars in the gay environment. They all played that kind of music. I guess you could say it imprinted on me—I have very strong affection for that sound.

"I was hired as waiter on Fire Island in the mid–'70s. At that time, they were playing tapes in the bars and clubs—mix tapes by Tom Moulton, Ray Yeates, Armando Galvez and all those great early DJs. Tom, of course, was more than just a DJ, but that's pretty much how he got his start as a remixer. They were playing the best music out there! It was the total soundtrack of the club scene back then. The era of DJs finding Motown records and European imports for people to dance to was pretty much over, and clubs were having music made expressly for them. All the producers were now conscious of the sound and making music expressly for the dance floor. 'Two Hot for Love' by THP Orchestra, 'Mellow Lovin'' by Judy Cheeks, Silver Convention, First Choice, Average White Band and B.T. Express were a few of the big [songs and artists] that began to cross over to the dance market," he says.

Leslie, like so many other industry professionals, credits the gay culture with breaking disco music. "Discothèques were initially very underground, and they were largely black, Puerto Rican or gay-oriented," he observes. "They were pretty much the breeding ground of the disco sound before it crossed over. Fire Island, the Pines, Cherry Grove—having predominantly gay populations in those communities brought the music to the area. So that's how it started. Then it turned out Fire Island became the testing ground for debuting new music. I remember they debuted Gloria Gaynor's 'Never Can Say Goodbye' and 'Love's Theme' by Love Unlimited Orchestra, for example. Huge records were played first at places like the Sandpiper, where I worked. The record labels knew we had a very savvy audience there, and they would come and bring their product and test market it. They'd see what the dance-floor response was. If it failed to generate excitement, they'd have to take the track back and tinker with it or perhaps not even sign it.

"I had worked in bars since 1974, but it wasn't until 1977 that I first got into the DJ booth. Up until then, I had enjoyed listening to the music, but I didn't have any designs on playing it. Once I got into the DJ booth and had that organic reaction, in other words watching the crowd respond to what I was playing and how to put it together, I was so hooked! I was immediately addicted to that amazing chemistry between the DJ and the dance floor. And remember, the experience could be good or bad. All it took was an empty dance floor to put the fear of God into you—or something worse: a hateful disco queen who was not happy!"

Robbie takes a moment to think about his gay audiences from the renowned summer beach community during that time. "What is it about disco that gay men identified with or caused them to resonate with that music?" he questions himself out loud. "I'm speaking in very general terms, because I know a lot of gay men who hate disco and never liked it, even back then. However, a big cross section of the community certainly was bitten by the disco bug. A lot of guys responded to the female vocalists that told it like it was. I think many gay men couldn't relate to rock lyrics, and a lot of disco lyrics were about romance and love—and that can push a button with gay people. Also, the gospel side of disco seemed to affect the gay community. The emotional delivery—especially in the

"Sometimes people have generalized, saying disco was pretty much the same formula, the same stuff, over and over. Not true," says Robbie Leslie, seen here behind the turntables that brought him fame in the disco era (courtesy Robbie Leslie).

songs of the early period—was very important. And much of disco is celebratory in nature. The full-on arrangements, the lyrical thrust, the positive messages—these components dovetailed perfectly with the new Gay Liberation movement and 'Out & Proud' mentality."

Having dropped the needle on literally thousands of disco records, Robbie considers the qualities intrinsic to most of the hits. "It's important to say at this point that sometimes people have generalized, saying disco was pretty much the same formula, the same stuff, over and over. Not true. What they tend to think about is that very familiar high-energy sound and beat that couldn't really cross over to radio. But disco music actually changed distinctly every year. There were two or three sounds that became popular every season or year, and a lot of it had to do with the producers and what they were favoring. Giorgio Moroder comes to mind most obviously because he was so groundbreaking with synthesizers. Once he opened that door, a colder more electronic sound became a more integral part of the scene. It wasn't the entire scene, but in the course of the night, there'd be a lot music played that had this electronic sound, almost like pre-techno.

"The producers knew what ingredients they had to put into their songs—obvious things like the four-four time and the drums," he continues, "but they didn't always get it right. Some of the producers didn't quite *get* disco, especially if they were coming in from other genres of music. And you needed a good engineer in the recording studio. And if you didn't have a great technician who handled the record mastering well and could make the record jump off the grooves—that was a handicap. The sound had to be bright and really pop! Lyrics were very important. If they were too corny, that could be a deal-breaker with the dance floor. A lot of times, if the DJ didn't like the lyrics, he just wouldn't play the record. And that would be the end of that. The disco formula came down to content, vocal artistry, the arrangement of the song, lyrics and the EQ of the record—how good it sounds at high volume. Little hooks could make the difference for the success of a song too. Like Amii Stewart's 'Knock on Wood.' That song was a variation from the normal steady drum. It had that really exciting 'boom-boom-boom' that people instantly recognized. I remember the mix of Musique's 'In the Bush' had that little intro melody, and the dance floor would just light up when it started."

As Leslie's reputation for spinning on the island grew, so did the demand for his work. Soon the DJ's name commanded higher fees and brought in huge crowds at New York City's top clubs and hot spots throughout the country. "Manhattan represented a more sophisticated audience," he says of the legions gyrating there to his mix sessions. "It was a more refined experience. I've worked everywhere over the years—big cities, small ones, very mainstream places and also very international types of clubs. In my time in New York, the crowds were very intelligent; they knew what they liked, and they had an attitude about music. If it were deemed to be too mainstream or popular, they'd shy away from it. They had an aversion to mainstream hits. You almost had to intentionally steer away from popular material that would be the peak records somewhere else, like New Jersey. The big songs, the ones that were hits on the radio or you would hear on *Solid Gold* or *Dance Fever* just couldn't be played on some New York City dance floors. So there was definitely a bit of snobbery in Manhattan, and you really had to change your program radically when you played different areas. I learned the hard way. I'd be trying to peak the room with a Cerrone song that was huge in Manhattan, and it would completely die in Atlanta. I learned by trial and error that different markets responded to different music.

"I think you could say in broad strokes, there were two types of DJs—ones that played for the audience and ones that played *to* the audience or for themselves," he asserts. "I think it had a lot to do with your personality. My own personal taste was always secondary to what I knew the floor would like, and I played accordingly. I think a DJ needs an innate gift to adapt instantaneously to an audience that is not responding to what he is doing. Depending on the place, you go in with an idea of what the crowd will want, and, if it doesn't work, you crash and burn the entire night or you adapt immediately. Hopefully you have the music with you that they want to hear. You needed to do your homework and get a feel for what your audience typically heard, what they've been groomed to enjoy. I'd ask some club owners for an idea of what their audiences liked and they'd say, 'Oh, just be Robbie Leslie, and they'll love it!' But that's like a sycophantic response—it's not a realistic answer. My secret to success was to play for the audience, not me, and, generally, I've done very well by that. I'm still doing it 35 years later."

The relevance of the artist performing the music was, to the DJ, often dependent upon a variety of factors he says. "There were some artists you could be pretty sure would always get a great dance-floor response, but it often had more to do with the producer of the record. With somebody like Giorgio Moroder, it didn't matter as much if it was

Suzi Lane, Debbie Harry or Donna Summer. We were paying attention to who was behind the production. The big ones of course were Giorgio, John Davis, THP, Jacques Morali and, in the mid-'70s, Norman Harris, Ronnie Baker, Earl Young, Vince Montana, Biddu, Barry White and Gamble & Huff.

"There were singers you could bank on, and in many ways they were like Hollywood stars. There are so many parallels between movie people and disco artists. There were artists you couldn't wait to get their next record. You knew the minute you put the needle down it was going to be great. There were surprises of course. Many artists just jumped out of obscurity. They may have one hit; they may have had a dozen. That was the magic, the wild card in the deck. Andrea True was one of those singers. When her songs came out ["More, More, More" and "NY, You Got Me Dancing"], everyone was titillated by the fact that she was a porn star. It was also a running joke that anyone could sing a disco record because here's a porn star, and she's doing it. That's not really fair, but that was the conventional wisdom of the day. Her producer, Gregg Diamond, had a lot of cachet that we as DJs always respected and appreciated."

Leslie's fame as a DJ is inseparable from his time spent spinning at the world's most famous discothèque—the one located at 254 West 54th Street in Manhattan. What began as an opera house in the 1920s became the epicenter of disco by the late '70s. Owned and operated at the height of the disco explosion by Steve Rubell and Ian Schrager, the opulent, theatrically designed club known as Studio 54 made millions and was the worldwide Mecca for celebrity partying. After Rubell and Schrager were arrested and served time for tax evasion, the club underwent various transformations and changed hands throughout the '80s and '90s, eventually housing Broadway shows in the 21st century.

"I worked at Studio 54 through all the owners," says Leslie. "I was there with Steve and Ian and then Mark Fleischman and then Frank Cashman. Each owner was totally different, and the club atmosphere changed during each of these runs. I can tell you at the time I started working there, it was probably one of the most stressful gigs I had. The DJ booth was like a cocktail party. There were people in and out of the booth all night long. Steve Rubell would bring all his VIPs up there to watch the dance floor from that perspective. Of course, I have all kinds of secret stories that I never tell anybody about—things that went on there—but more importantly it was a job that I admit I didn't really love at the time. I appreciated the prestige of working there and was proud of that, but at the time it was not the gig I would be all thrilled to hop in a cab and go to. I knew how difficult and exhausting it would be. However, I met everyone and saw amazing things. After all these years, I can say Studio 54 was the club that opened more doors for me than any of the others. It's just known everywhere. It's such a pop phenomenon. It's a media icon. I scratch my head sometimes. It's the hard jobs that stay with you because you have to put so much effort into them. Still, I was very lucky, and I'm fully aware of it."

The vices that permeated many clubs rarely went unnoticed by Leslie, but he again points out the individuality of each venue. "[The level of obvious drug use] depended on the club," says the DJ. "If we talk about clubs where the predominant drug was alcohol—I consider alcohol a drug—well, alcohol has been a bedmate of nightlife since the first bar opened. Harder drugs were largely relegated, I think, to the big cities, except maybe for cocaine. Designer drugs that people would dance on, whether it was MDA, ecstasy or mescaline back in the day, were found in the bigger metropolitan areas. Undeniably, these drugs enhanced the nightlife experience for many people. People doing them still had to be discreet, except for maybe at the big after-hours clubs that didn't even have a liquor license. There, people did take drugs quite out in the open. Tastes change over the years, cultures shift, and the beat goes on, so to speak. As a DJ now, I see very little drug use, except at the most enormous circuit parties."

Robbie acutely felt the dark days of the disco backlash in 1979, and he has his theory about what triggered it. "I feel that a certain segment of the young people that were going to clubs didn't connect to disco music. They felt like an outsider. There's no worse experience than feeling like you aren't included. After a while, you become resentful, and that leads to hostility. I think a lot of people felt they were left out of the disco experience. Not that they couldn't go to a disco and hear the music, but it didn't click for them. They resented all this attention that was surrounding the music. They became disenfranchised, and they started a 'disco sucks' movement. It was very damaging. When a record company sees a prevailing sentiment like that, they get spooked. They withdrew their support for the music, closed their dance departments, and it really crippled DJs. Companies weren't signing anything that sounded like disco."

"Historically, I think disco has jumped up the ladder as far as preeminence and prestige goes," says Robbie Leslie, who continues to spin for euphoric crowds (courtesy Robbie Leslie).

Leslie believes the tide has turned for this music. "I think because of the passing of time disco is being looked at again. Three quarters of what I do now are retrospective events. I think there's a nice warm glow of nostalgia surrounding disco. I think people that understand the true musicianship that went into these records and can hear the artistry behind them have always had that respect. We're talking about wonderful string sections and horns, great vocalists, beautiful background voices and incredible productions on the studio end. Historically, I think disco has jumped up the ladder as far as preeminence and prestige goes," he says with assurance.

The role of DJs in making disco the phenomenally emotional and physical experience it was cannot be overstated, and Robbie Leslie's ranking as one of music spinning's finest craftsmen has never been challenged. With nearly four decades spent in the nightclub business and numerous awards to his credit, his prestige and talent allow him to continue to spin for major club events throughout the world. The DJ also produces a weekly show on SiriusXM Studio 54 Internet radio, called *Robbie Leslie Presents*. Perhaps a reflection of his affection for the genre that brought him front and center, he has little hesitation when talking about his nightlife legacy. "I want people to smile when they think of me," he says warmly. "When I come up in conversation, I want people who heard me play and danced to the music to have a very good memory of the experience. I'm an entertainer, and my principal reason for being in this business is to make people happy and to see them dance and have a great night. I want them to remember when they were going out and heard I'd be playing—that it was very good news!"

W. Michael Lewis
"Cocomotion"

"That was one thing we liked about what we were doing. We tried to keep a sense of humor with our music."—W. Michael Lewis

W. Michael Lewis, who prefers the name Mike, is regarded as one of disco's premiere songwriters, musicians and producers, as well as one of its earliest innovators. His partnership with fellow producer and musician Laurin Rinder resulted in the creation of many of the genre's most celebrated and respected hits. They include the sensuous beats of St. Tropez, the bravado of disco-swingers Tuxedo Junction, the R&B groove of Le Pamplemousse, and their pièce de résistance—El Coco's "Cocomotion." With his visionary collaborator Ray Harris (who founded American Variety International Records, or AVI, with Ed Cobb, the producer/writer of Gloria Jones' "Tainted Love" and Brenda Holloway's "Every Little Bit Hurts" in the '70s), Lewis has achieved what few can lay claim to—a still flourishing music career filled with highly lauded accomplishments in classic disco. Michael talks about his success as the creator of a sound that has become synonymous with dance-floor pleasure.

"I was born in San Diego," Lewis says. "I'm a native Californian but I grew up all over the South. My dad was a civil engineer, so we moved to different cities every two years. I lived in Charleston, South Carolina, Mobile, Alabama, Miami, New Orleans—kind of all over. I started getting into music when I was a kid. I had very bad asthma, and the doctor recommended I learn a wind instrument to build up strength in my lungs. I took up the clarinet when I was nine years old, and that got me started. I took to it really well, and by the time I was 12, I knew I'd end up in the music business one way or another. I started out being a clarinetist in my high school band, and in college, I majored in music theory and composition at the University of Alabama. I was really into classical music at that point. While I was studying, I started doing weekend sessions at the Muscle Shoals Studios in Alabama, home to recordings by Wilson Pickett, Aretha Franklin, Millie Jackson and the Staple Singers, along with rockers the Rolling Stones, Elton John, Boz Scaggs and Paul Simon. I played on a lot of demos there, and that got the rock 'n' roll bug going in me. I decided I didn't want to be a classical player and turned my interest to rock because the music had a lot more improvisation to it. I also thought I could make a lot more money at it, and that's what kind of got me started.

"I moved out to California right out of college and played in the rock band the Devil's Brigade. Later, I joined Quicksilver Messenger Service, a well-known San Francisco acid rock band. But rock bands weren't doing all that well. I was signed to a management company, and one of the people there was named Ray Harris. He would come back from European trips in the early and mid-'70s and started telling me about this new music over there called disco and that he thought it would become huge here in the States."

Partner Ray Harris describes his introduction to the new music form and his vision of marketing it to American audiences. "I was in France for the early days of the MIDEM convention, a huge music conference in Cannes," Harris says. "I started going around to various clubs in the south of France, and there were quite a few at that time. There were many big clubs in Paris, such as Regine's, and I also went to several in London. I saw what they were doing—the DJs were extending the cuts or blending them at certain interludes. I thought it was quite interesting, and it kind of gave me an idea to do something like that in the U.S. I discussed it with my late partner, Ed Cobb (former member of the Four Preps), and he agreed that it seemed like longer versions might be a good idea. I attended a *Billboard* conference organized by Bill Wardlow in New York City, where DJs were talking about the same thing.

"I had noticed a label called Coco Records, a Latin music company, and they had a couple of records on the charts. It gave me the idea of calling a group El Coco. I had Michael start working directly with me in the A&R department of my label, AVI Records. I told him about these long versions of songs I'd been hearing in Europe with a melodic beat and let him hear some of the samples I had brought back. I said I wanted to make an album that would be a take off on the movie *Mondo Cane* and call it *Mondo Disco*. Donna Summer's 'Love to Love You Baby' had broken big, and I wanted to follow that pattern."

Michael agreed that Ray's plan was workable. "Ray brought me a few import albums to listen to, and he felt if I could do something musically similar to these albums, we could sell some records," says Lewis. "I said I thought I could do that kind of music. I got into disco right away. I grew up in the Deep South, Florida and Georgia, and I had always listened to a lot of R&B and blues. I realized with disco we could use some of those influences, and I thought if we could have some success in disco, anything that would further my career and get things going would be great. It really became a lot of fun right away. It was something different and it felt very fresh."

With a plan in place, Lewis melded his talents with those of Laurin Rinder, a drummer and a partner who was highly proficient at assembling and managing musicians. They began work on their first stellar contribution to disco's early history. "We went into the studio for about a week and came up with *Mondo Disco*, our first album as El Coco. I listened to Van McCoy, Barry White and the Love Unlimited Orchestra, and that seemed like the way to go. With my classical training, I knew I could write string and horn parts, and we treated the concept as if it were a live band. 'What would that entail?' we thought. We envisioned an eight or nine piece band and would enhance it with strings," Michael says of their formula.

Ray Harris had a concept for the marketing—he wanted to make the product look like it was European. DJs who could get free promos would often go to the key music store in their city and pay for European pressings of the same music or exclusive releases just because they believed it to be of better sonic quality. Shrewdly marketed or not, *Mondo Disco* was a big success, an enormously popular release in clubs both here and abroad.

Remembers Ray, "I came back to the U.S. after another trip to Europe and, seeing how big the record was there, told Michael we ought to start a second chapter on this El Coco phenomenon. He came up with a couple of ideas, and he and Laurin came back with a new El Coco LP. It was an instrumental record at first. I felt it had to have a vocal in there and asked them to tool it a bit with another songwriter [Merria Ross, who also sang on the track]. They came back with 'Let's Get It Together.' I had to figure out how to really market this record and was concerned it would otherwise be a flash in the pan. I have to give some credit to the Cayre Brothers' Salsoul Records label, which had been doing a lot of Latin releases. They were expanding into disco. The DJs were telling me that Salsoul was releasing (non-commercial) LP's with just one long cut on each side. I got an idea to start marketing singles on LP-sized discs, labeling them 'for discos.' Instead of doing them as 33 1/3 rpm, we'd get a deeper groove and a better sound by using 45 rpm. So we started releasing what we called 'The Giant 45.' It was very successful and kicked sales up another notch. 'Let's Get It Together' and 'Cocomotion' were released as Giant 45's.' To continue the concept of European marketing style, these 'Giant 45's' had all the writing on the cover in French. Label credits were printed on the sleeve itself. It added a lot to the cache of these releases to have that look of an 'import.'"

Next up for El Coco was the single "Cocomotion." "It started out as a spoof of 'Locomotion,'" admits Mike, "even though it had nothing to do with that song. We were always trying to come up with titles that had a double entendre meaning or a kind of humor. That was one thing we liked about what we were doing. We tried to keep a sense of humor with our music. No idea was sacred at all. We'd just go wherever the moment would take us in the studio. A lot of songs happened—were created—while we were actually in the studio. Honestly, we didn't really take it that seriously at first. But then El Coco sold about 120,000 copies, and we realized we were onto a good thing, something we needed to take seriously—and we did so for the next five years. We were lucky to be right there at the beginning of the genre, and I have to give that credit to Ray with his foresight to recognize disco music. He was right!"

Flush with success, the ideas for new concepts came fast and furious. Harris found inspiration in the unusual. "Barclay Records, a large French record company, was interested in getting a hit and approached me about producing something for them," Ray states. "I met with their A&R guy at a restaurant in France, and he ordered a drink called 'Le Pamplemousse,' which he said was grapefruit juice on ice. He asked me about the group idea I would bring to their label, and I said, 'Le Pamplemousse!' What else can it be?' We laughed, but that's how that group came to be. Keeping tongue firmly in cheek, the first cover featured a woman's body with two big grapefruits positioned where breasts should be. So now we had two groups. And, by the way, we only used our house musicians on these projects. There were never really two groups. They were all the same musicians under Mike Lewis' direction. He had his crew of guys who were on most of our records. We discovered some great artists in that group of musicians, like David Benoit who became a great jazz artist."

Mike laughs when thinking about Ray's Le Pamplemousse story. "Le Pamplemousse came right after the El Coco album," he says. "We knew we could keep writing material, but we couldn't just keep putting out El Coco releases. Ray came back from France and suggested a kind of street band theme to be called Le Pamplemousse. We asked, 'What the hell does that mean?' He said it meant 'The Grapefruit' in French and that he thought it was a great name. We thought, 'Why not?' We had the Brazilian theme going with El Coco and now we'd have this funky flavor with Le Pamplemousse."

Chicago DJ Rick Gianatos made Ray and Mike aware of a new dance breaking out called "The Spank." It became the inspiration for the hit title track of the 1977 Le Pamplemousse LP, *Le Spank*. Says Mike, "We were able to come up with that record within a week. I remember the cover of the album had a shot of a grapefruit tattoo on a woman's butt. I had to redo that!" Ray laughs. Chimes in Mike, "Because of that success, we went on to do the groups Saint Tropez and Tuxedo Junction for another label, Butterfly Records. We had four groups going all at once!"

"As we got a little bit of success, we started moving on to the A-list of a lot of publishers," Lewis claims. "We had access to excellent material other than what Laurin and I were writing, and that was great. I thought of [developing the music for these groups] like acting—where you go into character. So in my mind, we'd go into the studio and I would get into character for whatever act we were working on. Each act was a little bit different, and it was easy to keep the concepts different and separate in our minds. But when the outside song material would come in, we'd listen to it and say, 'This one is good for Saint Tropez' or 'Let's do this one with El Coco.' Laurin was the beat guy and everything was 50/50 as far as writing the music went. I would usually come up with the melody, and he was good with coming up with the hooks, whether it be the title of a song or how it starts off. Laurin was a little bit more into the business side, managing musicians and such, and I was a little more on the musical side, but we had a very good balance."

St. Tropez was another concept group by Rinder & Lewis that had a sophisticated European style and was enthusiastically embraced by DJs and dancers. According to Lewis, the group was comprised of vocalists Teresa Burton, Kathy Deckard and Phyllis Rhodes. They scored two Top 10 disco hits with a brilliantly orchestrated journey into erotica. The sultry classical-meets-disco triumph "J'Taime" in 1977 and the pop-fused "One More Minute" in 1978 were major successes. Tuxedo Junction was yet another female trio, this time with a highly stylized American feel that recreated the '40s swing sound. In January of 1978, the unlikely single "Chattanooga Choo Choo" hit the disco Top Five and made its way up the pop chart. "I'm pretty sure, if I remember right, Manhattan Transfer had just come out with a new album in the big band style," Michael recalls. "I'm not sure who came up with the idea, but we thought it would be cool to do big band swing songs with a disco beat. There had been some success with classical music done in a disco style [Walter Murphy's "A Fifth of Beethoven"] and that seemed to work, so why not this idea? A.J. Cervantes, who was overseeing Butterfly Records, was onboard with the idea, so we picked out some really cool swing material. I think initially we had about 20 or 30 songs picked out, and then we chose which ones would translate to a disco sound the best. We picked 'Moonlight Serenade,' although we weren't really sure about that one, and it ended up working well. 'Chattanooga Choo-choo' became a big crossover hit as well.

"As far as the singers were concerned, the idea was to have a group like the Andrews Sisters or the McGuire Sisters. We had a vocal contractor named Marilyn Jackson at AFTRA, and she put together the three singers to make that sound happen. We thought that because those songs for Tuxedo Junction were a little more complex, it would take a long time to get the vocals down. Marilyn became the first voice of the group and the other two ladies she brought in (Marti McCall and Sue Allen) were so good right off the bat. They read music so well. They knew the style very well, and it all came together very quickly and nicely. Marilyn had been with the Ray Charles Singers and she had done a lot of studio work. They were all highly professional. We used a different set of singers—the ones who had performed live as the group on tours—when we recorded the second Tuxedo Junction album. I stayed in the studio and created the music and I let the record company and managers or agencies run with the live concepts. I know as far as St. Tropez and Tuxedo Junction were concerned, the music and concept was created first and the act was created after the fact. Basically, they started out as fictitious groups and became real ones."

The freedom to focus on creativity and not have to worry about touring with his creations was appealing to Lewis. "We were doing well at the time and had nice budgets for our productions. Because we were writing a lot of the material, the royalties were good. Things kept moving well, and because I wasn't out having to perform live with any of these acts, I could stay in the studio and keep cranking out new material, which is what we did for about a four or five year period. It was amazing. I think we were able to put out 20-something albums overall. Everything we cut went out in some form or another. If we had a bunch of outtakes lying around from a project, we'd put them together and create a new concept. That's where things like Cheetah, Discognosis and Sweet Potato Pie came from," he says. The company released a large number of 12-inch singles that were welcome additions to DJ playlists.

Observes Harris, "This was the first time you had these really long versions coming out. The problem was, you usually had publishing rates that would increase as the song time got longer. Recognizing this, if I released anything on an album, it would go at the statutory rate, and if I put anything out on a 12-inch single, I added a clause in the contracts for songs we did not publish that we would maintain that standard rate. If you had an eight or 10-minute version of a song, other labels had to add in the increased publishing cost to the cost of manufacturing. Many of them couldn't get a handle on this. This problem ended up killing the giant single eventually because it became too expensive to commercially manufacture."

Like all producers, Rinder & Lewis needed to be commercially successful in order to keep the beats flowing. But it was only one measure of satisfaction. "We always wanted to get a chart record," Michael admits. "We started out on AVI, a very small label, so anything that hit and helped to get us more mainstream was always welcome. Club hits did sell a substantial number of copies. Clubs represented a vehicle that could make the songs cross over. If we could get a song into the Top 10 with the clubs, then it was pretty easy to get it to cross over to the mainstream chart. As far as how high up it would go—

that was another story. But having a club hit definitely gave you a shot at the Top 40, and that's exactly what happened with Tuxedo Junction's 'Chattanooga Choo Choo' and El Coco's 'Cocomotion.' I was always hoping it would happen, but I didn't dwell on it. We'd finish one album and move right on to the next one. We knew what we'd be working on about two or three months in advance, though we might not have all the material together yet. I didn't have much time to think about the charts. I left that up to AVI. I'd get a phone call from someone saying I was at such and such a spot on a chart in New York or Miami. Listen, as long as they didn't cut my budgets, I was happy! I remember being in New York City and getting in a cab and hearing 'Cocomotion' on the radio. I think it was the first time I had heard my work on mainstream radio, and that made me feel really good. I was with Ray and we heard 'Let's Get It Together' by El Coco blasting from someone's apartment balcony. That's when I knew it was all really working!"

Michael is quick to recognize the importance of gaining the approval of demanding gay audiences during the growth spurt of disco music. "When Laurin and I would visit the clubs and talk to the DJs personally and try to get their support, I did notice that the gay community and their response to our music was a very big factor in the success of our records. I think there was a big party going on for that lifestyle at the time, Studio 54 and all that, and when we were looking for subject matters to make our records, we tried to think of things that would give you a shot out on the dance floor—things that might appeal to the gay community and club goers in general."

Later in 1977, the duo decided to take a momentary break from working with groups to develop a more personal, albeit avant garde, project. It was an LP called *Seven Deadly Sins* and, performing under their Rinder & Lewis moniker, they hit the Top 10 on the dance chart with several tracks. "I gotta say, *Seven Deadly Sins* was probably the most fun because when we started that project we went to Ray and asked if we could forget the concepts and just go into the studio and see what we could create totally on our own. We wanted to see what would happen. He said we could go for it. We thought that wherever the moment would take us, that's where we'd go! We just wanted to make some sounds that people hadn't heard yet. That's probably my most favorite of the work we did. The Saint Tropez material was a lot of fun too because I could use my background in classical music in playing the string parts and handling the arrangements."

Late in '79, the tide began turning against disco. Observing the trend, Rinder & Lewis detoured away from the heavily orchestrated path they'd been traveling and released a funky remake of "Willie and the Hand Jive," which was a Top 20 success on the dance chart as a co-hit with their version of "Love Potion No. 9." "Laurin and I had a rock 'n' roll band going before disco called Joshua and we always performed the song 'Willie and the Hand Jive.' We knew it mostly from the Johnny Otis version from 1958. When we performed it live, people liked to dance to it, and so we decided to do it after the *Seven Deadly Sins* project. We were kind of moving on to the next level when we did the song. We weren't sure what was going on with music at the time, but it seemed like we were hearing things that were more minimalist, records that were a lot simpler. We started with that idea and then just added a little orchestration on top."

The offbeat style of "Willie and the Hand Jive" was perhaps fortuitous of the sharp decline in popularity of traditional disco music by the decade's end. Lewis, as others in the industry discovered, had to reinvent himself. With these changes came the end of the Rinder & Lewis partnership. "In the beginning, disco music was released by mostly independent record labels," Michael observes. "Everything was on a level playing field. When the major labels became aware of what was going on, they jumped into it, and then it made everything a lot harder. They had a lot of money and could promote easily, and that's when it started changing. I think the market got over saturated—too much disco stuff. As far as me—as a producer and writer and watching the genre slow down—I wondered what would be the next big thing. As a producer you want to keep working. After doing that type of music for over five years, I'm not going to say I was burned out, but it *was* getting harder to write disco music. We had already written so much. Laurin and I had a ton of songs, and it was getting tougher to come up with new ideas. Music changed in the '80s, and new wave was starting. I started performing live more. I had been in the studio so long I felt like I needed to get back out there and play."

Ray Harris says that, just as he had seen the dawn of disco, he was sensing the sun going down on the genre. "Once the majors started really getting involved in disco, and when Andy Williams came out with a disco record, I said, 'It's all over,'" he claims. "The major labels never really liked disco. They always thought it was sort of a bastardized sound. Only the independent labels really appreciated it, like AVI, T.K. and Salsoul. Even so, the producers generally stopped coming up with new innovations in disco music, and radio started dropping disco formats. Like the big band era, the disco era died. It had reached its plateau, and AVI started concentrating on its catalog music, blues and gospel."

"I haven't been in touch with Laurin that much over the last several years," Mike admits. "It's been about five years since we've seen each other. He moved into photography, and we have gone in different directions. So we stopped hanging together, but I expect I'll probably see him again fairly soon. We left on good terms. There was no weird break-up. We just did our thing together and then went separate ways. What amazes me is that I had no idea we still had such a large fan base after so many years. I look on YouTube, and I'm blown away. I think a lot of people are realizing disco was an integral part of the '70s, and it was an important musical contribution. A lot of the modern rap and R&B songs are borrowing those beats all the time. I'm very proud of my disco history, and I consider myself very fortunate."

Lewis has kept actively involved in music over the years and being a progressive thinker and innovator in the industry has kept him grounded, engaged and enthused. "Because of the music business, I think I'll always stay young. I am definitely more health conscious today and try to eat more healthy foods, but I think my lifestyle is pretty much the same. I started in music when I was a kid, and I've never done anything else but music, so I try to find ways of keeping it going. The whole music thing keeps you young as long as you stay active in it. My brain keeps working because I'm always absorbing the work of new artists. When I'm producing something, I always want to be current and keep up with what's going on. I have a recording studio up here in the Hollywood hills, and I'm running a record label with almost 200 releases on it. Ray Harris and I started the label Snailworx (snailworxmusic.com) about six years ago and geared it toward the Internet."

Their label features an eclectic mix of classical collections, oddities like the album

Favorite Gypsy Songs of Larry Talbot and rap artists like RoRo. There are blues acts from Bluesland Productions out of Nashville as well. "I take a lot of acts that have had trouble getting their music out there and remaster catalog from the '40s and '50s. It's fun!" says Mike. After his remarkable disco heyday, Lewis went on to write theme music for the *In Search of...* TV series and scored a number of Barbara Walters specials, *Cops*, *The Price Is Right* and other television programs. He's also recorded and performed with Vicki Carr, Liberace, Billy Preston, Tommy Sands, Rick Dees, Bobby Womack, Tavares, Air Supply, and many other celebrities. He has written arrangements for Rita Coolidge, Liberace, David Benoit, Mark Lindsay, Ice T and more.

Ray holds Lewis in high esteem today. "Those musical arrangements Mike did for El Coco and Le Pamplemousse were just fantastic. To this day, we still have a great working relationship. We were a great team in those days, and Mike Lewis led the way with the work we all did together. His contributions are sometimes not recognized as often as they should be."

With a remarkable string of disco hits to his credit, W. Michael Lewis, along with his partner Laurin Rinder, is widely acknowledged today as a progressive innovator who moved disco music forward in beautiful, often stirring ways. Together, their dance-floor classics remain masterpieces that defined the era and illustrated the complexity and artistry of a genre that was once maligned as simplistic and predictable. Of his musical legacy, Michael says, "As long as I know I made people smile and made them forget their problems for a few minutes, that's what I think it's all about! The fact that I got to write music that I liked and that other people enjoyed, well, that's incredible! I think a band mate in Quicksilver said it best to me. He said, 'You mean I can do what I love and get paid for it? What else is better in life?' That's the way it's been for me, too, and I'm a happy guy!"

•••••••••••••••••••••••••••••••

George McCrae
"Rock Your Baby"

"'Rock Your Baby' was one of the best songs I ever recorded. The song appealed to everyone, universally. Gay, straight, black, white, church people—everyone was enjoying it."—George McCrae

George McCrae believes that his 1974 number one single "Rock Your Baby," written, produced and arranged by Richard Finch and Harry Wayne Casey (KC and the Sunshine Band) has sold about 82 million copies to date. His best guess may not be that far off. Online sources have listed the tune as having moved anywhere from 11 to 52 million copies worldwide at the time of this writing. Whatever the true number of units sold, George's Grammy-nominated signature song was an astonishingly successful achievement, and it became an undeniable cornerstone in pop and disco music history. It's a disco classic that helped usher in the genre with unprecedented vivacity. Today, a mature and still handsome McCrae lives comfortably off his remarkable good fortune but never allows himself to be complacent. He is confident that, professionally, his best is still to come. He enjoys taking time out from his personal exploration of life to look back at his stellar accomplishments.

McCrae, a veteran of the Vietnam War, began his entertainment career as an R&B singer on the Florida circuit. "I signed my first contract with Henry Stone's Alston Records out of Hialeah back around 1970, when I was singing with my wife at the time, Gwen McCrae," says the artist. "We were an opening act for Betty Wright and Willie Clarke, who I believe was managing her. He liked us and told me about Alston Records. I signed a contract with them, and we became like a family. Henry had lots of R&B singers on his labels and was a great man. If it weren't for him, I wouldn't be the George McCrae you know. He worked with Ray Charles and James Brown, and I learned a lot from him. Our first recording together, Gwen and I, was a song called 'Three Hearts in a Tangle.'"

Though their partnership had been modestly successful, by 1974 the focus had largely fallen on Gwen, and George had begun looking at his career options. "That's when everything got started," he recalls. "Harry Wayne Casey (KC) and Rick Finch were two very young men. At the time, I was about 30 years old. Rick was handling recording, engineering—things like that—at T.K. Records [another subsidiary label of Henry Stone's franchise and reportedly named after Terry Kane, an engineer who had constructed Stone's eight-track studio]. KC was a musician who was also working in the warehouse of Henry's Tone Distributors. Singer Timmy Thomas ["Why Can't We Live Together"] had been doing some work up in the studio, and he had left his organ there. It was the same organ you hear on 'Rock Your Baby.'

"KC and Rick used to go up to the studio at night and fool around with their music and songs, creating new material. They found some old reel tape, and they recorded the instrumental for a new song using that organ. Rick played the bass and drums, and KC handled the keyboards. For some reason, the way they recorded it, it was too high a pitch for KC's voice to handle. It was set too high for KC to sing, but it was still a great track. Back then, once you put a song on reel-to-reel tape, you couldn't go back and redo it. You had what you had, you know? A few days later Rick came to me and said they had cut a song, and he thought with my high voice it would be perfect for me. I heard the song and said, 'Yeah, I can do that!' I went home with a cassette of the track, listened to it and practiced it. I asked some ladies how they liked a man to sing to them, and they said, 'You know, like Marvin Gaye, Sam Cooke, Smokey Robinson.' Well, those were the greatest vocalists—you know I grew up with them—and they were my idols. So I thought, oh shoot, I'll just be George McCrae and sing the song naturally. I recorded the vocals in one take."

Combining George's falsetto vocal style (which was not unlike that of his idol Robinson) with such an addictive arrangement turned out to be a remarkable feat acknowledged by everyone involved. "I recognized the song as sounding special," admits McCrae. "I was personally looking for something very, very different to sing, something fresh and young. Everything I was hearing on the radio at the time was the same. Especially in R&B—everybody was singing the same way. The women vocalists all wanted to be Aretha Franklin; the guys wanted to be like Wilson Pickett—those kinds of artists. I was looking for something totally different and something that would reach everybody, not just the R&B market. I wanted the pop market too. At the time, people were really starting to get back into dancing and romancing. So I needed a song that would get to all the ladies in that way. That was the idea, and, surprisingly enough, when they released it, you know, it just broke!"

Upon the song's release by T.K. Records, some sources cite a strong reaction first coming in from France. Others say it was local Miami phenomenon that simply spread. "Believe it or not, 'Rock Your Baby' broke in the gay market first," McCrae clarifies. "It started out as an underground hit. The gay community loved the music, and in the '70s the underground gay discos really got things started. The gay clubs were where disco songs were broken first. But I got the sense the record was going to be really big about two weeks after Henry Stone released the song in the Miami area to the local R&B stations. People started calling in more and more for it. Tone Distributors got a back order for 10,000 copies of the record just in the Florida area alone. The following week it went up to 50,000 copies. All of the sudden, I got a call from the *Palm Beach Post* in West Palm Beach asking for an interview. I was like, 'Why would they want to interview me?' I was once a paperboy for them, and here they are giving me an interview. The *Miami Herald* called too. Henry phoned me and asked me to come down to his office right away, saying he wanted to talk to me. He said, 'George, we have a smash on our hands!' When he said we had a hit record, I had no idea it would become as huge as it was. Internationally! I never dreamed it would go beyond the R&B stations. But soon the pop stations started picking it up."

"All this success was scary to me. I started to wonder if the record would be a blessing or a curse. It was a blessing, though, in retrospect," admits singer George McCrae, whose smash "Rock Your Baby" became one of disco music's biggest sellers (courtesy George McCrae).

By June of '74, the track began making waves well beyond the Florida region discothèques and entered the U.S. pop charts. Within a few weeks, the song had soared to the number one position in both America and in several European countries. An album, *Rock Your Baby*, was hastily recorded to support the single. The groundswell of publicity and fame that enveloped McCrae was staggering by anyone's measure. The artist seemed to be ready and looked the part, with a handsome face and a lean muscular body (he had abs long before they were fashionably hunky). George often appeared shirtless and wearing a sexy white fringe jacket and tight matching pants. However, despite possessing a seemingly self-assured persona, he vividly recalls his feelings of anxiety.

"Wow! I wasn't prepared at all; I was from a small town. I wasn't prepared for a tour and had no idea what to do. I was lost. I started meeting people coming out of the woodwork, people I'd never met before. Everyone was trying to be my friend. I got a call to tour with James Brown, and he was the first person I ever toured with. James Brown! I opened for him at Madison Square Garden in New York in 1975. It was unbelievable! Sold-out and packed! On my second tour, I opened for the Jackson 5. There were some incredible moments. One event that really stands out for me was performing later in South Africa during Apartheid. The whole audience was integrated, and my show amazingly went off without any incidents. Everyone together! Johannesburg, Cape Town. We played theaters, and the whole audience would be dancing. This was a time where the music industry said if you performed in South Africa, you'd be blacklisted. But I went anyway. I felt I had to. But still, all this success was scary to me. I started to wonder if the record would be a blessing or a curse. It was a blessing, though, in retrospect. At that point in time, however, the transition was very difficult."

The eddy of anxiety that came with his overnight success swirled close to home, where the singer's marriage was suffering. After *Rock Your Baby*, he recorded a duet album called *George & Gwen McCrae Together*, but it did little to distract the couple from the marital problems he and his wife were experiencing. Ironically, the duo released a single called "Winners Together or Losers Apart." Gwen had a major Top 10 pop hit of her own with "Rockin' Chair" in 1975, released on Stone's Cat label, but the two were undeniably moving in different directions. In 1976, George and Gwen divorced, and sometime later he moved to Canada for about 10 years. George entered another marriage, but it too failed. Despite the turmoil, the clubs were oblivious to McCrae's personal life and embraced many of his subsequent music releases, which were fine dance confections surprisingly independent of the "Rock Your Baby" sound.

In 1976, George tried working with a new producer, Gregg Diamond (who had been having great success with the Andrea True Connection and the hit "More, More, More"). Some of Gregg's ego may have been apparent in the titling of George's LP, *Diamond Touch*, but nobody could argue with the results. Their collaboration returned the artist to the top of the disco chart with the Top Five "Love in Motion," "I'm Gonna Stay with My Baby Tonight" and "Givin' Back the Feeling." The latter track was nearly two songs in one, brilliantly mixing funk-dance with a relentlessly catchy, high-energy hook. The album was a remarkably satisfying and solid disco-pop endeavor. He teamed with producers Ray Martinez and Willie Clarke in 1978 for a self-titled album and had a Top 20 club hit with "Kiss Me (The Way I Like It)." He returned to working with Casey and Finch in 1978 for the album *We Did It*. However, later that year, with the mainstream seemingly unmoved by his follow-up material, he hit bottom financially. The T.K. record label followed suite, collapsing by the beginning of the new decade.

"After 'Rock Your Baby,'" McCrae conjectures, "KC started creating his own sound and music with the Sunshine Band. I think he was kind of focused on getting some good songs for himself. The hits. He did a great job. I was just another artist on the label, and when he started having his own hits, he didn't really have as much time to concentrate on me or write a song that would hit the mark again for me. He had to also think about other new artists he was working with, like Jimmie 'Bo' Horne ('Dance Across the Floor'). I would have liked to record some of those songs.

"But I also had management problems at the time. I had to get rid of a few different managers who were ripping me off, and it's happened to others in the business too. You have a lot going on, and you don't always know the business. I also had my marital problems, and divorces and lawyers are expensive. That took away from my concentration on finding good songs. With the first two albums, we were more relaxed and having fun. We laughed more." George makes a gesture that brings his fingertips to his lips as if smoking and smiles devilishly. "After that, it's like everybody started taking things too seriously. Everyone was thinking too much about money. If we had been in the same frame of mind as we were with the first hit, we probably could have done a better job. If you do a great song, the song will sell itself."

He considers songs by other artists that he might have lent his voice to. "I never thought I could have done a song better than another artist. After all, they had the hit. But there are some I think I could have done a very nice job with and added my own little thing. Like 'Nice & Slow' [Jesse Green], 'Swing Your Daddy' [Jim Gilstrap] or the hits of Sylvester like '(You Make Me Feel) Mighty Real.'"

Eventually, McCrae picked himself up and brushed off his missteps. "At one point," he recalls, "I finally said enough is enough, and I took control over my life. I can't complain. I've been so blessed. Thanks to 'Rock Your Baby,' I have a beautiful home in Munstergeleen (a place in Holland), a beautiful spot in the paradise of Aruba and my home in the West Palm Beach, Florida, where my family and friends are. Life has been very good to me. I'm happy. My ex-wives are happy. We're all still friends. I've had kids with them, so we're all connected."

He does, however, acknowledge Gwen McCrae's difficult struggle to return from a stroke she suffered in England in 2012 and who now lives and continues to recuperate (at the time of this writing) in Pensacola, Florida. Mindful of his past relationships, he speaks warmly of his marriage today. "I eventually moved to the Netherlands because I fell in love with my third wife, Yvonne, and we've been together for 24 years. She was a fashion model who did some TV commercials and was Miss Holland in 1971. She later became the manager of a casino in Holland where I performed."

"I look back and reflect upon what I've done, and I look to see what I can do better," says George McCrae, who still makes performing and recording a top priority today (courtesy George McCrae).

George is the father of five children. All are young adults today, crafting their own musical sounds around the world. They include Sophia McCray (his oldest daughter, a gospel singer who spells her last name a bit differently), Leah McCrae, a vocalist in America with a hip, R&B vibe, and Jennifer McCray, who resides in Canada and Belgium but records pop-rock in Los Angeles. There is also Marcella McCrae, who's been forging a career as a German hip-hop artist. George's son, Shaka McCrae, is yet another rising star, presently recording island-fused hip-hop.

Throughout his career, Europe provided a vibrant fan base for McCrae during the '90s and into the 21st century. Regularly releasing new material that caters to the Euro-disco tastes of the continent, such as a spry 2013 retread of the Dieter Bohlen and Thomas Anders (Germany's Modern Talking) hit, "Don't Take Away My Heart," George remains an in-demand performer. "I can't tell the difference between American and European audiences," the singer claims. "People are people, you know? If they feel the music—they feel it! Regardless of whether they speak another language. I think, especially being a black artist, that I *do* have a more loyal fan base in Europe. Once you become a star there, you are always a star there. They may not hear from me for two or four years, but they never forget me. You go back on tour, and they all still come to see you and support you. I could stay in the United States and perform, but the music scene is way more fickle there. It's great when you're number one in America, but then it's out of sight, out of mind when you are not.

"Disco music and disco artists weren't treated quite the same as artists in other genres in the U.S.," he adds. "It's coming back a bit now. Over time, disco has gotten more respect than it used to receive. It's funny, I really feel that if it weren't for the George McCraes, the KCs, the Rick Finches, there would never have been a lot of the artists today who capitalize on the disco sound. I'm so proud that I was part of the pioneering process of disco and that it still exists today. Hip-hop came out of disco. With technology, [today's artists and DJs] are able to sample our work, loop it and stitch it all together. 'Rock Your Baby' has been reinvented so many times by other artists over the years. It's great, and I love that I'm sometimes invited to be a part of those new versions. I'm happy to do it!"

The year 2012 saw a popular take on the artist's signature song by Miami House Attack (featuring George McCrae) storm the clubs. McCrae recently put the finishing touches on a new LP, tentatively called *L.O.V.E.*, that he believes will mark a much needed return to his soulful dance roots. Though smoldering with a contemporary dance energy and appeal, the album's retro-soul undercurrent shows the singer to still be in exceptional vocal form on key tracks such as "Oh Baby Baby" and "We Got Love."

Today, McCrae's creativity springs from a markedly positive attitude and a strong philosophy about living well. He observes, "I think it's so important to be happy with yourself. I was in the U.S. Navy, and I was a Boy Scout. You learn to be prepared! I've been blessed to have far more positive things happen to me than negative. I look at the negatives and say, 'Okay, you got me. I learned from that!' You can't turn back the hands of time, so you just move ahead to the next thing. You try not to make those mistakes again, and you put them behind you. I always say, 'I don't have any problems. I only have solutions.' I look back and reflect upon what I've done, and I look to see what I can do better. 'Rock Your Baby' was one of the best songs I ever recorded. The song appealed to everyone, universally. Gay, straight, black, white, church people—everyone was enjoying it. It took me around the world three or four times, and I still perform it today. I can't go anywhere and leave the place without singing 'Rock Your Baby.' But I know I can *still* do something even better than that!"

While it's true thoughts of one's mortality may increase as a person becomes fully ensconced in middle age, reports of George's death have been greatly exaggerated (to borrow a familiar saying). "A rock 'n' roll history book published out of Minnesota reported that I had died of cancer in 1986. It was actually the Broadway and film singer Gordon MacRae who had died in '86. They eventually corrected the error, but I'm sure a lot of people thought I was long gone. I guess there were two people who rose from the dead—Jesus Christ and George McCrae!" he laughs.

George McCrae holds a unique place in disco history as one of its original frontrunners and as the singer of one of its all-time biggest hits. Still, it's never entirely easy for any artist to think about how he or she would like to be remembered when it all is said and done. McCrae pauses and looks slightly away in humility, as if it is difficult for him to admit the statement he is about to make.

"I just want to have been loved," he finally says softly. "That's always been my aim. We all want to be loved, right? With the way things are right now, it seems like so many people just hate each other for no good reason at all. They are forgetting all about love—loving each other and caring for each other. The new generation has to learn this. My music has brought a lot of people so much joy and love, and I am very, very proud of that. I'd like that to be what people remember."

•••••••••••••••••••••••••••••••

Denise Montana
"#1 Dee Jay"

"How can you be sad or upset when that music plays? It made everybody happy."—Denise Montana

She's a singer who Bob Perkins of Philadelphia's WRTI jazz radio described as having "a beautiful voice filled with passion that comes straight from her heart." That pure passion applies as much to Denise Montana's work in classic disco as it does to jazz. Few songs back in 1978 read like a love letter to the guys and gals spinning disco records in the clubs and on the radio better than "#1 Dee Jay." It readily identified the undeniable bond between the singer, the song, the vinyl and the record spinner. Still, it would never have attained classic status had Montana's song not passed the litmus test by packing dance floors to capacity. Estimated by some reports to have sold over a million copies, the song was a collaboration between Denise (known then as Goody Goody) and her world famous father, MFSB core member and the Salsoul Orchestra's musical maestro, Vincent Montana, Jr. She went on to build a varied and accomplished musical career and proudly says disco has remained close to her heart. Likewise, working with her father (who passed away on April 13, 2013) is a memory she cherishes and happily recalls today.

"I grew up with my mother and came from a very musical family," says Denise. "My mother's brother, Mike Pedicin, was sax player in a jazz band, and my father, Vince Montana, Jr., started out in Mike's band in the '50s. My uncle told my mother never to hang out with musicians, and he didn't want her to go out with any of them. But she ended up going out with Vince, and the next thing they knew, they fell in love. They got married, and they had me. They were together for a year or so, and they divorced. My mom and I then lived with my grandfather in Philadelphia. It wasn't easy. I wish I could say I had a magical childhood, but the truth is I didn't. My mother had difficulty making it on her own taking care of both my grandfather and I. As a child who didn't see her father often because of the divorce, I felt a sense of loneliness and alienation at times.

"Still, my mother tells me when I was four or five, I'd jump on a chair and just start singing! They tell me they were always entertained by me. I was also very much introverted and shy, but I guess I appeared to be extroverted. I remember having a little record player that my Uncle Mike bought me, and I would play my 45's over and over. Music was a savior for me, then and now. My mom remarried when I was about six years old, and they had a child, my brother Craig."

Once in her teens, the call to music began to strengthen in Denise. It didn't take long for her father to notice his daughter's gift for song. "My dad recognized I had potential as a singer when I started seeing him again at about the age of 14," she remembers. "He was part of the band on *The Mike Douglas Show*, and I was able to watch my dad play on the program. He took me out to lunch, and I guess there was a song playing on the radio, Diana Ross and some Motown songs I think, and I would sing along in the car. He asked me if I liked to sing, and I told him I loved it. He and I started doing some commercials together, with me singing and he creating the music. I had already been in some stage shows—talent shows, some Neil Simon plays, musicals, Greek tragedies (I even played Dorothy in a telecast of a Gene London production of *The Wizard of Oz*)—all things I did growing up before reconnecting with my dad."

Montana soon had her foot in the door over at Vince's stomping ground, Salsoul Records. She says, "One of my first opportunities was singing the demo for 'Runaway,' which would later be recorded by Loleatta Holloway. I can tell you she sang some of it in many respects the way I did, and I heard some licks in there that I had laid down. That often happens with demos. Of course, Loleatta put her own amazing spin on it, and she had a big hit with it. Ironically, I often sing the song in my own show today.

"In my early 20's, my dad asked me if I wanted to try singing a song called '#1 Man,' not '#1 Dee Jay,'" she remembers. "I gave it a try, and they liked it, but they ended up changing it to '#1 Dee Jay,' which turned out to be perfect. It became a song to give back to all the DJs who had recognized so many singers and musicians like my father. Atlantic picked up the record. My dad was really smart. He didn't want to just sell me as his kid and have people say, 'Sure Vince, your kid can sing.' He was trying to avoid being accused of nepotism I believe. He decided to call me by the name 'Goody Goody,' and then, later on, people got to know the vocalist was really I, Denise Montana. Not a lot of people knew that at the time, and that was fine. It didn't bother me. I think at that time there were a lot of pseudonyms being used by disco artists. There were groups like Chic and

Musique, and that may have influenced his decision to call me Goody Goody. Truthfully, it might have been better for my career if I had gone out as Denise Montana from the beginning. I had a DJ write to me recently saying he had no idea I was the voice of Goody Goody."

The opportunity to bond with her father through music was especially meaningful at this stage of Denise's life. "I had wanted to live closer to my dad, his wife Hilda, and my brother Vincent and sister Eileen (from my dad's marriage to Hilda). I knew he was doing so many great things in the business. I wanted to be around all of that. I picked up and moved closer to him—literally into his neighborhood. I loved doing music, and he was telling me he had some connections with people, and I felt I should grab the opportunity. The studio is one of my favorite places to be, besides performing on stage,

Denise Montana belts her hit single "#1 Dee Jay." *Inset:* Denise with her father, Vincent Montana, Jr., the late composer and arranger of many of Salsoul Records' biggest hits (courtesy Denise Montana).

because it's such a creative place. My father was so incredibly talented. As a producer and arranger, he knew how to get what he wanted out of a singer. We went through ['#1 Deejay'] and the arrangement, he would make suggestions for me to go back and sing it this way and then a different way, and we completed it in just two takes. That was it! If you have the heart and soul and voice, I don't think you usually have to go through it a million times.

"We didn't have any of the technology they have now to make sure you are singing in tune. We just cut it. He was a perfectionist and knew what he wanted to hear, and I was the same way. So you can be sure we would bump heads at times. But he knew music inside and out. He was a great person to work with, both professionally and as his daughter, even though we sometimes had our creative differences. Getting to know him better in the session—it was a beautiful thing that we connected through the music. I will treasure and keep that experience in my heart forever," she says, exhaling with emotion.

The track ended up a Top 20 disco chart hit late in 1978 and the *Goody Goody* album that followed, released by Atlantic Records, yielded two additional club hits with "Bio-Rhythms" and "Super Jock." Another track, "It Looks Like Love," was favored in Europe. "'It Looks Like Love' started out as commercial for a tuxedo company, and we decided to make a song out of it!" she laughs. And for the record jacket, take note that's *not* Denise yanking down a tank top to reveal a formidable bosom in the cover photograph, though the singer says the image went well with the times.

"We did a show for the Academy of Music in Philadelphia with my dad's 32 piece orchestra," Denise recalls with an excited voice. "It may have been 36 piece; I'm not sure. It was Chic, Musique, and the orchestra and I. We rocked out with 3,000 people in the audience! It was sometime in 1979 or 1980 I think. That was a big deal! It was also fun seeing my song go up the *Billboard* chart. I'm looking at some clippings as we speak. September 11, 1978—'#1 Dee Jay' is number eight, Goody Goody. On *Discothèque Reaction*, it was number two. I haven't seen these in a long time. I'm looking at ads for all the clubs I played. Perrillo's, Valentino's, Dillinger's, Emerald City. I remember doing a TV show called *Soap Factory Disco*. I'd love to see a clip from that show again!"

The artist recorded more for the Salsoul label, including the cut "Merry Christmas All" by the Salsoul Orchestra for the *Christmas Jollies* album. "It was huge!" she claims. "That sold millions of copies; I know it did! Neither my father nor I received the financial benefits that song earned, however. It's on tons of compilations, and it's a Top 100 Christmas song. And every December that song *still* gets airplay. I even sing it in the middle of July because I love it so much. [She begins to sing the track.] The reason we didn't name it 'Christmas Time Is Here' was because Vince Guaraldi and Snoopy had that name locked up from the *A Charlie Brown Christmas* show. So when I perform it, I always ask the audience, 'You know my Christmas song, right?' They usually stare at me like, 'Huh?' Then I start singing it, and everyone goes crazy because they *do* know it! They all start singing it with me no matter what time of the year it is. It's really cute."

According to the artist, she saw it all, the good, the bad, and the ugly, but never let the era's vices affect her experience. "Drugs were everywhere, all the time," she admits. "I saw a lot of people doing them. Everywhere I performed, Atlantic would send me a magnum of Dom Pérignon, so I guess alcohol is a drug too. After a gig, we'd party with the champagne! We'd do it up and go back out on the dance floor and dance it up! I think, for me, coke and whatever else a lot of these people were doing just wasn't something I wanted to be involved with. I did smoke pot when I was younger, but I would never perform high. I didn't do drugs, unless you consider pizza one. I admit I'm a bit of a food addict even today. It's always been a struggle to stay a certain weight, and food has always been something of a vice for me."

Denise says she had no hesitation about becoming a disco star. "Disco was it!" she exclaims. "I had sung in a small rock band, and I loved all music. Disco was really happening at the time. Even back then, my mantra was 'love to, have to, got to, wanna sing!' I had a ball. As a result of recording that song, I did a lot of television and went everywhere. Disco was what I was growing up with, and I loved singing in that style. We were supposed to get a deal for another album, this time with Columbia, but they dragged their feet, and then, by the early '80s, the music landscape had started to shift so much. The opportunity was lost. Suddenly, disco wasn't happening."

Following the disco meltdown, Montana began pursuing other musical ventures, and she's delighted that it's all come full circle. "I started doing jazz gigs and blues," she says. "I was still doing some Top 40 and disco at some clubs, but everything had changed quite a bit. I also had a son at the time and was starting my family, and it began to get tough to travel at that point. I have two sons now (Eli and John) and they are grown, so it's great. I also have a stepson named Damon from my husband Tom. I've been able to return to my music, and I can travel again and do more shows today. I think there are more opportunities opening up now. There are more and more disco shows. I'm just getting back into it, and disco is really in my heart. I started appearing at the Resorts World Casino in New York and on other disco diva shows, and I am really enjoying it. I don't have as many hits as, say, France Joli and Gloria Gaynor. But if I stick with it, I think people will get to know me again. I do covers of Karen Young's 'Hot Shot,' and I'm thinking of adding the O'Jays' 'I Love Music' (which I actually recorded in 1980 with my dad). I also have some unreleased disco tracks my father recorded and gave to me back in January and February of 2013, and it might be really something if I can build some new songs around those tracks or even record my vocals on them. It would be very cool!

"I'm ready! I have my show all ready to go. Music—being involved, performing, being in the studio, writing songs, being around musicians—it keeps me energized and feeling great. Music is in every fiber of my being. I won't say I get depressed when I don't sing, but if I don't for a while I have to go out and find some outlet where I can use my voice and create!" Montana acknowledges.

"Oh my God, everywhere I go DJs ask me, 'Am I your number one DJ?' And I love it! Of course they are!" beams Denise Montana today (courtesy Denise Montana).

Denise appreciates being connected with her legendary father, who she says was very proud of his work. "My dad and I come from the same mold in that we both love music. He started out playing jazz with Charlie Parker, Clifford Brown and Sarah Vaughan. Then he went over to Sigma Sound Studios in Philly. You can hear his vibes on all those Philly records. That's all he wanted to do. It didn't matter what form it took. 'Tangerine' [by the Salsoul Orchestra] was a great example of what he could do. My dad came from that era, the '40s and the '50s where that song was originally from, and he transformed it into a beautiful dance record. How can you be sad or upset when that music plays? It made everybody happy. And that made him very happy. But I have to say he didn't really know how many people loved him. He knew he was known worldwide, but he didn't get to see how many people wanted to express that love after he passed away."

Before his passing, Vince Montana was aware that he would be inducted into the Philadelphia Music Alliance Walk of Fame in 2013, which Denise says brought him immense joy.

In the year 2000, Vince Montana released a compilation CD that contained an assortment of tracks by his favorite Philly singers, including his daughter. On the back of the album, Vince had this to say:

> Denise Montana, my lovely daughter, has my musical genes. Denise is most noted for her club hits "# 1 Dee Jay," "It Looks Like Love," and "Goody Goody." Her jazzy sophistication is inherent in much of her other music, most notably "Merry Christmas All." She shares my love and respect for the great jazz era that produced such legendary singers as Ella Fitzgerald, Sarah Vaughan and Shirley Horn, to name a few. When Denise presently performs, her shows consist of great standards attributed to that timeless era. Although I did not spend as much time as I wanted with her, she cultivated and developed her own musical soul. My love for her is both fatherly and eternal, and my respect for her natural gift goes beyond my own artistic understanding.

Meanwhile, Denise Montana has secured her standing in disco history in her own right by having recorded a magnificent disco evergreen that embraced the DJs who had championed all of the genre's classics. "Oh my God, everywhere I go DJs ask me, 'Am I your number one DJ?'" she recounts with delight. "And I love it! Of course they are! The song was not a traditional love song, but '#1 Dee Jay' tells them how much they are appreciated for putting disco singers and our songs out there! I know my dad and I thought of this as we were making the song—we were trying to give something back to them! I tried to convey that in my performance, and I was giving it more than 100%! I think that people, my audiences, have felt that. I'd like to believe that everyone who has seen my show left feeling that I really loved my audience. I'd like people to know that I was, and am, grateful for the gift to sing and to be able to use my voice to make others feel their emotions! And disco made them feel *great*!"

Eddie O'Loughlin
"Doctor's Orders"

"I would say the record from the disco era that gave me the most satisfaction and that I enjoyed working on the most was Carol Douglas' 'Midnight Love Affair'..."

"I believe in staying fresh, new and aware of what's going on. I believe in staying curious. I continue to look for new directions and innovative ways to move forward," says producer, songwriter, remixer, label-owner and music industry executive Eddie O'Loughlin. Eddie was there from the very beginning of disco when he co-founded Midland International Records (later called Midsong International) and helmed the Midsong Music publishing company—and he's never stopped reinventing himself since. O'Loughlin was responsible for releasing a plethora of classic disco and dance records that became staples of the genre, from Carol Douglas' chart-topper "Doctor's Orders" to Salt 'n' Pepa's ground-breaking "Let's Talk About Sex." He successfully co-ran two major independent recording labels, including his exemplary start-up company Next Plateau Records, and he's expanded his list of accomplishments to include the challenges of discovering artists and repertoire for the NBC-TV network's *The Voice*. Though never content to live in the past, O'Loughlin doesn't mind a bit talking about his history and eagerly shares his memories of the disco revolution. He speaks with a calmness that is at the same time soothing and energizing, reflective of a man who has been able to successfully channel his positivity towards admirable goals for literally decades.

"That was a good era, a fun era and time of growth in America in the recording industry," O'Loughlin (sometimes called "Eddie O" in the business) says of the dawn of disco with a peaceful exhale. "It was a fresh time for music. I remember clearly, around May or June of 1974, a friend of mine named Steve Greenberg, who was a promoter for RCA Records, said that there was a new way of launching a record—through the clubs. He took me out with him one night to a club in New York called Le Jardin on 43rd and 6th I think. The place was packed—I thought it was amazing! The DJ was playing a lot of different beats, but not a lot of songs. There were a few Barry White tracks, and they seemed to be incorporating long beat segments into more popular records. Almost like forcing the rhythm with percussive beats. Then he took me to another club on 46th Street where Richie Kaczor was the DJ [later associated with Studio 54] and kind of the same thing was going on. A light bulb went on in my head, and I started to wonder if I could take songs and incorporate these great instrumental tracks or breaks into them. They were so wonderful—they had bounce and energy. I don't think anybody was even calling it disco yet. It was all so new!"

The seed planted in his fertile brain, Eddie went to work formulating what ended up being one of the earliest original hits of disco, a genre that was just beginning to enjoy commercial success with songs like B.T. Express' "Express" and the Hues Corporation's "Rock the Boat." "I had a song called 'Doctor's Orders' that I had found in England recorded by a girl named Sunny," O'Loughlin remembers. "I auditioned for a girl to sing it here in the United States, which turned out to be Carol Douglas. I took her to the studio with DCA (Disco Corporation of America), which was a great production company, and we made the song for Midland Records. I was a partner and co-owner of Midland along with Bob Reno." Eddie credits the collective creativity and arrangement skills of Meco Monardo and Lou DelGatto of DCA Records for the catchy musicality of Carol's debut record. "They also had helped create Gloria Gaynor's huge hit, 'Never Can Say Goodbye,'" he says. "Our publishing company was DCA's publisher, and we had the rights to all the songs they published with Jay Ellis and Tony Bongiovi. I had made that deal back in 1973 with them, and we were all working together. We built Midland into becoming a very successful publishing company, and we'd often have five of the Top 10 songs in any given week on the *Billboard* disco charts. On 'Doctor's Orders,' we added the percussive rhythm we needed, combined with a great, commercially viable singer and a very memorable song."

O'Loughlin's instincts and ability to recognize a hit were spot on. The song climbed to number two in the earliest days of the music industry's club surveys, quickly crossing over to pop, where it fell just shy of the Top 10 on *Billboard*'s best-selling singles chart. "It was such a new sound that when we released it in October of 1974; it was just an instant hit record. It sold over 100,000+ copies in the first five days! If a single was Top

5 in the clubs, you could sell between 100,000 and 175,000 copies or more without crossing over. And if you did crossover, you could easily sell 100,000 albums. All that changed over time of course.

"I thought Carol Douglas delivered all her records beautifully. Carol's voice was like a violin. It's like she just ice-skated over the tracks! I learned that with her smooth sound, she could just glide over the music. We did very well with her in the clubs. Later, I tried to give Carol a pure R&B sound, but we just couldn't find an audience for her. We did a killer R&B record with her called 'We Do It.' She sang it fantastically, and the song had been a former number one hit in England. But it just didn't work, and that was disappointing. Nas used that same track a few years ago and had a big single with it called 'Remember the Times.'

"Again, I don't think we had fully identified the music as disco yet," the producer recollects. "I think we were looking at these records as danceable R&B. We weren't calling Gloria Gaynor, Carol Douglas, Barry White and other artists like that 'disco singers.' The term 'disco' probably [became more widely used] a few months after that."

Eddie and his team knew they were on to something, and it wasn't long before the fledgling disco genre was clearly a sound to be taken seriously. The producer began looking for other artists and quality songs to launch in a hurry. "We were off to the races," he says, "because after I found Carol Douglas, I discovered an amazing group. I found out about them at a MIDEM [Marché International du Disque et de l'Edition Musicale] music convention in France, an international gathering that still takes place today. It was a place where record company executives would go to exchange ideas. I had gone to see some guys from Germany because somebody told me they had a really good record called 'Save Me' by a group called Silver Connection. I thought it was just amazing when I heard it, and everything about it sounded really, really good. Bob Reno and I signed them right away. The record did okay for us, but wasn't a big hit. Then they sent us their next single called 'Fly, Robin, Fly,' which was just incredible! In that time though, a group that was playing on cruise ships claimed that they owned the name Silver Connection so we changed our group to Silver Convention and we did just fantastic! We put those records out and just ducked!"

Silver Convention was comprised of female singers, usually reported as Jackie Carter (quickly replaced by Linda G. Thompson), Ramona Wulf and Penny McLean (who scored a disco hit on her own with "Lady Bump"). Rhonda Heath and Zenda Jacks were also members at various junctures in the group's history. Silver Convention initially floated around for a short time in the U.S. on Midland promo copies under the name "Silver Bird," with tracks produced by Michael Kunze and arrangements by Silvester Levay. O'Loughlin claims that one of the vocalists in the original formation singing "Fly Robin Fly" was actually Donna Summer. "We had a contract with her name on it, and we had to give her a release because she wanted to have her own solo deal," says Eddie. "The producers called us and said, 'Oh, you gotta let Donna go! She's got a great opportunity to do a record someplace else.' We did; we complied. She left the group just before 'Fly Robin Fly' came out. She's on that song and a few of the group's debut album cuts."

If it was Summer that O'Laughlin recalls being named on the contract (some reports indicate the singer may actually have been Roberta Kelly), the famed vocalist gambled wisely on her solo breakthrough, "Love to Love You Baby." But Silver Convention was not to be outdone. "Fly Robin Fly," with its simple lyrics, hard thump and powerful strings, won a Grammy, earned the number one spot on the pop and disco charts late in 1975 and went on to sell over a million copies. The group nearly duplicated the feat with the follow-up single, "Get Up and Boogie," which made it to number two on the pop side. With a new line-up of vocalists, the group later worked with legendary producer John Davis, who O'Loughlin calls his closest friend during the era. O'Loughlin's publishing division handled many of Davis' classic disco songs (recorded for the SAM Records label).

The catalog of successful dance-floor hits released by Midland grew steadily and carefully as O'Loughlin meticulously selected the artists, songs and albums his company chose to support. The label became home to Touch of Class (a John Davis production), Inner City Symphony (arranged in part by Warren Schatz of "Turn the Beat Around" fame), Silver Convention soloist Linda G. Thompson, Wardell Piper ("Super Sweet"), Ferrara (*Wuthering Heights* LP), and the Charlie Calello Orchestra ("Sing, Sing, Sing," a hit for Benny Goodman in 1938 and a track that spent almost six months on the disco chart in 1979). The company also released *Steppin' Out* (a compilation that featured hits by the Andrea True Connection, Liquid Pleasure and other stars of the day) and even a disco venture by Arthur Fiedler and the Boston Pops, with their LP called *Saturday Night Fiedler*.

Midland's reputation for successful endeavors expanded further with the arrival of an artist that became indirectly associated with disco music—though not as a singer. Teen heartthrob John Travolta of ABC-TV's *Welcome Back, Kotter* was on the fast track to stardom when he crossed paths with O'Loughlin. "I couldn't have predicted John Travolta would become the star that he did," Eddie admits. "He was playing the part of Vinnie Barbarino on *Welcome Back Kotter*. People would joke that my partner's name was Bob Reno and that it sounded like Barbarino. Someone brought John to our office, and we liked him. I had a song we had found in England that I couldn't get anyone to sing called 'Let Her In.' We asked John to sing it, and he became such a star it was amazing! I think we signed him [late in 1974] and forget it—his single just took off. The TV show was a smash, and then he went on to do *Saturday Night Fever*. He was a very impressive guy—very cool, very eager. Even though John wasn't really into recording, we achieved hits beyond our dreams with his [interpretations of tracks] from the *Grease* soundtrack like 'Sandy' and 'Greased Lightnin'. John's focus remained on acting, and he played to his strengths."

With his records breaking out of the discothèques more and more frequently, O'Loughlin began paying close attention to this new launching ground. He recalls, "We really started focusing on being club-based. The DJs started becoming very important. They'd come to the offices every week. The record pools started and those guys would come in, and we'd give them 35 or 40 copies of a new record. They'd pass them out to the other DJs. We started asking about what was happening in the clubs. We asked what were the DJs saying about the records. Then some of the good radio programmers, like Frankie Crocker of WBLS, would start hitting the clubs to see what was moving at the Paradise Garage or Studio 54. If a record was shaking the floor up or getting a great reaction, you can bet it would be on the radio—like hours later! Then these records would start to hit on R&B radio around the country.

"Disco wasn't in every city; some of them didn't even know what it was. My brother Jimmie promoted our records in Los Angeles to see what was happening there. He only found four clubs, and they all closed at something like 11 p.m. A lot of cities didn't have discos in those days—1974, '75. They didn't really start rising up until the following years. Boston was after New York. Montreal, Miami, Philadelphia—those were big cities for disco. But then it started spreading everywhere as the music became more popular."

Eddie saw many of the vices that plagued the emerging disco culture early on, but says he was able to keep his distance. "Midland was never a nightlife company. I wasn't in the clubs that much. I know there was rampant abuse of drugs in the DJ booths—I would see that when I went out. You'd see a pile of white powder in the recording studios too. But the people we worked with—Carol Douglas, John Travolta, John Davis—we never got into any of that. Like-minded people find each other I think. Myself, my team—frankly we were never the hippest, coolest people. We were focused on getting hit records."

O'Loughlin says he was always appreciative of the good fortune he experienced in those days, and he quickly recalls the moment when he realized he had moved into the big league. "We were publishers and had to learn the record business when we started up Midland in 1973. We had RCA Records [as a distributor] to hold our hand, truthfully, but in 1976 we had two records in the Top 10. Silver Convention's 'Get Up and Boogie' at number eight and John Travolta at number 10, either gold or platinum records. I remember thinking, 'We're doing *really* good!' We changed our advertising slogan from 'the little engine that could' to a play on Motown by saying something like 'the new sound of young America.' I have a lot of gold records. I moved a lot of them out of my office and to a closet in my basement—I don't know what to do with them!"

From this spectacular era of legendary disco classics, the producer pauses to consider the records of which he is most proud. He takes his time, almost as if he is thumbing through a vast record bin in his mind and says, "I would say the record from the disco era that gave me the most satisfaction and that I enjoyed working on the most was Carol Douglas' 'Midnight Love Affair,' followed by Carol's 'My Simple Heart.' I really owned every note of those records. I was on top of every nuance of every track (we started with 16-track and eventually went up to 24). I was focused on every dimension of how those songs were played. I knew what instruments were on each particular track. I really spent an enormous amount of time on both of them. I lived with those records for months until I felt they were right. I would do them over and over again until I felt they were perfect. That was unusual because there's a commerce factor involved, and these records have to earn money. But I didn't care, and I just stayed with them until I got them right. They were very popular in the clubs and on New York's WKTU. 'My Simple Heart' did very well in France—I loved that Bugatti and Musker song. It was a little too light for American audiences, but in Europe it found its way. These songs didn't cross over, but you heard them all the time!"

There wasn't so much a formula behind O'Loughlin's disco success as there was a standard by which he operated. "One talent that I possess is that I am very song-oriented," he claims. "So, regardless of the genre, the song and lyric must be memorable. I can dress it up to the current market sound. Disco rhythms enthralled me, but I was more interested in bringing real songs to that market. Silver Convention was very melodic, very beautiful.

The songs themselves were appealing to me, but not just for the reason that they could be classified as disco. I was never driven only by the track. I was always influenced by the voice and the melody and the lyrics. As to whether I'd pick up European singers like Silver Convention or cover a song by an American like Carol Douglas, it didn't really matter to me. I just looked for the best record. To this day, I still sign talent internationally, and I still create talent in America. It's a blend that I've been doing for something like 43 years. It's still the same formula, if you want to call it that, which I've always been using. When I moved into the rap era about 25 years ago, I always worked with artists who sang real songs, melody after melody, regardless of the musical category."

The media headlines proclaiming the so-called death of disco late in '79 had a rippling effect throughout the music industry, and Eddie felt the blow. He ponders the reasons for the slide and says, "I think disco just got overexposed. The majors started coming in around 1978, flooding the market. Quality control went down. The early records that were on the independent labels had a lot of love put into them. T.K. Records, Salsoul, Scepter, Midland—we were the companies that showed a lot of care in the making of disco records. Then the majors came in and collectively started throwing 50 of them out on the market every week. I think disco just got eaten up. It happens with every genre. It happened with rap 10 or 15 years later. By 1980, I was calling people up, and they wouldn't return my calls. I was like, 'This is bad!' People would make believe they didn't see me at a restaurant. People would cross the street rather than have to talk to me. They liked me still, but they felt bad for me and felt like I was part of something that was dead!

"I ended up leaving Midland Records in 1979. It was time for me to own more of my own destiny and search for a new sound I could do well in. Meanwhile, Prelude Records came in during the early '80s, and they did very well in dance music. But for many labels, it really dried up a lot. Personally, it was a very difficult time for me. I had to really reinvent myself. I produced a few hit dance records in that period for other labels with artists like Sharon Brown ('I Specialize in Love') on Profile and Jenny Burton (the album *In Black and White*) on Atlantic, but I still needed to try and figure out where to go next."

The producer refocused his energy, became an entrepreneur and managed to create a small recording dynasty that was integral to the development of '80s dance, rap and hip-hop. "I started Plateau Records, which later became Next Plateau," he says, his serious tone reflecting the difficulty of the venture. It was a hard-fought success story. "I started off trying electronic sounds and found a genius producer named John Robie, and he did a record for me by C-Bank called 'One More Shot,' which he produced in 1982 for my new label. He was also the man behind 'Planet Rock' (Afrika Bambaataa & Soulsonic Force) and 'Hip Hop, Be Bop' (Man Parrish). I always had confidence in myself, but I didn't realize how hard it would be. I was still a little too naive. I wasn't that clear on how rough having a brand new start-up could be. I had to learn a lot. I discovered people that once liked me weren't going to give me [financial] credit after working with them for eight or 10 years. But ours was a new company, and we had a new, unproven business. It was a very eye-opening, white-knuckle time and a very difficult five years for me. We always managed to come up with a record that sold 150,000 or 200,000 copies fortunately, and that kept us going. Eventually, I really had a great team assembled. Jenniene Leclercq became my partner in 1985. I don't know how brave we were, but it required tremendous perseverance and persistence to keep going without huge hit records. Then we made it to number one, ironically with Princess' 'Say I'm Your Number One' in 1986, and we never had to look back. After Jenniene and I partnered, she ran the business, and I made and promoted the records. We ended up producing something like 40 gold or platinum records over the next 12 years."

The team's breakthrough rap-dance smashes in the mid-'80s and early '90s illustrated the marketability of their winning formula. Biggest among them was with Salt 'n' Pepa, a Queens, New York, trio that reached number six on the *Billboard* dance chart with the gargantuan hit "Let's Talk About Sex." "With artists like Salt 'n' Pepa, Sweet Sensation, Sybil, Paperboy, Ultramagnetic MC's, 4PM, and KWS, we had a ten-year run together and sold over 12 million albums," Eddie says with pride. "Ultramagnetic MC's, one of the coolest hip-hop bands of all time, was a big critical success [with the LP *Critical Beatdown*], and Dr. Dre called that album a major influence on his work. I was, and am, always looking for great delivery and a great song. However, the industry has changed so much. The DJ is the star now, as opposed to the singer. The DJ is the draw, and all these great singers featured in their music are on the second tier."

The executive's learning process over so many years is one he continues to hone. O'Loughlin is especially cognizant of the importance of a positive mindset, regardless of aging. His attitude is not unlike those of progressive life-coaches and thinkers like Anthony Robbins or the late Earl Nightingale. "We all have to reinvent ourselves," he explains, "especially in today's world. You can end up reinventing yourself three or four times in a lifetime. I keep my ear to the ground every day and, by the way of example, I signed a record that just got added to Sirius' *BMP* this week. Sirius is *the* station that sells and breaks electronic dance music in America. I've had 20 records on their chart in the past three years."

O'Loughlin has continued to expand his horizons. "I saw a television show in Holland called *The Voice* about two years ago," he says. "I knew nothing about television, but I knew the show had great singers and songs. So I called the presidents of Universal Records, who are good friends of mine named Monte and Avery Lipman. I told them it looked like it could be a hit if it were to come out in America. I recommended they should try to get the music rights to the show. Well, they did, and I now work for the show as an A&R consultant for Universal Republic Records and as a talent producer. Right now I'm working with a singer from the show who is one of the greatest singers I've ever heard in my life. Judith Hill—she's at the level of Aretha, Chaka Khan, Patti Labelle. She's spectacular! I discovered her and got her on *The Voice*." The program features four stages of competition among unknown singers (though they don't stay that way for long) who are coached by luminaries like Adam Levine, Blake Shelton, Gwen Stefani, Usher and Shakira. It has been a ratings smash for NBC that outshines former institutions like FOX's *American Idol*. The show provides further evidence that O'Loughlin's instincts for what the public will savor are as sharp today as they were when disco was shaping up as the next big thing.

Eddie O'Loughlin's career was launched in disco. The evidence of his remarkable ability to identify quality music and his knack for pioneering some of the genre's most revered classics can still be heard on the radio and spinning from DJs' turntables worldwide.

Where this remarkable entrepreneur will end up in his ever-evolving musical journey is anyone's guess, but it's certain this warm and compassionate visionary will always be developing the very best talent the industry has to offer. When asked about his legacy, he doesn't call up any of his hits or remark on his stellar ranking in the business. Instead, Eddie says, "I would like to be remembered as a person who was very passionate about music and very caring about everybody I worked with. I hope they knew that I cared deeply about them—that's the truth."

Rob Parissi, formerly of Wild Cherry
"Play That Funky Music"

"There were also a lot of places where we'd go on stage, the lights would come up and the crowd would go, 'Oh my God, they're white!'"—Rob Parissi

Was disco some kind of evolution of soul and R&B best sung by black performers? Does any race or culture have the right to claim ownership of a music genre? Were different music styles somehow diametrically opposed to each other? These questions arose as dance music gained a formidable hold of pop culture in the mid–'70s. The fervid debate came to a head (of sorts) in 1976, when a relatively unknown band called Wild Cherry challenged popular conventions by releasing a remarkable song called "Play That Funky Music." By tacking the words "white boy" onto the end of its chorus, it became a sensation. The song took over the airwaves and dance floors of America, just when a tidal wave of increasingly fashionable disco songs had begun challenging rock's supremacy. Raised with rock music's serious-mindedness, introspection and intensity, the genre's fans were, to put it mildly, irked by disco's perceived lack of depth, sugary rhythms and obsession with carefree pursuits. They were also perturbed by disco's building momentum, which was increasingly nudging their beloved and once unstoppable sound out of the limelight. Throw in the ramifications of the friction that had resulted from disco's dicey melding of pop and soul with the notion of segregated sounds for blacks and whites and the eddy became even more powerful.

The group Wild Cherry, initially and somewhat unknowingly, swam against this current of racial stigma and music classification with its curious, yet exceptional, funk-rock song. Their signature hit became one of the period's biggest selling successes and an all-time classic. While often branded as a disco triumph, the song's writer and vocalist, Rob Parissi, looks back at the track decades later with reluctance to identify it as anything more than just a good old-fashioned bar band tune.

Born in Mingo Junction, Ohio, a steel mill town, Parissi started his musical journey at a very early age. "When I was five or six years old," the artist recalls, "I was just a sponge for music. I had an older sister, 10 years on me, and she'd bring her high school friends over, and they would play 45 rpm records on the turntable and dance. I was hearing the songs at such a young age, and I loved them! That was my introduction to rock 'n' roll—Buddy Holly and all the dance songs from the '50s. My father used to bring home records from the grocery store. My dad would play music composed by Mozart and Tchaikovsky, and so I also developed a love of all the classics. It just all grew from that. Music was something I always wanted to do—I wanted to be a musician. You either have that drive or you don't. I just knew it from the time I was a very small child," he says.

"I went through the ranks, and you just became a musician over time. You played and you practiced. You played out on the driveway; you played on the porch. You started to get better and you started to play in front of five people, 10, 20. So that's how it was for me, and I'm pretty sure it was the same for everybody else," he says.

Rob aligned himself with the local rock scene, singing and playing guitar in a succession of bands. "I came up through the ranks being in a band," he remembers. "We started doing instrumentals and then played a lot of Beatles. You learned how to sing better and start doing band songs. In Pittsburgh, even if you were a rock 'n' roll person, you had to have some soul in you, otherwise your band wouldn't be popular. Average White Band, for example, was very popular in Pittsburgh because they were in between that white/black thing. The Pittsburgh-Cleveland area was a great place to come from. The Del Vikings, George Benson, Perry Como, Macy Gray, Boz Skaggs, Devo, Joe Walsh, Rusted Root, Trent Reznor from Nine Inch Nails—they all came from there. You come from that area; you can't help but be influenced by both black and white people.

"We also learned to do whatever songs attracted girls to come to nightclubs—we learned that early on. I went through a couple of different bands, and it got to a point where the one I was with got to be pretty good. We were together four or five years, and then we broke up. I formed a new band, Wild Cherry [the name of which is said to have been derived from a box of cough drops]. To be honest, we were always a very popular band. My philosophy was just to get the girls in the club. When we made the transition from rock into the disco area, the girls moved with us. We were pretty popular guys. We always had a nice looking group of ladies with us, and, hey, look, if you're popular and you're doing your thing right, you can be ugly and the women will still come. Look at some of the guys in rock—they're scary looking! But the girls still want them; they marry them. It's like, *holy crap* sometimes!" he laughs.

Though wildly successful with their rock sound in the Pittsburgh area through the mid-'70s, Rob's band soon observed a dramatic musical undercurrent developing. "Disco music was coming out, and rock bands were going away," he remembers. "I finally told the guys in the band that we were gonna have to start playing more of this disco music because that's what was coming about. The guys didn't care about that and didn't want to play it. I told them if we were going to make a living, we'd have no choice. We started playing a bit more music like that, but it came to the point where I was forced to say we were going to have to do even more. The rock clubs were closing down, and the discos were opening up everywhere. Again, the band rebelled against that, and I said, 'Well, it's either that or we play a lot less! I can't afford to pay the salaries I'm handing out.' We all had our apartments, homes and cars, and nobody was anxious to give those up. I said we were gonna have to come up with 35 songs that we could play in both a disco and a rock club."

Brainstorming on a break during a club gig, Parissi's life-changing lyrical composition was scratched out on a small slip of paper. "My drummer spoke up and said something that someone had shouted at one of the discos we were playing in: 'Play that funky music, white boy!' I thought, 'Well that's a cool idea for a song,' and I thought maybe we'd put out a local record like that. I got one of those drink order pads, and I wrote about what was going on with us as a band at that time. I had the first verse written by the time I had gone back on stage after the break, and I wrote the last verse on the way home. That's how 'Play That Funky Music' came about," says Rob.

"We were a rock band, and that's all we were," he clarifies. "I wasn't even thinking I was writing a disco record or whatever. For me, it was a song that fell right in the middle of the whole disco-rock thing. I was writing about a rock band that was very popular, caught in [a transitional time]. Cleveland was a rock 'n' roll area, and Pittsburgh was an R&B town. I grew up in between both, which helped me appreciate Led Zeppelin, the Rolling Stones and Bad Company as R&B music. Coming up with 'Play That Funky Music' was no big deal because I grew up with those sounds.

"We went into the studio and recorded it as a planned B-side to another song we were covering, 'I Feel Sanctified,' which had been done by the Commodores," he explains. "Steve Popovich was head of A&R for Epic records at the time. He knew the guys at Sweet City, a production company out of Cleveland that was interested in our music. When Sweet City took 'Play That Funky Music' to Popovich, he loved it and signed those guys to a production/custom label deal (also called Sweet City). In turn, Sweet City signed us, and we also signed on with Epic Records. When the song came out, it went absolutely crazy!"

Almost serving as a shout-out to the rising influence of black culture in mainstream music (that had come further into vogue with the onslaught of disco fever), "Play That Funky Music" was an unexpected ultra-smash. As far as categorization was concerned, the single amazingly seemed to bridge the chasm that had developed between disco and rock fans and was eagerly embraced by both. "'Play That Funky Music' was number one for almost a month and on the R&B chart as well," Rob says, with a proud tone in his voice. "It was the second or third platinum record [at the time, honoring sales of over two million copies] issued in history! I think Johnnie Taylor's 'Disco Lady' was the first [also in 1976 and the first song to reach number one with the word 'disco' in its title]."

Wild Cherry was one of the few acts making waves on the disco frontier that didn't directly link the bulk of its newfound success to the gay community. "The gay guys would come see us with the girls," the artist says. "It didn't matter to us; that was fine! We had guys following us, and we knew they were gay. But to be honest, I was far more focused on the girls in our audience. Girls will dance with each other; guys won't unless they're really drunk," he laughs heartily. "Girls will start dancing with each other at 10 p.m. Guys won't dance with each other until one or two in the morning. That was just the way it was."

The path his band now found itself on was a tricky one to navigate. "The first thing that struck me, from the time they started playing the record on radio to the time we first started playing it live, was that people would get up and start dancing to it right away. I'd been performing for a while and never got that kind of reaction before. But it didn't always go smoothly. There was a guy in Toledo, the programming director of a radio station. We had gone to Ohio to promote [the record]. He told me he hated the song, and he was never gonna play it. I was like, 'Oh no, we need all the radio stations we can get!' So we went back to see him again, and he still wouldn't play it. We had gone through Toledo four or five times, and the song had climbed to something like number five in the country at that point, and we were nominated for two Grammys. He still kept saying he would never play that song. Well, I sang the song live on the Grammys, and I was thinking everybody likes this song but *that* guy.

"We had a lot of situations like that, where the song was met with resistance. There were also a lot of places where we'd go on stage, the lights would come up and the crowd would go, 'Oh my God, they're white!' We played with Average White Band, and there were almost riots going on different nights. We played Louisville one night with them, and some guy got shot in the second row. Average White Band played almost their whole set while the coroner came and proclaimed the guy dead. We got thrown out of the hotel we were staying at because they said we incited a riot. We had nothing to do with it; we were just trying to play some music. The riot was started because black and whites were pissed off at each other. They started fighting, and they chose our concert to do that. I just came up with a song—the way people would take it, well, I had no [control over that]. Black and white relations were what they were at that time, and when we would go onstage, some black people would become irate because we were white kids. I guess they just weren't expecting that. We were like, 'What?' But after we played for about 25 minutes, thinking we might not even live to the end of the set sometimes, we finished, and everybody started screaming for an encore. We were so stressed; we were like, 'No! We should probably just get out of here!'

"We found the same racial tension that black artists have said they found in front of white people," Parissi reveals. "For a while, I foolishly thought maybe I could be something like a white Dr. Martin Luther King, and everyone would say, 'There he goes! He's telling it like it is!' But it was not like that at all. I thought I was going to be more accepted. I really thought I was showing respect for black people. When I felt all that racial tension and animosity coming back at me, I was like, 'Where is that coming from?' What I was really saying with that song was if it weren't for black people in music, white people wouldn't be anywhere. I think Billy Joel even came out sometime later and said almost the same thing. You know it's true. If it weren't for the R&B element, Little Richard, Chuck Berry—that drive and creativity—where would rock 'n' roll be?"

Despite the controversy, the list of the hit song's far-reaching achievements continued to grow. The platinum-selling single may have sold as many as 2.5 million copies (or so reports Wikipedia). The song was a monster hit in the U.K. as well, cracking the Top 10 and enjoying similar success throughout Europe. "It's [on a list of] the biggest selling songs of the last 50 years," claims Parissi, citing a *Billboard* survey he had seen. "I also had lunch one time with a friend at Capitol Records back in 1980, and he pulled up the records and told me the Beatles had maybe three records that came close to being as big as 'Play That Funky Music.' It floored me. When I hear stuff like that, I have to pinch myself!" Parissi makes note that Vanilla Ice took a remake of the song, originally a B-side to his "Ice Ice Baby" hit, back into the Top Five in 1990.

"After the song was released, we started developing and recording the album," Rob remembers. "They asked me what kind of a logo I wanted for the band, and I thought the most recognizable logo at the time was [the one for] Coca-Cola. I let the artist come up with something that had that kind of a script. They came up with it, and then they came up with the album cover photo of the girl with the cherry in her mouth. They didn't want to show the band or let anybody know the band was white. I said that was a big mistake—I felt they should let everyone know right off the bat that we were white. They thought they'd sell more records if the public thought we were black, but how stupid can you be? I don't know, to me it was sort of racism in reverse. I check out our videos on YouTube, and every week somebody new posts, 'Oh my God, I didn't know you guys were white!' It is what it is. I always said, 'What difference does it make? Okay, yeah we're white, but so what?'"

Wild Cherry's self-titled LP was a hit, reaching the Top Five on *Billboard*'s pop album chart and number one on the R&B LP survey. The clubs latched onto "I Feel Sanctified," sending it and "Play That Funky Music" to the number one spot on the dance chart. "The single started to hit so fast that I had to finish the album quickly, but it was meant to just be an extension of the song. We wanted it to cross between the rock clubs and the discos. As I said, we got the 'I Feel Sanctified' song from the Commodores. [That group was] being played heavily in the disco clubs. The thing I noticed about their records was that they were like Detroit's the Funk Brothers—they were session musicians who had that real rhythm section sound. I thought we could do that with kind of a beefed-up Motown sound. Nobody in the white market really knew the Commodores, but I said to my band that this was the sound we needed. We just needed to turn up the guitars, more like Led Zeppelin. Crank it up! The media called us a punk band, and that didn't stick. Then a disco band, then something else, and that didn't work. I guess we were something different, and they didn't know how to pigeonhole us. I thought we were a funk-rock band; that's all we were, you know?"

No other material off their debut album made an impression on the public, but all eyes remained poised on the group's sophomore effort. There's a still-fresh sound of frustration in his voice as Parissi describes the game plan Wild Cherry's management laid out, which centered on the album *Electrified Funk* in 1977.

"The first thing the label wanted after 'Play That Funky Music,'" the artist says, "was for me to continue telling the story—what happened after the song. But 'Play That Funky Music' was *one* song. One song does not make a career. The song was done. I felt we had some other things to talk about and that we should move on. But they wanted me to make a career out of that one song, and I thought that was foolish. I didn't have that in me, but I did it anyway, and it turned out to be as dumb an idea as I told them it would be. But I just caved, and I did what they asked me to do. [The label] was having some problems with some other bands they had signed and, well, I tried to cooperate. I just should have said no. A song doesn't make a career, just like a band's name doesn't make the band. It's what they are doing that makes the band.

"'Baby Don't You Know' [the follow-up single that peaked at number 43 on the pop charts] was the worst thing we ever could have done, but they begged me to release it, and I complied when I never should have. We were two guitars, a bass, drums and maybe a keyboard player, and that's what all the bands were back in that time. But our thing was to do rhythm section kinds of sounds that would get girls dancing. That's what we did. Our band's songs could do that. I thought with the Wild Cherry thing, we should do an extension of that. I didn't want to move out of the clubs, whether it was discos or rock clubs. And my goal was to get the girls in there. The guys will come after that, I don't care what you're doing. Those are the guys that spend the money. If you're doing polkas, and the girls are in, they'll still be buying them drinks! Bar band songs were good for us. That's what we should have done."

Two more albums followed, 1978's *I Love My Music* and 1979's *Only the Wild Survive*, but each did progressively less to further the act's presence on the mainstream pop charts.

Then the disco backlash kicked in, and Wild Cherry, like so many other artists who had once found favor under the glitter ball, found themselves out in the cold. Parissi observes, "Everybody went through the same thing after the disco backlash—the whole disco record-burning thing in Chicago. Even KC [of KC and the Sunshine Band], a guy that had so many hit records in disco. I read somewhere recently that for a 10-year period he was made to feel like the Rodney Dangerfield of the music business—same as a lot of us. It was like [some people felt] that the whole disco era destroyed the music business, and we were all accessories to the crime! Nobody wanted anything to do with KC. They wanted even less to do with me from 1979 until about 1989, when George Michael eventually covered our song on his tour. *Rolling Stone* hated everything we ever did, but when George came out with his rendition, they said he was doing 'such classics' as 'Play That Funky Music.' Ten years later—how things changed.

"But for a long time, everyone associated with that disco era was considered—*not* cool. We didn't classify ourselves as a disco band, even though everyone else did, when you have one hit record in the genre. For some reason, by the '90s it turned around a bit, and people started saying, 'No, this doesn't really suck.' But artists from the disco genre and that era were treated like crap up until then. We all were!"

Over time, Parissi has accepted that the media corrals him with one-off artists like Nena, Soft Cell, Toni Basil and A-ha. "VH1 came at least twice here to do interviews," he says, "and in one of them, they asked me what I thought of being a one-hit wonder. The first thing that came out was: 'Well, it's probably not as good

"There's gotta be life afterwards, you know? You gotta pull things along. You have to try to do something you like but not lose people," says Rob Parissi of life after Wild Cherry. The artist is an accomplished jazz music composer and musician today (courtesy Rob Parissi).

as being a two-hit wonder, but better than being a no-hit wonder. Besides, who cares about two-hit wonders as much as one hit wonders? Now a three-hit wonder—you're on to something!"

Following the break-up of the band in 1979, Parissi moved to Miami and formed a tour band with Bobby Caldwell. From there, he relocated to New York and enjoyed success as a songwriter with Ellie Greenwich and Jeff Kent and co-produced material for Gary U.S. Bonds with Bruce Springsteen. Today, he's back to living in Florida and writing and recording albums like *East Coast Vibe*, a smooth jazz collection.

"If you listen to the early Wild Cherry stuff," he observes, "you'll hear a lot of jazz influence. I used a lot of jazz musicians all along. I've always liked that sound. My change to jazz music today is not really a big stretch. My latest album [*The Real Deal*] is a vocal album in the adult contemporary and dance–Top 40 genres. There's gotta be life afterwards, you know? You gotta pull things along. You have to try to do something you like but not lose people. If you can do that, you're a winner. I'm a musician first, and I'm always trying to do things on the cutting edge." Parissi also recently recorded a jazz version of "Play That Funky Music" with Steve Oliver.

Long past the era that brought him so much fame, Rob, recently married and residing in Florida, has sharp wisdom for handling life and career goals, no matter what direction one takes. "Follow your gut!" he says firmly. "It's the best advice. For example, I had people ask me to take the words 'white boy' out of that record. I went through that with CBS Records. They were afraid of using those words. They said they were getting some kind of racial backlash or whatever, and some people were complaining. I said, 'You take those words out and you're gonna kill it.' I had to remove the words and replaced them with the words, 'yeah, funky music' for a radio station in Boston where we were having trouble getting airplay. The next week they got so many requests that they didn't really need to worry about it anymore. But there's a version of 'Play That Funky Music' floating around out there without the 'white boy.' I think if you follow your gut and use common sense, you're always good to go."

Now in middle age, it might seem easy for Parissi to take his success for granted, but he vehemently claims he doesn't. He relates a recent experience that stirs up emotion. "The [former] president of the Rock and Roll Hall of Fame, Terry Stewart, asked me to come up there to do a fundraiser about three years ago. He told me how much he thought of 'Play That Funky Music' and that he even thought it should be the theme for the place. I didn't even know him, but I just broke down right in front of him. He just affected me so much. He has been one of my biggest allies and fans. I was on a show with a lot of huge names, and he said he wanted *me* to close the show! It just choked me up. My father was a diesel mechanic and I came from real humble beginnings, and I will never forget where I came from. For someone to say something like that to me means so much to me. It really brings me to tears. I don't have that kind of ego where I think, 'Yeah, you should love me!' Anyone I ever encountered who had that kind of ego, I always thought, 'What the hell is wrong with you?'"

He suddenly recalls one more anecdote. "The jacket and shoes I wore in the video for 'Play That Funky Music' and the original piece of paper containing the lyrics for the song are in revolving rotation on display and on loan to the Rock and Roll Hall of Fame for as long as they want!"

For a while in 1976, Rob Parissi and his band Wild Cherry managed to eradicate both racial and musical segregation on the dance floor. The group found themselves unexpectedly contributing to disco history, while making a profound social statement that remains relevant today. The singer, songwriter and musician seems to enjoy pondering his legacy. He reiterates that it's unlikely he will ever allow himself to become indifferent to his good fortune.

"'Play That Funky Music' has done many wonderful things for me. It has gotten me into this book and afforded me a wonderful life. I've been lucky, and I've been blessed. Everyone says you can't live off one song, but when it comes to a song like *that*, yeah, you can. I've been happy for a long time because I was able to retire 22 years ago. Since then, it's just been icing on the cake. But that doesn't stop you from working and wanting to work. Life is what you make it; it all depends on you. If you're done after your big event, you're done. If you have more than that in you and have more to say, you appreciate what that event is, give thanks, and you say, 'Wait till you see what else I want to do!' I just want to try and always come up with something better. Even if I do manage to come up with something better than 'Play That Funky Music,' I'm always gonna be thinking about what's next after that. I'm just that kind of person. I want to be remembered as somebody who just tried to do the best that he could.

"On my tombstone I'd like it to read: 'Live Band! Free Beer! No Cover!' That will always draw people to my grave," he laughs.

•••••••••••••••••••••••••••••••••••

Bonnie Pointer
"Heaven Must Have Sent You"

"When I saw people dancing in clubs to my music later on, it felt so great! It was like, 'Wow! I just wanna dance with them!'"—Bonnie Pointer

"It felt like a dream come true—it felt like heaven!" Bonnie Pointer exclaims proudly of reaching the top of the charts with her disco classic "Heaven Must Have Sent You." A scalding, hook-fused extravaganza unleashed at the peak of the glitter ball era, the song featured wild guitar riffs, a banjo gone mad, stabbing strings, bells ringing and stomping sound effects against a driving beat. One of the track's most distinctive elements was the artist's stylish vocal urgency, a remarkable display of gut-felt emotion. The song became one of the most beloved classics of the genre, and it captured the brilliance and excitement of disco at its energized best! Pointer's unique gift for delivering tantalizing music began with her original formation of the Pointer Sisters and quickly expanded into a well-regarded solo career. Her path has been peppered with both enviable recording accomplishments and a smattering of scandals. But the artist's competitive spirit and drive to move forward has made her stronger than any challenges that have arisen from life in the spotlight. She speaks of her many years in show business with a youthful enthusiasm that is most genuine.

She was born Patricia Eva Pointer and says the name "Bonnie" was bestowed upon her by a family friend. "She named me that because she wanted me to be her baby, and I was her little Bonnie," she laughs. Pointer's childhood seems to have been a relatively short one as her anxiousness to enjoy adulthood prompted early independence. "My sisters and I were born in Oakland, California. My mother and father were both ministers. My father was 23 years older than my mother, and his name was Elton. My mother's name was Sarah. My sisters and I started out singing in the church as we were growing up. I was the next to youngest of six kids.

"Halloween was always my favorite time of year because it allowed me to dress up like the sexy girl I was born to be. I got to put on nail polish and my wig and would dress up the way I wanted. I got to wear lipstick and all that stuff that I wanted to wear but couldn't most of the time—being a minister's daughter. I also had two brothers. My youngest brother, Fritz, is now a professor at Contra Costa College (San Pablo, California) and my oldest brother, Aaron, is the commissioner of parks and recreation in Tacoma, Washington. I have a cousin named Paul Silas, who was a standout player and coach with the NBA. He also played with the Boston Celtics and Seattle SuperSonics. His son Stephen is an assistant coach with the Charlotte Bobcats. We are a family of high achievers, and we all like competition.

"I had decided to go out in the world and seek my fortune in my late teens," Bonnie remembers. "I went on to find myself in music by living life on the streets of Frisco. Before we became famous, I was a Haight-Ashbury hippie. I was the one who started the Pointer Sisters. I was just trying to make it or break it. I guess I had a lot of guts. I started off singing alone, and then I got my sister June to join me. We became 'Pointers–A Pair.' Then Anita came on board a few years later, and we became the Pointer Sisters. Ruth was the last one to join the group.

"One time, we got into my sister's boyfriend's car, and he said he had some work for us in Texas. It was Anita, June and myself. It turned out he wasn't going to get us work at all, and we had this big ol' blow out. We left him and started to make our way back to California. The car of some guy who was driving us back broke down on the way. I had this number in my wallet of a man named David Rubinson, and I called him. He didn't really know who I was, but I said if he would help us get out of Texas, we would show him what we could do. So he sent us three plane tickets to get back to California. We ended up recording for the first time with him, and David gave us our start. A lot of people had told me that it would never happen, but that just gave me more determination. We were backup singers for many performers in those days, including Elvin Bishop, Taj Mahal, Grace Slick and Sylvester [James]. A lot of groups had fallen by the wayside or faded [at that time]. My idea was to fill that void. The Pointer Sisters just blew up bigger than I ever thought we could."

The Pointer Sisters' rise to fame was rooted in a series of funky soul, jazz and pop jams (with a touch of swing and rock 'n' roll) recorded for Blue Thumb Records. Part of the sisters' charm, aside from their savory harmonies and authentic visual style, was the fact that one never knew what to expect next from the girls. Songs like the hit "Yes We Can Can" helped to further establish their energized reputation. Slowly, the pop music landscape became dotted with more and more danceable R&B material from the Pointer Sisters.

"I didn't really see disco emerging in the early '70s," Bonnie says. "We were recording music with sort of an 'honesty is the best policy' attitude. I felt it was just important to be true to the rhythm in our souls. If people were dancing to our music and making noise for the Lord, it was all good!" Around this time, Anita began writing the song "Fairytale." She and Bonnie finished the song together, which Elvis Presley recorded on his last album (*Elvis in Concert*, 1977). The song won a Grammy Award for Best Country Performance by a Duo or Group in a ceremony held in March of 1975.

Bonnie says she began having mixed feelings about being part of a group. "I didn't really want to leave the group," she admits, "but I wanted to try something on my own to see what would happen. I didn't have any skills other than singing and songwriting. I didn't want to do any other kind of job. I wanted to see what I could do on my own if, God forbid, anything ever happened to my sisters and I had to keep my career going. I wanted to establish a foundation for myself so that I could always earn a living, and I needed to see what I could do on my own."

Jeffrey Bowen was an accomplished producer, songwriter and musician who worked with many giants of the industry, including Marvin Gaye, Rick James, the Temptations and Chairmen of the Board. He met and married Pointer in 1978. "He was the number one producer at Motown," says Bonnie, "and we were married for 20 years. He produced the Commodores, DeBarge, Freda Payne and many others. Jeffrey knew that I had some songs I wanted to try out, and he set me up with Berry Gordy. Motown—Berry Gordy really—offered me the opportunity to record solo. He liked my songs and voice—and it all just began."

Bonnie's self-titled debut album, featuring a striking cover painting of the artist against a red background, was released in 1978. A highly unique collection of songs sung and orchestrated with a retro–Motown feel, the album was an audio feast for those craving the Northern Soul style that disco had superseded. The clubs, no surprise, were the first to notice Bonnie, sending the banjo-popping, funky and infectious track "Free Me from My Freedom/Tie Me to a Tree (Handcuff Me)" soaring up the disco chart. But there was more to come.

"I really liked the Elgins' song 'Heaven Must Have Sent You,'" Pointer recalls. "We recorded it at the Record Plant in Los Angeles, and Berry Gordy and my husband were there. The whole Los Angeles Philharmonic Orchestra was there in the studio playing the violins and other instruments. In those days, that's how they did these productions. When we first recorded it, it was a different kind of rhythm—a basic standard four-four. I recorded the disco version after hearing the Village People's 'Y.M.C.A.' I was driving down Sunset Blvd., and I heard their hit, and I thought, 'That's the way I want to do "Heaven Must Have Sent You."' Jeffery asked me to go in and re-record it—*and I just did it!* We recorded the disco version about a month or two after the original was done. Carolyn Franklin, Aretha's sister, sang background with me on that song. She was my only backup singer. She died of cancer some time later, but I was so proud to have her on that record, as she was very close to my sisters and myself. I ad-libbed the scatting part in the studio.

"The disco version of 'Heaven Must Have Sent You' was the first digital remix ever recorded," claims Pointer. "It was done on some kind of IBM recording equipment. I don't know who actually engineered it, but I do know it was the first song to be remixed digitally. After we did it, it became commonplace. I felt the new version could be a hit when I heard the disco arrangement, but what did I know?"

Her instincts were on the mark. "Heaven Must Have Sent You," thanks to its new disco mix, was a monster hit, quickly crossing from Top 10 status on the club charts (where it was a fixture for almost six months) to *Billboard*'s pop chart, where it peaked at number 11. A new version of the album was issued containing the smash retake. Bonnie had found the confirmation of her talent that she had longed for. "I was in awe, in a daze. It was kind of shocking to me that it did so well. It was a beautiful thing. It verified my feelings and gave me a sense of individuality and a certain respect for myself. I needed that confidence to feel my dreams could come true.

Bonnie Pointer stirs up the masses on Fire Island in 1979, as her hit "Heaven Must Have Sent You" tops the charts (photograph by Charles R. Moniz, used by permission).

"Berry Gordy was the executive producer of the single. I have heard so many bad things about him over the years, but for me he gave me the chance of a lifetime. I really appreciate that to this day! Motown was the label that every black artist strove to be associated with. To be able to say that I had recorded on Motown was the greatest thing that's happened in my life. Growing up in the '50s and '60s with that music—it was incredible that I became a part of it!"

The media became highly focused on Bonnie's fast track to stardom. With her newfound success, the artist knew she had arrived. "I think I felt like I had really made it when I was on the cover of *Jet* magazine, *The Hollywood Reporter* and *Cashbox*—alone, just me. Those things really meant a lot to me, especially being an African American. I think I was the first person ever seen in a bathing suit on the cover of *Cashbox*. *The Hollywood Reporter* voted me as one of the most beautiful women in Hollywood. I was in *Vogue* and a lot of great magazines, and I just loved it. It was fantastic! At the time, Motown was really pumping me up. I was the new baby!"

The so-called "purple album" (known as *Bonnie Pointer II* in the U.K.) was released late in 1979 and was equally well received by fans, if not by all critics. Pointer sang and arranged all the background vocals on the set, a collection once again comprised mostly of vintage Holland-Dozier-Holland covers that followed the successful formula of her solo debut. The artist composed (with Donald Baldwin) the sole original track on the album, "Deep Inside My Soul," a masterfully written love song that brimmed with raw, late hour emotion. She also contributed lyrics to the track "When the Lovelight Starts Shining Through His Eyes." Sly Stone supplied the foot-stomping effect on the cut "Jimmy Mack." "I just did what I liked to do," Bonnie says, dismissing any notions about anxiety that might have been attached to the sophomore project. "I let them do what they do best, and they let me do my thing. I appreciated that they let me include my song. I was afraid to sing something like 'Deep Inside My Soul,' and they convinced me it was good. I wrote that track like it was going to be sung by Al Green. I wrote it for him, but I ended up singing it myself."

Pointer achieved her highest charting single on the disco charts with "I Can't Help Myself (Sugar Pie, Honey Bunch)" from the album. The electrifying remake of a previous Four Tops hit was arranged and mixed in a similar fashion to "Heaven Must Have Sent You" (though it was critically maligned by some for that very reason). The track cracked the *Billboard* Top 40 on the pop side, no small accomplishment during the upheaval of disco's post-boom days.

"I was very comfortable reinterpreting 'I Can't Help Myself,'" she says. "Since I had been with Motown, I was doing a lot of covers of material by their male artists. I liked it because I could add in my Marilyn Monroe–style campiness. It wasn't really one of my top song choices to sing, though. I was just sort of going with the flow because I was still new to the game. I wanted to do what *they* wanted me to do. Motown knew what they were doing. Berry Gordy was legendary, and I let them have their way. At the same time, they let me arrange the songs in the way I was comfortable. I always liked Judy Garland and Marilyn Monroe movies, and I think that influenced the theatrical aspects of my songs—the drama! I love show biz!

"I had appeared with my sisters on incredible shows like *The Carol Burnett Show*, Helen Reddy's show, *Sonny & Cher*, and now I was being featured on programs like *Don Kirshner's Rock Concert* as a solo artist. I don't remember half the stuff I did to be honest. Half of it is a blur. I know I did *Dance Fever* with Deney Terrio, Dick Clark's *American Bandstand*—but I can't say I really *remember* it," she laughs. "When I see myself on YouTube and things like that, my first reaction is 'Ewwww!'"

Bonnie was delighted to become one of disco's most notable divas, and she embraced her sizable gay following warmly. "I had been into disco and dancing for a long, long while by the time 'Heaven Must Have Sent You' came out," she states. "I once dated a gay man named Daniel, and we would go to the clubs every single night in San Francisco. The gay community was part of me. When I saw people dancing in clubs to my music later on, it felt so great! It was like, 'Wow! I just wanna dance with them!' It wasn't a feeling of power. It was pure joy. Just to have people feeling the same thing you're feeling and making other people happy and see them dancing—it's an amazing sensation! What could be better? I lived for that!

"The gay and lesbian community absolutely supported my music! I give them all the credit. I was so campy, and I loved dressing up. They identified with that. I used to raid Sylvester's closet on a daily basis. We were the best of friends! [My sisters and I] did a lot of work for him as backup singers. We were way before Two Tons of Fun," says the artist.

Pointer's connection to the gay community was evident in her first two albums, perhaps in a way that eluded most fans. The artist's unique LP covers were designed both to promote her identity and to act as a homage to the underground culture she had embraced. "I was doing the colors of the gay flag on my album covers," claims Bonnie. "That's what it started out to be. I didn't want a title for either album. I didn't want the albums to be bought because of my outfits or anything. I kept it simple. I intended to have a red album, a purple album, a blue one, a green one—just like the gay flag. My albums were going to look like a rainbow on the record store racks. I didn't want a title on them, and neither did Motown or my husband. They wanted me to be recognized as someone separate from the Pointer Sisters. They wanted to make sure there were no distractions, and they wanted to show only my face—me as an individual. Just Bonnie Pointer—no big hair, no wild clothes, just colors. That's how we were going to do it. Phyllis Morris, the wonderful artist and designer, did the cover painting on my second album. I never knew what happened to those illustrations. I think I heard one was sold in Las Vegas. It would be nice if I had them."

Bonnie took a break from recording for a few years and re-launched her career in 1984 with a style that reflected the times. She released the album *If the Price Is Right* on a new label, but musically stayed true to the genre with which she had found so much success (adding an '80s flair). However, this time the artist's sleek, ultra-toned body was also shown on the LP's cover, scantily clad in a provocative, liquid style one-piece swimsuit. Produced again by Jeffrey Bowen, the set featured co-production by Greg Perry and Brian Holland and several songs co-written by Bonnie, including the club hit "Tight Blue Jeans." Sisters Anita and Ruth handled backup vocals on the track "Johnny," and the 12-inch version of the first single, "Your Touch," scored well in the clubs. "I signed with Private I Records, who bought my contract from Motown. They signed me to do a deal for the album, and I also did the soundtrack to the film *Heavenly Bodies*, which was a *Fame*-styled movie." DJ's welcomed Pointer's return, which fit right in with the soul-fused electronic dance beats that were dominating the period in which her sisters were having such gargantuan success with "I'm So Excited," "Jump" and "Neutron Dance."

"They made me change my original lyrics in 'Tight Blue Jeans' because they said it was a little too risqué," Pointer confesses. "A lot of my songs were like that. Now it would be okay, of course, but back then, you know, I was kind of a nasty girl. But that's okay!" she says playfully. "I remember 'Free Me from My Freedom/Tie Me to a Tree (Handcuff Me)' from my first album was banned from radio in many places. I wasn't thinking of that song in a raunchy way at the time. I was thinking, 'If I want to leave, tie me up 'cuz I'm stupid!' That song became a big hit for me because it went underground. Kind of a cult hit."

Pointer's solo career had been tied to Jeffrey Bowen for many years, but their marriage had begun to show signs of wear, according to the singer. "I did think about doing music with other people, but it was hard at the time because we were married. He was kind of controlling, and I was kind of like a trophy wife. I separated from him after the last album. It was a bad time in my marriage, and I had to leave. One time, I told him I was going to get some ice down the hall at the hotel, and I never came back. I was on the road after that and doing songs, ghostwriting for other people. I am still doing all of that. I do backgrounds for many artists as well. I've recorded a lot of music, but not all of it gets released. I did a movie not long ago called *The Road to Nowhere*, and I try to stay pretty busy. I released an album in 2011 called *Like a Picasso*." Pointer's latest single, "Eyes Don't Lie," was a substantial digital hit after being reinvented in numerous dance mixes. Most recently, she joined Ben Wilkins on his single "Day to Day."

Tabloids and television gossip shows like *TMZ* have taken to reporting some of the artist's public difficulties with drugs and alcohol in recent years. The artist doesn't shy away from the subject. Pointer says, "Back when I was growing up in the music business, it *really* was sex, drugs and rock 'n' roll, you know? Everyone did drugs. I was at Haight-Ashbury, and I went to Woodstock; I went with my sisters to Africa with Muhammad Ali. It's been a long journey, and it included drugs. I wasn't able to do drugs when I was growing up, but when I turned 19—after seeing it all around me—I ended up doing it. But after a while, it gets old and played out.

"It's the best thing in the world to be associated with 'Heaven Must Have Sent You' and disco music," says singer Bonnie Pointer, who enjoys an active touring schedule today (courtesy Bonnie Pointer).

"I was at Smokey Robinson's Lifetime Achievement Award event and went to get a $20 package of powder, and I got busted with it. I got taken to jail, and, while I was handcuffed in the patrol car, they were playing 'I'm So Excited.' I remember they were singing 'He's So Shy' when I was crying in my cell. I asked if I could leave my wig on so I wouldn't look like James Brown. They said okay. It's like—you know." She laughs somewhat reluctantly without finishing the thought. "Okay, so now I go to drug counseling, and I'm trying to become a leader. I'm telling young people all about this problem I had. Maybe that helps them to live differently.

"It's funny, because most of the songs I wrote that were successful I wrote when I was high or smoking grass. I asked my counselor how to deal with that. Bottom line—I have to find another way to stimulate my mind besides drugs, plain and simple. I never got on stage high and never travelled with anything. I used to relax and wind down with it, and it did help me do some creative things. I'll be honest; I didn't think I had a problem but, you know, I'm learning a lot through what I'm experiencing right now. I'm 62 years old, and I feel like I've lived a long life. I've learned a lot. But I've discovered I am *still* learning, and I can appreciate the education I'm getting now from the drug courses I'm taking and the counseling I am receiving. I'm really trying to clean up my act and get myself together. I have a very good counselor named Mark Davidson who has been very, very helpful to me."

Pointer has a great deal of energy, yet she is poised and articulate as she expresses her observations about life today. "I'm still very competitive! Competition drives me forward, and I love it! I love to compete in sports and compete with new singers, sort of in a creative way. I love to push myself to the limit. I love my creative side—I love to draw and paint. I have a flair for crafts. You know, I also just enjoy playing, swimming—things that I never really got to do in my childhood. I still go dancing, and I go to clubs. I just sprained my ankle hiking, and I loved it because it happened when I was out doing things and being active. I get up at six every morning and start my day exercising—dancing, walking, eating right. I enjoy being healthy, happy and having fun—even though I'm old and everything," she says with a laugh. "It's okay. I don't let anything stop me. I'm working with some new rappers and on a CD for myself called *My Hair*. [Bonnie starts singing a melody with clever lyrics that are instantly catchy.] One of the songs is called 'Drop Those Pants!'" She laughs again.

She is anxious to make her musical legacy a part of her future. "It's the best thing in the world to be associated with 'Heaven Must Have Sent You' and disco music. I'm still touring as a result of it. I just did some shows with Tavares, the Trammps and France Joli." While Bonnie addresses her substance abuse issues, Anita has faced the challenges of recovery from cancer treatment. The siblings continue to help each other on the road to recovery and write music together. "Today, my sisters and I have a beautiful relationship, and it's much better than it used to be. These days, we are really loving each other—we're planning to work together when I graduate from the [drug rehab program]. We'd like to do some kind of a reunion thing, some of the old and new stuff. That will be something to make people jump—pun intended!" she says playfully.

Bonnie Pointer is a true artist. A distinctive vocal style, polished songwriting skills and flair for style have made her one of the music industry's most unique, accomplished and memorable entertainers. She still possesses the aura of charming innocence and sly spirit that's been part of Bonnie's appeal since her first hits made their mark on the dance floor. The uplifting power that radiates from the disco classic "Heaven Must Have Sent You" is as much a mixture of the pure fire that burns inside of the artist as it is the craftsmanship of a brilliant record.

She gives a playful "ahhhh" sound and blushes a bit before saying, "I'd like to be remembered as someone who cared about people and had a great deal of passion for her work. I would like to be thought of as someone who made a lot of people happy with my music!"

Warren Schatz
"Turn the Beat Around"

"I must have released 120 singles by that time and never had more than a marginal hit. Nothing like 'Turn the Beat Around.' It was huge!"—Warren Schatz

Warren Schatz, to say the least, has a long and distinguished history in disco music. First and foremost, we can thank him for bringing the amazing vocal talents of Vicki Sue Robinson front and center with the classic dance-pop juggernaut "Turn the Beat Around." Though he started his career as a delivery boy at a recording studio and then began singing on records of his own, his accomplishments behind the scenes (producing, engineering, writing, arranging, and marketing such notables as Evelyn "Champagne" King, Viola Wills, the New York Community Choir and his own breakthrough studio act, the Brothers) has earned Schatz his ranking as one of the genre's most important pioneers. He's quick to admit that his success was a combination of luck, timing and a natural gift for creating music. He speaks with warmth and affection for an industry that's been his inspiration for decades.

"My dad knew I was into music and recording when I was a boy," Schatz remembers, "and for my tenth birthday he gave me the opportunity to see a real recording session. A friend of my father's, Nat Schnapf, owned a studio called Associated Recording Studios, and they let me sit in the back of the horn section during a session. I was overwhelmed! While I was there, I noticed people taking packages to and from the reception area and found out they were sending demos to publishers, writers and record companies. I asked what these messengers were paid, and Nat said they got about $40–50 a week. I said, 'What if I did it in the summer for about $25 a week?' He said sure! So I became a delivery boy at Associated, and after school I would go into the city and deliver demo acetates in the afternoon.

"When I was 13, one of the engineers didn't show up for a recording session for Hal David, Burt Bacharach and Dionne Warwick. I went to Nat and told him that I could do it, and he asked Hal. Hal, being gracious, said sure, as long as Nat stood by to supervise me. So that was my first recording session. It was just a piano vocal demo, but by the time I was 15, I was working on projects for Carole King and Gerry Goffin, Barry Mann and Cynthia Weil, Mort Shuman and Doc Pomus, Barry Manilow, Jeff Barry and Ellie Greenwich, Paul Simon, Neil Diamond, the Lovin' Spoonful and many others. It was really fabulous! One of the engineers at Associated, Nancy Cesare, knew that I sang a bit, and when she was asked by Charles Strouse and Lee Adams to make a recommendation for a young person to sing the demos for a new Broadway show, 'Bye Bye Birdie,' she suggested me. I wound up singing the demos and shortly after started recording my own records. It was very exciting for me. I would come up with these songs and get all the musicians from the studio together, and they would play on my records for something like $25 apiece. I was friendly with the group the Tokens ('The Lion Sleeps Tonight'), and they would do all my background vocals. I even had a few flirtations with the pop charts with my version of 'Here Comes Summer' under the name the Whispers on Laurie Records, 'Goodbye Girl' as Ritchie Dean for the newly formed Capitol Records' Tower label and 'Younger Girl' by the Warmest Spring on Cameo Parkway."

Though Schatz managed to get a little bit of attention for his musical accomplishments, which included releases for Columbia Records in the early '70s and the Press Prize at the Sopot song festival in Poland, his singing career hadn't taken off. "My Columbia album was a real stiff," he readily admits.

"To jump ahead," he says, "I had just arranged the strings and horns on three cuts for Tony Orlando and three for Frankie Valli. 'Our Day Will Come' by Valli was the first real hit I had. Then one of the publishers I had worked for, Allen Stanton, who was now in charge of publishing at RCA Records, called me and asked me if I wanted a job. I met with him at a small crepe restaurant on 56th Street. After a six-hour interview, where he asked me why I never had a hit, he hired me. I had just finished producing an album with Scott Fagan (*Many Sunny Places*), which I sold to Ethel Gabriel at RCA. Vicki Sue Robinson had sung the background vocals on Scott's album.

Warren Schatz began life in the music business as a delivery boy, struggled as a recording artist and eventually became a top executive at RCA Records (courtesy Warren Schatz).

"One night, I had a dream where I saw Vicki was number three with a bullet on a *Cashbox* chart singing 'Baby, Now That Found You,' a song by the Foundations. I woke up and thought, 'What the heck!' I didn't really know Vicki that well and thought it was the strangest dream. I called my boss and said, 'Allen, you're gonna think I'm crazy, but I had this dream last night, and I have to record this girl named Vicki Sue Robinson singing 'Baby Now That I Found You.' He said, 'Oh Warren, what are you doing to me? We don't even publish that song.' I said, 'If I can't sell it within two hours of recording it, I will pay you back every penny out of my salary,' which was ridiculously low at the time. He finally said yes, and I actually sold it to RCA Records. The sale happened almost immediately, to both Allen's and my amazement. The record came out in 1975 and was well received, but it wasn't a hit."

The vision of a hit single for Vicki, who was signed with RCA's black music department, stayed with Schatz, who was just beginning to get his feet wet in the emerging disco genre. Says the producer, "It was a period where singer/songwriters were really in vogue. I kept doing various demos with Vicki using different songwriters. I went to Tom Draper [National VP of Urban Music for RCA], and he agreed to do an album with her saying I should to do a few more sides [an industry term for tracks]. I had just had a disco hit with a group called the Brothers, which was comprised of my friend Ben Lanzaroni, a bunch of our fellow musicians, and me. We did a song called 'Are You Ready for This' [a Top 20 club sensation in 1975]. It was a huge dance hit that nobody expected. We had put it out on a mid-price LP called *Disco-Soul*, which contained our versions of 'Never Can Say Goodbye,' 'Doctor's Orders' and other songs that were big in the clubs at the time. The budget was just $6,000, but I needed something to be happening. Nobody had any money for an untried producer back then, but Ethel Gabriel gave me a shot. In fact, I couldn't even pay Ben, and he was (and is) such a great friend that he did all the arrangements for free. He and I wrote 'Are You Ready for This' and 'In the Pocket' for the album, which made us a little money. The whole entertainment business is built on gatekeepers. It's like professional sports. You have to prove yourself before you can reach the major leagues and have them be willing to take a money shot on you. Nobody ever said, 'Hey Warren, go and do disco!' It was pure desperation so that I could keep my job! I had to study what people were calling disco music. Even our first Brothers album was just Ben and me taking songs that were popular in the clubs, which were just starting to get hot back then. It was a good way to practice figuring out what people liked.

"To be honest," Schatz confesses, "RCA was not well thought of by people in the industry at the time. They would laugh when you mentioned RCA. RCA was on board with disco after I introduced them to the music, and they saw that it could sell records. They didn't care what they were selling; they didn't know. Any label only knows what works for them once they've seen that it racks up sales. It was my time, and I personally got lucky with that. I was no expert on dance records, but they didn't want me to do anything else. I was the outsider looking for more work, and I was seeing Gloria Gaynor doing well and then Carol Douglas, etc. RCA wasn't aware of any of that, and this trend towards disco was just starting to happen. The only things out there at the beginning were radio records that the early dance community connected with. Disco just got built out of rhythmic R&B records. Nobody was calling them disco records then. Disco became my niche because RCA didn't want me to do the pop/rock or post-psychedelic music I had done before. I got comfortable with dance music and with the beats and the feeling.

"The Brothers' success helped to get me known as a 'disco producer,' but it was all very accidental and pretty much out of desperation," he adds. "The hit songs we wrote on the album were really just Ben and me standing on the shoulders of those who had done the original versions. Nobody thought it would be a hit, and RCA sold it at a mid-line price. We ended up selling 40,000 units, and the label president wondered why it wasn't being sold at a regular album price. But who knew? They gave me a chance to do a second Brothers album [*Don't Stop Now* in 1976], and that was a classic—and as close to a 'masterpiece' (other people's opinion, not mine) as I had done so far. It was released as a regular priced album. So I started getting a little bit of a reputation and had some credibility when I went to Tom Draper about Vicki."

Given the green light to produce Vicki Sue Robinson, Schatz laid down the first cuts for his new star at RCA Studios. Schatz's buddy Ben handled keyboards, and the producer incorporated conga and percussion work by Ray Armando. "We recorded some tracks, and the last one we did was on a Friday, after a very depressing week of rain in New York City. It was 'Turn the Beat Around.' *I hated it!* I listened to it in my office, and I just couldn't get it. It had been such a bad week that I just couldn't hear anything with an open mind. Then David Todd, the head of disco promotion at RCA, came into my office, and he went crazy over the track! He convinced me to finish it as soon as possible. He had also recognized the potential of my Brothers' track, 'Are You Ready for This.' David was very much responsible for making sure these songs were successful.

"I had written four full arrangements out on score paper before I finally combined a little of each into the final arrangement of 'Turn the Beat Around.' I never collaborated with Vicki on the arrangement—this was at a time when she would just sing and I would just do my thing. She did want to have a guitar solo part and wanted to use Elliot Randall, and so we did use him for those solos. Pete and Gerald Jackson wrote the song. Vicki loved it, and she and her boyfriend, Al Garrison, who worked for me at Sunbury-Dunbar, RCA's music publishing company, were the ones who found the song to begin with. She added her own nuances to the song, and I can tell you 'Turn the Beat Around' would have been nothing without her! She did all the background voices for the track as well. All you have to do is hear her sing this song. You'd have to ask yourself, 'Who could have done that but her?'

"'Turn the Beat Around' is what I call a 'record song,'" says Schatz. "My job was to set a background that she'd be comfortable with and just let her go. There is a lot of ad-libbing; the twists and turns and that way she sings 'rat-tat-tat-tat' is all Vicki's energy. That record was really one of a kind! People were making long versions out of three-minute songs back then. I believe this was the first time that I know of that someone actually wrote out a breakdown for a song. Things were created to happen at certain times in the music, so I didn't have to rebuild it from pieces of something else. I always found that piecing things together from existing parts was a bit stagnant in early disco records. She had such a distinctive and amazing style, and it was perfect for the song. She sang 'Turn the Beat Around' the way it was written, but I've heard others sing it and found their renditions a bit understated and boring to me. I really feel Gloria Estefan copied every lick that Vicki did, because it was *that* good. Vicki was brilliant! Don't get me wrong, though. We had our differences and some difficulties at times, but, overall, the experience with her was wonderful."

Warren seems to take delight at thinking about Robinson and begins laughing. "Vicki was a wild child, man! I remember taking her to her apartment on the Westside, and we stopped at a little grocery store. She jumped out of the cab and said, 'Warren, come with me!' Then, all of the sudden, she was ducking out the back door of a bodega on the corner of 72nd Street and West End Avenue to avoid paying the cab driver. She was wild, like a street kid! It was like nothing for her to do that. She grew up in the streets of New York after all, running around with all of her friends," he says with affection.

Vicki's days of stiffing cabbies came to an end, Warren admits with a smile. In early 1976, "Turn the Beat Around" reached the top position of the disco chart and stayed there for nearly a month as it climbed to number 10 on *Billboard's* pop singles survey. Proclaimed a classic nearly overnight, the song was featured on almost every disco music compilation LP released in the years that followed. Divas Gloria Estefan, Laura Branigan and others covered the track later, but Robinson's Grammy-nominated version has remained supreme. Schatz and Robinson released her debut album, *Never Gonna Let You Go*, which climbed halfway up *Billboard's* Hot 100 albums chart. The LP spawned only one other major club hit with the track "Common Thief," but critics generally lauded the collection as a stellar debut.

"I must have released 120 singles by that time and never had more than a marginal hit," Warren admits. "Nothing like 'Turn the Beat Around.' It was huge! I was in shock and very happy over the song's success. For me, it was amazing. Vicki got very busy, and she was appearing all over the place. I didn't see her very much until it was time to do the next album. She was aware of her gift, but she wasn't stupid about it. She was just happy that something had happened. The Grammy nomination was a big thing for me, but I never got the feeling from her that she was nearly as excited as I was."

Robinson followed up with a series of albums under the watchful eye of Schatz. They included a self-titled LP late in '76, *Half and Half* in '78, and *Movin On*, produced by T. Life (Evelyn "Champagne" King's producer) at the decade's end. She enjoyed numerous club hits (including "Daylight," "Should I Stay" and "Trust in Me") while working with Warren, but nothing had quite the impact of her beat-turning smash. Observes Schatz, "I had been in the music business for almost 20 years, so I had seen people have hits and nothing after that. I knew that it could be a fleeting moment as far as that kind of success was concerned. All of her albums sold very well, however. My success with Vicki opened up every door for me at other places. So, for me, it was exciting as a musician to have the freedom to do what I wanted. After that success, I did the New York Community Choir, which had a huge hit with the song 'Express Yourself,' and I had a big dance record with Gordon Grody ['Living with You']. I then worked with Evelyn 'Champagne' King. Because of my commercial successes, I was asked to handle more of the A&R function at RCA."

Schatz began climbing the corporate ladder at the label giant. "The head of black A&R left RCA, and Ken Glancy, the president, needed someone to oversee that department," he remembers. "He said, 'Warren does those black records,' and he asked me to take over it. I said, 'No, that's ridiculous.' I finally said I would only run it from downstairs in the publishing department and that I didn't want the title or the office on the 8th floor (execs only). I said I'd do the job, not as head of black A&R, but as part of my job at the publishing company's production company, Sunbar Productions.

"Nancy Jeffries, then the head of A&R administration, had been sitting with a demo tape that the producer T. Life had brought to her of Evelyn 'Champagne' King. The minute I made this change of job, she played me the tape. I, of course, said yes! I said to T. Life, 'Look, let's do four sides within a budget, and if it's all good, we'll stretch it out into an album.' That's how Evelyn's LP *Smooth Talk* came about. She was a joy. Another gifted—really gifted—human being. She was just about 16 or 17 and very sweet and kind. She'd come into the city with her parents, and I got friendly with them. We tried to take care of Evelyn—we liked her a lot," Schatz says fondly.

To all outward appearances, RCA Records seemed very "pro-disco" during the genre's heyday and was more likely to nurture its disco stars than other labels of the time. This may account for King and Robinson's long-standing contracts with the company. Schatz claims some responsibility for the label's nurturing disposition and disco-friendly corporate vision.

"A year after I started helping in the Urban A&R department, Mike Berniker, who was the head of pop A&R at RCA, left. RCA asked me and Neil Portnow (currently the president of the Grammys) to share the position. I stayed in New York, and Neil went to California. During this time, I ended up having some big hits, and at one point I had a large number of records in the Hot 100. A year later, I was promoted to VP of National A&R. I had taken a different tack when I was running the department. A lot of labels signed artists and dropped them as soon as they got cold. That's not how I wanted to run the department. I had looked at very successful labels like A&M and Warner Brothers that kept their artists for three or four albums to see what would happen. I wanted to have that kind of reputation. The artists we picked were chosen carefully, and our lives were all commingled, and it mattered that we built something together. By the time I left RCA, that idea had taken hold with them, especially with artists with whom they had enjoyed success. Long after I left, they continued to have hits with Evelyn.

"RCA eventually had me reporting to someone new, and I just didn't get a sense of the autonomy I once had," Schatz admits, choosing his words slowly and carefully. "I was finding out what other people at other companies were making. I was looking at the success I had signing rock acts like Triumph, Toby Beau, Kristy & Jimmy McNichol and Bonnie Tyler to the label, and I started believing my own press. I was thinking I was the greatest thing since sliced bread. People started coming out of the woodwork making me offers, and I left RCA around the beginning of 1980 to go run Ariola America. That decision was really me just thinking that I deserved more."

Ariola had made significant inroads on the charts in previous years with the popular disco single "Love Rush" by Ann-Margret, Amii Stewart's gargantuan number one hit "Knock on Wood," and two albums by the Three Degrees, produced by Giorgio Moroder. Schatz' move to the label (following the downturn of classic disco) afforded him the opportunity to sign the latest album recorded by Viola Wills, *If You Could Read My Mind*, in 1980.

"Viola was signed to Hansa Records in Germany," he says. "Ariola America had entered a venture with Arista Records, and I worked in the same building as Clive Davis, who had signed his deal with BMG at the same time I did. He had first crack at everything, and Arista wound up distributing Ariola product. He passed on Viola, and he definitely didn't understand dance music. But I liked her album. So I took that record over. That album came to me finished, and I identified it as a potential hit, but I didn't do anything creative on it. I was the repository of the good luck, you might say. Clive had also passed on the Swiss hard rock group Krokus, so I signed them as well. I also signed Vicki to Ariola, but gave the production over to Clayton Ivey and Terry Woodford. They recorded the Michael McDonald song 'Nothin' But a Heartache' in Muscle Shoals, Alabama, with Vicki using the same rhythm section that was on all the great Aretha records. It was a wonderful record, but not a dance record. Not my smartest decision, but I wanted Vicki to be happy, and she wanted to try something new.

"Ariola should have been successful as a label, but it only lasted three years. The deal we had with Arista was that we'd build the records to a certain level, and then Arista would take over the marketing and promotion. We made Viola's record a really successful dance hit, but it didn't matter what I did. They never stepped in and did what they were supposed to do. It should have been bigger than it was. We sold about 50,000 albums, which was pretty good at that point, but I think it could have sold half a million if Arista had gotten behind it. They didn't, and that was really disheartening for me because I felt it was a great LP," he says with disappointment. Wills' extended single version of "If You Could Read My Mind," a remake of the Gordon Lightfoot hit, was a tremendous success in the clubs and remained on DJ playlists for almost all of 1980.

"When I decided to close Ariola—and a lot of people decided that with me—I said, 'Now what?' I happened to have synthesizers and a very cool drum and percussion track I had done, and Vicki Sue Robinson and I wrote a song on the spot. I did it on an eight-track, not even a 24-track, and it turned out to be a pretty big hit called 'Hot Summer Night.' I knew the guys at Prelude, and they immediately said, 'Oh! Okay!' and grabbed it. Vicki and I tried a couple of other singles on my own label, but I didn't have the money to properly promote them, so we moved to Profile Records, which was owned by my friend Cory Robbins. We made two big dance records for Profile—'To Sir with Love' and 'Everlasting Love.' Warren mentions that Vicki recorded both tracks in the bathroom of his apartment, where the acoustics happened to be just right.

"Viola Wills and I stayed friends," says the producer. "I wound up producing three more sides for her that Hansa paid for and that I put out on my own small label here in New York called Perfect Records. Hansa put them out in Germany, and they did pretty well. We did 'I Can't Stay Away from You,' 'If You Leave Me Now,' and 'The More I See You' (which featured Vicki on background vocals). Viola was another gem—charming, warm, gifted—a lovely person. She moved to Minneapolis, and I eventually fell out of touch with her. I never knew she'd fallen in a bad way."

Viola had a series of personal problems and succumbed to cancer in 2009. Vicki Sue Robinson had also fallen victim to cancer, passing nine years earlier.

"Vicki and I were friends until the day she died," Warren says. It is clearly a subject that stirs up emotions for her former producer. "I was at her bedside until a week before she passed. She had become a very big jingle singer for about five years before that. She was doing very well at it financially. She was still performing club dates singing her hits, but she was making a fortune singing commercials for Pepsi and Coke and things like that. She volunteered at her church to help kids. She was so grateful to everyone and had become such a mellow, gracious, and sweet woman. She knew she was sick and was in bed all the time towards the end, but she still tried to make us laugh. It was something to behold—the transition from this kid in the wild to a lovely, glowing woman, so generous of spirit. I had a lot of respect for her. She was married and lived in Connecticut. I knew her mom, but she didn't have a large family. Her friends were her family. She had a great passion and spirit, and it was hard to keep up with her. As she became older, she was quite spiritual in the way she'd radiate kindness. I never met anyone like Vicki—*ever*."

In a manner of speaking, the cycle of life and death also extended itself to the realm of dance music. Schatz remembers the media-sparked cries for the death of disco. But instead of disco vanishing, he says the music evolved, as it had been for decades, into a broader form of dance music.

"It's like anything else," Schatz remarks, "when things are new and people are exper-

Music industry veterans and friends gather to reminisce in 2013. Left to right: Eddie O'Loughlin, Warren Schatz and Cory Robbins (courtesy Warren Schatz).

imenting, really interesting things happen—especially musically. There's energy, it's new, and it's fresh. Then, finally, all the big record companies see a trend and jump on the bandwagon. They just sign anything and everything. It happened in disco, and it's true of every genre. Whoever had the biggest name at the label that was in this trend would get tons of dollars behind them. Others suffered. Everything got so watered-down; the style got homogenized into the general social psyche. Because it was so diluted and the passion of the productions got lost, people could hear that and became disinterested. Some of the disco records towards the late '70s and early '80s period were pretty boring. I just moved on and worked with the emerging trends.

"I became one of the main producers at Profile Records in the mid–'80s. The emerging electronic and drum machine sound influenced Cory Robbins and I. I engineered, produced and arranged 'Memory' [from the Broadway musical *Cats*] by Ménage in 1983, which was huge, and also 'I Love Men' by Cinema, on my own Promise label, which Profile distributed. I was using drum machines, but I used real guitars and horns and strings as well. But our music was drum machine–based because that's what was happening at that time. Soon people stopped using strings and horns because of small budgets or whatever, and they started using synthesizers to generate sounds. That became new, and that became interesting."

Schatz doesn't need to reflect long in order to identify the crowning moment of his accomplished career. "'Turn the Beat Around' was my best work. Aside from Vicki's vocal work, I knew if the arrangement wasn't vibrant, it wouldn't stand out. I think I'm very attached to the things I've worked hardest on, and I think I worked pretty hard for that song. It was my first big hit, and the song was really at the core of who I am. So when I was finally accepted in the music business as a producer, I didn't have to try to be anybody else anymore. People wanted me now for something I was actually good at. I also did an album by Inner City Symphony on Midland International that I did with Ben and my friends that I was very proud of. I was finally given a decent budget of $25,000 to do that record.

"When cable TV first came to New York City, there would be a blue screen on your TV set for a time. For two years they played music off the Inner City Symphony album as the 'official music of the blue screen,'" he laughs. "This was before they had agreements with ASCAP or BMI to pay people for music usage like that. I would be a millionaire if I'd been paid for all that borrowing."

Warren's philosophy for enjoying life today is simple, and it's one that has always served him well. "Follow your gut as much as you can!" he insists. "I've reinvented myself five or six times. Just be willing to change; don't stay in one place. Now I make my living doing corporate videos, and I do marketing support for a large data company and other consulting firms. I still have a record company distributed through E-One, the former Koch label, and I'm still involved in music, though it's mostly crossover classical material. But even if you change your path in life to something different from what you've been doing, don't be afraid of it. You never lose the core of who you are. If the core is true and passionate, that's the person you are. It may manifest itself in music for a time, and then it comes out in helping people in some other way later on. The core always stays, no matter what you do. When Cory Robbins of Profile Records had a falling out with his partner over the record company, I asked him what he would do if he didn't have his company. He looked at me as if I was missing the obvious and shrugged, 'What do you mean? I'd do something else!' That was all he said. He had no attachment to having to be *anything*. I thought that was brilliant!

"There was a time in my life when there was a lot I wanted to musically and lyrically communicate to the world. But after recording 'Memory' by Menage, I started to feel like I didn't have anything more to say. It had reached the point where all anyone wanted from me anyway was another 'Turn the Beat Around.' I could have continued to do dance music right up to this day, but I really didn't want to. Instead, I moved to other forms of music, like jazz and classical. It's like I said, sometimes your path in life changes," he says quite casually.

It's difficult to imagine the disco genre without the influence of Warren Schatz. The world might never have discovered the talents of Vicki Sue Robinson or Evelyn "Champagne" King, and there'd be far fewer classic songs in its energized arsenal of hits. Schatz brought style and unparalleled creativity to his productions, and he literally made millions of people dance until dawn. His irresistible songwriting, hook-laden arrangements and remarkable creativity remain prime examples of disco music at its artistic and commercial finest.

"I'd like to be remembered as someone who lived a passionate life and found people with talent, who made *my* life and work something worth remembering." He pauses a moment. "I've been lucky enough to be able to follow my heart." Warren laughs before rushing off to his next project, adding, "I want them to say that even if I was a jerk sometimes, I was always willing to clean up the messes that I made! That's what I'd like them to remember!"

Debbie Sledge, Joni Sledge and Kim Sledge of Sister Sledge
"We Are Family"

"I remember we liked 'He's the Greatest Dancer,' and they told us that 'We Are Family' was written specifically for us, so we liked that concept.... I'm not sure we really caught that they were 'disco songs' at the time."—Kim Sledge

It's difficult to imagine artists who represent the "family values" of disco better than Sister Sledge. In the glory days of this effervescent music, such values might best be illustrated by the all-encompassing love and elation that was found on so many dance floors. Each person moving so joyfully to the beat of the sisters' chart-topping music was a kindred spirit, sharing in the revelry of the uplifting songs and divine voices of this highly unique group of women. Originally comprised of four siblings born and raised in Philadelphia, Sister Sledge enjoyed a modicum of success with their very first recordings. But once their paths crossed with those of producers Nile Rodgers and Bernard Edwards, this innocent quartet was transformed into world famous pop and dance music superstars. From their inspired collaboration came one of the most recognized and beloved songs from the disco era—the triumphant "We Are Family." Debbie, Joni and Kim Sledge (fellow sister Kathy was not available for this interview) reveal the essence of their chemistry and what's at the heart of one of disco's most memorable female ensembles.

The Sledge sisters started their musical careers blissfully ignorant of the incredible adventures that lay ahead of them. "Believe it or not, we began singing in glee club," says Joni, "which nobody really knows. Debbie, who has a really brilliant ear, taught us four-part harmony while we were in school. In addition to that, our grandmother was a lyric soprano opera singer, Viola Williams, who was also a student of Juilliard. She taught us how to sing, breathe properly and how to use our voices. Debbie led us into singing as a group after learning songs in school and church.

"A lot of people don't realize we were performing for a while before we ever worked with Nile and Bernard. [One of the] very first singles we did was a song that Debbie led called 'The Weatherman.' Debbie has such a beautiful voice—she has what you might call a jazz voice. I call it 'the waterfall' because it has no edge. It's just very smooth and beautiful. I believe Tony Bell and Phil Hurtt produced that song [aka the Young Professionals, a team which also included LeBaron Taylor]. The first album that we recorded was *Circle of Love*, with producers Bert 'Super Chart' De Coteaux and Tony Silvester [released in 1975]. It was released in Japan as well as the U.S., and that's where we had our first really big hit. We were still in school, and we didn't even understand what having a hit meant—what being considered a star was all about. When we first went to Tokyo and got to the airport, there were all these kids with posters of us on sticks. We were like, 'Why are they doing this?' It was an interesting, fun experience. When we got back home, we just were normal, regular kids again. Nobody believed we were having this success in Japan."

The sisters were a stateside hit on the dance chart with the single "Love Don't You Go Through No Changes on Me" (one of several songs on the album composed by Gwen Guthrie and Patrick Grant). They reached the Top Five of the disco survey just before the new year. The tracks "Pain Reliever" and "Protect Our Love" also fared well. The album was followed by the LP, *Together*, a production helmed by Silver Convention's Michael Kunze and Sylvester Levay. Despite the production team's track record, the LP received little attention. "Those early days were a great experience, and I just want to give credit to all those producers. They were excellent and very cool to work with," Joni says.

Though club DJs had welcomed the girls, the sisters say their group hadn't fully identified with the disco genre as a possible niche. Their introduction to producers Nile Rodgers and Bernard Edwards, who had been enjoying tremendous success in disco with the group Chic, changed all that. "When we met up with Nile and Bernard," says Joni, "we were something of an experiment for them. They were a new production team at Atlantic Records, and they were asked by the label to produce our group. Actually, I think they were given several groups to choose from, and they may have requested to work with Sister Sledge.

"We weren't familiar with them," she adds. "It was an interesting experience working with them because they were used to working with a certain method, and we were used to our own way. I think the combination really worked though. But it wasn't always easy. They would sometimes have ideas and basic melodies and tell us to interpret them. So we would have to interpret the songs the way they presented them to us. It wasn't like we had anything to follow."

Debbie chimes in, "Nile and Bernard were not singers, and they were creating as they would go along. When they'd try to sing something, it would have a certain sound. We'd have to try and figure out what notes they were actually trying to convey. In some cases, even they weren't sure."

Rumors and publicity stories at the time had suggested that Sister Sledge had been considering breaking up just prior to their collaboration with Chic's producers. Not precisely, say the sisters. "We weren't thinking of breaking up exactly," Joni recalls. "We were tired and frustrated at that point in our career. It actually takes a lot of work to be in the business. If we can give some advice to young people looking to explore music careers—you have to be really willing to roll up your sleeves and dig your hands in the dirt. You have to rehearse endlessly; you have to deal with a lot of disappointment; you have to be able to *not* take 'no' for an answer. You really have to keep going. We were at a point when we met Nile and Bernard that we were looking at other goals and ambitions. Eventually we all went to college, but we didn't know if music was going to be our destiny.

That's what it was. It wasn't a conflict; it was more that we were asking ourselves if this was the route we should be taking. And right in that same year, a lot of miraculous things started happening, and we were like, 'Wow, I guess it *is* the right thing.'"

Adds Debbie, "We were never thinking of breaking up. We were always going to be family. We were as strong as ever as far as unity among sisters goes."

Sister Sledge's *We Are Family* album on Cotillion Records was a colossal success. The well-timed debut single, "He's the Greatest Dancer" (which name checked designer clothing labels and celebrated the joys of nightclubbing), reached the number one spot on the disco chart early in 1979. The song soon climbed the R&B charts and made its way into the Top 10 on the pop side. Filled with occasionally sketchy lyrics, Debbie confirms that the frequently misunderstood exclamations heard just before the title of the song were, "Oh-what-wow!" "Everybody always asks about that," laughs Joni.

Parent label Atlantic was pressed to quickly release the rapidly accelerating follow-up track "We Are Family" as a single, which had already joined "He's the Greatest Dancer" at the number one position on disco surveys and on a 12-inch single. The title track was a sensation, reaching the number two position on *Billboard*'s pop chart. The four sisters' youthful and earnest harmonies blended seamlessly with the so-called "Chic sound," and the song became a nationwide anthem. It was a gold-certified single adopted by the Pittsburgh Pirates (who won baseball's World Series that year) to symbolize their unity. "We Are Family" soon stood beside Gloria Gaynor's "I Will Survive" and Donna Summer's "Last Dance" as one of disco's most highly regarded achievements. "Thinking of You" and "Lost in Music" were also major club hits off the set.

"Nile and Bernard were totally different people," recalls Joni. "Nile was a lot more easygoing and more fun to work with than Bernard. Bernard kind of reminded me of Debbie a little bit because Debbie is kind of a perfectionist when it comes to harmony. Bernard was kind of a perfectionist when it came to his interpretation of ideas. As Debbie said, a lot of times they didn't really have melodies. They had strong hooks. You had to really interpret what they were going for and be creative at the same time. You had to create the melody and interpret the emotion. That can be very challenging."

Adds Debbie, "There was some difficulty working with them, but only to the degree that I was, at the time, the group leader as far as vocals were concerned. I had a little bit of a conflict because at one point they wanted to use other backing vocals. I said, 'Why? We're a self-contained group. What do you mean?' They'd say, 'You're not singing it the way we want it.' I'd say, 'Well, tell us the way you want it!'" she laughs. "We could have sung anything they wanted. So, in that sense, there was a communication conflict. When I look back on them now, those conflicts were meaningless because it turned out to be a great, great project. There was, in the end, a joining of creative minds—the artists and producers."

"Eventually Debbie and Bernard became great friends," Joni clarifies, "and we all ended up having a lot of respect for each other. But sometimes you have to go through some difficulties to make that happen. You have to develop and earn that respect and that's what happened here."

"It was a very exciting time for us; it really was," Kim recalls. "Everything was a whirlwind. Having been recording artists for some time already, Nile and Bernard's method of teaching and reviewing the songs that we were going to do was very different for us, as Joni said. We had learned early on from our grandmother's training that you get your song down pat and memorize it so that it's second nature to you. But their whole perspective was different. They were perfectionists, but yet very spontaneous. I guess they were looking for nuances that you just catch when you start recording. I didn't quite understand it then, and we kept saying, 'What do they want from us?' I can't say we had a lot of freedom because they had a plan and a formula. I have to say it was a great formula, a formula of warmth, and they were confident that we could deliver it. We were as well. It's not that the songs were very difficult for us to sing; it's just that the environment was very rigid. It was a little frustrating at times, but it was also very exciting.

"I liked the songs on the *We Are Family* album," she continues, "and thought they were fun to do, but they were definitely different and had their own kind of feel. I didn't recognize at all how huge these songs were going to be. I remember we liked 'He's the Greatest Dancer,' and they told us that 'We Are Family' was written specifically for us, so we liked that concept. They were a different style from what we had been singing, and I'm not sure we really caught that they were 'disco songs' at the time."

Even today, the *We Are Family* album is sometimes first identified as a product of Nile and Bernard before the Sledge sisters get their rightful due. However, Debbie, Joni and Kim agree the project reflects their cohesiveness and energy as a unique group of performers. Debbie anxiously addresses the pecking order issue. "You could tell," she says, "that even Nile and Bernard initially looked at this as a Chic project. Especially back in those days, when artists, especially female artists, were not given the proper level of credit. The producer would take credit for everything. But even Nile and Bernard were shocked at the popularity of our album, and they *had* to give at least partial credit to the group for its success."

Adds Joni, "We always felt the album was a really good example of who Sister Sledge was. However, I think we are so much more than just the vocals on the album. I think we are the *unity* of the album."

"Yes, it's the performance!" Debbie chimes in. "Nile and Bernard were extremely impressed by our performance, and it shocked them. ['We Are Family'] is a Sister Sledge interpretation that just happened to fit us very well."

Kim agrees. "I don't think I ever looked at that album as a Nile and Bernard project because we were chosen because of who we were and how we would complement the way they wanted to present their songs," she says earnestly. "They could have chosen anyone to do this album, but they specifically chose us because of our talents. I think it was a great marriage. I really believe that's why it worked so well."

Having such a gargantuan worldwide hit was a life-changing event for the siblings. "We went on a tour that lasted almost three years," says Joni. "It just kept growing and growing. We were something unique out there. Most girl groups were wearing gowns and looking very feminine. Not that we weren't, but for a while we never ever put on gowns. We wanted to dance and absolutely loved it. So I think that was one way we changed the idea of female groups. Today, of course, the girls are really getting down. So, we may have led the way, and we feel really good about that.

"I think in our live performances we showed much more diversity than on our albums. Touring gave us a chance to travel internationally and broaden our base and share our energy with audiences. One of our biggest learning experiences of that time was just discovering how to connect with people. We found out that everybody in the whole world has the same desire for love and a connection with other people. The fact that 'We Are Family' was such a big hit, well, it ended up reflecting a message that was stronger than the song. That message, to us, is something we continue to benefit from, and it continues to help us learn and grow. I can't even really explain it. A lot of people have hit songs, but I have the feeling that this song will be around long after we're gone. And our kids and their kids and their kids will all be a part of it. It was more than the beat and the rhythm. It was the essence of the song—what family means—whether it's by blood or spirit. That's the kind of reaction we got from having that hit, and that's what made it so miraculous for us."

Debbie agrees. "We talked a bit about whether or not Sister Sledge represents the 'We Are Family' song or the song represents Sister Sledge. I think one of the things Joni is saying is that the message of family is who we are, and that's what we want to share through our music. Rather than talk quite so much about the song 'We Are

Kim, Joni and Debbie continue to bring the uplifting music of Sister Sledge to a worldwide audience in 2016 (courtesy Sister Sledge).

Family,' we've always preferred to talk about the message Sister Sledge is trying to promote."

"We should do a book about the stories people share with us because of the 'We Are Family' song," adds Joni. "But Debbie is right. We actually represent the concept she described, and we are so honored to be in a position to help spread that kind of love—and we like to do that with every song we perform. As a matter of fact, Debbie and I write a lot of our songs, and that is still our goal. My icon is Stevie Wonder. I think all of his songs represent a similar message of love and strength and connection. Whenever I feel down, I'll go and listen to one of his albums, like *Songs in the Key of Life*. Instantly, I connect with my own soul. Hopefully we are doing that for others, and we can continue to expand on that."

As a group, Sister Sledge had a genuine family vibe that was palpable and extremely appealing to their fans. Maintaining an individual sense of self while forging a collective identity was something the members of many ensembles found difficult, but the sisters agree they managed to navigate the challenge. Kim is quick to identify their secret. "I'd say there's two sides to each of us. One side is established from the moment we are born, and each of us has his or her own personality. My sisters and I moved around as one entity constantly, but our individual places within our family have always been maintained. Our individuality always flourished. For instance, Debbie has always had a gift for music and perfect pitch, even going back to when we were very small. She always kind of guided us, and you could depend on her. Joni was always full of energy and had extremely creative ideas. Sometimes they were way over the top, but if you put all of us into her concept, it was always a great idea. Kathy was always a funny person, a jokester, and she still is. So there was always laughter, thanks to her.

"Me," she continues, "I guess I was the rebellious one. I was always my sisters' protector—even in conflicts with tour managers when we became successful. There were some managers and backstage people who weren't very nice when we went on tour with other artists. They were people who thought they had to give off a certain attitude. I didn't stand for that or anything that would hurt one of my sisters. So we all had our personalities and each part made up the whole, and we all worked together to keep it in balance. There were, of course, some different aspirations that each of us had that were difficult to pursue. As you mature, that can create a conflict because there are things you want to do. It wasn't always easy. But the group always came first, and that was the commitment we made."

Though their Rodgers and Edwards–produced follow-up LP, *Love Somebody Today*, had been highly anticipated, the album was caught smack in the middle of the disco backlash, which was in full swing by 1980. The tracks "Got to Love Somebody" and "Reach Your Peak" garnered some attention in the clubs and on the R&B charts, but the album failed to catch the mainstream current. The sisters admit a number of factors worked against the project.

"[I think the album's lack of success] was the result of ineffective promotion," concedes Debbie. "Although it's not widely known, Nile and Bernard took on the promotion of the *We Are Family* album themselves. They wanted to make sure that the album had the correct exposure and promotion. They knew the record company wouldn't do what *they* could do. With the second album, they did not take that path. The record company was not supportive as far as promotion goes."

Adds Joni, "The clubs demanded our first record with Nile and Bernard. The disco movement was empowering, and radio stations were forced, you might say, to play our records. The public demanded it. Debbie, Kim and I know that record label budgets for promotion back then were very small. Rock acts got tremendous budgets, but R&B acts did not. We were very happy we had that huge fan support for our songs from *We Are Family*, but on our second album we had to have meetings with the label. Their attitude was let's throw it up against the wall and see if it sticks. That's the truth. Rather than taking advantage of the track record we had already built, that's what happened. The proof of it was this—our live performances started increasing, tripling. The locations, the venues, and what we could demand for shows were all on the upswing. There was a total imbalance with the radio airplay we were getting from promotion. We sort of started having a cult following without the help of the record company. Eventually, we left that label, but that is exactly what happened. However, we never felt pressure [to have a big follow-up hit], and we were still having fun. As long as we were being true to our art, doing our best and receiving the kind of gratitude and love we were getting from audiences, we weren't pressured. It was fun!"

Kim also recognizes the importance of the group's live shows. "It's interesting," she observes. "Having performed for so many years before all this success, I have to say we were kind of prepared because of our upbringing to some extent—at least as far as what it would take to maintain the position we had achieved. The success of the songs happened overnight, but more important to us than the hits (which we were very grateful for) was our live show. It was so wonderful to be able to perform music that we loved, but even more important to be able to translate that love into a live performance. We started doing shows for huge audiences, and the accolades we received were very fulfilling.

"We were raised to believe it is a gift to give—and I'm really being honest—a gift to be able to sing. To me, singing is another form of worship. When you sing, it's a form of worshipping God and glorifying Him. You are bringing a gift He's given you to someone else. To be able to give this to an audience who is already prepared for a great experience because of our hits—it was just amazing. The goal was always to look in the eyes of the audience and make a connection and to help them receive something. They want you to take them to a different place. And it was never one-sided. We would try to give to them and they would give to us."

Joni has a very definite theory about the thick anti-disco fog that the sisters and so many other artists were forced to contend with as the decade wound down. "Music used to be very segregated, and there were many radio stations that only dealt with certain artists and specific target audiences," she conjectures. "They had sponsors who only wanted those audiences. When disco came out, the clubs started dictating what people would hear, not the radio. It caused a lot of problems for record companies and radio stations and their bottom-line revenues. It was like the people were empowering the artists instead of the radio stations. As a result, I believe the industry started a negative campaign against disco—disco sucks and things like that. Prior to this, we had been looking at all these charts and seeing how the pop and rock acts dropped and watching the disco artists climbing. Those in power had no control over it. I think the backlash was a contrived effort to darken the name of disco. I don't think it had anything to do with the music or these great artists who were doing wonderful stuff. I remember those charts with Chic, Donna Summer, Giorgio Moroder—there were some really great musical contributors. Yes, there were some fakes trying to get hold of that energy, but you have that in every music form. I think the backlash was all about the business and the industry. That's my take on it."

"Because we were never fighting so hard to become huge stars," adds Kim, "our experiences were just another form of life. We were doing something we loved. I don't think we recognized we had been pigeonholed into disco at that time. I know I personally didn't realize the media had turned against it until much later. We continued to do music that we felt was good and that we would be proud to sing. The disco backlash didn't deter me or concern me. I don't believe we ever thought of ourselves exclusively as disco artists."

By the early '80s, dance music had largely retreated to the underground clubs and the gay culture from which it had evolved, but artists venturing back into this musical territory gradually began to make small dents on the mainstream U.S. pop chart. Leaving behind Rodgers and Edwards, Sister Sledge's *All American Girls* set was released in 1981. Narada Michael Walden ("I Shoulda Loved Ya," "Tonight I'm Alright") produced the LP, which managed to crack the Top 50. The set yielded two Top 10 dance hits, "All American Girls" and "He's Just a Runaway," the latter remixed as a reggae style 12-inch single in tribute to Bob Marley upon his passing.

"Narada was an interesting choice as a producer, and he was once again chosen by the record company," remembers Debbie. "We had the type of contract that the record company could really dictate who would produce us."

Says Joni, "It was definitely a company decision rather than ours. We weren't even familiar with Narada. I think what he tried to do was duplicate the *We Are Family* album instead of expanding on what we had to offer. That's just my opinion. It was a good experience, but it was not as fun working with him. I remember wanting to contribute a lot of great ideas, but they were rejected. There was such a resistance to our viewpoints. We were supposed to co-produce that album. I think the album was good, and I have respect for him as a producer, but it could have been a lot better. After that, we did produce an album on our own [1982's] *The Sisters*. It did well on the pop chart, and I remember later running into Narada, who offered his congratulations. I said thank you. Certain things just forced you to grow. We learned a tremendous lot about the business—the importance of owning publishing and mastering—things like that. Now, as business women, we know how it works, and while we might not have as big a hit today, if you own your material and understand where you should spend your money and how to protect your rights, you can have a lot more satisfaction and still do well."

"It goes back to those challenges," Debbie believes. "We were women, and the record company did not want to hear our ideas. Today, we produce our own music. Back then, we wrote many songs, but management didn't want to see or hear any of our ideas. As Joni said, that's a challenge as an artist because you want people to know who you are. *Who you are is your art.* Today, we know the value of being able to do it ourselves and expressing our ideas. When you are a creative person, that all needs to come out. When you are blocked because you are a woman or an artist, it is extremely frustrating."

The ladies went on to have more hits, both here and abroad. In 1982, the single

"My Guy" (a remake of the Mary Wells hit) was a Top 30 pop success that also reached the Top Five of the New Zealand charts. England took a liking to Nile and Bernard's remixes of "Lost in Music" and sent the song back up the British pop charts in 1984. The following year, Sister Sledge reached number one in the U.K. with the single "Frankie," a retro-pop dance charmer that formally reunited them with producer Rodgers. The track was part of their 1985 album *When the Boys Meet the Girls*. Great Britain favored the sisters once again in 1993 when the songs "We Are Family" and "Lost in Music" were given the "Sure Is Pure" remix treatment and vaulted to the top of the country's music surveys.

"I do believe Europeans are very appreciative of disco," Kim asserts. "Here in the U.S., music can be a lot like the holidays. Christmas comes, then a week later you see Valentine's cards and flowers everywhere. Then Easter and Mother's Day. The music industry is like that—something is in, then it's out. The people who truly appreciate disco aren't like that. The people who make the songs and the people who want them and buy the songs are passionate about it. On the executive level, it's all about the dollars. How fast can they turn it over and how much can they make. I believe that those who truly love the art are the ones who want to savor it. It's like a good movie. I think of *Ben Hur*, which is one of my favorites. I've watched it thousands of times, and I'll watch it again. It's an old movie, but it's not old for me. It's the same with disco and those who love it."

Debbie believes the music of dance artists may have been better marketed in Europe. "I think the U.S. has a whole different way of connecting with audiences," she says. "The exposure is different. In England, it's much simpler. You aren't judged by the way you look or the fact that you are older. They either like your music, or they don't. In the United States, if you don't get the right exposure, the audiences only know you in a limited way based on what they've seen. In the U.K. and overseas, you are accepted for who you are as an artist. I think in some ways music plays a more important role in their lives."

"That's very true about Great Britain," agrees Joni. "I would say the same of Japan. They are extremely polite people. They will sit there and watch your whole show, and then at the end, they suddenly jump up and shower you with gifts. You think for a while maybe they aren't really into it, but they were just being polite. All audiences are different. New York, London, Paris, all the major cities—you better come with a good show. They are so used to seeing so much great stuff. We performed on six of the seven continents. We've performed all over the world except for Antarctica. That's why all this has less to do with us than it has with giving love and getting love from audiences. We just try to reciprocate that, and we just feel blessed all around and grateful. It's not that we're here to show audiences what we've got; it's that we are privileged to share *with* them—to smile and laugh and dance and sing with them."

It's clear the sisters take a great deal of satisfaction from their live performances, often returning to the subject and emphasizing the importance of their shows to their overall career. "You have to be naked when you do a show—by that I mean *real*," Joni explains. "You can't fake it. When you are performing, you have to take the wall down and look in their eyes. You have to expose your soul. Why else be up there? I'm not saying every show can be hunky-dory. There are times when you ask yourself, 'Am I being honest?' They can feel it when you're not. Even if you make mistakes, the fans are with you. I remember when Kim fell into an orchestra pit," she laughs. "It was really funny. She fell right in—bam! She was okay, thank God. It was her great attitude when she got back up on stage that made the audience love her even more."

"You can't go out there with any walls up," Debbie concurs. "You're coming out to share love. I make a great connection with the audience because I look directly in their eyes. I point out people; I wave to them directly. It makes all the difference."

Kathy Sledge (the group's primary lead vocalist) left the group in 1989 to pursue a solo career. The sisters say they understood her desire to take a new path and were confident the change would represent an exciting new beginning for Sister Sledge. "Our initial reaction was, 'Okay, fine, we support you,'" Debbie recalls. "We didn't agree with the decision at first because our interest was in retaining a family unit. But we recognized early that each of us has so much to offer. We actually moved forward in many ways because [her departure] allowed the three of us to expand as artists and become an even stronger unit."

One result of this recharged union was an album recorded in Italy in the early '90s called *And Now.... Sledge.... Again*. The set featured well-crafted Euro-House remakes of some of their earlier hits and a highly regarded original single called "World, Rise & Shine," which became an in-demand import among U.S. DJs and fans. The song was written by Joni and J.P. "Bluey" Maunick from the group Incognito and was number one on the dance charts in Italy. The sisters also released a 1997 set called *African Eyes*, which featured many songs co-written by Joni. Though the album fell under the commercial radar, the collection was critically acclaimed.

Debbie jumps at the opportunity to discuss a bit about her philosophy for managing aging, being successful and the overall evolution of Sister Sledge. "Right away I want to say we know we have to have a connection with life itself, with God. And by God, for Joni, Kim and I, I am referring specifically to Jesus Christ. We have a connection with the creator Himself. And we're artists, right? So creativity and the creator will always keep us young. We're gonna always stay young. We're going to take care of our bodies and stay young at heart. And we are going to love and enjoy life. God is life—that's the key. That's the formula."

"I do think that being connected to the power of love, which is God, is very important," Joni agrees. "You have ups, and you have downs, but I don't think anyone can survive the rollercoaster of life without being connected to the power of love. Love is the most powerful force in this universe. We've been taught that to understand God's love is to understand love that supersedes our human understanding of the term. I think love inspires creativity and allows you the opportunity to connect on a deeper level. I think if I just wanted to design shoes tomorrow, I would just draw on that same creativity I've used for music, that same love. I'd do it and move forward. When you have that connection, I think that failure just means, 'next?' You're not afraid of failure, and you're not afraid of pitfalls.

"I read somewhere that there are two kinds of people in the world, or rather two kinds of approaches to success. One is the person who avoids pitfalls. That's a person who won't take a certain road because they are afraid of the risks. Consequently, their road is very crooked, but it's a way of perhaps finding success. The other philosophy is to just go for it. If you fall, you pick yourself up, and you try not to fall that way again.

You don't avoid the pitfalls; you learn from them. To me, that is mastering life. So I'm on the road to mastery. Sometimes we pray together for guidance. We pray for help removing our own opinions and the opinions of others from our hearts and minds and we just ask God, 'What is your will for us?' And sometimes, in doing so, you find miracles."

Faith is equally important to Kim. "I am a believer in Jesus Christ as my Lord and Savior. I believe in the Father and the Holy Spirit. I will say this boldly—I'm a Christian, but I get a bit concerned regarding the motives behind organized religion. I love the Word of God (the Bible), but religion has been so twisted and used to hurt people, and it's so political. That's not who God is. We can be young at heart by continuing to grow, give and love. It's kept me young. It gives me hope, and it's what has kept me stable and given me joy. I can't help but want to give that joy to others. My life is not perfect by any means. But even though we have all this stuff that goes on around us, and we have our struggles, and we feel that so many things aren't right, there is a truth and a presence that will come and help us move beyond what we have to deal with. And that is God."

Today, Sister Sledge still performs around the world and continues to enjoy media coverage, including a recent spot on Neil Patrick Harris' NBC prime-time program, *Best Time Ever*. They are actively working on new recordings, and in the Spring of 2016 the sisters plan to release an empowering new track called "WAMOW (Women Are the Music of the World)." These are the latest developments in careers that have spanned decades and collectively remains one of disco's greatest success stories. Meanwhile, they continue to take pride in their disco history.

"It was a wonderful era, and people were free," insists Joni. "All nationalities—they just all connected. It was amazing. I don't object to our group being associated so strongly with disco. There were some negative connotations that people put out there, but it just ended up being called dance music. I think being a part of anything that generated that kind of freedom, love and fun is great—I'd say it's historic. And disco pays a lot of bills," she laughs.

"We had no problem being called a disco act," adds Debbie, "and the quality of disco music was nothing to sneeze at. The genre should be respected just as much as any other type of music. But it does not define who Sister Sledge is. I think that's another angle. If you saw our live act back in those days, it was so much more than just disco. A lot of people don't realize that, and it's important to remember."

Adds Kim, "I think many of the songs from the disco era were so exciting. I think disco was a wonderful genre of music and it bridged every possible gap."

Sister Sledge's stunning contributions to disco music have stood not only as timeless dance gems representing the very best combination of creativity, stellar production and sumptuous vocal harmonies, but as valuable songs of empowerment and solidarity. Forever and proudly linked to "We Are Family," the sisters' voices are now synonymous with the joyous sound of humanity united. Kim, Joni and Debbie take a moment to consider their musical legacy and how they would like Sister Sledge to be remembered. Their aspirations turn out to be quite simple.

Says Debbie, "I would hope Sister Sledge is remembered for unity and sisterhood."

Joni speaks next, saying, "I'd like us to be remembered as sisters who incited people to experience joy in their lives—that we inspired them to go for it and just have fun!"

Kim concludes the conversation, saying, "I hope our legacy will be that Sister Sledge came into people's lives, reconciled families back to each other and that we helped bring the world back to each other and back to God."

Arthur "Pooch" Tavares of Tavares
"Heaven Must Be Missing an Angel"

"We didn't want our whole R&B background to disappear, but once we got into that whole disco thing [our careers] took off. It was hard to avoid it."—Arthur "Pooch" Tavares

"If disco came around for a second time, I'd do it again. I'm just proud that Tavares was involved with something that helped make us a household name. Disco did that for us, I'm proud of that, and I always will be," declares Arthur Tavares, more commonly known as "Pooch." He comes from a six-brother family comprised of Victor, Ralph Vierra, Antone Lawrence (Chubby), Feliciano Vierra (Butch) and Perry Lee (Tiny). As an ensemble called Tavares, they became synonymous with disco following a string of successful crossover dance hits in the '70s. The songs "It Only Takes a Minute," "Don't Take Away the Music," "More Than a Woman," "Whodunit" and the number one disco smash "Heaven Must Be Missing an Angel" featured the brothers' scintillating harmonies wrapped around infectious beats. These hook-laden classics made them fixtures at the top of all the major music charts of the day. Pooch settles back to give his take on the group's remarkable joyride in disco land.

The first thing to tackle are the unusual nicknames. "It's a thing in our family," says Pooch. "The aunts and uncles all liked to put nicknames on most of us when we were kids. Just about everybody in our family has a nickname. Believe it or not, I have no idea where mine came from, but it stuck! Maybe I was cuddly like a puppy! Whatever—everybody calls me that."

The Tavares brothers are often credited with originating from New Bedford, Massachusetts, but Pooch says the New England region is more accurate. "My dad, being a musician, moved around quite a bit. My brother Ralph was born in Waterbury, Connecticut, Chubby and I were born in Providence, Rhode Island, and Tiny, Butch and Victor were born in New Bedford. We were very young kids, maybe four or five years old, when we started singing around the house while my dad played guitar. We'd harmonize with him, and when we got to the age where we were listening to the radio, that's where we had to part company," he laughs. "We sang with the Boy's Club and have really been doing it all our lives. It was really second nature to us."

Honing their skills in early incarnations of their group, it wasn't long before their unique vocal style caught the ear of the music business. "We had a friend from Providence who was the A&R man for Capitol Records," Tavares recalls. "He used to come see us in nightclubs and the venues we played on the Eastern Seaboard. We were in Toronto performing and got a call from him asking us if we were still interested in recording for

Capitol. Well, of course we were! That was about 1973. We've been in the recording industry since then." The group's first album release was called *Check It Out*, produced by Johnny Bristol. The title track became an R&B hit. According to Pooch, it was at this point that brother Victor decided to leave the group, and Tavares was introduced to the world as a five-man act.

"We all have lead singing voices. Chubby did a lot of the leads on our early songs, but when Butch and I would coordinate together for a lead later on, it always worked well and was a good choice. He and I did 'She's Gone,' 'A Penny for Your Thoughts,' and 'Words and Music.' But we all could do leads very well. At the same time, our father taught us how to do backgrounds, and we picked up a lot of our singing chords because of our father's playing on the guitar. When we went into the studio to sing our harmonies, people would be amazed. Normally, singers didn't use the kind of voicing you heard from us—but all we were doing was using the voicing our father had taught us." "She's Gone" reached the top of the R&B chart just as disco music was beginning to make its presence known in 1974.

Soon, all the major labels began to notice the success singers like KC and the Sunshine Band, Carol Douglas, Hues Corporation, Van McCoy and Gloria Gaynor were beginning to enjoy, as their hits crossed from clubs to mainstream pop. Says Pooch, "We started out doing R&B—Gladys Knight and the Pips, the Four Tops—those were our idols. My biggest idol was Jerry Butler. We all had our person or group that we wanted to sing like. We started working with Johnny Bristol and a lot of people that gave us fantastic music. Then we started doing upbeat songs like 'It Only Takes a Minute' and 'Heaven Must Be Missing an Angel' with producers and arrangers like Freddie Perren, Michael Omartian, Brian Porter and Dennis Lambert. We never thought of it as 'disco.' I think we had our minds set on it as danceable R&B music. We did some slow songs, but our overall sound made the producers move us in a different direction—the energized sound that was coming from the clubs.

"We strove to sing a lot of different types of music. We'd go to Vegas and perform Broadway songs, believe it or not. We would do anything the audience wanted to hear. Our father taught us to sing a lot of different styles—not just music that would appeal to a black audience. He wanted us to learn everything from A to Z in music. I don't think we ever worried about what we were recording—whether it was disco or any other style. I think we were just excited to be recording artists. We didn't care as long as the song sounded good and we felt good performing it. We didn't want our whole R&B background to disappear, but once we got into that whole disco thing [our careers] took off. It was hard to avoid it," he says.

Tavares became celebrities in 1975, scoring a Top 40 pop album with *In the City* and a Top 10 hit with "It Only Takes a Minute." They also enjoyed hugely successful tours with KC and the Sunshine Band and the Jackson 5. The momentum continued with follow-up albums *Sky-High!* and *Love Storm*, as well as 1976's infectious disco triumph, "Heaven Must Be Missing an Angel," which stayed active on the club charts for almost six months. Other tracks that stirred the masses included "Don't Take Away the Music" featuring Butch and Tiny (which hit the Top Five in the U.K.) and 1977's pop and R&B smash, the clever "Whodunit" (a celebration of famous case-solvers like Charlie Chan and Ellery Queen), with leads by Chubby, Tiny and Butch.

Freddie ("I Will Survive") Perren wrote the disco classic "Heaven Must Be Missing an Angel" (with Keni St. Lewis) and arranged the track. Chubby and Butch sang the lead on it. "Freddie was very meticulous," the singer remembers. "It's funny, his team would make us try to do things other artists wouldn't do—special chords and things like that. They told us we recorded quicker than anybody they had ever worked with. They told us we were so easy to work with in the studio. We may have had a few arguments over who would do lead, but if a producer like Freddie came up with the idea that he wanted two voices, then that's what we did. Sooner or later, everybody sang lead. We just wanted to sing. I don't think too many groups were capable of copying the sound we came out with. The harmonies were so intricate. Things haven't changed that much over time. Our voices may have changed a bit with age, but I have to say mine sounds the same as when I started," he laughs.

"Seeing our songs go to the top of the charts was the greatest feeling in the world. My mom and dad always wanted that for us. Man, when I was riding around town on a Friday or Saturday with my friends and one of our songs came on the radio, everybody would go crazy talking about how excited they were to know us personally and all that. That's a great feeling. Imagine you are chasing some beautiful girl, and one of your songs comes on the radio. It's the best feeling I've ever had. Even now and then, we still get those accolades, and that means more to me than anything in the world! When you get on that stage and see the smiles of the audience and the brightness of their eyes—it's the most rewarding feeling you could ever imagine in your life," Pooch says almost breathlessly.

Now firmly in the company of other popular artists and top male groups heating up the disco scene, Tavares stood proud wherever they performed. "We never had a problem with another group or with any artists we did shows with," he claims. "We usually become friends with most of the artists we work with. Some agents and promoters like to set up a show in such a way that one artist or group opens; another closes. We didn't care where they put us. You know what our feeling was? No matter where they put us, someone's gonna have to follow us. We'd go up there and give 120 percent, and whoever followed us would have to be ready for that. We loved to entertain, and we worked very hard for the audience. We liked clubs because they're more intimate, and you can get close to the audience. Big clubs and venues—you couldn't do that. You can only give them what you can give from the stage. At nightclubs, you can get out into the audience a bit more, and you really feel that closeness and warmth from them.

"Man, we performed with some of the best—Evelyn 'Champagne' King and the Trammps. We worked with them a lot. We did shows with Yvonne Elliman, Maxine Nightingale, Gloria Gaynor, KC and the Sunshine Band. We worked with them all, and we still enjoy seeing them today, and we all love having a good time with each other. We built up a very good bond with the people we worked with in disco. Disco introduced us to so many great people and artists," he adds.

Tavares fit in so comfortably with the disco environment thanks to the slick combination of their finely tuned sound, sharp onstage moves and possessing the look of champions. "Most black artists when they were getting started had to get their moves down," observes Pooch. "We had to try and keep up with our choreography on stage and do a little extra just to make ourselves known and leave people with that 'wow' feeling.

My brother Butch handled most of our choreography when we were younger. When we got up to the period of 'Heaven Must Be Missing an Angel,' that's when our manager from Capitol Records brought in Charlie Atkins to take our moves to the next level. I think they wanted to add a little more polish, but I think we already had that. I give Butch a lot of credit because he was a very good dancer, and he knew what steps to keep adding in. He put together our choreography for 'More Than a Woman,' and he was pretty good at it. We don't dress up quite as much as we used to today, like using all the same colors and things like that, because that's a bit dated now. But back then, we had many designers submitting their ideas to us, and we'd pick the outfits we liked."

Pooch readily admits the vices of the disco era were literally everywhere, but states Tavares never fell into any of the traps. "Drugs were always around," he says of life behind the scenes. "We were five Catholic brothers working together. Yes, we did our drinking, but when it came to any kinds of drugs—no way. And if you came into our dressing room and tried to do that or offer us that stuff, we'd throw you out. That's the God's honest truth—we'd physically throw you out. We were a bunch of big brothers—who can stand up to that? I think this attitude we had came from our parents and the way we were brought up. The singing was from our hearts, and the drug thing just wasn't in us. I am so proud of the fact that we didn't do any of that stuff because it was so prevalent—especially during the disco era. I take great pride in being able to say we have never had a drug problem in our family."

The film *Saturday Night Fever* upped the ante for the disco genre and nearly everyone involved with the Robert Stigwood project, including Tavares. "We were doing a show at Madison Square Garden," the artist recalls, "and the Bee Gees were on the bill. They wanted to meet us, and I believe they told our road manager that they had a song they really wanted us to do. They were a family too, and I guess they felt that we as a family, with our voices and harmony, could do this song justice. It was 'More Than a Woman.' We struck up a relationship with the Bee Gees and started practicing the song and eventually recorded it. Having the song in the movie *Saturday Night Fever* was the last thing we expected to happen in our careers at that point. Robert Stigwood really wanted the song in the movie, and the only reason why there are two versions, one by the Bee Gees and one by us, is because we were out of the country when they needed that particular song actually placed into the movie. So our version wasn't finished in time and they took the Bee Gees' version and put it in the film itself. We had signed a contract, so they ended up including our version on the soundtrack, but the powers that be weren't worried at all about putting two versions of the song on the album. This was okay with us because it ended up being one of the biggest selling albums in the world. We ended up winning a Grammy for the song, and I *still* hear it on the radio all the time. We definitely earned that Grammy, hands down. We were also nominated for a Grammy a couple of years later for the song 'A Penny for Your Thoughts,' but we missed out on that one. We lost out to the Dazz Band, I believe, but at least we were nominated again."

As swiftly as the disco rollercoaster car climbed the tracks, it came hurtling down late in 1979. However, according to the artist, the negative press for all things disco and the challenges of a new decade left Tavares relatively unconcerned. "We didn't worry about the disco backlash. We were a very versatile group and were as comfortable with

R&B as we were with disco. We never had a problem. People wanted to hear our music. I think that our being the type of group we were, people just identified disco music with us as something we did during that period. It has never hurt us. I can tell you that we ran into more problems with our trip to South Africa in the '80s during Apartheid than we ever did because of disco. We didn't go to Africa because we wanted to defy anyone or create controversy; we just went because we wanted to play our music for our fans there. It wasn't to make a statement. We made sure there would be mixed audiences when we did those shows."

Tavares left Capitol Records and signed with RCA, a move that unfortunately resulted in fewer chart hits. Their final major LP release was 1983's *Words and Music*, produced by an assortment of notables including Leon Sylvers III, Dana Meyers and Kenny Nolan. Says Pooch, "My personal feeling was that, as a group, we shouldn't have left Capitol Records. But everyone else in the group may have had a different feeling. I believe we were the first black group that Capitol ever had, and we did them proud. I think if we had stayed with Capitol, who knows—we might still be making albums today. We went over to RCA with our new management at the time, Weisner-DeMann Entertainment. At that time, the Jacksons were getting ready to leave their company, and so they may have been trying to get another family group on their roster. I was against the idea, but we were a family and, you know, when everybody is trying to stick together, you stick together. We had some good songs and writers with RCA and, really, we made a good living from all of our records. It helped if you were a songwriter. However, I was never a writer—I'd rather sing a song than sit down and write one."

The group continued touring, enjoying an exceptionally warm reception from their fans in Europe. Audiences worldwide never seemed to tire of Tavares, especially the ladies. "Listen, even before we started recording, we used to play clubs in New York, Miami, Boston, all over, and we always drew more women than men. I don't know why. But I'll tell you—all the guys would come out too because they knew the girls would be at our shows. Still today, we draw more women than men. I guess we still have some charisma and sex appeal, and that's a good feeling. And the guys are still gonna come and chase the girls! That happens no matter what age people are," he laughs.

"There's no place we go that we don't get requests for those signature songs, especially 'Don't Take Away the Music.' Especially in Europe—if we don't do 'Don't Take Away the Music,' they will boo us off the stage. The music changed so fast here in the U.S. [when the disco backlash hit]. In Europe, the people listened to the songs longer, and they idolized us and stayed with us. In America, everything was changing so fast, and somebody new was always coming up—you'd get lost in the shuffle. One thing about Europe, we never stopped performing there—especially Holland and the U.K. They were a huge audience for us, and they were very loyal. We would go to Holland, Germany, Belgium and the U.K. four or five times a year," he says with pride.

The European division of Capitol Records saw the potential to mine some further gold from Tavares in 1985 and '86. Special British remixes of "Heaven Must Be Missing an Angel" and "It Only Takes a Minute" by Ben Liebrand, along with a revved up retake of "Don't Take Away the Music" became monster chart hits all over again throughout the continent. "It was a good feeling," observes Pooch, "because they tried to make them a hit all over again and it worked. That showed we had something timeless that people really enjoyed and all they had to do was enhance it a bit. We had no involvement with those remixes—I imagine somebody at Capitol in England got the idea to see if they could make the song a big seller again, but we weren't a direct part of it."

Some of the Tavares brothers continue to actively tour today, and the fans that crowd their shows demonstrate the same level of enthusiasm the gentlemen enjoyed decades earlier. Their hits in disco music have bonded them with their followers, and their sound remains as invigorating as ever. "I'm very, very proud of our work in disco," he says with a strong tone of earnestness. "I'm very proud of what we did in the genre. I just love singing. The biggest worry I have today is handling the business side of things for the group. But once we're booked, and I get to where I am going with my brothers, and it's time to perform—I become a different person. I am proud to be singing our songs. It's wonderful that we still sound strong. I'll just say that if our track goes out during a show, we can still sing it! There aren't too many young artists out there today that can do that. That's an accomplishment that nobody can take from us."

Tavares, with their irresistible harmonies and songs that have become hopelessly locked into the most pleasant memories of disco fans worldwide, are ineffaceably a part of this genre's rich history. Pooch Tavares is delighted by that fact and hopes there is more to come, saying, "I think as a group and as a family, I hope we can put out a few more songs that have the warmth and the feeling that Tavares is known for. My brother Butch is still writing, and we are still always in and out of the studio. I can tell you that before I leave the music business, I still want to get one more hit that gets played on the radio and gives people another shot of that joy Tavares loves to deliver."

••••••••••••••••••••••••

Richie Weeks, formerly of Weeks & Co.
"Rock Your World"

"Musically, disco music moved on, and dance music evolved from it. Dance was just disco with a new spin..."—Richie Weeks

Take a catchy hook phrase, mix it with an infectious, urban beat and you had the kind of irresistible dance music hit that the masses were eager to scoop up during the post-disco days of 1981. A former New Jersey public school math teacher, songwriter Richie Weeks, along with associates Roy Bermingham and Jorge Barreiro, tapped into the public's desire for a fresh, funky dance sound with the single "Rock Your World," a jazzy house and disco hybrid that was a Top 10 dance chart smash. The track brought the group Weeks & Co. applause from all corners of the world. Richie has fond memories of these exciting days and is joined by vocalists Trudy Miller and Lynná Davis, part of the Weeks & Co. touring ensemble, to reminisce about the jubilant history and times the group shared.

"My dad wrote a song by Dion and the Belmonts called 'I Wonder Why,'" Weeks recalls. "He took me to the studio, and I really enjoyed it, playing around and kind of singing. He thought I could really sing. I went to a Catholic school, and they would have these talent shows. I did my little act, and people went crazy over it; they went ecstatic over my performance. I was only seven years old, and I didn't really know what was going on," he laughs. "But after that, things started progressing. As I got older, I got into local groups, street corner harmony. I learned how to differentiate between tenor, midrange and baritone, and it was a real education for me. I started to play guitar, then drums, and then I discovered keyboards—piano and synthesizers. From there, I got some help from guys in the industry, including Patrick Adams.

"I had written a song and Patrick liked it, and he put me in the studio where I started to produce tracks—laying them down, mixing them and running them back past Patrick. He was my mentor in those early days. I was getting very serious about my production work, and I started to meet more professionals in the industry, like the group Black Ivory and Leroy Burgess [a writer and Black Ivory's lead vocalist for many years, who also worked with Adams' Bumble Bee Unlimited and Inner Life groups]. Leroy also helped me hone my skills. But the person that showed me how to really play keyboards was a gentleman named Harris Punyon. We played professionally with a lot of bands."

From there, Weeks teamed up with Jorge Barreiro, a fellow songwriter, and they began to formulate the future hit "Rock Your World." "Barreiro was much more accomplished than I at the time," says Richie, "and he played many instruments. We collaborated on different arrangements, and we worked well together. We got some great music tracks down, and then he said, 'Okay, now we gotta come up with some songs.' My daughter kept telling me there was this hip saying, 'I'm gonna rock your world.' I started working on some lyrics with that in mind. I met up with a gentleman named Roy Bermingham (aka Roy B), and he became part of the production team, along with Jorge. We got together in the studio, and we developed the song further. Then we called the girls in to sing." Among the vocalists enlisted to record the track was Jocelyn Brown, according to Richie.

"Rock Your World," released in the U.S. by the indie label Chaz Ro, was an almost instant hit, quickly garnering broad pop and R&B radio airplay and staying in heavy rotation on the club circuit for nearly four months. "We brought in a different team of girls to handle the live performances," says Weeks. "Cyré Rodriguez [who later had a huge freestyle hit in 1987 with 'Last Chance'], Trudy Miller and Lynná Davis became the onstage performers. We travelled the world—Holland, France, Germany, Belgium—and we had great chemistry. By the way, I should note [these ladies who performed live] were no Milli Vanilli—they had great voices and really sang!"

"I had been a roommate and a very good friend of Norma Jean Wright, Chic's original lead vocalist, and I was doing some studio session work and a bit of writing," recalls Lynná Davis. "I had been doing backup work and choreography with the singer Eloise Laws and doing choreography work out at the Great Adventure amusement park in New Jersey. Coincidentally, Nile Rodgers was one of the first guitar players that we hired to play with us out there. It was one of those jobs people would do before they became successful. When he started talking about putting Chic together, I was being considered to be one of the girls. I suggested Norma Jean go in and also audition for Chic and, as it turned out, she got the job. A few years later, I did some backup work for Denroy Morgan ['I'll Do Anything for You']. I had heard about an audition for Weeks & Co. It was one of those word-of-mouth auditions to be an onstage member of the group. The music had already been recorded. When I met Richie, I thought he was just so vivacious, always smiling and a lot of fun. He'd always say, 'The way you girls look, the way you sound and the way this song is catching on out there, we're gonna do some big things together!' He was a just a very pleasant, talented human being."

"I started singing in the church and at a Catholic school," recalls Trudy Miller. "I belonged to a few small groups and performed in clubs when I got a bit older. I went to college in Queens, New York, and that was kind of a Mecca for music at the time. I worked with the songwriter, drummer and producer Trevor Gale, did some tours like *Bubbling Brown Sugar* and sang with Norma Jean Wright. Later, I too worked with Denroy Morgan. There are so many jobs you do, and they kind of all blend together. Truthfully, I have trouble remembering exactly how I came to be in Weeks & Co. I know I went to the audition and got the job. The record was done, and they wanted to get the tour going right away. Six weeks in France? Yeah, I could do that!" she laughs. "I thought Richie Weeks was the sweetest guy! He was always smiling and happy, and there was never any drama. He was just a great guy overall."

Now a smash hit, the song's magnetic draw created a huge demand for Weeks & Co. and the group began touring the biggest and best clubs and venues throughout the United States and Europe. Says Richie, "Studio 54, Paradise Garage, New York New York, the Funhouse and Bonds International—man, we played them all. Bonds really scared the hell out of me because there were so many people there. We performed at Madison Square Garden, too. We did a lot of shows overseas as well. We racked up nice numbers over there. We did shows with Kurtis Blow, D-Train and Shalamar, and we were on a roll."

"I was with the group for roughly two or three years, and I agree that the Bonds International show was really a highlight," Lynná confirms. "Every group in the world wanted to play there, and then we got booked there one night. It was an amazing show. And then we went on a 14-city tour of France. We rocked the world in the U.S., but I have to say it was red carpet all the way in Europe. As a matter of fact, they had nicknamed me 'Little Diana Ross' over there, which was very nice for me. I was also a prominent roller-skater, and I would open the show with a skating routine then run backstage, change clothes and join the group back on stage."

"There's a funny thing about the whole cultural aspect of our success," adds Trudy. "At the time, Americans tended to think of the French as being a little bit snooty. If we'd go to a restaurant in France, we might not even get served because we didn't speak fluent French. But once we got on that stage, folks would break their necks to get near us, speaking any kind of broken English they could to communicate with us. It was very funny and ironic. They'd also sometimes pinch our butts as we'd go onstage—it was their way of saying they loved us, I guess—and they did! You'd have thought we were Earth, Wind & Fire or something. Red carpets, V.I.P. rooms—all of that when they knew who we were.

"I think in terms of liking the song, Americans and Europeans were pretty much the same, equal," Trudy observes further. "The physical response of Europeans to our song was extremely strong, however, and they seemed to appreciate us more as a group. They are your fans for life—whether your group is together for two weeks or 20 years. It didn't matter. In the U.S., fans move on and forget much quicker, unless you are a gigantic name."

Richie's voice has a youthful enthusiasm as he describes the merits of his hit. "The song made people just jump up and go 'Yo! Yo!' This happened everywhere we went—it didn't matter what country we were in. It was so much fun. I can even say I know what it's like to hear my song on the radio when someone drove by. A guy went by on a bicycle, and I actually heard my song playing on his radio. I would get calls from friends, girl-friends, family, co-workers—'Richie, your song is on the radio!' It was a good feeling. To get to number one on the dance charts blew me away. We were right there on the charts with Prince and Earth, Wind & Fire."

"I think 'Rock Your World' resonated with people because it said that with whatever talents, goals or ideas you have inside of you, you can really have an impact. You can really 'Rock Your World.' Everyone wanted to have their world get rocked, and they wanted to do that for others," believes Lynná.

Weeks & Co. released a self-titled album in 1983 on Salsoul, along with a handful of popular singles like "If You're Looking for Fun." Still, "Rock Your World" reigned as the ensemble's supreme effort and became the song for which the group is best known to this day. "His song is a classic!" Trudy says eagerly. "There are people in their 20s and 30s that know 'Rock Your World,' and Richie's right—they instantly start shouting, 'Yo! Yo!' Musically, Richie was amazing! It was great working with him, live musicians, doing takes over until we got it right. Today, it's all synthesized, and there's none of that. Back in those days, working with Richie and Bert Reid (from Crown Heights Affair) was wonderful. I was really blessed to have been accepted [by these great professionals] and to be in the midst of such positive people."

Weeks says that the anti-disco sentiment that lingered in the years that followed the crash of classic disco in 1979–80 left him untroubled. "Everything has a lifecycle, but I wasn't worried about disco and dance music," he says. "I managed to get a lot of songs out there, and I hit the charts about seven times. Right after 'Rock Your World,' I got two other deals. I produced the Jammers' self-titled album, which was a big hit for Salsoul Records. My brother, Sheldon Weeks, was the lead singer for that one, along with a great singer named Debra Blackwell, and we had big hits with 'And You Know That' and 'Be Mine Tonight' [which cracked the disco chart Top 20 in 1982.] I also worked with Instant Funk [as a backup vocalist, keyboard player, writer and arranger] for their 1983 album *Instant Funk V*. In 1988, I produced an album with Lloyd Price [with his group the LPO Band], and we had a hit with the single 'Love Go 'Round,' and I also worked with Vaughan Mason. I changed my name to Major Weeks and sounded almost like a preacher on 'Don't Give Up' [a Top 40 dance hit] in 1989 [on Epic Records]. Today, I still work with new artists and am writing new songs for a production company called Quemaxx. We're making mostly dance music, and I'm always hoping for another hit."

Trudy opines, "Music changes, and you just have to go with the flow [ironically, the name of the group's 1982 club hit on Prelude Records]. Musically, disco music moved on, and dance music evolved from it. Dance was just disco with a new spin, and as far as Weeks & Co. went, I don't think we ever noticed any negativity toward our music."

Richie believes the secret of his success was rooted in determination. "You just have to take things one day at a time and feel sure of yourself," he asserts. "In the music industry, you have to have product that you really believe in. It doesn't matter what other people say about it—*you* have to believe in it. Go with your dream and what you think will work. But no matter what you do, you always have to have business savvy. I had my own publishing company and was lucky that I knew I had to hang onto those rights. My philosophy is to remember that if you march to a different drummer, make sure your music is still relevant to the times.

"I still get accolades from all over the world to this very day," he adds. "DJs still play my stuff, and I get constant feedback for 'Rock Your World.' I was lucky that the song went down in posterity. I have met so many people in the industry over the years that I've grown to love and respect, too—Shep Pettibone, who mixed many of my tracks, 'The Crazy Frenchman' Reynald Deschamps, drummer John Cooksey [who also worked with Venus Dodson, Ashford & Simpson, Phyllis Hyman, and others]—and many more talented musicians and vocalists. My son just got out of the military, and he's following in my footsteps now as well. That also makes me proud."

"I'm blessed that I still get a lot of work today," says Lynná. "I still get singing and roller skating offers. I recently did a gig with Joyce Sims—she had a new CD out, and I was hired to grace the stage with her. I never thought I'd skate and sing all over the world, as far away as Japan and Mexico, and I constantly thank God for that. When I first started out, I wanted all my dreams to come true. You know, you start off thinking casting directors or producers will see you on the street and say, 'You're exactly what I've been looking for.' Of course, that's not the way it goes. I think I learned that when I wasn't chosen for something, it wasn't personal—I just wasn't the type they were looking for. You move on to the next thing. You learn to be ready though, so when the call comes you can grab the opportunity."

"It seems like it all went by in about a week," admits Trudy, who continues to sing with bands today. "It was a great time in my life because these people were very, very cool. We all worked together well, and even when we weren't performing, we'd hang out. We'd go rollerblading with Lynná, which was popular in Europe at the time. I remember being on the rink while Stevie Wonder's 'Do I Do' was playing. We laughed and had one continuous good time. We were young, so what else did we have to do? Touring Europe, hit records—what could be bad about that?"

Richie Weeks, through the joyful energy of his productions with Weeks & Co. and other acts, has left his mark in dance music history. His motivation for creating such hits was in perfect harmony with the stellar results he achieved. "I just tried to make everybody happy," the artist humbly admits. "I wasn't in it for the money back then—I just got a huge kick out of being on the radio and in the clubs and everybody listening to my songs. I loved that they liked my work and that it wasn't all in vain. It was wonderful that in such a competitive industry I was able to have my talent recognized, and I have always appreciated that. I was blessed, and I love dance music so much! Just remember that I was true to the game, and I'll be doing this till the day I die!"

James "D-Train" Williams
"You're the One for Me"

"They hated 'You're the One for Me.' They said I couldn't sing and that we needed to take my voice off the record and hire a girl. Columbia Records, all the labels—nobody liked it. Man, they all hated me!"—James "D-Train" Williams

"My father always said, 'Personality is what defines you when everyone else is around. Character defines you when they are gone,'" recalls James Williams, better known as "D-Train." He's a man who says he has always been driven to uphold his ethics and esteem in an industry that often seemed to make decency seem, well, indecent. As a singer, songwriter and creative spirit over the past three decades, he has remained a creative and determined individual. Williams acquired the nickname D-Train in high school, where his power as a football player was formidable. His impact on the post-classic disco music scene (especially with the single "You're the One for Me") was felt like a bulldozer thundering across worldwide dance floors in 1981. His deep, growling voice, combined with the electrifying beats of his partner, Hubert Eaves III, topped the charts and helped moved disco out of its overkill-induced slump into a new dimension of funky energy. Williams has seen the heights of fame and endured more than his share of low points on his personal and artistic journey. But he has developed a wisdom that can only come with experience, and he doesn't hesitate to share it.

"I started singing when I was six years old in the Washington Temple Church in Brooklyn," says Williams. "Ronnie Dyson was our choir director, Al Sharpton was my junior church minister, and Rev. Timothy Wright was the choir's musical director. There was genius all around me growing up as a kid, and I had a lot of people to look up to on the music side. I made my first professional recording at the age of 15, singing with Reverend Wright."

While still in college, James connected with Hubert Eaves III, an aspiring producer and keyboardist who had an idea for a hit. Williams remembers, "I was going to Brooklyn College, and Will Downing was doing a demo in 1980 called 'Real Deal' at Sound Lab Recording Studios. I got a gig working on that. Hubert Eaves was producing it, and he heard me singing and doing ad-libs and he was like, 'Whoa!' My voice apparently fit the bill for a sound he was looking for. He played a rough song that he was working on for me at his house and said it was his first attempt at song writing. [James starts singing 'You're the One for Me.'] It was raw, and he kept rewinding the quarter inch tape and playing it back, over and over again. We started to get more ideas for it. I grabbed a pen, and we ended up writing the whole song in about an hour. The rest is history. We started writing together two days a week. He came up with the [new arrangement] to 'Walk on By,' and we started recording some of these songs. We started to really click as songwriters. We wrote 'Keep On' and started 'Tryin' to Get Over.'

"We recorded 'You're the One' on a 16-track and overdubbed the crap out of it so it sounded just like the version everyone knows. We started bringing the track around to different record companies, and most of them rejected it. They hated 'You're the One for Me.' They said I couldn't sing and that we needed to take my voice off the record and hire a girl. Columbia Records, all the labels—nobody liked it. Man, they all hated me!" Williams claims.

Undaunted, the duo began a grassroots effort to get their music noticed. "I remember it well—February 1981!" he says, vividly recalling the memory as if it happened yesterday. "We first built the record up on the street before we ever brought it to Prelude Records. Hubert knew about the Paradise Garage and gave the record to the DJ there named Larry Levan. Larry broke the record that night, and the gay population in the club blew D-Train through the roof. He put the song on, and it was like somebody set off a bomb at the Paradise Garage. There were about 2,000 people there, and they lost their minds! I remember we were there with him in the DJ booth, and he announced, 'We have this new track from D-Train called 'You're the One for Me' right here at the Paradise Garage! Come on children; get up!'

"This was my first time at a gay club because, you gotta remember, I came from the church. I didn't know anything about that lifestyle. Everyone jumped out on that floor! They even came running out of the bathroom. That dance floor got packed! Soon, it seemed like everywhere we went, the clubs had to play the song twice a night. Then we took it to Frankie Crocker at WBLS, and he broke the record for us on radio. After 'You're the One for Me' was released on Prelude and became a hit, I remember we were doing *Top of the Pops* with Sting and the Police over in London. They had a bar across the street, and we went in there, and they were playing our record. We went down the street to another, and they were playing it too! Then a third club was playing it! That's how popular the record was, and that's the God's honest truth. Later, we performed the song again on *Pops* with the JoBoxers, and the third time the song was featured on the show I performed it with Paul Hardcastle, after Hubert had moved on. Paul had done a new arrangement of it, and it went up to number 15 in the U.K. in 1985."

Gay clubs were among the first to break D-Train, and they remained a loyal following during his Prelude years. Issues of sexuality were of little concern to Williams. "I learned that all people have the same needs, whether they are straight or gay. We all need love. As kids, we are sexual, and we're told this is right, and this is wrong. In my day, it was that whole 'Adam and Eve, not Adam and Steve' thing, and you grew up with that kind of thinking until you met someone who *was* gay. Everyone needs food, clothes on their back, a roof over their head, and somebody that believes in them. Gay or straight. At the end of the day, we all want the same things.

"Sexual preference doesn't matter to me. In New York, I've probably played more gay clubs than straight ones. People are people, and my job is to get on the stage and have you leave the place feeling better than when you came in. The music was their savior in those clubs. You know, not everyone is gonna go to church to hear 'Precious Lord, Take My Hand.' But many people *did* go to the clubs and listened to 'Keep On' because there was no religious pretext behind it. The song just inspired you to rise to the top of yourself, no matter what your circumstances were. Fight another day, no matter how many times you get knocked down. I'm not going to judge you because of who you are or what you do. The club is a nonjudgmental place. The clubs were the churches of everybody—where everyone could go and be accepted!"

By December of 1981, "You're the One for Me" had reached the number one spot on the *Billboard* dance chart. The duo released an album by the same name (mixed by

Eaves and Francois Kevorkian). For the next year, tracks like "Keep On," "Walk on By" (a cover of the Burt Bacharach–Hal David hit) and "D-Train (Theme)" (with backing vocals by Lisa Fischer) became essential floor-fillers in the clubs and staples of R&B and dance radio.

"Other than singing, I didn't work [on other elements of the album] with Hubert in the beginning," James says. "The production side was all him. On the first album, he ended up just adding live drums. He called up Howard King, who played drums on every D-Train record. The first album was all Hubert and Howard. On later albums we brought in other musicians and artists, including the Institutional Choir of Brooklyn (on the 'Children of the World' track from the album *Music*). Eaves was a genius in the studio, and as technology grew, our options grew in the studio. I eventually started programming keyboards in addition to singing."

D-Train delivered two more albums to Prelude Records, *Music* (1983) and *Something's on Your Mind* (1984). The single "Music" was a gospel-tinged club hit in the U.S. and did even better in Europe. "Something's on Your Mind" gave the team their first crossover hit, reaching the lower regions of *Billboard's* pop chart. A greatest hits album followed in 1985. Despite their success, Williams says the music industry was clouded with dishonesty. "When 'You're the One for Me' was a hit, the agency that sends out the gold records was sending them to the Prelude label," James claims. "They never sent it to us in the studio and I wondered if it was to draw attention away from the fact that we sold over half a million records. You end up just leaving it alone. There's a saying—when it comes to money, the room gets smaller. The more money that came in, greed set in, and people (the executives) just didn't want you to know about it."

Still, the artist was able to bask in the rush of fame that had come his way for quite a while as his hit records kept him in the spotlight. He recalls, "Promoters would put big posters of you up all over Manhattan. There was a street on 10th Avenue at 34th Street, which I remember was somewhat known for prostitution at the time and called the 'Ho Stroll.' Well, anyway, there were posters of me all the way from 10th Avenue to 8th Avenue announcing my performance at the club Bond. I'm in the car seeing this, and I'm thinking, 'Holy crap, that's me!' And then the first time I saw myself on *Soul Train*, I thought, 'That's nice; that's cool!' I think everyone gets that 'ah-ha!' moment when they see themselves on television."

Dance music was particularly prone to the "here today, gone tomorrow" syndrome, especially in the U.S. at the time, and D-Train was cognizant of the limitations of the genre. He examines the subject of a singing career in dance music with the wisdom and perspective of age. "I performed on *Soul Train* four times and in hundreds of clubs and, having done all that and having hit the charts on both sides of the pond, they eventually archive you as a viable entity in music," observes the singer. "The 40- or 50-year-olds in Europe know your music, and so do their children. In America, it doesn't translate as well. Here, the 40- or 50-year-olds sometimes remember your music, but their kids have no idea who you are. They only think of the subway line. Most Americans don't know me.

"If you didn't go to Europe early on in your career," he goes on, "man, forget it—they have no base for you if you try to go now. They can't be loyal to what they've never known. If you're 60 and going to try and break yourself there, forget it—you're too old.

What I've also learned in life is that success is what happens when preparation meets opportunity. Some singers limited themselves to the next gig, the next record. They looked at paying their rent, paying their mortgage, paying for their car, putting their kids through school. And then you wake up one day, and your last hit record was 30 years ago, and all you can get is the oldies but goodies show in Atlantic City and some gigs in Europe. You stopped bringing in $100,000–150,000 a year. What you make now is not enough to sustain you for the rest of your life. You are lucky if you bring in $25,000 in later years."

By the mid–'80s, his partnership with Hubert Eaves amicably ended (they remain friends to this day), and the artist explored a solo career, often dropping the "D-Train" from his name. He continued working with Eaves, who sometimes served as a producer or musician. Williams released an album on Columbia Records in 1986 called *Miracles of the Heart,* which returned him to the R&B chart with the funky single "Misunderstanding." The artist remained hot with his follow-up album, *In Your Eyes,* whose title track fell just shy of the R&B Top 10. However, this seemingly opportune resurgence failed to become the lucrative venture for which he had hoped.

He says, "By 1988, I had no shows for my band, I was falling behind in my bills and rent. With the record industry, you can spend three to five months in the studio working on an album, like I did at Columbia Records. One day your song has climbed the charts, and you're at the top, right behind Bobby Brown. Then one of their top artists gets ready to release his record, and you become the tax write-off for the label. It's like they never saw my record. The same thing has happened to many artists. The label says, 'We'll get it on the next one.' Well, what happens to the four months of my life I took to record this one? They don't care. They figure they gave me a little money from the budget, and they'll just shelve the record. So if your album cost $175,000, they give that to their hottest act and they do that with five or six other artists at the same time. That gives the person they are hot on a huge budget. That was the downside of the record industry.

"Then I got a new opportunity thanks to a man named Bill Eaton. He was a top jingle writer, producer and songwriter for a lot of R&B groups. I was able to start doing commercial jingles through him. I welcomed it. I didn't have to track down shifty promoters for my money; I didn't have to fight with record companies for my royalties. Everything with record companies becomes such a struggle. You fight with your manager because he isn't getting you enough work; you fight with everyone. With the jingles, they call you to the studio, you sing the song, and you get checks in the mail. It was like hitting lotto! The first time I did a Budweiser commercial and started getting all these checks, I called the guy who did the commercial thinking it was a mistake. The gentleman said, 'No, that's right, but if you don't want the money, I'll take it!'" he laughs. "You get these big checks, and you fall in love with your mailman! It's a new type of lifestyle, and I had a good run in it. I did jingles for the next 18 years, working for companies like Saatchi & Saatchi and Grey Advertising, and I learned how the industry works."

Williams is quick to point out that, like pop music, the jingle industry wasn't without its darker side. "I had a commercial pulled from the air. I had sung on a Hanes pantyhose commercial and sang something with their catch phrase, something like 'Wait till we get our Hanes on you.' A teacher had written to the ad agency saying that a black man singing about getting his Hanes on you made white women susceptible to rape. She threatened to stop supporting the parent company of Hanes [and all its products] at the time. She threatened to make a public protest. They ended up removing my voice from the commercial and had a white woman sing it. That was one of the worst days of my life.

"As great as our country is, the thing that still separates us is racism. When people learn that our differences are what bring us together, this will be a better world. I learned long ago that if someone doesn't like me because I'm black, that's their problem to deal with. They can keep on hating me, and I'm gonna keep on doing what I do. I'm not going to sit there and try to fight someone else's hatred because I'll just end up becoming ignorant myself. Racism is just ignorance. If you knew who I was and could walk a mile in my shoes, you wouldn't hate me. You'd probably love and respect me for being the man that I am."

Despite the incident, Williams had a good run with jingles until the business dried up around 2000. "I got another phone call from B.J. Stone, who used to produce Ashford & Simpson's show on WBLS radio," he remembers. "He asked me to come over to a New York radio station and offered me my own radio show. He said he'd train me for three months, and then I'd be on my own. I went in there with the belief that I'd have one of the number one shows on their R&B platform, and I did! It was on SiriusXM satellite radio. I was there from 2001–2008, and it really blossomed for me. I was doing shows out of New Orleans, live concerts in New York and had Lionel Richie and many others perform live on our *Up Close & Personal* series. It was a wonderful experience having Roberta Flack and Jet Li come on my show, and I learned how to sit on the other side of the table and learned how to be the interviewer. That was a big lesson because it taught me how to listen. Singers are used to talking. We don't really listen. Being in radio taught me how to keep my mouth shut and listen. You gain a lot more knowledge that way, and it was really interesting."

Williams is adamant about remaining flexible to handle life's challenges, and he relates his philosophy about the importance of being able to reinvent one's self. "Write on one side of a sheet of paper everything good about you, everything you do well," he suggests. "Everything bad that's happened to you, write on the other side. On a third sheet of paper, write how you overcame those difficulties. You'll realize how far you've come and that you're a better person than you actually thought. It's not what happens to you, it's your response to what happens to you. I read a lot of Anthony Robbins. When you spend time with your mind, you can reach the pinnacle of success. I have had to learn all of this over time. I've come through a tough divorce. You ask God, or the universe, or whatever you choose to believe in, to help you accept what has happened to you, and say that it's time for you to make your move. And if you write down your affirmations about what you are determined to become and you speak it as if it has already happened and believe it—it will happen.

"I lived in a crappy basement apartment for a time not that long ago—just not a great place to live. I had been financially hurt by the divorce. After you pay lawyers and your ex-wife, you have nothing. My girlfriend said she found us a really great place to live, and if we believed in it, we could do better and live better. I started looking for something to focus on that could change my hopes into a reality. We looked at the apartment, and it was incredible, but I thought, 'How the heck are we gonna get this place?'

The only thing I could focus on was the beautiful hardwood floor. I saw it when I went to bed at night and when I woke up in the morning. I prayed about it, and every day I went to work, and I focused on that hardwood floor. My finances and credit were crap because of the divorce, but I didn't think about that—I just focused on the floor. Well, I ended up getting the apartment with no credit check and at a lower price than we expected. It's amazing how far you can go when you believe. I remember saying, 'Holy crap! It worked!'

"Now, I ask, what's next? If I can get a great apartment, why not a seven million dollar mansion someday? So I focus on just the gate at the end of that mansion's driveway. And I'm gonna work hard to see that this happens. In the music industry, we tend to see ourselves only as musicians, only as a singer, and we use just a tiny portion of our brain instead of thinking that we can do other things, like manage our investments. How many singers set him or herself up with IRAs when they were making money? How many invested in stocks? Mutual funds? They never let the money work for them—they worked for the money. Many never set themselves up and put the money from some of their gigs towards investing. Some die and their families have to put together a fundraiser, instead of the singer being able to take care of his own funeral. Your music lasts forever, but all you end up with is a song on the radio.

"I've had every label put on me under the sun. I've been called a legend of disco, a legend of R&B. Some people call me that simply because I'm over 50," says James "D-Train" Williams today (courtesy James Williams).

"It's partially because of the industry and partly the singer's responsibility," Williams goes on. "The industry has robbed artists since the beginning. Even in gospel music. It's gone on forever and ever. Do you think Gladys Knight ever made what Kanye West has in the bank? I'm pretty sure Gladys didn't make that kind of money working as hard as she did for much of her early career. She lives a good life now because she eventually did Vegas and she toured a lot, but does she live like some newcomer who signs a huge contract right out of the gate? I don't think so.

"I say all this meaning you have to be smart and realize diversification is the key. And you have to remember money isn't the catalyst to happiness. Like I said, money makes the room smaller. You make a million dollars, and I hate to sound paranoid, but everyone is gonna want to be your friend. You have to be smart about your dealings and keep your mouth closed. Don't go telling everyone how much money you have. I hate to say it, but that's a model that mobsters use. Make the money, keep your mouth shut, and live your life," he advises.

D-Train laughs at the idea of being considered a legend. "I've had every label put on me under the sun," he says dismissively. "I've been called a legend of disco, a legend of R&B. Some people call me that simply because I'm over 50. Everyone calls you a legend. What constitutes that? I sure don't live a legend's lifestyle, that's for sure—I take the bus just like everyone else. A celebrity once said if you can just hang around long enough and they can still hear and see you, that's what gives you that legend title. Disco and dance means the clubs. Just about every dance club or DJ has played my music at some time. Well, not everybody can say that, I guess."

Williams has returned to recorded music in recent months. "I've come full circle, and I'm back doing music. When one door in life closes, another one opens, and it's always been that way for me. God has always provided for me. I'm working with Lenny Kravitz on his new album. We did nine songs already with Tawatha Agee and Cindy Mizelle," he says proudly, very much aware that his reinvention has taken him back to his roots.

The original Prelude recordings that made James "D-Train" Williams a star are now owned by Canada's Unidisc label, which acquired the catalog in the '90s. Meanwhile, "You're the One for Me" continues to be sampled and played on radio and in clubs in virtually every corner of the globe. It's an enviable legacy, but the singer is far more concerned with the impact his music has had on the spirits of his fans.

"There's a part of me that lives in people that I will never meet before I die," he says slowly. "My music left the pages that were in Hubert's basement and became a record that was played on the radio and entered other people's souls. When you hear a good song, you remember where you were, what you were doing, whether you were laughing or crying. And every time you hear that song, you relive that moment. When everyone hears 'You're the One for Me' or 'Keep On,' they relive something in their lives. Maybe they were at the Paradise Garage that night it was played for the first time or maybe they were in London at the Camden Palace.

"What happens is they take something home with them from your music that they can really feel. Every time I hear Michael Jackson's music, I remember his brilliance and why I got into the industry. It was because of him and his brothers. His legacy lives on in me and in everyone else who believed in what he did. So if there's enough people who believe in what I've done, what I'm doing now, and what I will do in the future, that's good enough for me! If I was able to take them to a higher plane within themselves—and as long as I believe that some people are in a better place than where they were before I got here—I've done my job!"

Afterword
by Henry Stone, Founder of T.K. Records

Henry Stone was in the music business, operating out of Miami, Florida, for over 50 years and was widely regarded and respected as one of the undisputed founding fathers of disco. He owned several record labels, including Alston, Brownstone, Cat, Dash and Marlin, and founded one of the most beloved disco music production companies of all time, T.K. Records. Stone was responsible for a string of over 20 gold and platinum records and worked with and recorded many great artists, including Latimore, Sam & Dave, Bobby Byrd, Clarence Reid, Sonny Thompson, J. P. Robinson, Roach Thompson, Betty Wright and many others. He recorded some of the earliest works of Ray Charles and collaborated with James Brown for many years.

Stone fostered the development of disco music from its infancy when he discovered Harry Wayne Casey (better known as "KC" of KC and the Sunshine Band), who had been working in one of his warehouses. He recorded many other legendary disco artists, including Gwen McCrae, Timmy Thomas, T-Connection, Peter Brown, Foxy, Fern Kinney, Dorothy Moore, the Ritchie Family, Anita Ward and George McCrae, whose number one smash single, "Rock Your Baby," became one of the genre's most successful recordings. His so-called "Sound of Miami" further became the signature of quality disco music, a floor-filling beat that Stone's camp delivered for many years.

Henry composed this afterword in 2013 at the age of 92. At the time, he was feeling sharp and energized and was still fully engaged in his business, continuing to release CD compilations of his vintage recordings.

Stone, a true pioneer of disco, passed away on August 8, 2014.

* * *

How can I tell you about disco?

To be honest, I was really just making music—*great* music.

I never set out to make "disco" music, but I did have the world's first American-born international disco hit with George McCrae's "Rock Your Baby." Well, that was a little bit before the term disco was being widely used. Basically, T.K. Records and I helped pave the way for disco with the funky dance records we were releasing at the time. Our music had great beats, and we had wonderful artists like Funky Nassau and Betty Wright doing well on the charts. We were there at the very beginning, when KC's earliest releases, such as "Sound Your Funky Horn" in 1973 (even before he and Richard Finch came up with "Rock Your Baby"), were clicking around in the dance clubs as the genre was just beginning to develop.

Then along came 1974. "Rock Your Baby" and George McCrae shook the world up—actually, it seemed like George took over the world—and disco became a reality. During a visit to Cannes, I took a supply of "Rock Your Baby" records in my hand and distributed them to all the clubs I went through in France. After the DJs put the record on their turntables, I never saw so many people get up and swarm to the dance floor in my entire time in the record business! That's the impact that record had—it was really so powerful! I know "Rock Your Baby" sold well over 20 million copies around the world, probably much more. I never saw another record that could compare to it.

I never even knew who invented the word disco, and I don't remember the first time I heard the term, but I knew our records were exploding thanks to this new genre. The dance movement became enormously popular in gay and straight clubs throughout the world. We started making wonderfully orchestrated disco records with great arrangements and outstanding singers, including the hits of KC and the Sunshine Band. His group earned an unheard of five consecutive number one disco records that, even more remarkably, also became chart-topping pop records. T.K. released one disco smash after another, such as T-Connection's "At Midnight" and Peter Brown's "Dance with Me" (and its follow-up, "Crank It Up"), which filled the dance floors of clubs worldwide. We had tremendous pop and disco success with Foxy ("Get Off") and Anita Ward with "Ring My Bell." We produced these records with the dance floor in mind but ended up crossing over and reaching the summit of the pop charts.

Ultimately, disco could *not* be ignored. These songs and singers became so huge in the clubs that radio started playing the edited versions more and more. But radio had been very resistant to playing disco and dance records from the very beginning. Undaunted, we took the 12-inch single to DJs in the clubs, and, in turn, they broke these records for us even without radio airplay. I was always into quality sound, and if you listen to my records, they sound fantastic to this day! That's why the 12-inch single came into play. The sound was so great on those pressings, and the DJs loved the convenience of a big, LP-sized single. Boom, boom, boom—it was a whole domino effect! Disco music hit the top spot all around the world, and T.K. Distribution became a leader in the disco market in the United States, with Columbia Records handling our product throughout much of Europe and beyond.

As the disco era progressed, T.K. started to develop strong relationships with foreign dance music makers, such as the group Voyage ("Souvenirs") and Boris Midney (producer of Beautiful Bend's "That's the Meaning"). They helped solidify our presence as a label in the disco world. Disco reached its crescendo with the *Saturday Night Fever* film, and I even managed to be a part of that! I had recorded a jazz artist by the name of Ralph MacDonald and released the hit "Calypso Breakdown" in 1976, which became a hit on the disco charts and then was featured on the legendary *Saturday Night Fever* soundtrack.

I have many wonderful memories of the disco revolution. One unusual recollection that stands out for me from the '70s was the consistent arrival of busloads of German and Japanese tourists that used to come to T.K.'s headquarters to take pictures of the artists and the studios! We were like a big tourist attraction! They loved it, especially seeing where all this music was made, who made it and how it was made from 1973 to 1980 or so. If KC happened to be there recording, or Peter Brown or Foxy, there would always be a frenzy of tourists snapping pictures. Bobby Caldwell ("What You Won't Do for Love") was one of our artists, and he had one of his biggest records in Japan. You can imagine the excitement he created when the tourists spotted him!

The disco sound created in the '70s is still heard today around the world—on the radio, in clubs, supermarkets, boutiques—you name it. The T.K. and Miami disco sound, which was engraved into music history, is very much a part of modern-day dance and hip-hop music, and our hits are often sampled and re-envisioned by contemporary artists. There is one major difference today. Our artists were in the spotlight in the disco era, and DJs often worked for little or nothing back then. Eventually, the DJs took over with their mixes and now make $5,000 to $10,000 a night! Times have changed. But, you know, it really was disco that made the club DJ important, and it all goes back to those wonderful and historic early days on Fire Island and the first legendary clubs of the era.

It all goes back to disco. It all goes back to my musical creations in the '70s—and I am very, very proud of that.

What did disco mean to me? It represented my love of dance music, and it still means the world to me!

The Turntable: Recommended Listening

The following is an extremely small sampling of some noteworthy disco tracks generally released between 1974 and 1984 by artists not prominently featured elsewhere in the books *First Ladies of Disco* or *Legends of Disco*. Some are well-known classics, some are a bit more obscure, and some may have been completely missed by disco aficionados the first time around. However, all are significant products of the disco era by important artists and worthy of a spin.

ABBA—"Dancing Queen," "Lay All Your Love on Me," "Super Trouper," "On and On and On," "The Winner Takes It All," "The Visitors"
Addrisi Brothers—"Slow Dancin' Don't Turn Me On"
Alma Faye Brooks—"Stop, I Don't Need No Sympathy," "Don't Fall in Love," "Gimme Your Love," "It's Over"
Angela Clemmons—"Give Me Just a Little More Time"
Arabesque—"Friday Night," "Rock Me After Midnight," "City Cats," "Parties in a Penthouse"
B.B. Band—"All Night Long"
B.T. Express—"Express"
Barrabas—"Hi-Jack," "Desperately"
Barry Manilow—"Copacabana"
Beautiful Bend—"That's the Meaning"
Belle Epoque—"Black Is Black," "Miss Broadway"
Bette Midler—"Married Men"
Billy Ocean—"Nights," "Stay the Night," "Caribbean Queen," "Love Really Hurts Without You"
Bimbo Jet—"El Bimbo"
Bizzy & Co.—"Take a Chance"
Blondie—"Heart of Glass"
Boney M.—"Daddy Cool," "Rivers of Babylon," "Rasputin," "Ma Baker"
Brick—"Dazz"
The Brothers Johnson—"Stomp!"
Bryan Adams—"Let Me Take You Dancing"
Captain & Tennille—"You Never Done It Like That," "Happy Together"
Carl Carlton—"Everlasting Love," "She's a Bad Mama Jama," "Baby, I Need Your Loving"
Carol Lloyd—"Score," "Showdown," "Shake Me, Wake Me"
Celi Bee—"Fly Me on the Wings of Love," "Boomerang," "Superman"
Cerrone—"Love in C Minor," "Supernature," "Je Suis Music," "Tripping on the Moon"
Chakachas—"Jungle Fever"

Change—"A Lover's Holiday," "Angel in My Pocket," "The Glow of Love," "Searching," "Paradise," "Change of Heart"
Cheryl Lynn—"Star Love," "Got to Be Real," "Shake It Up Tonight"
Cissy Houston—"Think It Over," "Warning—Danger," "Somebody Should Have Told Me," "You're the Fire"
Coati Mundi—"Me No Pop I"
Colleen Heather—"On the Run"
The Crusaders—"Street Life"
Cut Glass—"Without Your Love"
D.C. LaRue—"Cathedrals," "Don't Keep It in the Shadows," "Do You Want the Real Thing," "Hot Jungle Drums and Voo Doo Rhythm"
Dan Hartman—"Instant Replay," "Hands Down," "Vertigo," "Relight My Fire"
David Naughton—"Makin' It"
Delores Hall—"Snapshot"
Deniece Williams—"I've Got the Next Dance," "What Two Can Do," "Let's Hear It for the Boy"
Denise McCann—"I Have a Destiny," "Tattoo Man"
Don Armando's 2nd Avenue Rhumba Band—"Deputy of Love"
The Doobie Bros.—"What a Fool Believes"
Dschinghis Khan—"Moskau"
Duncan Sisters—"Sadness in My Eyes," "Boys Will Be Boys," "Outside Love"
Earlene Bentley—"The Boys Come to Town," "I'm Living My Own Life"
Earth, Wind & Fire—"Sing a Song," "Getaway," "Boogie Wonderland," "September"
Ebony, Ivory & Jade—"Samson"
Eddie Holman—"This Will Be a Night to Remember"
Eloise Whitaker—"Don't Turn Your Back on Love"
Emotions—"Best of My Love"
Evie Sands—"Keep My Lovelight Burnin'"
The Fatback Band—"Spanish Hustle"
Festival—"Don't Cry for Me Argentina"
5000 Volts—"I'm on Fire," "Motion Man"
Frankie Avalon—"Venus"
G.Q.—"Disco Nights"
Gary Criss—"Rio De Janeiro"
Gene Chandler—"Get Down"
Gene Page—"Close Encounters of the Third Kind," "Love Starts After Dark"
Gibson Brothers—"Cuba," "Que Sera Mi Vida"
Gino Soccio—"Dancer," "Dance to Dance," "Try It Out," "Remember," "It's Alright"
Gladys Knight and the Pips—"On and On"
Gonzalez—"I Haven't Stopped Dancin' Yet"
Herb Alpert—"Rise," "Garden Party," "Paradise Cove," "True Confessions," "Red Hot"
Hot—"If That's the Way That You Want It"
Hot Chocolate—"You Sexy Thing," "Every 1's a Winner"
Imagination—"Just an Illusion," "Flashback," "Burnin' Up"
Instant Funk—"I Got My Mind Made Up," "Bodyshine," "Slap, Slap, Lickedy Lap"
Janice McClain—"Smack Dab in the Middle"
Jean Carn—"Was That All It Was," "What's on Your Mind"
Joe Simon—"I Need You, You Need Me"
Johnny Bristol—"Hang on in There Baby"
Julie Budd—"All Night Man"
Kano—"I'm Ready," "It's a War," "Can't Hold Back"
Kathy Barnes—"Fun and Games"
Kebekelektrik—"Magic Fly"

Recommended Listing

The Kinks—"Superman"
Larry Elgart and His Manhattan Swing Orchestra—"Hooked on Swing"
Lectric Funk—"Shanghaied"
Lipps, Inc.—"Funky Town," "All Night Dancing," "How Long," "Designer Music," "Choir Practice"
Liquid Gold—"My Baby's Baby," "Dance Yourself Dizzy"
Love and Kisses—"I Found Love (Now That I've Found You)"
Luv'—"He's the Greatest Lover"
M—"Pop Muzik"
Mai Tai—"History," "Female Intuition"
Margaret Reynolds—"Keep on Holdin' On," "Day After Day," "All Day All Night"
Marshall Hain—"Dancing in the City"
Martha High—"Don't Ask My Neighbors"
Mavis Staples –Tonight I Feel Like Dancing"
The Mike Theodore Orchestra—"High on Mad Mountain"
Moment of Truth—"Helplessly"
The Nick Straker Band—"A Little Bit of Jazz," "NSB Radio," "A Walk in the Park"
Norman Connors—"Once I've Been There"
Ohio Players—"Love Roller Coaster"
The O'Jays—"I Love Music"
Ottawan—"D.I.S.C.O."
Patrick Juvet—"Got a Feeling," "I Love America"
Peaches & Herb—"Shake Your Groove Thing," "Roller-Skatin' Mate," "Funtime"
People's Choice—"Boogie Down U.S.A.," "Do It Any Way You Wanna"
Peter Brown—"Do You Wanna Get Funky with Me," "Dance with Me," "Crank It Up (Funk Town)," "They Only Come Out at Night"
Peter Jacques Band—"Fire Night Dance," "Walking on Music"
Phylicia Allen—"Two Loves Have I (J'ai Deux Amours)," "Medley: Saint Louis/Broadway/Star of Paris"
Prince—"I Wanna Be Your Lover," "Dirty Mind," "Controversy," "1999," "Little Red Corvette"
The Raes—"A Little Lovin' (Keeps the Doctor Away)"
Ram Jam—"Black Betty"
The Real Thing—"Can't Get by Without You," "Can You Feel the Force"
Ren Woods—"Everybody Get Up," "Straight to Love," "I'm Hooked on a Love Groove," "Sweeter as the Day Goes By," "You Are the One"
Risque—"The Girls Are Back in Town"
Rod Stewart—"Da Ya Think I'm Sexy"
Rolling Stones—"Miss You"
Rosebud—"Have a Cigar"
Roy Ayers Ubiquity—"Running Away"
The Royal Philharmonic Orchestra—"Hooked on Classics"
Rozalin Woods—"Flashback," "Whatcha' Gonna Do About It"
Rufus & Chaka Kahn—"Do You Love What You Feel"
Samantha Sang—"You Keep Me Dancing"
Santa Esmerelda—"Don't Let Me Be Misunderstood"
Saturday Night Band—"Come on Dance, Dance"
Shalamar—"Uptown Festival," "The Second Time Around," "Right in the Socket," "Make That Move," "A Night to Remember," "Dead Giveaway," "Dancing in the Sheets"
Stargard—"Which Way Is Up," "Disco Rufus," "What You Waitin' For"
Stars on 45—"Stars on 45," "The Star Sisters Medley"
Sweet Cream—"I Don't Know What I'd Do (If You Ever Left Me)"
T-Connection—"Do What You Wanna Do," "At Midnight"
Taka Boom—"Mr. DJ, You Know How to Make Me Dance" (*with Glass Family*), "Night Dancin'," "Red Hot," "Anything You Want"

Tantra—"Hills of Katmandu," "Hallelujah"
Tata Vega—"I Just Keep Thinking About You Baby"
Technique—"Can We Try Again," "Tonight"
Telex—"Moskow Diskow"
Theo Vaness—"No Romance"
Timmy Thomas—"Stone to the Bone"
Vaughan Mason and Crew—"Bounce, Rock, Skate, Roll"
Voyage—"From East to West," "Souvenirs," "Let's Fly Away," "Let's Get Started," "Follow the Brightest Star"
Watson Beasley—"Breakaway," "Don't Let Your Chance Go Bye"
Witch Queen—"Bang a Gong"
The Wonder Band—"Whole Lotta Love"
Yambu—"Sunny"
Young & Co.—"I Like What You're Doing to Me"

Index

Adams, Patrick 7, 9, 11, 13, 16, 75–77, 80, 216
Aller, Michelle 85–86, 90
American Bandstand 32, 95, 186
Anderson, Alfa 8, 18–28
Anderson, William 28–36, 119
The Andrea True Connection 1, 3, 148, 160, 171
Ashford & Simpson 5, 61–63, 86, 219, 224

Bathé, Clare 36–41
Baynard, James vi, 28–36
Bellotte, Pete 104, 120
Belolo, Henri 123–126, 129
Benson, George 23, 176
Blacksmith, LA 28–36
Blecman, Marty 57
Bogart, Neil 88–89, 124, 126–127
Bonds International 217
Boney M 9, 231
Bowen, Jeffrey 184, 187
Briley, Alex 123, 125
Brooks, Alma Faye 98, 231
Brooks, Anthony 42–46
The Brothers 190, 192–193

Caldwell, Bobby 229
Can't Stop the Music 125, 127
Carr, Allan 127
Casablanca Records 7, 17, 85–86, 88–90, 123–124, 127
Casey, Harry Wayne (KC, KC and the Sunshine Band) 7, 51, 92–94, 96, 118, 157–158, 160, 180, 211–212, 227–229
Causi, Joe 7–18
Caviano, Ray 76, 78
Cermanski, Ed 46–53
The Charlie Calello Orchestra 171
Cher 15–16, 40, 84, 88–91
Cheri 100–101
Clifford, Linda 131
Cowley, Patrick 57

Cox, Tyrone 28–36
Crocker, Frankie (WBLS/NY) 71, 118, 171, 221, 224
Crown Heights Affair 28–38, 50, 119
Cucuzella, George 106, 137–138, 140–141

D-Train 220–226
Daft Punk 15, 26
Darnell, August 36–38, 40
Dash, Sarah 53–59
Davis, Clive 195
Davis, John 59–66, 148, 171–172
Davis, Leonard 28–36
Davis, Lynná 215–219
De-Lite Records 33–34
DeSario, Teri 7–18
Diamond, Gregg 148, 160
Disco '77 3, 72
Dodson, Venus 7, 75–81, 219
Dorhan, Carlita 109–110
Dorris, Joy (Joy Winter) 81–84, 140
Double Exposure 16, 66–75
Douglas, Carol 1, 3, 60, 62–63, 168–170, 172–173, 192, 211
Duke, George 79, 113, 120

Eaves, Hubert, III 220–223, 226
Edwards, Bernard 8, 19–26, 37, 199–207
El Coco 150–153, 155, 157
Ellis, Jimmy 46–47, 51–52
Erotic Drum Band 137
Eruption 7, 9–11
Esty, Bob 84–92

Finch, Richard 93–94, 157–158, 160, 162, 228
Fishof, David 128
Funhouse 139, 217
Fuqua, Harvey 5

Gamble, Kenny 42, 46, 130, 132–134, 148

Gardner, Taana 34
Gaynor, Gloria 3, 15, 50–51, 145, 167, 169, 170, 192, 201, 211–21
Gibb, Barry 7
Gibb, Maurice 5
Gibb, Robin 5
Goody Goody 163–168
Gordy, Berry 134, 184–186
Got Tu Go Disco 64–65
Green, Tony 1, 98–99, 116–119, 141
Greenwich, Ellie 181, 190

Hale, Dr. Cecil 113
Harris, Joe 66–75
Harris, Norman 46, 51, 148
Harris, Ray 150–157
Hartman, Dan 128
Hayden, Tom 139–140
Hendryx, Nona 54, 57
Hodo, David 123, 125
Horne, Jimmie Bo 92–97, 161
Houston, Thelma 1, 44, 84, 106
Hubertz, Rob 83
Hues, Glenn 5, 123, 125, 129
Hues Corporation 3, 30, 169, 211
Huff, Leon 42, 46, 130, 132–134, 148
Hunt, Geraldine 97–102

Inner City Symphony 178, 198

Jabara, Paul 85–87, 89, 91
Jackson, Michael (Jackson 5/Jacksons) 5, 11, 17, 47, 72, 94, 99, 120, 134, 160, 211, 214, 226
James, Freddie 99–101, 117, 137
James, Rick 5
Jiani, Carol 97, 99, 102–108, 141
Johnson, Janice Marie 108–115
Joli, France 1–2, 10, 16, 28, 34, 83, 98–99, 115–123, 141, 167, 189
Jones, Grace 124

Index

Jones, Randy 123–130
Jones, Shirley 130–135
The Jones Girls 130–135

Kat Mandu 137
Kelly, Roberta 85, 89, 91, 170
Kersey, Ron 46–47, 51, 68–69, 74
Kibble, Perry 109–111
King, Evelyn "Champagne" 8, 83, 190, 194, 198, 212
Kirshner, Don 32, 55, 126, 186
Kool & the Gang 31, 79

Labelle, Patti (Labelle) 53–55, 57, 59, 174
La Greca, Joe 102–104, 106–107, 137–138, 141, 143
Lanzaroni, Ben 192
LePage, Denis (Nini Nobless) 81–84, 97–99, 102–104, 135–144
LePage, Denyse 81–84, 99, 103, 137, 138–142
Le Pamplemousse 131, 150, 152–153, 157
Leslie, Robbie 144–150
Lewis, W. Michael 104, 150–157
Lime 81–84, 135–144
Lipetz, Mark 28–38

MacDonald, Ralph 228
Machine 36–41
Marsh, Chris 82
Martin, Luci 8–17
Mayfield, Curtis 130
McCrae, George 3, 93–95, 157–163, 227–228
McCrae, Gwen 93, 160
McFadden, Gene 5–6, 43, 132
Megatone Records 57
Melvin, Harold (and The Blue Notes)/Harold Melvin's Blue Notes 42–46
Miller, Trudy 215–219
The Monster Orchestra 60–64
Montana, Denise 163–168
Montana, Vincent, Jr. 68, 74, 148, 163, 165, 168
Morali, Jacques 123–125, 129, 148
Morgan, Denroy 34–35, 217
Moroder, Giorgio 65, 86–87, 120, 146–148, 195, 206
Moulton, Tom 47–50, 56, 145
Musique 7, 9, 76, 147, 165–166

O'Loughlin, Eddie 60, 63, 168–175

Le Pamplemousse 131, 150, 152–153, 157
Parissi, Rob 175–182

Payne, Hazel 109
Pendergrass, Teddy 42, 44–45
Perren, Freddie 211–212
Peters, Jon 89–90
Piper, Wardell 63, 171
Pointer, Bonnie 16, 182–189
The Pointer Sisters 84, 134, 182–189
Prelude Records 34, 118–119, 173, 196, 218, 221–222, 226

Reid, Raymond 28–29, 33–35, 119
Rinder, Laurin 150–157
Robbins, Cory 8–17, 196–198
Robinson, Vicki Sue 1, 8, 33, 105, 157, 190–198
Rodgers, Nile 8, 10, 14, 19–21, 25–26, 37, 57, 199–200, 204, 206–207, 216
Roller Boogie 90
Rose, Felipe 123–125, 129
Ross, Diana 5, 25, 60–61, 63–64, 85–86, 90, 95, 97, 130–131, 138, 164, 217
Rubell, Steve 8, 18, 148

Saint Tropez 150, 153–155
Salsoul Orchestra 68, 71, 167
Salsoul Records 51, 60, 67–74, 103, 152, 156, 164–166, 173, 218
SAM Records 60
Saturday Night Fever 18, 31, 49–50, 67, 87, 101, 171, 213, 228
Schatz, Warren 171, 190–199
Schrager, Ian 8, 148
Silver Convention 145, 171–173, 175, 200
Simpson, Ray 123
Sister Sledge 7, 23, 25, 134, 199–210
Sledge, Debbie 199–210
Sledge, Joni 199–210
Sledge, Kathy 199, 204, 208
Sledge, Kim 199–210
Soul Train 32, 72, 95, 99
Spelling, Aaron 65
Starr, Edwin 5
Stewart, Amii 28, 34, 78, 100, 147, 195
Stone, Henry 93, 96, 158–159, 227–229
Stovall, Jay 36–38
Streisand, Barbra 1, 5, 15, 89–90, 116, 118
Studio 54 8, 10, 14, 17–18, 23, 56, 77, 81–82, 105, 144, 146, 148–158, 169, 217
Sugarhill Gang 24
Summer, Donna 1–2, 5, 15, 17, 23, 26, 51–52, 55, 62, 86–87, 89,
98, 105, 117–188, 124, 148, 151, 170, 201, 206
Suzy Q 106
Sylvers, Edmund 5
Sylvester (Sylvester James) 5, 56–57, 105, 131, 134, 161, 183, 187
Syreeta 90

A Taste of Honey 108–115
Tavares 13, 31, 51, 157, 189, 210–215
Tavares, Arthur 210–215
Taylor, Johnnie 5
Thank God It's Friday 86–87
Thomas, Phil 28–38
Thomas, Timmy 95, 158, 227
T.K. Records 17, 76, 93, 95–96, 156, 159–160, 173, 227–229
The Trammps 9, 11, 31, 46–53, 67, 74, 189
Travolta, John 49, 171–172
Tuxedo Junction 150, 153–155

Upchurch, Robert 46–53

Vandross, Luther 5, 21, 25–27, 134
Village People 5, 23, 61, 90, 123–130, 184

Walden, Narada Michael 7, 206
Warner Communications (Warner Bros., RFC, Atlantic, Cotillion) 20, 22–23, 47–48, 50, 61, 76, 78, 106, 117, 164–166, 173, 195, 200–201
Wash, Martha 5, 8, 18, 84
Waters, Ruth "Silky" 63
The Weather Girls 84, 90, 134
Weeks, Richie 215–219
White, Barry 6, 16, 151, 169–170
White, Maurice (Earth, Wind & Fire) 6
Whitehead, John 5–6, 43, 132
Wilbur, Sandy 102–104, 141
Wild Cherry 175–182
Williams, Carol 68
Williams, James (D-Train) 220–226
Willis, Victor 61, 123–125
Wills, Viola 190, 195–196, 199
Wilson, Precious 7, 9, 10, 12, 15, 17, 19
WKTU/NY 7–9, 118, 172
Wright, Norma Jean 8, 21–22, 25, 28, 37–38, 41, 216

Young, Earl 46–49

Zulema 5

www.ingramcontent.com/pod-product-compliance
Ingram Content Group UK Ltd.
Pitfield, Milton Keynes, MK11 3LW, UK
UKHW051958220725
461058UK00019B/240